Urban Transportation Planning in the United States

History, Policy, and Practice

Third Edition

Edward Weiner

Urban Transportation Planning in the United States

History, Policy, and Practice

Third Edition

 Springer

Edward Weiner
US Department of Transportation
Washington, DC
USA

ISBN: 978-0-387-77151-9   e-ISBN: 978-0-387-77152-6
DOI: 10.1007/978-0-387-77152-6

Library of Congress Control Number: 2008926765

Preface

Urban transportation planning is carried out primarily by state and local agencies. Over the years, much experience has been gained in the planning and evaluation of urban transportation systems. This knowledge can be useful to planners and decision makers in the development and implementation of transportation system changes. In this context, it is important to understand the transportation and planning options that have been tried, and how they developed into the approaches we have today. This book describes the evolution of urban transportation planning over the last 70 years.

This is the third edition of this book which was first published in 1987. The earlier edition discussed urban transportation planning up to mid-1997. This edition updates the evolution of urban transportation planning and policy up to mid-2006. It also contains some additions and revisions to the earlier edition. This book is an updated version of *Evolution of Urban Transportation Planning* which was first published in 1979 as Chap. 15 in *Public Transportation Planning, Operations and Management*, edited by George E. Gray and Lester L. Hoel (Weiner, 1979). It was revised and published in 1992 as Chap. 3 in *Public Transportation*, second edition, edited by George E. Gray and Lester L. Hoel.

The book focuses on the key events in the evolution of urban transportation planning including developments in technical procedures, philosophy, processes, and institutions. But, planners must also be aware of changes in legislation, policy, regulations, and technology. These events have been included to provide a more complete picture of the forces that have affected and often continue to affect urban transportation planning.

Summarizing so much history in a single book requires difficult choices. The efforts of many individuals and groups made important contributions to the development of urban transportation planning. Clearly, not all of these contributions could be included or cited. This book concentrates on the key events of national significance and thereby tries to capture the overall evolution of urban transportation planning. Focusing on key events also serves as a convenient point to discuss developments in a particular area.

The book is generally arranged chronologically. Each period is titled with the major theme pervading that period as viewed by the author. Not all key events fit precisely under a particular theme, but many do. The discussion of the background

v

for some events or the follow-on activities for others may cover more than one time period and is placed where it seemed most relevant.

The book takes a multimodal perspective and attempts to provide a balanced view among a number of subject areas including:

Significant Federal legislation
Major, relevant Federal regulations and policies
Highway concerns
Transit concerns
Environmental issues
Energy issues
Safety issues
Relevant conferences
Technological developments
Transportation service alternatives
Manuals and methodological developments
National transportation studies
National data resources
Local events with national significance

Over the years, the author has discussed these events with many persons in the profession. Often they had participated in or had firsthand knowledge of the events. The author appreciates their assistance, even though they are too numerous to mention specifically.

In preparing this book, the author was directly aided by several individuals who provided information on specific events. Their assistance is appreciated: Jack Bennett, Barry Berlin, Susan Binder, Norman Cooper, Frederick W. Ducca, Sheldon H. Edner, Christopher R. Fleet, Charles A. Hedges, Donald Igo, Anthony R. Kane, Thomas Koslowski, Ira Laster, William M. Lyons, James J. McDonnell, Florence Mills, Camille C. Mittelholtz, Norman Paulhus, Elizabeth A. Parker, John Peak, Sam Rea, Carl Rappaport, Elizabeth Riklin, James A. Scott, Mary Lynn Tischer, Martin Wachs, Jimmy Yu, and Samuel Zimmerman.

The author appreciates the review comments provided by: Donald Emerson, David S. Gendell, James Getzewich, Charles H. Graves, Thomas J. Hillegass, Howard S. Lapin, Herbert S. Levinson, Alfonso B. Linhares, Gary E. Maring, Ali F. Sevin, Gordon Shunk, Peter R. Stopher, Carl N. Swerdloff, Paul L. Verchinski, and George Wickstrom.

Any errors of fact or interpretation are the responsibility of the author.

Edward Weiner
Washington, DC

Contents

Abbreviations

AASHO	American Association of State Highway Officials
AASHTO	American Association of State Highway and transportation Officials
AGT	Automated Guideway Transit
ANPRM	Advanced Notice of Proposed Rulemaking
APTA	American Public Transit Association
ATA	American Transit Association
BART	Bay Area Rapid Transit
BMS	Bridge Management System
BOB	Bureau of the Budget
BPR	Bureau of Public Roads
BRT	Bus Rapid Transit
BTS	Bureau of Transportation Statistics
3C	Continuing, Comprehensive, and Cooperative
CAFE	Corporate Average Fuel Economy
CAMPO	Capital Area Metropolitan Planning Organization
CATI	Computer-Assisted Telephone Interviewing
CATS	Chicago Area Transportation Study
CBD	Central Business District
CEQ	Council on Environmental Quality
CFS	Commodity Flow Survey
CMS	Congestion Management System
COG	Council of Governments
CTRMA	Central Texas Regional Mobility Authority
CUTD	Characteristics of Urban Transportation Demand
CUTS	Characteristics of Urban Transportation Systems
DEIS	Draft Environmental Impact Statement
DMATS	Detroit Metropolitan Area Traffic Study
DOE	Department of Energy
DOT	Department of Transportation
DPM	Downtown People Mover

EIS	Environmental Impact Statement
E.O.	Executive Order
EPA	Environmental Protection Agency
ERGS	Electronic Route Guidance System
FAF	Freight Analysis Framework
FARE	Uniform Financial Accounting and Reporting Elements
FAUS	Federal Aid Urban System
FHWA	Federal Highway Administration
FOIA	Freedom of Information Act
FONSI	Finding of No Significant Impact
FTA	Federal Transit Administration
FY	Fiscal Year
GARVEEs	Grant Anticipation Revenue Vehicles
GIS	Geographic Information Systems
GRT	Group Rapid Transit
GRTA	Georgia Regional Transportation Authority
HCM	Highway Capacity Manual
HEW	Department of Health, Education, and Welfare
HHFA	Housing and Home Finance Agency
HHS	Department of Health and Human Services
HOV	High Occupancy Vehicle
HPMS	Highway Performance Monitoring System
HP&R	Highway Planning and Research
HRB	Highway Research Board
HUD	Department of Housing and Urban Development
ICE	Interstate Cost Estimate
IM	Instructional Memorandum
I/M	Inspection/Maintenance Program
IMS	Intermodal Transportation Facilities and Systems Management System
IPG	Intermodal Planning Group
IRT	Institute for Rapid Transit
ISTEA	Intermodal Surface Transportation Efficiency Act of 1991
ITE	Institute of Transportation Engineers
ITLUP	Integrated Transportation and Land-Use Package
ITS	Intelligent Transportation Systems
IVHS	Intelligent Vehicle-Highway Systems
JARC	Job Access and Reverse Commute Program
LCI	Livable Communities Initiative
LPO	Lead Planning Organization
LRT	Light Rail Transit
LRV	Light Rail Vehicle

LUTRAQ	Making the Land Use, Transportation, Air Quality Connection
MIS	Major Investment Study
MPO	Metropolitan Planning Organization
MSA	Metropolitan Statistical Area
NARC	National Association of Regional Councils
NCHRP	National Cooperative Highway Research Program
NEPA	National Environmental Policy Act of 1969
NHS	National Highway System
NMI	National Maglev Initiative
NPRM	Notice of Proposed Rulemaking
NPTS	Nationwide Personal Transportation Study
NRC	National Research Council
NTS	National Transportation System
OMB	Office of Management and Budget
OTA	Office of Technology Assessment
PATS	Pittsburgh Area Transportation Study
PCC	Electric Railway Presidents' Conference Committee
PLANPAC	Planning Package (of computer programs)
PMS	Pavement Management System
PPM	Policy and Procedure Memorandum
PRT	Personal Rapid Transit
PTMS	Public Transportation Management System
QRS	Quick Response System
3R	Resurfacing, Restoration, and Rehabilitation
4R	Resurfacing, Restoration, Rehabilitation and Reconstruction
RMA	Regional Mobility Authority
SAFETEA-LU	Safe, Accountable, Flexible, Efficient Transportation Equity Act: A Legacy for Users
SEWRPC	Southeastern Wisconsin Regional Planning Commission
SHRP	Strategic Highway Research Program
SIB	State Infrastructure Bank
SIP	State Implementation Plan
SLRV	Standard Light Rail Vehicle
SLT	Shuttle Loop Transit
SMD	Service and Methods Demonstration
SMS	Safety Management System
SMSA	Standard Metropolitan Statistical Area
SOV	Single Occupancy Vehicle
STIP	Statewide Transportation Improvement Program
STP	Surface Transportation Program

SUV	Sport Utility Vehicle
TAG	Transportation Alternatives Group
TAZ	Transportation Analysis Zone
TCM	Transportation Control Measure
TCP	Transportation Control Plan
TCQSM	Transit Capacity and Quality of Service Manual
TCRP	Transit Cooperative Research Program
TCSP	Transportation and Community and System Preservation Pilot Program
TDM	Transportation Demand Management
TEA-21	The Transportation Equity Act for the Twenty-First Century
TIFIA	Transportation Infrastructure Finance and Innovation Act
TIGER	Topologically Integrated Geographic Encoding and Reference
TIP	Transportation Improvement Program
TMA	Transportation Management Association/Transportation Management Area
TMIP	Travel Model Improvement Program
TOD	Transit-Oriented Design
TOPICS	Traffic Operations Program to Improve Capacity and Safety
TRANSIMS	Transportation Simulation and Analysis System
TRB	Transportation Research Board
TRO	Trip Reduction Ordinance
TSM	Transportation System Management
TTC	Texas Transportation Commission
UMTA	Urban Mass Transportation Administration
UPWP	Unified Planning Work Program
UTCS	Urban Traffic Control Systems
UTPP	Urban Transportation Planning Package
UTPS	Urban Transportation Planning System
VMT	Vehicle Miles of Travel

Chapter 1
Introduction

Fifty years have passed since the Federal-Aid Highway Act of 1962 created the federal mandate for urban transportation planning in the USA. The act was the capstone of two decades of experimentation and development of urban transportation procedures and institutions. It was passed at a time in which urban areas were beginning to plan the Dwight D. Eisenhower National System of Interstate and Defense Highway routes through and around their areas. The 1962 Act, combined with the incentive of 90% federal funding for Interstate highway projects, caused urban transportation planning to spread quickly throughout the USA. It also had a significant influence on urban transportation planning in other parts of the world.

In some ways, the urban transportation planning process and planning techniques have changed little over the 50 years. Yet, in other ways, urban transportation planning has evolved over these years in response to changing issues, conditions, and values, and a greater understanding of urban transportation phenomena. Current urban transportation planning practice is considerably more sophisticated, complex, and costly than its highway planning predecessor, and involves a wider range of participants in the process.

Modifications in the planning process took many years to evolve. As new concerns and issues arose, changes in planning techniques and processes were introduced. These modifications sought to make the planning process more responsive and sensitive to those areas of concern. Urban areas that had the resources and technical ability were the first to develop and adopt new concepts and techniques. These new ideas were diffused by various means throughout the nation, usually with the assistance of the federal government and professional associations. The rate at which the new concepts were accepted varied from area to area. Consequently, the quality and depth of planning is highly variable at any point in time.

Early highway planning concentrated on developing a network of all weather highways connecting various portions of the nation. As this work was being accomplished, the problems of serving increasing traffic grew. With the need to plan for urban areas came additional problems of dispersed land use development patterns, dislocation of homes and businesses, environmental degradation, citizen participation, energy consumption, transportation for the disadvantaged, and infrastructure deterioration. More recently have been the concerns about traffic congestion,

E. Weiner, *Urban Transportation Planning in the United States, Third Edition*, doi:10.1007/978-0-387-77152-6, © Springer Science+Business Media, LLC 2008

intermodal connectivity, performance measures, sustainable development, environmental justice, climate change, and national security.

Urban transportation planning in the USA has always been conducted by state and local agencies. This is entirely appropriate since highway and transit facilities and services are owned and operated largely by the states and local agencies. The role of the federal government has been to set national policy, provide financial aid, supply technical assistance and training, and conduct research. Over the years, the federal government has attached requirements to its financial assistance. From a planning perspective, the most important has been the requirement that transportation projects in urbanized areas with population of 50,000 or more be based on an urban transportation planning process. This requirement was first incorporated into the Federal-Aid Highway Act of 1962.

Other requirements have been incorporated into federal legislation and regulations over the years. Many of these are chronicled in this report. At times, these requirements have been very exacting in their detail. At other times, greater flexibility was allowed in responding to the requirements. Currently, the emphasis is on increasing state and local flexibility in planning implementation, and in making the planning process more inclusive for all groups and individuals.

Over the years, a number of federal agencies have affected urban transportation planning. (Table 1.1) The US Bureau of Public Roads (BPR) was part of the US Department of Commerce when the 1962 Highway Act was passed. It became part of the US Department of Transportation (DOT) upon its creation in 1966, and its name was changed to the US Federal Highway Administration (FHWA). The federal urban mass transportation program began in 1961 under the US Housing and Home Finance Agency, which became the US Department of Housing and Urban Development in 1965. The federal urban transit program was transferred to DOT in 1968 as the US Urban Mass Transportation Administration (UMTA). The name was changed to the US Federal Transit Administration (FTA) by the Federal Transit Act Amendments of 1991. The US Federal Railroad Administration (FRA) was created at the same time as DOT. The National Traffic and Motor Vehicle Safety Act of 1966 established the National Traffic Safety Agency, and the Highway Safety Act of 1966 established the National Highway Safety Agency both in the US Department of Commerce. The two safety agencies were combined by Executive Order 11357 in 1967 into the National Highway Safety Bureau in the newly created DOT. In 1970 it became the National Highway Traffic Safety Administration (NHTSA).

Other federal agencies became involved in urban transportation planning as new issues arose. The US Department of Labor (DOL) became involved in 1964 to administer the labor protections provisions of the Urban Mass Transportation Act. The Advisory Council on Historic Preservation was established in 1966 to administer national historic preservation programs. The Bureau of the Budget (BOB), later to become the Office of Management and Budget (OMB), issued guidance in 1969 to improve coordination among programs funded by the federal government. In later years, OMB issued guidance on many issues that affected urban transportation. To address environmental concerns that were increasing in the latter part of the 1960s, the

Table 1.1 Dates selected federal agencies were established

1849	Department of Interior
1913	Department of Commerce
1913	Department of Labor
1916	Bureau of Public Roads
1921	Bureau of the Budget
1947	Housing and Home Finance Agency
1953	Department of Health, Education and Welfare
1965	Department of Housing and Urban Development
1966	Department of Transportation
1966	Federal Highway Administration
1966	Federal Railroad Administration
1966	Advisory Council on Historic Preservation
1967	National Highway Safety Bureau
1968	Urban Mass Transportation Administration
1969	Council on Environmental Quality
1970	National Highway Traffic Safety Administration
1970	Office of Management and Budget
1970	Environmental Protection Agency
1977	Department of Energy
1979	Department of Health and Human Services
1991	Federal Transit Administration
1992	Bureau of Transportation Statistics
2000	Federal Motor Carrier Safety Administration
2001	Transportation Security Administration
2002	Department of Homeland Security
2005	Research and Innovative Technology Administration

Council on Environmental Quality (CEQ) was created in 1969 and the US Environmental Protection Agency (EPA) in 1970. The US Department of Health, Education and Welfare (HEW), now the US Department of Health and Human Services (HHS), became involved in urban transportation as a result of the Rehabilitation Act of 1973 as part of its function to eliminate discrimination against handicapped persons in federal programs. With the passage if the Endangered Species Act of 1973, the Department of Interior and the Department of Commerce became involved in some aspects of urban transportation planning. In 1977, the US Department of Energy (DOE) was created to bring together federal energy functions.

The Bureau of Transportation Statistics (BTS) was created by the Intermodal Surface Transportation Efficiency Act of 1991 for data collection, analysis, and reporting and to ensure the most cost-effective use of transportation monitoring resources. It was merged into the Research and Innovative Technology Administration (RITA) in 2005 by the Norman Y. Mineta Research and Special Programs Improvement Act. The Federal Motor Carrier Safety Administration (FMCSA) was established as a separate administration within the US DOT in 2000 by the Motor Carrier Safety Improvement Act of 1999 to reduce crashes, injuries, and fatalities involving large trucks and buses. The US Transportation Security Administration (TSA) was created in the US DOT in 2001 by the Transportation Security Act to protect the nation's transportation systems by ensuring the freedom of movement for people and commerce. It was merged into the Department of Homeland Security (DHS) when it was created by the Homeland Security Act of 2002.

The involvement of these and other agencies at the federal, state, and local levels created an increasing challenge to agencies conducting urban transportation planning to meet all the requirements that resulted. Local planners devoted substantial resources to meeting requirements of higher level governments, which often detracted from their ability to address local needs and objectives. These requirements, however, were also used by local agencies as the justification to carry out activities that they desired but for which they could not obtain support at the local level.

This report reviews the historical development of the urban transportation planning process in the USA from its beginnings in early highway and transit planning to its current focus on intermodal connectivity, sustainable development, and broad participation in the planning process.

- Chapter 2 discusses the early beginnings of highway planning.
- Chapter 3 covers the formative years of urban transportation planning during which many of the basic concepts were developed and the beginning of the National System of Interstate and Defense Highways.
- Chapter 4 focuses on the 1962 Federal-Aid Highway Act and the sweeping changes it brought in urban transportation planning in the USA. It also describes early federal involvement in urban public transportation.
- Chapter 5 discusses efforts at intergovernmental coordination, the beginning of the federal highway and vehicle safety programs, a deeper federal role in urban public transportation, and the evolution to "continuing" transportation planning.
- Chapter 6 describes the environmental revolution of the late 1960s and the increased involvement of citizens in the urban transportation planning process.
- Chapter 7 addresses the events that led to integrated planning for urban public transportation and highways. These included major increases in federal transit programs as well as increased flexibility in the use of highway funds.
- Chapter 8 focuses on the Arab oil embargo of 1973 which accelerated the transition from long-term system planning to short-term, smaller scale planning. It also discusses the concern for cost effectiveness in transportation decisions and the emphasis on transportation system management techniques.
- Chapter 9 highlights the concern for the revitalization of older urban centers and the growing need for energy conservation. It describes the expanding federal requirements on environmental quality and transportation for special groups.
- Chapter 10 describes the efforts to reverse federal intrusion into local decisions and to scale back federal requirements.
- Chapter 11 discusses the expanded interest in involving the private sector in the provision of transportation services and the decline in public resources to address transportation planning.

- Chapter 12 focuses on strategic planning to the year 2000 and into the next century, and the renewed interest in new technological options. It also discusses the growing concern for traffic congestion and air pollution and the efforts at transportation demand management.
- Chapter 13 describes how the increasing concern for the effects of transportation on living quality and the environment grew, and on broader approaches of the transportation planning process to address the relationship of transportation to sustainable development.
- Chapter 14 focuses on expansion of a participatory transportation decision-making process to include a wide range of participants in the process, including individuals and citizen groups.
- Chapter 15 highlights the beginning of a new century that ushered in a drive to preserve and effectively operate the transportation system, assure that expenditures achieved solid results, and find adequate resources to meet growing needs.
- Chapter 16 provides the summary and concluding remarks.

Chapter 2
Early Highway Planning

Early highway planning grew out the need for information on the rising tide of automobile and truck usage during the first quarter of the twentieth century. From 1904, when the first automobiles ventured out of the cities, traffic grew at a steady and rapid rate. After the initial period of highway construction, which connected many of the nation's cities, emphasis shifted to improving the highway system to carry these increased traffic loads. New concepts were pioneered to increase highway capacity including control of access, elimination of at grade intersections, new traffic control devices, and improved roadway design.

Early highway planning was devoted to the collection and analysis of factual information and applying that information to the growing highway problems in the period prior to World War II. It was during this period that scientific and engineering principles were first used to measure highway traffic and capacity and to apply that knowledge to the planning and design of highways.

Federal Highway Act of 1921

In the early years of highway construction, the automobile had been regarded as a pleasure vehicle rather than an important means of transportation. Consequently, highways consisted of comparatively short sections that were built from the cities into the countryside. There were significant gaps in many important intercity routes. During this period, urban roads were considered to be adequate, particularly in comparison to rural roads that were generally not paved.

As the automobile was improved and ownership became more widespread, the idea of a highway network gained in strength. The concept of a national system of highways was recognized in the Federal Highway Act of 1921. The act required that the state highway departments designate a system of principal interstate and inter-county roads, limited to 7% of the total mileage of rural roads then existing. The use of Federal-aid funds was restricted to this system. The Federal government would pay 50% of the construction cost while the states would pay the other 50%. This concentration of attention on a carefully selected system of roads had a large influence on the rapid development of an integrated, nationwide network of improved highways.

E. Weiner, *Urban Transportation Planning in the United States, Third Edition*, doi:10.1007/978-0-387-77152-6, © Springer Science+Business Media, LLC 2008

The concept of a continuous national system of highways was reinforced in the Federal-Aid Highway Act of 1925 with the requirement for a US numbered highway system composed of important through routes extending entirely across the nation. Instead of using names and colored bands on telephone poles, this new system would use uniform numbers for inter-state highways and a standardized shield that would be universally recognizable. This was not a formal highway system but simply a basis for route marking as a guide for motorists. The US number highway system was adopted in 1926.

With the adoption of a Federal-aid system, in the Federal-Aid Act of 1921, and the marking of through routes, the focus of highway construction was on "closing the gaps." By the early 1930s, the objective of constructing a system of two-lane roads connecting the centers of population had largely been completed. It was then possible to travel around the country on a smooth, all-weather highway system (US Federal Works Agency, 1949).

With the completion of this "pioneering period" of highway construction, attention shifted to the more complex issues resulting from the rapid growth in traffic and increasing vehicle weights. Figure 2.1 shows the growth in vehicle registrations, motor fuel consumption, highway expenditures, and tax receipts during the period (US Dept. of Commerce, 1954a). Early highways were inadequate in width, grade, and alignment to serve major traffic loads, and highway pavements had not been designed to carry the numbers and weights of the newer trucks.

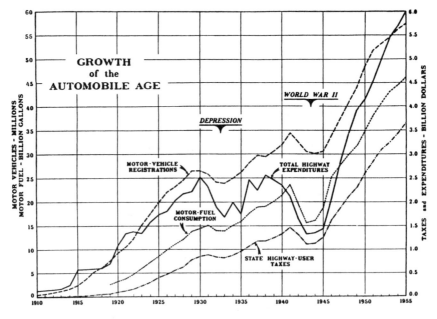

Fig. 2.1 Motor vehicle registrations, fuel consumption, user taxes, and highway expenditures, 1910–1955 (Source: US Dept. of Commerce, 1954)

It became clear that these growing problems necessitated the collection and analysis of information on highways and their use on a more comprehensive scale than that had ever before been attempted (Holmes and Lynch, 1957). A systematic approach to the planning of highways was needed to respond to these problems.

Early Parkways

The growing number of automobiles and the expansion of cities into nearby suburbs in the early part of the century created the need for specialized roadways. In New York, the city's growth was rapidly extending northward into Westchester County. Property along the Bronx River was coming into the market, and the subdivision of this land into smaller plots and the development was polluting the river. The Bronx River Commission was established in 1907 to acquire the necessary lands and to build the Bronx River Parkway as a joint undertaking between New York City and Westchester County.

The Bronx River Parkway Reservation was the first public parkway designed explicitly for automobile use. The project began as an environmental restoration and park development initiative that aimed to transform the heavily polluted Bronx River into an attractive linear park. With the addition of a parkway drive, the project became a pioneering example of modern motorway development. It combined beauty, safety, and efficiency by reducing the number of dangerous intersections, limiting access from surrounding streets and businesses, and surrounding motorists in a broad swath of landscaped greenery. The Bronx River Parkway Reservation, which parallels the parkway, was the first parkland in Westchester County (Bronx River Parkway – Historic Overview).

The parkway drive accommodated four lanes of traffic on a **40'-wide pavement and included several important design features that would soon become hallmarks of parkway design. These included the avoidance of excessive grades and dangerous curves; the replacement of at-grade intersections with grade-separated crossings; and the division of traffic into two one-way drives separated by a landscaped median divider. Bridges were built for permanence with architectural treatment in harmony with their natural surroundings. Many of these features were duplicated by designers of other projects and became the hallmarks of parkways (Bronx River Parkway – Historic Overview).

The continued expansion of automobile ownership and the technological advances in automobiles soon required additional parkways. During the 1920s and 1930s, a number of new parkways were built including the Hutchinson, Saw Mill, Grand Central, and the Taconic north of the New York City, the Henry Hudson Parkway in New York, and the Palisades and the Palisades Parkway in New Jersey. On Long Island, there were the Meadowbrook, Northern and Southern State, and Wantagh State Parkway. By 1934, there were some 134 miles of parkways in Queens, Nassau, and Westchester Counties under the direction of Robert Moses (Walmsley, 2003). Also, in the 1930s, the modern parkway movement expanded out of New York with construction of several Federal parkways including Skyline Drive in Virginia, Blue Ridge Parkway in North Carolina and Tennessee, and the Merritt Parkway in Connecticut (Loukaitou-Sideris and Gottlieb, 2003).

Radburn, New Jersey

The industrialization of the USA after World War I led to migration from the rural areas and a striking growth of the cities during the 1920s. This population shift led to a severe housing shortage. The automobile, which was becoming a mainstay in American life, added a new problem to urban living. Changes in urban design were necessary to provide more housing and to protect people from automobile traffic. To address these needs, Radburn, the "Town for the Motor Age," was created in 1929 in Fairlawn, New Jersey, outside of New York City.

Radburn was designed by Henry Wright and Clarence Stein using Wright's "Six Planks for a Housing Platform":

- Plan simply, but comprehensively. Don't stop at the individual property line. Adjust paving, sidewalks, sewers, and the like to the particular needs of the property dealt with – not to a conventional pattern. Arrange buildings and grounds so as to give sunlight, air, and a tolerable outlook to even the smallest and cheapest house.
- Provide ample sites in the right places for community use: playgrounds, school gardens, schools, theatres, churches, public buildings, and stores.
- Put factories and other industrial buildings where they can be used without wasteful transportation of goods or people.
- Cars must be parked and stored, deliveries made, waste collected – plan for such services with a minimum of danger, noise, and confusion.
- Bring private and public lands into relationship and plan buildings and groups of buildings with relation to each other. Develop collectively such services as will add to the comfort of the individual, at a lower cost than is possible under individual operation.
- Arrange for the occupancy of houses on a fair basis of cost and service, including the cost of what needs to be done in organizing, building, and maintaining the community (Gatti, Ronald, 1969–1989).

The primary innovation of Radburn was the Road System Hierarchy that separated pedestrian and vehicular traffic. This was accomplished by doing away with the traditional grid-iron street pattern and replacing it with an innovation called the superblock. The superblock was a large block of land surrounded by main roads. The houses were grouped around small cul-de-sacs, each of which had an access road coming from the main roads. The remaining land inside the superblock was park area, the backbone of the neighborhood. The living and sleeping sections of the houses faced toward the garden and park areas, while the service rooms faced the access road.

The idea of purely residential streets was a new idea at that time. The Radburn plan used the cul-de-sac as a rational way to escape the limitations of the checkerboard plan, in which all streets were through streets, with the possibility of collisions between cars and pedestrians every 100 m. The Radburn cul-de-sac lane was designed at a 100–130-m length, with only a 10-m wide right of way, as opposed to the prevailing 16–20-m width. The plan further reduced the paved driving lane to 6 μ and allowed for the 2-m utility strip on each side to be landscaped and thus visually part of the garden. Building setbacks were 5 m and provisions were made for street parking.

The walks that surround the cul-de-sacs on the garden side of the houses divided the cu-de-sacs from each other and from the central park area. These paths crossed the park when necessary. Finally, to further maintain the separation of pedestrian and vehicular traffic, a pedestrian underpass and an overpass, linking the superblocks, was provided. The system was so devised that a pedestrian could start at any given point and proceed on foot to school, stores, or church without crossing a street used by automobiles.

Another innovation of Radburn was that the parks were secured without additional cost to the residents. The savings in expenditures for roads and public utilities at Radburn, as contrasted with the normal subdivision, paid for the parks. The Radburn type of plan used small property lots and less area of street to secure the same amount of frontage. In addition, for direct access to most houses, it used narrower roads of less expensive construction, as well as smaller utility lines. The area in streets and length of utilities was 25% lesser than that in the typical American street. The savings in cost not only paid for 12–14% of the total area that went into internal parks, but also covered the cost of grading and landscaping the play spaces and green links connecting the central block commons. The cost of living in such a community was therefore set at a minimum for the homeowner, and the cost to the builder was small enough to make the venture profitable (Gatti, Ronald, 1969–1989).

Radburn was unique because it was envisioned as a town for better living, and it was the first example of city planning that recognized the importance of the automobile in modern life without permitting it to dominate the environment. None of the Radburn design features were completely new. Yet, their synthesis and integration into a comprehensive layout was a breakthrough in subdivision form. It was the first time in the USA that a housing development was attempted on such a large scale, proceeding from a definite architectural plan resulting in a complete town. Radburn was also important to builders because of the unique way that the parks and grading were funded.

The Radburn idea, however, watered down, became the suburban model of choice. Planners enshrined it in cluster zoning ordinances. Developers who had never heard of Radburn or its planning principles grouped buildings around cul-de-sacs and marketed their product from "community centers." Their projects routinely included "common open space," a swimming pool, and sometimes tennis courts, indoor exercise facilities, and children's play equipment (Garvin, 1998).

Federal-Aid Highway Act of 1934

Beginning with the Federal-Aid Highway Act of 1934, the Congress authorized that 1½% of the amount apportioned to any state annually for construction could be used for surveys, plans, engineering, and economic analyses for future highway construction projects. The act created the cooperative arrangement between the US Bureau of Public Roads (now the US Federal Highway Administration) and the state highway departments, known as the statewide highway planning surveys. By 1940, all states were participating in this program (Holmes and Lynch, 1957).

As an initial activity, these highway planning surveys included a complete inventory and mapping of the highway system and its physical characteristics. Traffic surveys were undertaken to determine the volume of traffic by vehicle type, weight, and dimensions. Financial studies were made to determine the relationship of highway finances with other financial operations within each state, to assess the ability of the states to finance the construction and operation of the highway system, and to indicate how to allocate highway taxes among the users. Many of the same types of activities are still being performed on a continuing basis by highway agencies (Holmes, 1962).

Electric Railway Presidents' Conference Committee

Electric railway systems were the backbone of urban mass transportation by World War I with over 1,000 street railway companies carrying some 11 billion passengers by 1917 (Mills, 1975). After 1923, ridership on the nation's electric railways began to decline as the motor bus, with its flexibility to change routes and lower capital costs, quickly began replacing the electric streetcar (N.D. Lea Transportation Research Corporation, 1975). With rising costs and the inability to raise fares to cover costs, the financial condition of street railway companies worsened.

In 1930, the heads of 25 electric railway companies formed the Electric Railway Presidents' Conference Committee (PCC). The goal of the PCC was to develop a modern streetcar to match the comfort, performance, and modern image of its competitors, and stem the decline of the street railway industry. The effort took 5 years and $750,000. It was one of the most thorough and efficiently organized ventures in urban mass transit. The product, known as the "PCC car," far surpassed its predecessors in acceleration, braking, passenger comfort, and noise (Mills, 1975).

The first commercial application of the PCC car was in 1935 in Brooklyn, New York. By 1940 more than 1,100 vehicles had been purchased. By 1952, when production was first halted, about 6,000 PCC cars had been produced. The PCC cars did improve the competitive position of streetcars and slowed the conversion to buses, but without other improvements, such as exclusive rights of way, it could not stop the long-term decline in street railways. By 1960, streetcars remained in only about a dozen cities in the USA (Vuchic, 1981).

Manual on Uniform Traffic Control Devices

As the highway system was expanded and upgraded to meet the growth in automobile traffic, the need for highly uniform standards for traffic control devices became obvious. These traffic control devices included signs, traffic signals, markings and other devices placed on, over, or adjacent to a street or highway by a public body to guide, warn, or regulate traffic. In 1927, the American Association of State Highway Officials published the *Manual and Specifications for the Manufacture, Display and Erection of U.S. Standard Road Markers and Signs.* The manual was developed for application of rural highways. Then, in 1929, the National Conference of Street and Highway Safety published a manual for use on urban streets.

But the necessity for unification of the standards applicable to different classes of road and street systems was obvious. To meet that need, a joint committee of the AASHO and the National Conference of Street and Highway Safety combined their efforts and developed the first Manual on Uniform Traffic Control Devices, which was published by the BPR in 1935.

Over the years since that first manual, the problems and needs of traffic control changed. New solutions and devices, as well as the standards to guide their application, were developed. The original joint committee continued its existence with occasional changes in organization and personnel. In 1972, the Committee formally became the National Advisory Committee on Uniform Traffic Control Devices to the FHWA. The Committee has been responsible for periodic revisions to update and expand the manual in 1942, 1948, 1961, 1971, 1978, 1988, and 2000 (US Dept. of Transportation, 2000a,b; Upchurch, 1989).

AASHO Policy on Geometric Design of Rural Highways

As new knowledge became available on the performance of vehicles and highway design features, there was a need to incorporate it into practice. The Committee on Planning and Design Policies of the American Association of State Highway Officials (AASHO) was formed in 1937 for this purpose. The committee's mode of operation was to outline a program of work that was performed by the BPR under the supervision of the Committee Secretary. The BPR gathered known information and developed draft guidance, known as policies, which were revised by the committee. The policies were finally approved by a two-thirds favorable vote of the States.

In the period from 1938 to 1944, the Committee under Secretary Joseph Barnett produced seven policies related to highway classification, highway types, sight distance, signing, and intersection design for at-grade rotaries and grade separations. These policies were reprinted without change and bound as a single volume in 1950 (American Association of State Highway Officials, 1950).

The policies were updated, expanded, and rewritten as a single cohesive document and issued as "A Policy on Geometric Design of Rural Highways" in 1954

(American Association of State Highway Officials, 1954). The policy contained design guidance on the criteria determining highway design, vertical and horizontal alignment, cross-section elements, at-grade and grade intersections, and inter-changes. The volume, which became known as the "Blue Book," went through seven printings by 1965. It received wide acceptance as the standard guide for highway design. The policy was again reissued in 1966 in revised and updated form to reflect more current information (American Association of State Highway Officials, 1966).

Much of the material in the 1954 Rural Policy applied to both urban and rural highways. As new data and research results became available on urban highways, the AASHO Committee decided to issue a separate policy for the geometric design of urban highways (American Association of State Highway Officials, 1957).

The development of these policies typified the approach to highways standards. Research engineers collected data on the performance of vehicles and highways. These data were brought together in the form of design standards, generally by staff of the BPR under the guidance of the AASHO. Eventually, they became part of highway design practice through agreement of the States. As a result of their factual basis and adoption through common agreement, the policies had immense influence on the design of highways in the USA and abroad.

Toll Road Study

By the mid-1930s, there was considerable sentiment for a few long-distance, con-trolled-access highways connecting major cities. Advocates of such a highway sys-tem assumed that the public would be willing to finance much of its cost by tolls. The US Bureau of Public Roads was requested by President Roosevelt in 1937 to study the idea, and 2 years later it published the report, Toll Roads and Free Roads (US Congress, 1939).

The study recommended the construction of a highway system comprising direct, interregional highways with all necessary connections through and around cities. It concluded that this nationwide highway system could not be financed solely through tolls, even though certain sections could. It also recommended the creation of a Federal Land Authority empowered to acquire, hold, sell, and lease land. The report emphasized the problem of transportation within major cities and used the city of Baltimore as an example (Holmes, 1973).

Highway Capacity Manual

During the 1920s and early 1930s, a number of studies were conducted to deter-mine the capacity of highways to carry traffic. Early efforts were theoretical, but gradually, field studies using observers, cameras, and aerial surveys created a body of empirical data on which to base capacity estimates. By 1934, it was clear that a coordinated effort was needed to integrate the results of the various studies and to collect and analyze additional data. The BPR launched such an effort from 1934 to 1937 to collect a large quantity of data on a wide variety of roads under different conditions (Cron, 1975a).

In 1944, the Highway Research Board organized the Committee on Highway Capacity to coordinate the work in this field. Its chairman, O.K. Normann, was the foremost researcher on highway capacity at that time. By 1949, the Committee had succeeded in reducing the enormous volume of factual information on highway capacity to a form that would be usable to highway designers and traffic engineers. The results were first published in *Public Roads* magazine, and then as a separate volume entitled, the *Highway Capacity Manual* (US Dept. of Commerce, 1950). The manual defined capacity, and presented methods for calculating it for various types of highways and elements under different conditions. This manual quickly became the standard for highway design and planning. More than 26,000 copies of the manual were sold, and it was translated into nine other languages.

The Committee on Highway Capacity was reactivated in 1953, again with O.K. Normann as chairman, to continue the study of highway capacity and prepare a new edition of the manual. Much of the work was done by the staff of the BPR. The new manual, which was issued in 1965, placed new emphasis on freeways, ramps, and weaving sections because they had come into widespread use. A chapter on bus transit was also added. Other types of highways and streets continued to receive complete coverage. This manual, like its predecessor, was primarily a practical guide. It described methods to estimate capacity, service volume, or level of service for a specific highway design under specific conditions. Alternately, the design to carry a given traffic demand could be determined (Highway Research Board, 1965).

The third edition of the *Highway Capacity Manual* was published by the Transportation Research Board in 1985. It reflected over two decades of empirical research by a number of research agencies primarily under the sponsorship of the National Cooperative Highway Research Program and the FHWA. The procedures and methodologies were divided into three sections on freeways, rural highways, and urban streets, with detailed procedures and work sheets. The material in the third edition offered significantly revised procedures in many of the areas, and included entirely new sections on pedestrians and bicycles (Transportation Research Board, 1985c, 1994).

The most recent revised edition of the *Highway Capacity Manual* (HCM) 2000 was published in metric units, as well as in the US customary system units used in the traditional manual. In addition to improvements in current analysis methodologies, HCM 2000 included a chapter on interchange ramp terminals, several chapters with material for planning uses of the manual, and a discussion of when simulation models should be used instead of the manual. The HCM 2000 was also published as a CD-ROM. In addition to the text and exhibits of both versions of the book, the CD-ROM included tutorials, narrated example problems, explanatory videos, navigation tools, hyperlinks between sections of the manual, and easy access to application software (Transportation Research Board, 2000).

Interregional Highway Report

In April 1941, President Roosevelt appointed the National Interregional Highway Committee to investigate the need for a limited system of national highways to improve the facilities available for interregional transportation. The staff work was done by the US Public Roads Administration, which was the name of the Bureau of Public Roads at that time, and in 1944 the findings were published in the report, Interregional Highways (US Congress, 1944). A system of highways, designated as the "National System of Interstate and Defense Highways," was recommended and authorized in the Federal-Aid Highway Act of 1944. However, it was not until the Federal-Aid Highway Act of 1956 that any significant work on the system began.

This study was unique in the annals of transportation planning, and the implementation of its findings has had profound effects on American lifestyles and industry. The study brought planners, engineers, and economists together with the highway officials responsible for implementing highway programs. The final route choices were influenced as much by strategic necessity and such factors as population density, concentrations of manufacturing activity, and agricultural production as by existing and future traffic (Holmes, 1973).

The importance of the system within cities was recognized, but it was not intended that these highways serve urban commuter travel demands in the major cities. As stated in the report, "…it is important, both locally and nationally, to recognize the recommended system…as that system and those routes which best and most directly join region to region and major city to major city" (US Congress, 1944).

The report recognized the need to coordinate with other modes of transportation and for cooperation at all levels of government. It reiterated the need for a Federal Land Authority with the power of excess condemnation and similar authorities at the state level.

Chapter 3
Launching Urban Transportation Planning and the Interstate Highway System

During World War II, regular highway programs stopped. Highway materials and personnel were used to build access roads for war production and military needs. With rationing of gasoline and tires, and no new automobiles being manufactured, the use of transit mushroomed. Between 1941 and 1946, transit ridership grew by 65% to an all-time high of 23.4 billion trips annually (American Public Transit Association, 1995). (Fig. 3.1).

When the war came to an end, the pent-up demand for homes and automobiles ushered in the suburban boom era. Automobile production jumped from a mere 70,000 in 1945 to 2.1 million in 1946, 3.5 million, and 3.5 million in 1947. Highway travel reached its prewar peak by 1946 and began to climb at 6% per year, which was to continue for decades (US Dept. of Transportation, 1979a). Transit use, on the other hand, declined at about the same rate it had increased during the war. By 1953, there were fewer than 14 billion transit trips annually (Transportation Research Board, 1987).

The nation's highways were in poor shape to handle this increasing load of traffic. Little had been done during the war to improve the highways and wartime traffic had exacerbated their condition. Moreover, the growth of development in the suburbs occurred where highways did not have the capacity to carry the resulting traffic. Suburban traffic quickly overwhelmed the existing two-lane formerly rural roads (US Dept. of Transportation, 1979a). Transit facilities, too, experienced significant wear and tear during the war from extended use and deferred maintenance. This resulted in deterioration in transit's physical plant by war's end. Pent-up wage demands of transit employees were met causing nearly a 50% increase in average fares by 1950. This further contributed to a decline in ridership. These factors combined to cause serious financial problems for many transit companies (Transportation Research Board, 1987). The postwar era concentrated on dealing with the problems resulting from suburban growth and resulting from the return to a peacetime economy. Many of the planning activities that had to be deferred during the war resumed with renewed vigor.

To meet this growing demand for travel, the nation embarked on the largest public works program, building the National System of Interstate Highways. This massive undertaking launched a new era of highway expansion that brought with it wide-ranging economic, social, and environmental impacts.

E. Weiner, *Urban Transportation Planning in the United States, Third Edition*,
doi:10.1007/978-0-387-77152-6, © Springer Science+Business Media, LLC 2008

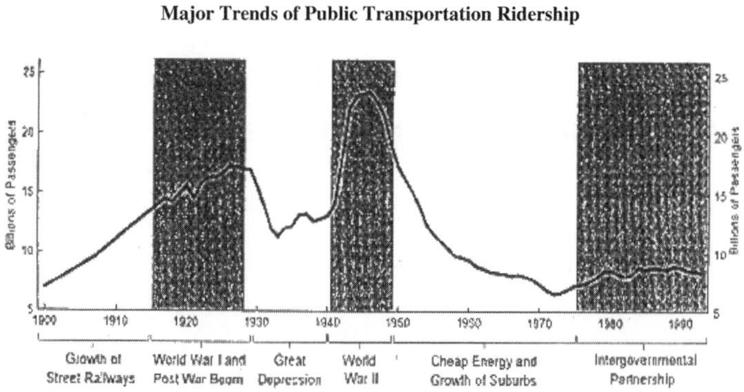

Major Trends of Public Transportation Ridership

Fig. 3.1 Major trends of public transportation ridership (Source: American Public Transit Association, 2007)

Federal-Aid Highway Act of 1944

The Federal-Aid Highway Act of 1944 was passed in anticipation of the transition to a postwar economy and to prepare for the expected growth in traffic. The act significantly increased the funds authorized for federal-aid highway programs from $137,500 in 1942 and 1943, no funds in 1944 and 1945, to $500,000 annually for 1946 through 1948. The act also recognized the growing complexity of the highway program.

The original 7% federal-aid highway program was renamed the Federal-aid Primary system, and selection by the states of a Federal-aid Secondary system of farm-to-market and feeder roads was authorized. Federal-aid funding was authorized in three parts, known as the "ABC" program with 45% for the primary system, 30% for the secondary system, and 25% for urban extensions of the primary and secondary systems.

The act continued the allocation of funds by means of formulas. For the primary system, funds were allocated using area, total population, and postal route miles as factors. For the secondary system, the same formula was used except that rural population was substituted for total population. For the urban extensions, urban population was the only factor. For the first time, federal-aid funds up to one-third the cost could be used to acquire right-of-way.

A National System of Interstate Highways of 40,000 miles was authorized. The routes were selected by the states with BPR approval. However, but no special funds were provided to build the system beyond regular federal-aid authorizations.

Early Urban Travel Surveys

Most urban areas did not begin urban travel surveys until 1944. It was during that year that the Federal-Aid Highway Act authorized the expenditure of funds on urban extensions of the federal-aid primary and secondary highway systems. Until that time, there was a lack of information on urban travel, which could be used for the planning of highway facilities. In fact, no comprehensive survey methods had been developed that could provide the required information. Due to the complex nature of urban street systems and the shifting of travel from route to route, traffic volumes were not a satisfactory guide to needed improvements. A study of the origins and destinations of trips and the basic factors affecting travel was needed (Holmes and Lynch, 1957).

The method developed to meet this need was the home-interview origin–destination survey. Household members were interviewed to obtain information on the number, purpose, mode, origin, and destination of all trips made on a particular day. These urban travel surveys were used in the planning of highway facilities, particularly expressway systems, and in determining design features. The US Bureau of Public Roads published the first manual, Manual of Procedures for Home Interview Traffic Studies, in 1944 (US Dept. of Commerce, 1944). Figure 3.2 shows the internal trip report form from a home interview survey. In 1944, the interviewing technique was used in Tulsa, Little Rock, New Orleans, Kansas City, Memphis,

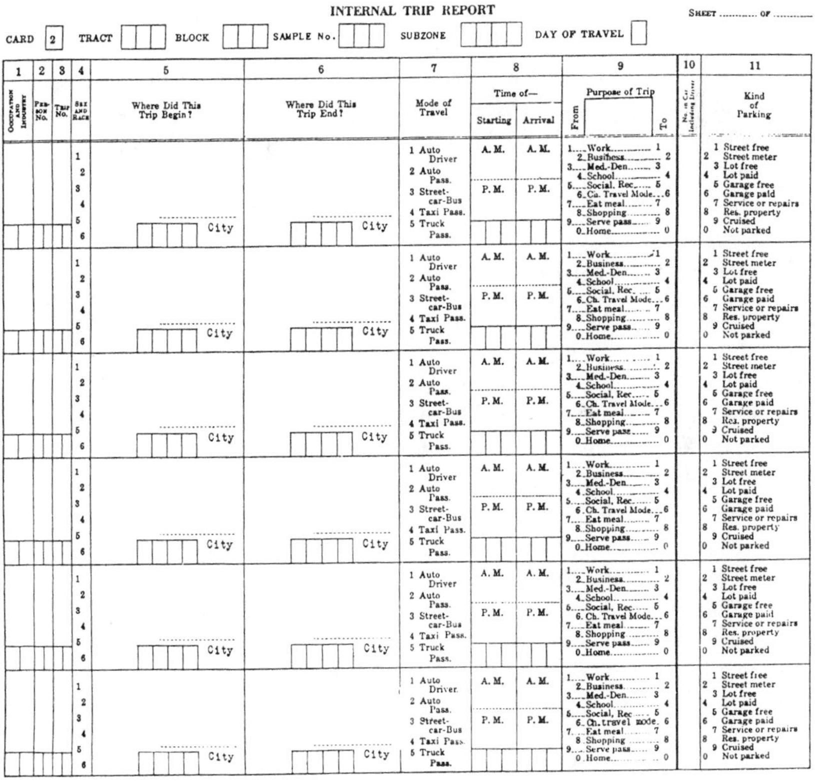
INTERNAL TRIP REPORT

SHEET .... OF ....

CARD 2 TRACT BLOCK SAMPLE No. SUBZONE DAY OF TRAVEL

1	2	3	4	5	6	7	8		9	10	11
Occupation and Industry	Person No.	Trip No.	Sex and Race	Where Did This Trip Begin?	Where Did This Trip End?	Mode of Travel	Time of— Starting	Arrival	Purpose of Trip (From / To)	No. in Car Including Driver	Kind of Parking
			1 2 3 4 5 6	.... City	.... City	1 Auto Driver 2 Auto Pass. 3 Street-car-Bus 4 Taxi Pass. 5 Truck Pass.	A. M. / P. M.	A. M. / P. M.	1 Work 1; 2 Business 2; 3 Med.-Den. 3; 4 School 4; 5 Social, Rec. 5; 6 Ch. Travel Mode 6; 7 Eat meal 7; 8 Shopping 8; 9 Serve pass. 9; 0 Home 0		1 Street free 2 Street meter 3 Lot free 4 Lot paid 5 Garage free 6 Garage paid 7 Service or repairs 8 Res. property 9 Cruised 0 Not parked
			1 2 3 4 5 6	.... City	.... City	1 Auto Driver 2 Auto Pass. 3 Street-car-Bus 4 Taxi Pass. 5 Truck Pass.	A. M. / P. M.	A. M. / P. M.	1 Work 1; 2 Business 2; 3 Med.-Den. 3; 4 School 4; 5 Social, Rec. 5; 6 Ch. Travel Mode 6; 7 Eat meal 7; 8 Shopping 8; 9 Serve pass. 9; 0 Home 0		1 Street free 2 Street meter 3 Lot free 4 Lot paid 5 Garage free 6 Garage paid 7 Service or repairs 8 Res. property 9 Cruised 0 Not parked
			1 2 3 4 5 6	.... City	.... City	1 Auto Driver 2 Auto Pass. 3 Street-car-Bus 4 Taxi Pass. 5 Truck Pass.	A. M. / P. M.	A. M. / P. M.	1 Work 1; 2 Business 2; 3 Med.-Den. 3; 4 School 4; 5 Social, Rec. 5; 6 Ch. Travel Mode 6; 7 Eat meal 7; 8 Shopping 8; 9 Serve pass. 9; 0 Home 0		1 Street free 2 Street meter 3 Lot free 4 Lot paid 5 Garage free 6 Garage paid 7 Service or repairs 8 Res. property 9 Cruised 0 Not parked
			1 2 3 4 5 6	.... City	.... City	1 Auto Driver 2 Auto Pass. 3 Street-car-Bus 4 Taxi Pass. 5 Truck Pass.	A. M. / P. M.	A. M. / P. M.	1 Work 1; 2 Business 2; 3 Med.-Den. 3; 4 School 4; 5 Social, Rec. 5; 6 Ch. Travel Mode 6; 7 Eat meal 7; 8 Shopping 8; 9 Serve pass. 9; 0 Home 0		1 Street free 2 Street meter 3 Lot free 4 Lot paid 5 Garage free 6 Garage paid 7 Service or repairs 8 Res. property 9 Cruised 0 Not parked
			1 2 3 4 5 6	.... City	.... City	1 Auto Driver 2 Auto Pass. 3 Street-car-Bus 4 Taxi Pass. 5 Truck Pass.	A. M. / P. M.	A. M. / P. M.	1 Work 1; 2 Business 2; 3 Med.-Den. 3; 4 School 4; 5 Social, Rec. 5; 6 Ch. Travel Mode 6; 7 Eat meal 7; 8 Shopping 8; 9 Serve pass. 9; 0 Home 0		1 Street free 2 Street meter 3 Lot free 4 Lot paid 5 Garage free 6 Garage paid 7 Service or repairs 8 Res. property 9 Cruised 0 Not parked
			1 2 3 4 5 6	.... City	.... City	1 Auto Driver 2 Auto Pass. 3 Street-car-Bus 4 Taxi Pass. 5 Truck Pass.	A. M. / P. M.	A. M. / P. M.	1 Work 1; 2 Business 2; 3 Med.-Den. 3; 4 School 4; 5 Social, Rec. 5; 6 Ch. travel mode 6; 7 Eat meal 7; 8 Shopping 8; 9 Serve pass. 9; 0 Home 0		1 Street free 2 Street meter 3 Lot free 4 Lot paid 5 Garage free 6 Garage paid 7 Service or repairs 8 Res. property 9 Cruised 0 Not parked

Fig. 3.2 Internal trip report (Source: US Dept. of Commerce, 1944)

Savannah, and Lincoln. By 1954, metropolitan area traffic studies by the home interview method had been conducted in more than 100 metropolitan areas located in 36 states (US Dept. of Commerce, 1954b).

Other elements of the urban transportation planning process were also being developed and applied in pioneering traffic planning studies. New concepts and techniques were being generated and refined in such areas as traffic counting, highway inventories and classification, highway capacity, pavement condition studies, cost estimating, and system planning. The first attempt to meld many of these elements into an urban transportation planning process was in the Cleveland Regional Area Traffic Study in 1927, which was sponsored by the US Bureau of Public Roads. But, even in this study, traffic forecasting was a crude art using basically linear projections (Cron, 1975b).

In the Boston Transportation Study, a rudimentary form of the gravity model was applied to forecast traffic in 1926, but the technique was not used in other areas. In fact, the 1930s saw little advancement in the techniques of urban transportation planning. It was during this period that the methodology of highway needs and financial studies was developed and expanded (US Dept. of Transportation, 1979a).

By the 1940s, it was apparent that if certain relationships between land use and travel could be measured, these relationships could be used as a means to project future travel. It remained for the development of the computer, with its ability to process large masses of data from these surveys, to permit estimation of these relationships between travel, land use, and other factors. The first major test using this approach to develop future highway plans was during the early 1950s in San Juan, Puerto Rico, and in Detroit (Silver and Stowers, 1964; Detroit Metropolitan Area Traffic Study, 1955/6).

Early Transit Planning

During this period, transit planning was being carried out by operators as part of the regular activities of operating a transit system. Federal assistance was not available for planning or construction, and little federal interest existed in transit. However, financial problems increased as transit ridership declined, and there were no funds available to rehabilitate facilities and equipment. In some urban areas, transit authorities were created to take over and operate the transit system. The Chicago Transit Authority and the Metropolitan Transit Authority in Boston were created in 1947, and the New York City Transit Authority in 1955.

It was at this time that the San Francisco Bay area began planning for a regional rapid transit system. In 1956, the Rapid Transit Commission proposed a 123-mile system in a five-county area. As a result of this study, the Bay Area Rapid Transit District (BARTD) was formed among the five counties. BARTD completed the planning for the transit system and conducted preliminary engineering and financial studies. In November 1962, the voters approved a bond issue to build a three-county, 75-mile system, totally with local funds (Homburger, 1967).

Dawn of Analytical Methods

Prior to the early 1950s, the results of early origin–destination studies were used primarily for describing existing travel patterns, usually in the form of trip origins and destinations and by "desire lines," indicating schematically the major spatial distribution of trips. Future urban travel volumes were developed by extending the past traffic growth rate into the future, merely an extrapolation technique. Some transportation studies used no projections of any sort and emphasized only the alleviation of existing traffic problems (US Dept. of Transportation, 1967b).

Beginning in the early 1950s, new ideas and techniques were being rapidly generated for application in urban transportation planning. In 1950, the Highway Research Board published Route Selection and Traffic Assignment (Campbell, 1950), which was a compendium of correspondence summarizing practices in identifying traffic desire lines and linking origin–destination pairs. By the mid-1950s, Thomas Fratar, at the Cleveland Transportation Study, developed a computer method for distributing future origin–destination travel data using growth factors. In 1956, the Eno Foundation for Highway Traffic Control published Highway Traffic Estimation (Schmidt and Campbell, 1956), which documented the state of the art and highlighted the Fratar technique.

During this period, the US Bureau of Public Roads (BPR) sponsored a study on traffic generation at Columbia University, which was conducted by Robert Mitchell and Chester Rapkin. It was directed at improving the understanding of the relationship between travel and land use through empirical methods, and included both persons and goods movement. Mitchell and Rapkin state as a major premise of their study:

> Despite the considerable amount of attention given in various countries to movement between place of residence and place of work, the subject has not been given the special emphasis suggested here; that is, to view trips between home and workplace as a "system of movement," changes in which may be related to land use change and to other changes in related systems of urban action or in the social structure. (1954, p. 65)

They demonstrated an early understanding of many of the variables that effect travel patterns and behavior; for example:

> Systems of round trips from places of residence vary with the sex composition and age of the individual members of the household. The travel patterns of single individuals, young married couples, families with young children, and households consisting of aging persons all show marked differences in travel behavior. (Mitchell and Rapkin, 1954, p. 70)

They also anticipated the contribution of social science methods to the understanding of travel behavior:

> However, inquiry into the motivations of travel and their correspondence with both behavior and the actual events which are consequences of travel would make great contributions to understanding why this behavior occurs, and thus to increase the possibility of predicting behavior. (Mitchell and Rapkin, 1954, p. 54)

They concluded with a framework for analyzing travel patterns that included developing analytical relationships for land use and travel and then forecasting them as the basis for designing future transportation requirements.

AASHO Manual on User Benefit Analysis

Toward the end of the 1940s, the AASHO Committee on Planning and Design Policies, with the assistance of BPR, undertook the development of generally applicable analytical techniques for performing economic analysis of highway projects. The work grew out of a survey of state highway departments on the use of economic analysis, which found a definite lack of similarity in such procedures and their use (American Association of State Highway Officials, 1960).

Building upon earlier work on highway economic analysis, the committee developed a manual for conducting benefit–cost analyses (American Association of State Highway Officials, 1952a). The basic tenet of the manual was "…that a profit should be returned on an investment applies as well to highway projects as to general business ventures." Unlike previous methods of analysis that only measured construction, right of way, and maintenance costs, the manual included the costs to the user of the highway as a necessary and integral part of the economic analysis. Up to the publication, no data existed to perform such an analysis.

The manual defined the benefit to cost ratio as the difference in road user costs (between alternate routes) divided by the difference in costs. Road user costs included fuel, other operating costs (i.e., oil, tires, maintenance, depreciation), time value, comfort and convenience, vehicle ownership costs, and safety. The value of time was specified at $1.35 per vehicle h or $0.75 per person h. The value of comfort and convenience was included as an increasing cost for greater interference with the trip and varying according to the type of road. It ranged from 0 cents per mile for the best conditions to 1.0 cents per mile for the worst conditions. The manual included tables and charts containing specific values for these components of costs and benefits, and the procedures to conduct benefit–cost analyses.

The manual was updated in 1960 with the same analytical methodology but new unit cost data (American Association of State Highway Officials, 1960). A major update of the manual was issued in 1977 after a number of research efforts had been completed on analytical techniques and unit cost data (American Association of State Highway and Transportation Officials, 1978). The manual was also expanded to address bus transit improvements. The manual recognized that benefit–cost analysis was only an element in the evaluation of transportation projects and that it fit within the larger urban transportation planning process.

The revised edition, *A Manual of User Benefit Analysis for Highways*, 2nd Edition, was published in 2003 which updated the 1977 edition and the theoretical and empirical basis of highway improvement evaluations. It provided analytic tools to evaluate costs and benefits associated with transportation improvement projects. It was published in Paperback with a Windows CD-ROM (American Association of State Highway and Transportation Officials, 2003).

Breakthroughs in Analytical Techniques

The first breakthrough in using an analytical technique for travel forecasting came in 1955 with the publication of a paper entitled, "A General Theory of Traffic Movement," by Alan M. Voorhees (Voorhees, 1956). Voorhees advanced the gravity model as the means to link land use with urban traffic flows. Research had been proceeding for a number of years on a gravity theory for human interaction. Previously, the gravity analogy had been applied by sociologists and geographers to explain population movements. Voorhees used origin–destination survey data with driving time as the measure of spatial separation and estimated the exponents for a three-trip purpose gravity model. Others conducting similar studies soon corroborated these results (US Dept. of Commerce, 1963a).

Another breakthrough soon followed in the area of traffic assignment. The primary difficulty in traffic assignment was evaluating the driver's choice of route between the origin and the destination. Earl Campbell of the Highway Research Board proposed an "S" curve, which related the percent usage of a particular facility to a travel–time ratio. A number of empirical studies were undertaken to evaluate the theory using diversion of traffic to new expressways from arterial streets. From these studies, the American Association of State Highway Officials published a standard traffic diversion curve in "A Basis for Estimating Traffic Diversion to New Highways in Urban Areas" in 1952 (Fig. 3.3). However, traffic assignment was still largely a mechanical process requiring judgment (US Dept. of Commerce, 1964).

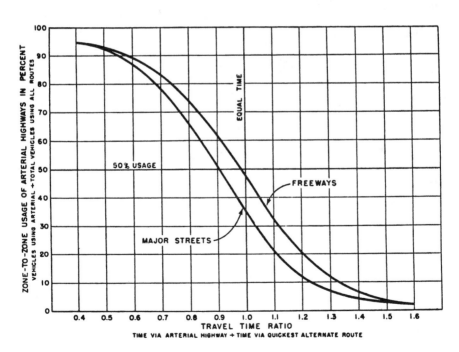

Fig. 3.3 Traffic diversion curves for urban arterial highways (Source: US Dept. of Commerce, 1964)

Then, in 1957, two papers were presented that discussed a minimum impedance algorithm for networks. One was titled, "The Shortest Path Through a Maze," by Edward F. Moore, and the second was, "The Shortest Route Problem," by George B. Danzig. With such an algorithm, travel could then be assigned to minimum time paths using newly developed computers. The staff of the Chicago Area Transportation Study under Dr. J. Douglas Carroll, Jr. finally developed and refined computer programs that allowed the assignment of traffic for the entire Chicago region (US Dept. of Commerce, 1964).

National Committee on Urban Transportation

While highway departments were placing major emphasis on arterial routes, city street congestion was steadily worsening. It was in this atmosphere that the Committee on Urban Transportation was created in 1954. Its purpose was, "to help cities do a better job of transportation planning through systematic collection of basic facts… to afford the public the best possible transportation at the least possible cost and aid in accomplishing desirable goals of urban renewal and sound urban growth" (National Committee, 1958–59).

The committee was composed of experts in a wide range of fields, representing federal, state, and city governments, transit, and other interests. It developed a guidebook, *Better Transportation for Your City* (National Committee, 1958–59), designed to help local officials establish an orderly program of urban transportation planning. It was supplemented by a series of 17 procedure manuals describing techniques for planning highway, transit, and terminal improvements. The guidebook and manuals received national recognition. Even though the guidebook was primarily intended for the attention of local officials, it stressed the need for cooperative action, full communication between professionals and decision-makers, and the development of transportation systems in keeping with the broad objectives of community development. It provided, for the first time, fully documented procedures for systematic transportation planning.

Housing Act of 1954 – "701" Comprehensive Planning Program

An important cornerstone of the federal policy concerning urban planning was Section 701 of the Housing Act of 1954. The act demonstrated congressional concern with urban problems and recognition of the urban planning process as an appropriate approach to dealing with such problems. Section 701 authorized the provision of federal planning assistance to state planning agencies, cities, and other municipalities having a population of less than 50,000 persons and, after further amendments, to metropolitan and regional planning agencies (Washington Center, 1970).

The intent of the act was to encourage an orderly process of urban planning to address the problems associated with urban growth and the formulation of local plans and policies. The act indicated that planning should occur on a region-wide basis within the framework of comprehensive planning. The program was instrumental in developing consistency in planning criteria and guidelines, and working toward the objective of establishing a single agency for all comprehensive and transportation activities in a metropolitan area.

The program encouraged state, local, and regional officials to make planning and management a continuous process to formulate, analyze, evaluate, and implement polices and objectives related to community development. The comprehensive planning programs helped provide a rational basis for community derisions relating to area-wide transportation and comprehensive planning objectives. The plans developed under the 701 Comprehensive Planning Program became the foundation for a metropolitan area's highway and transit plans (US Department of Transportation and US Department of Housing and Urban Development, 1974).

The program was initially funded at $1 million per year and rose to its heights in the early 1970s with $100 million per year in appropriations. The program ended in 1981 as the focus of urban programs shifted to other priorities (Feiss, 1985).

Pioneering Urban Transportation Studies

The developments in analytical methodology began to be applied in pioneering urban transportation studies in the late 1940s and during the 1950s. Before these studies, urban transportation planning was based on existing travel demands or on travel forecasts using uniform growth factors applied on an area-wide basis.

The San Juan, Puerto Rico, transportation study begun in 1948 was one of the earliest to use a trip generation approach to forecast trips. Trip generation rates were developed for a series of land-use categories stratified by general location, crude intensity measures, and type of activity. These rates were applied, with some modifications, to the projected land use plan (Silver and Stowers, 1964).

The Detroit Metropolitan Area Traffic Study (DMATS) put together all the elements of an urban transportation study for the first time. It was conducted from 1953 to 1955 under Executive Director Dr. J. Douglas Carroll, Jr. The DMATS staff developed trip generation rates by land use category for each zone. Future trips were estimated from a land use forecast. The trip distribution model was a variant of the gravity model with airline distance as the factor to measure travel friction. Traffic assignment was carried out with speed and distance ratio curves. Much of the work was done by hand with the aid of tabulating machines for some of the calculations. Benefit/cost ratios were used to evaluate the major elements of the expressway network (Detroit Metropolitan Area Traffic Study, 1955/1956; Silver and Stowers, 1964; Creighton, 1970).

In 1955, the Chicago Area Transportation Study (CATS) began under the direction of Dr. J. Douglas Carroll, Jr. It set the standard for future urban transportation studies.

The lessons learned in Detroit were applied in Chicago with greater sophistication. CATS used the basic six-step procedure pioneered in Detroit: data collection, forecasts, goal formulation, preparation of network proposals, testing of proposals, and evaluation of proposals. Transportation networks were developed to serve travel generated by projected land-use patterns. They were tested using systems analysis considering the effect of each facility on other facilities in the network. Networks were evaluated based on economic efficiency – the maximum amount of travel carried at the least cost. CATS used trip generation, trip distribution, modal split, and traffic assignment models for travel forecasting. A simple land-use forecasting procedure was employed to forecast future land-use and activity patterns. The CATS staff made major advances in the use of the computer in travel forecasting (Chicago Area Transportation Study, 1959–1962; Swerdloff and Stowers, 1966; Wells, et al., 1970).

Other transportation studies followed including the Washington Area Traffic Study in 1955, the Baltimore Transportation Study in 1957, the Pittsburgh Area Transportation Study (PATS) in 1958, the Hartford Area Traffic Study in 1958, and the Penn–Jersey (Philadelphia) Transportation Study in 1959. All of these studies were transportation planning on a new scale. They were region wide, multidisciplinary undertakings involving large full-time staffs. Urban transportation studies were carried out by ad hoc organizations with separate policy committees. They were not directly connected to any unit of government. Generally, these urban transportation studies were established for a limited time period with the objective of producing a plan and reporting on it. Such undertakings would have been impossible before the availability of computers (Creighton, 1970).

The resulting plans were heavily oriented to regional highway networks based primarily on the criteria of economic costs and benefits. Transit was given secondary consideration. New facilities were evaluated against traffic engineering improvements. Little consideration was given to regulatory or pricing approaches, or new technologies (Wells, et al., 1970).

These pioneering urban transportation studies set the content and tone for future studies. They provided the basis for the federal guidelines that were issued in the following decade.

Federal-Aid Highway Act of 1956

During this early period in the development of urban transportation planning came the Federal-Aid Highway Act of 1956. The act launched the largest public works program yet undertaken: construction of the National System of Interstate and Defense Highways. The act was the culmination of two decades of studies and negotiation. As a result of the Interregional Highways report, Congress had adopted a National System of Interstate Highways not to exceed 40,000 miles in the Federal-Aid Highway Act of 1944. However, money was not authorized for construction of the system. Based on the recommendations of the US Bureau of Public Roads and the Department of Defense, a 37,700-mile system was adopted in 1947 (Fig. 3.4).

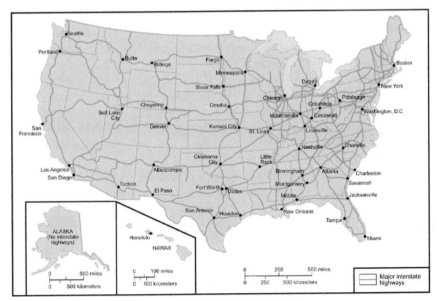

THE INTERSTATE HIGHWAY SYSTEM

Fig. 3.4 National system of interstate highways (Source: US Dept. of Commerce, 1957)

This network consisted primarily solely for of the most heavily traveled routes of the Federal-Aid Primary System. The remaining 2,300 miles were reserved for additional radials, by-pass loops, and circumferential routes in and adjacent to urban areas. Studies of urban area needs were made by the states with the cooperation and aid of city officials. The urban connections were formally designated in 1955 (US Dept. of Commerce, 1957).

Funds were appropriated by then, but at very low levels: $25 million annually for 1952 and 1953 with a 50% federal share, and $175 million annually for 1954 and beyond with a 60% federal share. To secure a significant increase in funding, a major national lobbying effort was launched in 1952 by the Highway Users Conference under the title, "Project Adequate Roads." President Eisenhower appointed a national advisory committee under General Lucius D. Clay, which produced a report, A Ten-Year National Highway Program, in 1955. It recommended building a 37,000-mile Interstate System using bonds to fund the $23 billion cost (Kuehn, 1976).

Finally, with the Federal-Aid Highway Act of 1956, construction of the National System of Interstate and Defense Highways shifted into high gear. The act increased the authorized system extent to 41,000 miles. This system was planned to link 90% of the cities with populations of 50,000 or greater and many smaller cities and towns. The act also authorized the expenditure of $24.8 billion in 13 fiscal years from 1957 to 1969 at a 90% federal share. The act provided construction standards and maximum sizes and weights of vehicles that could operate on the system. The system was to be completed by 1972 (Kuehn, 1976).

The companion Highway Revenue Act of 1956 increased federal taxes on gasoline and other motor fuels and excise taxes on tires, and established new taxes on retreaded tires and a weight tax on heavy trucks and buses. It created the Highway Trust Fund to receive the tax revenue that was dedicated to highway purposes. This provision broke with a long-standing congressional precedent not to earmark taxes for specific authorized purposes (US Dept. of Commerce, 1957).

These acts have had a profound effect on urban areas. They established an assured funding source for highways, through user charges, at a time when federal funds were not available for mass transportation. They set a 90% federal share that was far above the existing 50% share for other federal-aid highways. About 20% of the system mileage was designated as urban to provide alternative interstate service into, through, and around urban areas. These provisions dominated urban transportation planning for years to come and eventually caused the development of countervailing forces to balance the urban highway program.

Sagamore Conference on Highways and Urban Development

The availability of large amounts of funds from the 1956 Act brought immediate response to develop action programs. To encourage the cooperative development of highway plans and programs, a conference was held in 1958 in the Sagamore Center at Syracuse University (Sagamore, 1958).

The conference focused on the need to conduct the planning of urban transportation, including public transportation, on a region-wide, comprehensive basis in a manner that supported the orderly development of the urban areas. The conference report recognized that urban transportation plans should be evaluated through a grand accounting of benefits and costs that included both user and nonuser impacts.

The conference recommendations were endorsed and their implementation urged, but progress was slow. The larger urban areas were carrying out pioneering urban transportation studies, the most noteworthy being the CATS. But few of the smaller urban areas had begun planning studies due to the lack of capable staff to perform urban transportation planning.

To encourage smaller areas to begin planning efforts, the American Municipal Association, the American Association of State Highway Officials, and the National Association of County Officials jointly launched a program in early 1962 to describe and explain how to carry out urban transportation planning. This program was initially directed at urban areas under 250,000 in population (Holmes, 1973).

Housing Act of 1961

The first piece of federal legislation to deal explicitly with urban mass transportation was the Housing Act of 1961. This act was passed largely as a result of the growing financial difficulties with commuter rail services. The act inaugurated a small, low-interest loan program for acquisitions and capital improvements for mass transit systems and a demonstration program (Washington Center, 1970).

The act also contained a provision for making federal planning assistance available for "preparation of comprehensive urban transportation surveys, studies, and plans to aid in solving problems of traffic congestion, facilitating the circulation of people and goods on metropolitan and other urban areas and reducing transportation needs." The act permitted federal aid to "facilitate comprehensive planning for urban development, including coordinated transportation systems, on a continuing basis." These provisions of the act amended the Section 701 planning program that was created by the Housing Act of 1954.

Chapter 4
Urban Transportation Planning Comes of Age

Urban transportation planning came of age with the passage of the Federal-Aid Highway Act of 1962, which required that approval of any federal-aid highway project in an urbanized area of 50,000 or more in population be based on a continuing, comprehensive urban transportation planning process carried out cooperatively by state and local governments. This was the first legislative mandate requiring planning as a condition to receiving federal capital assistance funds. The US Bureau of Public Roads (BPR) moved quickly to issue technical guidance interpreting the act's provisions.

Through the mid-1960s urban transportation planning went through what some have called its "golden age." Most urban areas were planning their regional highway system, and urban transportation planning methodology had been designed to address this issue. The BPR carried out an extensive program of research, technical assistance, and training to foster the adoption of this process and the new methodologies. These efforts completely transformed the manner in which urban transportation planning was performed. By the legislated deadline of 1 July 1965, all 224 of the then existing urbanized areas that fell under the 1962 Act had an urban transportation planning process underway.

This was also a period in which there was early recognition of the need for a federal role in urban mass transportation. This role, however, was to remain limited for a number of years to come.

Joint Report on Urban Mass Transportation

In March 1962, a joint report on urban mass transportation was submitted to President Kennedy, at his request, by the Secretary of Commerce and the Housing and Home Finance Administrator (US Congress, Senate, 1962). This report integrated the objectives for highways and mass transit, which were comparatively independent up to that point but growing closer through cooperative activities. The report was in a large part based on a study completed in 1961 by the Institute of Public Administration (IPA) entitled Urban Transportation and Public Policy

E. Weiner, *Urban Transportation Planning in the United States, Third Edition*,
doi:10.1007/978-0-387-77152-6, © Springer Science+Business Media, LLC 2008

(Fitch, 1964). The IPA report strongly recommended that urban transportation was a federal concern and supported the need for transportation planning.

The general thrust of the report to Congress, as it related to planning, can be summarized by the following excerpt from the transmittal letter:

> Transportation is one of the key factors in shaping our cities. As our communities increasingly undertake deliberate measures to guide their development and renewal, we must be sure that transportation planning and construction are integral parts of general development planning and programming. One of our main recommendations is that federal aid for urban transportation should be made available only when urban communities have prepared or are actively preparing up-to-date general plans for the entire urban area which relate transportation plans to land use and development plans.
>
> The major objectives of urban transportation policy are the achievement of sound land-use patterns, the assurance of transportation facilities for all segments of the population, the improvement of overall traffic flow, and the meeting of total transportation needs at minimum cost. Only a balanced transportation system can attain these goals - and in many urban areas this means an extensive mass transportation network fully integrated with the highway and street system. But mass transportation in recent years experienced capital consumption rather than expansion. A cycle of fare increases and service cuts to offset loss of ridership followed by further declines in use points clearly to the need for a substantial contribution of public funds to support needed mass transportation improvements. We therefore recommend a new program of grants and loans for urban mass transportation. (US Congress, Senate, 1962).

President Kennedy's Transportation Message

In April 1962, President Kennedy delivered his first message to Congress on the subject of transportation. Many of the ideas related to urban transportation in the message drawn upon in the previously mentioned joint report. The President's message recognized the close relationship between the community development and the need to properly balance the use of private automobiles and mass transportation to help shape and serve urban areas. It also recognized the need to promote economic efficiency and livability of urban areas. It also recommended continued close cooperation between the Department of Commerce and the Housing and Home Finance Administration (HHFA) (Washington Center, 1970).

This transportation message opened a new era in urban transportation and led to passage of two landmark pieces of legislation: the Federal-Aid Highway Act of 1962 and the Urban Mass Transportation Act of 1964.

Federal-Aid Highway Act of 1962

The Federal-Aid Highway Act of 1962 was the first piece of federal legislation to mandate urban transportation planning as a condition for receiving federal funds in urbanized areas. It asserted that federal concern in urban transportation was to be integrated with land development and provided a major stimulus to urban transportation planning. Section 9 of the act, which is now Section 134 of Title 23 states:

> It is declared to be in the national interest to encourage and promote the development of transportation systems embracing various modes of transport in a manner that will serve the states and local communities efficiently and effectively. (US Dept. of Transportation, 1980a)

This statement of policy directly followed from the recommendations of the Sagamore conference and President Kennedy's Transportation Message. Moreover, the section directed the Secretary of Commerce to cooperate with the states:

> ...in the development of long-range highway plans and programs which are properly coordinated with plans for improvements in other affected forms of transportation and which are formulated with due consideration to their probable effect on the future development of the urban area... (US Dept. of Transportation, 1980a)

The last sentence of the section, which required that urban highway construction projects be based upon a planning process, legislated the planning requirement:

> After July 1, 1965, the Secretary shall not approve under section 105 of this title any programs for projects in any urban area of more than fifty thousand population unless he finds that such projects are based on a continuing, comprehensive transportation planning process carried out cooperatively by states and local communities in conformance with the objectives stated in this section. (US Dept. of Transportation, 1980a)

Two features of the act are particularly significant with respect to the organizational arrangements for carrying out the planning process. First, it called for a planning process in urban areas rather than cities, which set the scale at the metropolitan or regional level. Second, it called for the process to be carried on cooperatively by the states and local communities. Because qualified planning agencies to mount such a transportation planning process were lacking in many urban areas, the BPR required the creation of planning agencies or organizational arrangements that would be capable of carrying out the required planning process. These planning organizations quickly came into being because of the growing momentum of the highway program and the cooperative financing of the planning process by the HHFA and the BPR (Marple, 1969).

In addition, the act restricted the use of the 1½% planning and research funds to only those purposes. If not used for planning and research, the state would lose the funds. Previously, a state could request that these funds be used instead for construction. This provision created a permanent, assured funding source for planning and research activities. In addition, the act provided that a state could spend another 0.5% at their option for planning and research activities.

Hershey Conference on Urban Freeways

In response to the growing concern about freeway construction in urban areas, the Hershey Conference on Freeways in the Urban Setting was convened in June 1962 (Freeways, 1962). It concluded, "Freeways cannot be planned independently of the areas through which they pass. The planning concept should extend to the entire sector of the city within the environs of the freeway." The conference recommendations reinforced the need to integrate highway planning and urban development.

The findings recognized that this planning should be done as a team effort that draws upon the skills of engineers, architects, city planners, and other specialists. Freeway planning must integrate the freeway with its surroundings. When properly planned, freeways provide an opportunity to shape and structure the urban community in a manner that meets the needs of the people who live, work, and travel in these areas. Further, the planning effort should be carried out in a manner that involves participation by the community (Freeways, 1962).

Implementation of the 1962 Federal-Aid Highway Act

The BPR moved quickly to implement the planning requirements of the 1962 Federal-Aid Highway Act. Instructional Memorandum 50-2-63, published in March 1963 (US Dept. of Commerce, 1963c) and later superseded by Policy and Procedure Memorandum 50-9 (US Dept. of Transportation, 1967a), interpreted the act's provisions related to a "continuing, comprehensive, and cooperative" (3C) planning process. "Cooperative" was defined to include not only cooperation between the federal, state, and local levels of government but also among the various agencies within the same level of government. "Continuing" referred to the need to periodically reevaluate and update a transportation plan. "Comprehensive" was defined to include the basic ten elements of a 3C planning process for which inventories and analyses were required (Table 4.1).

These memoranda and further refinements and expansions upon them covered all aspects for organizing and carrying out the 3C planning process.

Through its Urban Planning Division, under Garland E. Marple, the BPR carried out a broad program to develop planning procedures and computer programs, write procedural manuals and guides, teach training courses, and provide technical assistance.

Table 4.1 Ten basic elements of a continuing, comprehensive, cooperative (3C) planning process

1. Economic factors affecting development
2. Population
3. Land use
4. Transportation facilities including those for mass transportation
5. Travel patterns
6. Terminal and transfer facilities
7. Traffic control features
8. Zoning ordinances, subdivision regulations, building codes, etc.
9. Financial resources
10. Social and community-value factors, such as preservation of open space, parks, and recreational facilities; preservation of historical sites and buildings; environmental amenities; and aesthetics

Source: US Dept. of Commerce, 1963c

The effort was aimed at developing urbanized area planning organizations, standardizing, computerizing and applying procedures largely created in the late 1950s, and disseminating knowledge of such procedures.

The BPR defined the various steps in a 3C planning process. These steps had been pioneered by the urban transportation planning studies that were carried out during the 1950s. It was an empirical approach that required a substantial amount of data and several years to complete. The process consisted of establishing an organization to carry out the planning process, development of local goals and objectives, surveys and inventories of existing conditions and facilities, analyses of current conditions and calibration of forecasting techniques, forecasting of future activity and travel, evaluation of alternative transportation networks resulting in a recommended transportation plan, staging of the transportation plan, and identification of resources to implement it. The product of these 3C planning studies was generally an elaborate report describing the procedures, analyses, alternatives, and recommended plans.

To foster the adoption of these technical procedures, the BPR released a stream of procedural manuals that became the technical standards for many years to come: (Calibrating and Testing a Gravity Model for Any Size Urban Area (U.S. Dept. of Commerce, 1963b), (Calibrating and Testing a Gravity Model with a Small Computer (October 1963), Traffic Assignment Manual (U.S. Dept. of Commerce, 1965b). Population Forecasting Methods (Herman, Frank, 1964), (Population, Economic, and Land Use Studies in Urban Transportation Planning July 1964), (The Standard Land Use Coding Manual January 1965), (The Role of Economic Studies in Urban Transportation Planning (Meck, Joseph, 1965), (Traffic Assignment and Distribution for Small Urban Areas, September 1965), (Modal Split Documentation of Nine Methods for Estimating Transit Usage, December 1966), (Fertal, et al., 1966), and (Guidelines for Trip Generation Analysis, June 1967).

The BPR developed a 2-week "Urban Transportation Planning Course" that was directed at practicing planners and engineers. It covered organizational issues and technical procedures for carrying out a 3C planning process as it had been conceptualized by the BPR. The course used the BPR manuals as textbooks and supplemented them with lecture notes to keep the information current and to cover material not in manual form. In addition, personnel from the BPR provided hands-on technical assistance to state and local agencies in the applying these new procedures to their own areas.

This effort to define the "3C planning process," to develop techniques for performing the technical activities, and to provide technical assistance completely transformed the manner in which urban transportation planning was performed. By the legislated deadline of 1 July 1965, all the 224 existing urbanized areas that fell under the 1962 Act had an urban transportation planning process underway (Holmes, 1973).

Conventional Urban Travel Forecasting Process

The 3C planning process included four technical phases: collection of data, analysis of data, forecasts of activity and travel, and evaluation of alternatives. Central to this approach was the urban travel forecasting process (Fig. 4.1). The process used

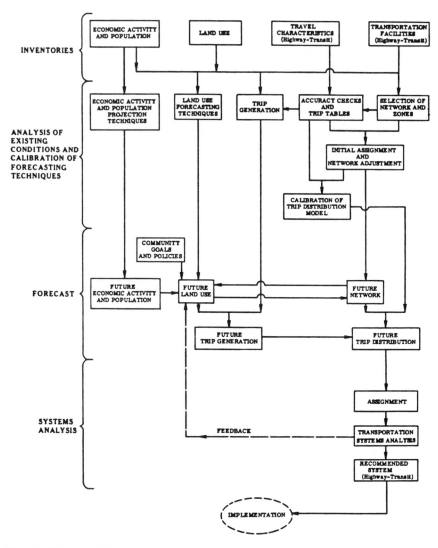

Fig. 4.1 Urban travel forecasting process (Source: US Dept. of Transportation, 1977c)

mathematical models that allowed the simulation and forecasting of current and future travel. This permitted the testing and evaluation of alternative transportation networks.

The four-step urban travel forecasting process consisted of trip generation, trip distribution, modal split, and traffic assignment. These models were first calibrated to replicate existing travel using actual survey data. These models were then used to forecast future travel. The forecasting process began with an estimate of the variables that determine travel patterns including the location and intensity of land use, social and economic characteristics of the population, and the type and the extent of transportation facilities in the area. Next, these variables were used to estimate the number of trip origins and destinations in each sub-area of a region (i.e., the traffic analysis zone), using a trip generation procedure. A trip distribution model was used to connect the trip ends into an origin–destination trip pattern. This matrix of total vehicle trips was divided into highway and transit trips using a modal split model. The matrices of highway and transit trips were assigned to routes on the highway and transit networks, respectively, by means of a traffic assignment model (US Dept. of Transportation, 1977a).

In using these models to analyze future transportation networks, forecasts of input variables were used for the year for which the networks were being tested. Travel forecasts were then prepared for each transportation alternative to determine traffic volumes and levels of service. Usually only the modal split and traffic assignment models were rerun for additional networks after a future year forecast had been made for the first network. But occasionally the trip distribution model was also rerun.

Travel forecasting on a region-wide scale required a large computing capability. The first generation of computers had become available in the mid-1950s. The BPR had taken advantage of them and adapted a telephone routing algorithm for traffic assignments purposes that would operate on the IBM 704 computer. Additional programs were developed to perform other functions. The second generation of computers, circa 1962, provided increased capabilities. The library of computer programs was rewritten for the IBM 709 computer and then for the IBM 7090/94 system. The BPR worked with the Bureau of Standards in developing, modifying, and testing these programs. Some programs were also developed for the IBM 1401 and 1620 computers. This effort was carried out over a number of years, and by 1967 the computer package contained about 60 programs (US Dept. of Transportation, 1977c).

This approach to travel forecasting, which later became known as the "conventional urban travel forecasting process," came quickly into widespread use. The procedures had been specifically tailored to the tasks of region-wide urban transportation planning, and BPR provided substantial assistance and oversight in applying them. Moreover, there were no other procedures generally available, and urban transportation study groups that chose not to use them had to develop their own procedures and computer programs.

Southeastern Wisconsin Regional Planning Commission

In most urbanized areas, ad hoc organizational arrangements were created to conduct the urban transportation planning process required by the Federal-Aid Highway Act of 1962 and the Bureau of Public Roads' guidelines. In some urbanized areas, however, the urban transportation planning process was carried out by existing regional planning agencies. This was the case for the urbanized areas of Milwaukee, Racine, and Kenosha in Southeastern Wisconsin.

The Southeastern Wisconsin Regional Planning Commission (SEWRPC) was created under State enabling legislation by Executive Order of the Governor of Wisconsin in 1960 upon petition of the County Boards of the seven constituent counties. It was directed to prepare and adopt master plans for the physical development of the Southeastern Wisconsin region on the basis of studies and analyses. The Commission itself was formed with 21 citizen members, serving for 6 years without pay, 3 from each county, with 1 member from each county appointed by the County Board and the other 2 members appointed by the Governor (Bauer, 1963).

The Regional Land Use-Transportation Study, which began in 1963, was the Commission's first long-range planning effort. The staff proceeded under the guidance of the Intergovernmental Coordinating and the Technical Coordinating Committees (Fig. 4.2). The 3½-year, $2 million study covered the development of goals and objectives, inventory of existing conditions, preparation and analysis of alternative plans, and selection and adoption of the preferred plan (Southeastern Wisconsin Regional Planning Commission, 1965–66). SEWRPC prepared three alternative land use plans for the year 1990. The "controlled existing trend plan" continued the low-density residential development trend with the imposition of land use controls to minimize leap-frog development and reduce encroachment on environmentally sensitive areas. The "corridor plan" concentrated medium- and high-density residential development along transportation corridors interlocked with recreation and agriculture wedges. The "satellite city plan" focused new residential development into existing outlying communities in the region. A transportation

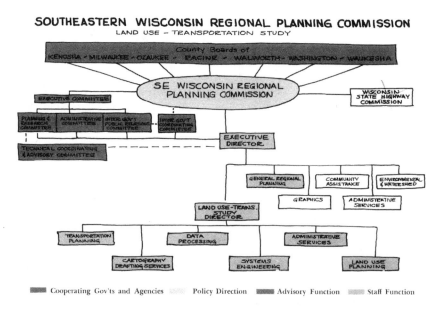

Fig. 4.2 Southeastern Wisconsin regional planning commission (Source: Highways and Urban Development, 1965)

plan was developed for each of the land use plans that primarily consisted of the existing plus committed highway and transit systems with additions, including an extensive bus rapid transit system with an exclusive busway.

The recommended "controlled existing trend plan" was adopted by the full commission and eventually by most of the county boards and local units of government. In 1966, SEWRPC began the continuing phase of the land use-transportation study that provided support to implement the plan, monitored changes in the region and progress in implementing the adopted plan, and conducted periodic reappraisals of the plan in light of the changes in the region.

In the ensuing years, SEWRPC conducted a wide range of planning studies including those related to watershed development and water quality, air quality, highway functional classification, public transportation, parks and open space, port development, libraries, airport use, and prepared many local plans in cooperation with the local jurisdictions. Moreover, it provided extensive technical assistance to local governments on a variety of planning issues.

Highway Planning Program Manual

As part of its extensive efforts to provide technical guidance for carrying out highway planning, the BPR developed the *Highway Planning Program Manual*. The manual was designed to consolidate technical information on highway planning practice and make it readily available. Much of that information on highway planning practice and many of the manuals had been developed by the BPR.

The *Highway Planning Program Manual* was first issued in August 1963 (US Dept. of Commerce, 1963d). It was directed primarily at the highway engineers in BPR's field offices who needed information to administer highway planning activities that were being carried out by State highway departments and by urban transportation planning groups with federal-aid highway planning funds. It also provided valuable information to those performing the actual planning activities in state and local agencies.

The manual covered the basic elements of a highway planning program that included administration and control, highway inventory, mapping, traffic counting, classifying and weighing, travel studies, motor vehicle registration and taxes, highway fiscal data, road life expectancy and costs, and urban transportation planning. The goal for the overall highway planning process was to develop a master plan for highway development. This was to consist of a functionally classified highway system, an estimate of highway needs, a long-range development program to meet the needs with priorities, and a financial plan to pay for the development program.

The section of the manual devoted to urban transportation planning was equally detailed. It covered various aspects of the urban transportation planning process including organization, use of computers, origin destination studies, population studies, economic studies, land use, street inventory and classification, evaluation of traffic services, traffic engineering studies, public transportation, terminal facilities, travel forecasting, traffic assignment, developing the transportation plan, plan implementation, and the continuing planning process.

The Federal Highway Administration continued to update the *Highway Planning Program Manual* and add appendices, which included recent version of relevant procedure manuals, until the early 1980's. The manual was eventually rescinded by FHWA in 1985.

Urban Mass Transportation Act of 1964

The first real effort to provide federal assistance for urban mass transportation development was the passage of the Urban Mass Transportation Act of 1964. The objective of the act, still in the spirit of President Kennedy's Transportation Message, was "...to encourage the planning and establishment of areawide urban mass transportation systems needed for economical and desirable urban development" (US Dept. of Transportation, 1979b).

The act authorized federal capital grants for up to two-thirds of the net project cost of construction, reconstruction, or acquisition of mass transportation facilities and equipment. Net project cost was defined as that portion of the total project cost that could not be financed readily from transit revenues. However, the federal share was to be held to 50% in those areas that had not completed their comprehensive planning process, that is, had not produced a plan. All federal funds had to be channeled through public agencies. Transit projects were to be initiated locally. Section 13(c) of the act protected employees in transit properties from the potential adverse effects of federal transit assistance so that they would not be fired or lose their collective bargaining rights.

A program of research, development, and demonstration was also authorized by the 1964 act. The objective of this program was to "...assist in the reduction of transportation needs, the improvement of mass transportation service, or the contribution of such service toward meeting total urban transportation needs at minimum cost" (US Dept. of Transportation, 1979b).

Congress, however, did not authorize much money to carry out this legislation. Not more than $150 million per year was authorized under the 1964 act and the actual appropriations fell short of even that amount (Smirk, 1968).

Urban Development Simulation Models

With the growth of urban transportation planning came an increasing interest in understanding urban phenomena and in constructing urban development simulation models. Such models would enable planners to evaluate alternative urban development patterns, and to produce information on population, employment, and land use for use in estimating travel and transportation requirements. Land use simulation models that developed in early urban transportation studies were rudimentary and focused on the effect of transportation access on the location of activities (Swerdloff and Stowers, 1966).

During this period, many cities were actively engaged in developing work plans to eliminate slums and urban blight through Community Renewal Programs (CRPs) that were partially funded by the Housing and Home Finance Agency (HHFA). These CRPs provided an additional impetus for the development of urban simulation models. It was as part of one of these CRPs that a significant breakthrough occurred. Between 1962 and 1963, Ira S. Lowry developed a land use allocation model for the Pittsburgh Regional Planning Association as part of a modeling system to generate alternatives and aid decision-making (Lowry, 1964).

The "Lowry model," as it came to be known, was the first large-scale and complete urban simulation model to become operational. The model was attractive because of the simplicity of its causal structure, the opportunity to expand it, and its operationality (Goldner, 1971). The underlying concept of the model used economic base theory in which employment was divided into "basic" employment that was devoted to goods and services exported outside the region, and "retail" or "nonbasic" employment that served local markets. Basic employment was located outside the model, while nonbasic employment by the model was located on the basis of its accessibility to households. Households were located on the basis of accessibility to jobs and availability of vacant land. The model proceeded in an iterative fashion until equilibrium was reached (Putman, 1979).

The conceptual framework developed by Lowry stimulated an era of model development during the mid-1960s, much of which concentrated on elaborations and enhancements of the original Lowry model concepts (Goldner, 1971; Harris, 1965; Putman, 1979). The Lowry model evolved through further development in Pittsburgh and the San Francisco Bay Area Simulation Study, and other efforts by a number of researchers. Most of this work, however, did not result in models that did not become operational (Goldner, 1971). After a period of dormancy, work began anew and resulted in the development of the integrated transportation and land-use package (ITLUP). This set of models performed land use activity allocation, incorporating the effects of transportation on land use, and the feedback effects of land use on transportation (Putman, 1983).

Williamsburg Conference on Highways and Urban Development

By 1965 there was concern that planning processes were not adequately evaluating social and community values. Few planning studies had developed goal-based evaluation methodologies. A second conference on Highways and Urban Development was held in Williamsburg, Virginia, to discuss this problem (Highways and Urban Development, 1965). The conference concluded that transportation must be directed toward raising urban standards and enhancing aggregate community values. Transportation values such as safety, economy, and comfort are part of the total set of community values and should be weighted appropriately.

The conference resolutions highlighted the need to identify urban goals and objectives that should be used to evaluate urban transportation plans. It emphasized that many values may not be quantifiable but, nonetheless, should not be ignored. The conference also endorsed the concept of making maximum use of existing transportation facilities through traffic management and land use controls.

Residential Location and Urban Mobility

During the 1960s, the US Bureau of Public Roads contracted with the University of Michigan, Survey Research Center to conduct several surveys on the attitudes of families toward residential location and travel preferences. By surveying consumer attitudes, transportation planners were attempting to understand the direction of the leading indicators for future residential patterns and travel decisions. The Survey Research Center conducted two waves of interviews for a statistically selected sample (exclusive of the New York metropolitan area) during the mid-1960s (Lansing et al., 1964).

The findings of this research provided a benchmark of consumer attitudes in the mid-1960s (Lansing, 1966; Lansing and Hendricks, 1967).

- The existing pattern of residential location was strongly influenced by family income and stage in the family life cycle.
- There was a strong preference of single family homes. The entire 85% of the families surveyed preferred to live in a single family home.
- The preference for a large lot size was evident. The preferred lot size was about three-tenths to five-tenths of an acre compared to the then existing average of two-tenths of an acre.
- The features most recent movers were looking for in their new homes were related primarily to needs for space.
- While a majority of people liked their present location, more preferred to move further out than closer in.
- The number of automobiles a family owned increased with their incomes and with lower density areas.
- The number of miles a family traveled annually increased with their income and the number of adults in the household.
- The average journey to work was 5 miles in the cities studied. It took 20 min by car and twice that long by common carrier. About half as many workers headed away from the center of the metropolitan area as toward it.
- Most people preferred to go to work by car than by common carrier. If the time and cost of the two modes were the same, nine out of ten people would prefer to go by car. People indicated that they liked the freedom of movement and the convenience of travel by car; they disliked common carriers because they were crowded.

This study captured the preferences of the American population in the postwar era when the force of rising incomes launched the spread to the suburbs, the rise of automobile ownership, the expansion of automobile usage, and the low density pattern of development that evolved over several decades.

Chapter 5
Improving Intergovernmental Coordination

As the number and scope of federal programs for urban development and transportation projects expanded, there was increasing concern over the uncoordinated manner in which these projects were being carried out. Each of these federal programs had separate grant requirements that were often developed with little regard to the requirements of other programs. Projects proceeded through the approval and implementation process uncoordinated with other projects that were occurring in the same area.

During this period, several actions were taken to alleviate this problem. First was an attempt to better integrate urban development and transportation programs at the federal level by bringing them together in two new Cabinet level departments, HUD and DOT. Second was the creation of a project review process to improve intergovernmental coordination at both the federal and local levels. States and local governments also moved to address this problem by consolidating functions and responsibilities. Many states created their own departments of transportation. In addition, states and local communities created broader, multifunctional planning agencies to better coordinate and plan area-wide development.

The urban transportation planning process transitioned into the "continuing" phase as most urban areas completed their first plans. There was a new interest in low capital approaches to reducing traffic congestion using techniques such as reserved bus lanes, traffic engineering improvements, and fringe parking lots. It was also during this time that national concern was focused upon the problem of highway safety and the enormous cost of traffic accidents. Environmental issues became more important with legislation, addressing the preservation of natural areas and historic sites, and providing relocation assistance for households and businesses.

Housing and Urban Development Act of 1965

The Housing and Urban Development Act of 1965 created the Department of Housing and Urban Development (HUD) to better coordinate urban programs at the federal level. In addition, the act amended the Section 701 urban planning assistance

E. Weiner, *Urban Transportation Planning in the United States, Third Edition*,
doi:10.1007/978-0-387-77152-6, © Springer Science+Business Media, LLC 2008

program established under the Housing Act of 1954 by authorizing grants to be made to "...organizations composed of public officials whom he (the Secretary of HUD) finds to be representative of the political jurisdictions within a metropolitan area or urban region..." for the purposes of comprehensive planning (Washington Center, 1970).

This provision encouraged the formation of regional planning organizations controlled by elected rather than appointed officials. It gave impetus to the formation of such organizations as councils of governments (COGs). It also encouraged local governments to cooperate in addressing their problems in a regional context.

1966 Amendments to the Urban Mass Transportation Act

To fill several gaps in the 1964 Urban Mass Transportation Act, a number of amendments were passed in 1966. One created the technical studies program, which provided federal assistance up to a two-thirds federal matching share for planning, engineering, and designing of urban mass transportation projects or other similar technical activities leading to application for a capital grant.

Another section authorized grants to be made for management training. The third authorized a project to study and prepare a program of research for developing new systems of urban transportation. This section resulted in a report to Congress in 1968, Tomorrow's Transportation: New Systems for the Urban Future (Cole, 1968), which recommended a long-range balanced program for research on hardware, planning, and operational improvements. It was this study that first brought to public attention many new systems such as dial-a-bus, personal rapid transit, dual mode, pallet systems, and tracked air-cushioned vehicle systems. This study was the basis for numerous research efforts to develop and refine new urban transportation technologies that would improve on existing ones.

Highway and Motor Vehicle Safety Acts of 1966

In 1964, highway deaths amounted to 48,000 persons, 10% more than that of 1963, and the death rate was increasing. In March 1965, newly Senator Abraham Ribicoff, Chairman of the Subcommittee on Executive Reorganization of the Government Operations Committee, held hearings on the issue of highway safety to focus national concern on this national tragedy. Ralph Nader who was already working on highway safety volunteered to assist Senator Ribicoff's committee. He provided much material to the committee based on his research and a book that he was writing on traffic safety (Insurance Institute for Highway Safety, 1986).

In the July hearings, General Motors' president admitted that his company had only spent $1.25 million on safety in the previous year. Following that disclosure,

President Johnson ordered Special Assistant Joseph Califano to develop a transportation package. In November 1965, Mr. Nader's book, *Unsafe at Any Speed*, was published with criticism of both the automobile industry and the traffic safety establishment.

In February 1966, President Johnson told the American Trial Lawyers Association that highway deaths were second only to the Vietnam War as the "gravest problem before the nation." A month later, the President's message requested the Congress to establish a department of transportation. His message also outlined a national traffic safety act to require the establishment of motor vehicle standards, provide for state grants in aid for safety programs, and fund traffic safety research. By August, both houses unanimously passed a motor vehicle standards bill and, with only three dissenting votes in the Senate, passed state program legislation. The final bills were signed by President Johnson on 9 September 1966.

The National Traffic and Motor Vehicle Safety Act of 1966 established the National Traffic Safety Agency in the Department of Commerce. It required the establishment of minimum safety standards for motor vehicles and equipment, authorized research and development, and expanded the National Driver Register of individuals whose licenses had been denied, terminated, or withdrawn. According to the act, each standard was required to be practical, meet the need for motor vehicle safety, and stated in objective terms. In prescribing standards, the Secretary was required to consider: (1) relevant available motor vehicle safety data, (2) whether the proposed standard is appropriate for the particular motor vehicle or equipment for which it is prescribed, and (3) the extent to which the standard contributed to carrying out the purposes of the act (Comptroller General, 1976).

The Highway Safety Act of 1966 established the National Highway Safety Agency in the Department of Commerce. It was designed to provide a coordinated national highway safety program through financial assistance to the states. Under this act, states were required to establish highway safety programs in accordance with federal standards. Federal funds were made available under Section 402, to be allocated by population and highway mileage, to assist in financing these programs with a 75% federal and 25% matching ratio (Insurance Institute for Highway Safety, 1986).

The two safety agencies were combined by Executive Order 11357 into the National Highway Safety Bureau in the newly created DOT. By 1969, the Bureau, under Dr. William Haddon Jr., had established 29 motor vehicle standards and 13 highway safety standards, and all states had established highway safety programs. By the end of 1972, the agency had issued a total of 43 motor vehicle standards, covering vehicle accident prevention and passenger protection, and 18 highway safety standards, covering vehicle inspection, registration, motorcycle safety, driver education, traffic laws and records, accident investigation and reporting, pupil transportation, and police traffic services (Insurance Institute for Highway Safety, 1986).

These two safety acts provided the basis for a practical, comprehensive national highway safety program to reduce deaths and injuries caused by motor vehicles.

Department of Transportation Act of 1966

In 1966, the Department of Transportation (DOT) was created to coordinate transportation programs and to facilitate development and improvement of coordinated transportation service utilizing private enterprise to the maximum extent feasible. The Department of Transportation Act declared that the nation required fast, safe, efficient, and convenient transportation at the lowest cost consistent with other national objectives including the conservation of natural resources. DOT was directed to provide leadership in the identification of transportation problems and solutions, stimulate new technological advances, encourage cooperation among all interested parties, and recommend national policies and programs to accomplish these objectives.

Section 4(f) of the act required the preservation of natural areas. It prohibited the use of land for a transportation project from a park, recreation area, wildlife and waterfowl refuge, or historic site unless there was no feasible and prudent alternative and the project was planned in such a manner as to minimize harm to the area. This was the earliest statutory language directed at minimizing the negative effects of transportation construction projects on the natural environment.

The DOT Act left unclear, however, the division of responsibility for urban mass transportation between DOT and HUD. It took more than a year for DOT and HUD to come to an agreement on their respective responsibilities. This agreement, known as Reorganization Plan No. 2, took effect in July 1968. Under it, DOT assumed responsibility for mass transportation capital grants, technical studies, and managerial training grant programs subject to HUD certification of the planning requirements for capital grant applications. Research and development (R&D) was divided up. DOT assumed R&D responsibility for improving the operation of conventional transit systems and HUD assumed R&D responsibility for urban transportation as it related to comprehensive planning. Joint responsibility was assigned for R&D on advanced technology systems. The Reorganization Plan also created the Urban Mass Transportation Administration (UMTA) (Miller, 1972).

National Historic Preservation Act of 1966

Through the 1950s and 1960s, while the federal government funded numerous public works and urban renewal projects, federal preservation law applied only to a handful of nationally significant properties. As a result, federal projects destroyed or damaged thousands of historic properties. Congress recognized that new legislation was needed to protect the many other properties that were being harmed by federal activities (Advisory Council on Historic Preservation, 1986).

The National Historic Preservation Act of 1966 was passed to address these concerns. The act established the Advisory Council on Historic Preservation to provide advice on national preservation policy. Section 106 of the act required federal agencies to take into account the effects of their undertakings on historic preservation, and to afford the Council the opportunity to comment on such undertakings. Section 110 required federal agencies to identify and protect historic properties under their control.

The Section 106 review process established by the Council required a federal agency funding or otherwise involved in a proposed project to identify historic properties that might be affected by the project and find acceptable means to avoid or mitigate any adverse impact. Federal agencies were to consult with the Council and State Historic Preservation Officers, appointed by the Governors, in carrying out this process.

Demonstration Cities and Metropolitan Development Act of 1966

With the growth in federal grant programs for urban renewal, highways, transit, and other construction projects, there was a need for a mechanism to coordinate these projects. The Demonstration Cities and Metropolitan Development Act of 1966 was enacted to ensure that federal grants were not working at cross purposes. Section 204 of that act was significant in asserting federal interest in improving the coordination of public facility construction projects to obtain maximum effectiveness of federal spending and to relate such projects to area-wide development plans.

Section 204 required that all applications for the planning and construction of facilities be submitted to an area-wide planning agency for review and comment. The area-wide agency was required to be composed of local elected officials. The objective was to encourage the coordination of planning and construction of physical facilities in urban areas. Section 204 was also designed to stimulate operating agencies with narrow functional responsibilities to examine the relationship of their projects to area-wide plans for urban growth. Procedures to implement this act were issued by the Bureau of the Budget in Circular No. 82, "Coordination of Federal Aids in Metropolitan Areas Under Section 204 of the Demonstration Cities and Metropolitan Development Act of 1966" (Bureau of the Budget, 1967).

In response to these review requirements, many urban areas established new planning agencies or reorganized existing agencies to include elected officials on their policy boards. By the end of 1969, only six metropolitan lacked an area-wide review agency (Washington Center, 1970).

Dartmouth Conference on Urban Development Models

Land use planning models were developed as an adjunct to transportation planning to provide forecasts of population, employment, and land use for transportation forecasting models. From the mid-1950s, there was rapid development in the field stimulated by newly available computers and advances in operations research and systems analysis (Putman, 1979). Developments were discussed at a seminar at the

University of Pennsylvania in October 1964 that was documented in a special issue of the *Journal of the American Institute of Planners* (Harris, 1965).

By 1967, the Land-Use Evaluation Committee of the Highway Research Board determined that there was need for another assessment of work in the field, which was progressing in an uncoordinated fashion. In June 1967, a conference was held in Dartmouth, New Hampshire, to identify the areas of research that were most needed (Hemmens, 1968).

The conferees recommended that agencies sponsoring research on land use models, generally the federal government, expand the capabilities of their in-house staff to handle these models. They recommended steps to improve data acquisition and handling. Further research on broader models that included social goals was recommended. Conferees recommended that research on the behavioral aspects of the individual decision units be conducted. Concern was expressed about bridging the gap between modelers and decision-makers. Professional standards for design, calibration, and use of models was also encouraged (Hemmens, 1968).

The early optimism in the field faded as the land development models did not perform up to the expectations of researchers and decision-makers, particularly at the small area level. Modelers had underestimated the task of simulating complex urban phenomena. Many of these modeling efforts were performed by planning agencies that had to meet unreasonable time deadlines (Putman, 1979). Models had become more complex with larger data requirements as submodels were added to encompass more aspects of the urban development process. They were too costly to construct and operate, and many still did not produce usable results. By the late 1960s, land use modeling activity in the USA entered a period of dormancy that continued until the mid-1970s.

Freedom of Information Act of 1966

The Freedom of Information Act (FOIA), which was passed in 1966, established a presumption that records in the possession of agencies and departments of the executive branch of the US Government were accessible to the people. This had not always been the approach to Federal information disclosure policy. Before enactment of the FOIA, the burden was on the individual to establish a right to examine these government records. There were no statutory guidelines or procedures to help a person seeking information. There were no judicial remedies for those denied access.

With the passage of the FOIA, the burden of proof shifted from the individual to the government. Those seeking information were no longer required to show a need for information. Instead, the "need to know" standard was replaced by a "right to know" doctrine. The government now had to justify the need for secrecy. The FOIA set standards for determining which records must be disclosed and which records may be withheld. The law also provided administrative and judicial remedies for those denied access to records. Above all, the statute required Federal agencies to provide the fullest possible disclosure of information to the public. The history of the act reflected that it was a disclosure law. It presumed that requested records will be disclosed, and the agency must make its case for withholding, in terms of the act's exemptions to the rule of disclosure. The application of the act's exemptions was generally permissive – to be done if information in the requested records required protection – not mandatory. Thus, when determining whether a document or set of documents should be withheld under one of the FOIA exemptions, an agency should withhold those documents only in those cases where the agency reasonably foresaw that disclosure would be harmful to an interest protected by the exemption. Similarly, when a requestor asked for a set of documents, the agency should release all documents, not a subset or selection of those documents.

The FOIA required agencies to publish in the Federal Register, later modified to require that such information be made available online, as well: (1) descriptions of agency organization and office addresses; (2) statements of the general course and method of agency operation; (3) rules of procedure and descriptions of forms; and (4) substantive rules of general applicability and general policy statements. The act also required agencies to make available for public inspection and copying: (1) final opinions made in the adjudication of cases; (2) statements of policy and interpretations adopted by an agency, but not published in the Federal Register; (3) administrative staff manuals that affect the public; (4) copies of records released in response to FOIA requests that an agency determined had been or would likely be the subject of additional requests; and (5) a general index of released records determined to have been or likely to be the subject of additional requests. The 1996 FOIA amendments required that these materials, which an agency must make available for inspection and copying without the formality of a FOIA request, must be made available electronically and in hard copy.

The FOIA also required federal agencies to publish in the Federal Register notice of changes to programs, and the Administrative Procedure Act established formal rulemaking processes for notifying the public and making changes to federal programs, including soliciting comments about proposed changes. The FOIA substantially improved the transparency of government decision-making.

Reserved Bus Lanes

As construction of the Interstate highway progressed, highway engineers came under increasing criticism for providing under-priced facilities that competed unfairly with transit service. Critics were also concerned that the 3C planning process was not giving sufficient attention to transit options in the development of long-range urban transportation plans.

The first official response to this criticism came in April 1964 in a speech by E. H. Holmes, Director of Planning for the Bureau of Public Roads. Mr. Holmes stated, "Since over three-quarters of transit patrons ride on rubber tires, not on steel rails, transit has to be for highways, not against them. And vice versa, highways have to be for transit, not against it, for the more that travelers patronize transit the easier will be the highway engineer's job." He went on to advocate the use of freeways by buses in express service. This would increase bus operating speeds, reduce their travel times, and thereby make bus service more competitive with car travel. The BPR position was that the reservation of a lane for buses was reasonable if its usage by bus passengers exceeded the number of persons that would be moved in the same period in cars, for example, 3,000 persons per h for a lane of freeway (Holmes, 1964).

This position was formalized in Instructional Memorandum (IM) 21-13-67, "Reserved Bus Lanes," issued by the Federal Highway Administration (FHWA) in August 1967. In addition to reiterating the warrant for reserving of lanes for buses, the IM stated the warrant for preferential use of lanes by buses. Under preferential use, other vehicles would be allowed to use the lane but only in such numbers that they do not degrade the travel speed of the buses. The number of other vehicles would be controlled by metering their flow onto the lane. The total number of persons using the preferential lanes was to be greater than that would be accommodated by opening the lanes to general traffic.

The FHWA actively promoted the use of exclusive and preferential bus treatments. Expenditures for bus priority projects on arterial highways, including loading platforms and shelters, became eligible for federal-aid highway funds under the Traffic Operations Program to Improve Capacity and Safety (TOPICS), which was initiated as an experimental program in 1967. Reserved lanes for buses on freeways were eligible under the regular federal-aid highway programs.

Many urban areas adopted bus priority techniques to increase the carrying capacity of highway facilities and make transit service more attractive at a limited cost. By 1973, one study reported on more than 200 bus priority projects in the USA and elsewhere. These included busways on exclusive rights-of-way and on freeways, reserved freeway lanes and ramps, bus malls, reserved lanes on arterial streets, traffic signal preemption, and supporting park-and-ride lots and central city terminals (Levinson, 1973).

National Highway Needs Studies

The expected completion of the Interstate highway system in the mid-1970s led to consideration of new directions for the federal-aid highway program. Recognizing the need for information on which to formulate future highway programs, the US Senate, in section 3 of the Senate Joint Resolution 81 (approved 28 August 1965), called for a biennial reporting of highway needs beginning in 1968.

In April 1965, the US Bureau of Public Roads had requested the states to prepare estimates of future highway needs for the period 1965–1985. The states were given only a few months to prepare the estimates and they relied upon available data and rapid estimating techniques. The results were documented in the 1968 National Highway Needs Report. The estimated cost of $294 billion to meet the anticipated highway needs was a staggering sum. It included another 40,000 of freeways in addition to the 41,000 miles in the Interstate system (US Congress, 1968a). The supplement to the report recommended the undertaking of a nation-wide functional highway classification study as the basis for realigning the federal-aid highway systems (US Congress, 1968b).

The 1968 report paid greater attention on urban areas than in the past. The supplement recommended that a larger share of federal-aid highway funds should be made available to urban areas. As a means to accomplish this, the supplement discussed expanding the urban extensions of the primary and secondary highway systems to include all principal arterial routes into a federal-aid urban system. To overcome the difficulties of urban area decision-making among fragmented local governments, it suggested requiring the establishment of area-wide agencies to develop 5-year capital improvement programs. The agencies would be governed by locally elected officials (US Congress, 1968b).

The supplement also recommended the use of federal-aid highway funds for a parking research and development projects, and for construction of fringe parking facilities. The establishment of a revolving fund for advance acquisition of right-of-way was recommended as well. The supplement advocated joint development adjacent to or using airspace above or below highways. Such projects should be coordinated jointly by DOT and HUD (US Congress, 1968b).

Many of the recommendations in the Supplement to the 1968 National Highway Needs Report were incorporated into the Federal-Aid Highway Acts of 1968 and 1970. Section 17 of the 1968 act called for a systematic nation-wide functional highway classification study in cooperation with state highway departments and local governments. The manual for this functional classification study stated that, "All existing public roads and streets within a State are to be classified on the basis of the most logical usage of existing facilities to serve present travel and land use" (US Dept. of Transportation, 1969b). This was the first major study to collect detailed functional system information on a nation-wide basis.

The supplement to the 1970 National Highway Needs Report detailed the results of the 1968 functional classification study, which covered existing facilities under current conditions of travel and land use. The results showed that there was wide variation among states in the coincidence of highways classified functionally and which federal-aid system they were on. This disparity was greater in urban areas than that in rural areas. The report demonstrated that arterial highways carried the bulk of highway travel. For example, in urban areas in 1968, arterial highways constituted 19% of the miles of facilities and carried 75% of the vehicle miles of travel (US Congress, 1970) (Fig. 5.1).

The 1972 National Highway Needs Report documented the results of the 1970–1990 functional classification study. It combined a projected functional classification for 1990 with a detailed inventory and needs estimate for all functional classes including local roads and streets. It recommended the realignment of federal-aid highway systems based upon functional usage in a subsequent year such as 1980. This recommendation for realignment was incorporated into the Federal-Aid Highway Act of 1973. Highway needs were estimated for the 20-year period to 1990 under nationally uniform "minimum tolerable conditions." Of the estimated

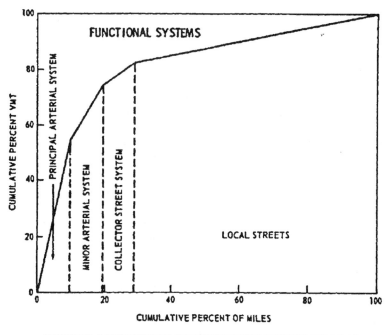

NATIONAL DISTRIBUTION OF MILES VERSUS VEHICLE-MILES OF
TRAVEL SERVED ON THE FUNCTIONAL SYSTEMS IN URBAN AREAS - 1968

Fig. 5.1 National distribution of miles versus vehicle-miles of travel served on the functional systems in urban areas – 1968 (Source: US Congress, 1970)

$592 billion in needs, 43% were on federal-aid systems as they existed in 1970. Over 50% of these needs were considered to be "backlog," that is, requiring immediate attention (US Congress, 1972b,c).

The 1974 National Highway Needs Report updated the needs estimates that were reported in the 1972 report. The 1974 Highway Needs Study was conducted as part of the 1974 National Transportation Study. The 1974 highway report analyzed the sensitivity of the needs estimates to the changes of reduced forecasted travel and a lower level of service than minimum tolerable conditions. The report clarified that the highway needs estimates are dependent upon the specific set of standards of highway service and highway design on which they are based.

The highway needs studies represented an ongoing process to assess the nation's highway system and quantify the nature and scope of future highway requirements. The studies were carried out as cooperative efforts of the federal, state, and local governments. The extensive involvement of state and local governments lent considerable credibility to the studies. Consequently, the highway needs reports had a major influence on highway legislation, and the structure and funding of highway programs (US Congress, 1975).

Federal-Aid Highway Act of 1968

The Federal-Aid Highway Act of 1968 established the Traffic Operations Program to Improve Capacity and Safety (TOPICS). It authorized $200 million each for fiscal years 1970 and 1971. The federal matching share was set at 50%. The program was designed to reduce traffic congestion and facilitate the flow of traffic in urban areas. Prior to the act, the Bureau of Public Roads had initiated TOPICS as an experimental program. IM21-7-67, which established guidelines for TOPICS, divided urban streets into two categories. Those on the federal-aid Primary and Secondary systems were considered Type 1. Other major streets were under Type 2. Only traffic operations improvements were allowed on Type 2 systems (Gakenheimer and Meyer, 1977).

The TOPICS program grew out of a long history of the BPR's efforts to expand the use of traffic engineering techniques. In 1959, the BPR sponsored the Wisconsin Avenue Study to demonstrate the effectiveness of various traffic management methods when applied in a coordinated fashion (US Dept. of Commerce, 1962).

TOPICS projects were to result from the 3C urban transportation planning process. By October 1969, there were 160 cities actively involved in TOPICS and another 96 cities in preliminary negotiations expected to result in active projects. Even so, the level of planning detail for TOPICS projects was not totally compatible with the regional scale of the planning process (Gakenheimer and Meyer, 1977).

The TOPICS program was reauthorized for fiscal years 1972 and 1973 at $100 million per year. But the Federal-Aid Highway Act of 1973 ended further authorizations and merged the TOPICS systems into the new federal-aid urban system. TOPICS had accomplished its objective of increasing the acceptance of traffic engineering techniques as a means of improving the efficiency of the urban transportation system. It also played an important role in encouraging the concept of traffic management (Gakenheimer and Meyer, 1977).

In addition to launching the TOPICS program, the Federal-Aid Highway Act of 1968 incorporated several provisions designed to protect the environment and reduce the negative effects of highway construction. The Act repeated the requirement in Section 4(f) of the Department of Transportation Act of 1966 on the preservation of public park and recreation lands, wildlife and waterfowl refuges, and historic sites to clarify that the provision applied to highways. Moreover, the act required public hearings on the economic, social, and environmental effects of proposed highway projects and their consistency with local urban goals and objectives. The act also established the highway beautification program. In addition, a highway relocation assistance program was authorized to provide payments to households and businesses displaced by construction projects. Additionally, a revolving fund for the advanced acquisition of right-of-way was established to minimize future dislocations due to highway construction and reduce the cost of land and clearing it. Also, the act authorized funds for a fringe parking demonstration program.

Many of the provisions of the act were early responses to the concern for environmental quality and for ameliorating the negative effects of highway construction.

"Continuing" Urban Transportation Planning

By 1968, most urbanized areas had completed or were well along in their 3C planning process. The Federal Highway Administration turned its attention to the "continuing" aspect of the planning process. In May 1968, IM 50-4-68, "Operations

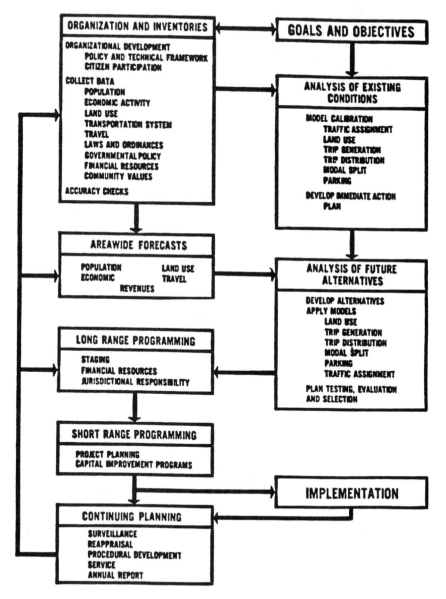

Fig. 5.2 The continuing urban transportation planning process (Source: US Dept. of Transportation, 1968)

Plans for 'Continuing' Urban Transportation Planning" was issued. The IM required the preparation of an operations plan for continuing transportation planning in these areas. The objective was to maintain the responsiveness of planning to the needs of local areas and to potential changes (US Dept. of Transportation, 1968).

The operations plans were to address the various items needed to perform continuing planning, including the organizational structure, scope of activities and the agencies that were responsible, a description of the surveillance methodology to identify changes in land development and travel demand, a description of land use and travel forecasting procedures, and work remaining on the ten basic elements of the 3C planning process (US Dept. of Transportation, 1968).

Guidelines were provided identifying the five elements considered essential for a continuing planning process (Fig. 5.2). The "surveillance" element focused on monitoring changes in the area in development, sociodemographic characteristics, and travel. "Reappraisal" dealt with three levels of review of the transportation forecasts and plans to determine if they were still valid. Every 5 years the plan and forecast were to be updated to retain a 20-year time horizon. The third element, "service," was to assist agencies in the implementation of the plan. The "procedural development" element emphasized the need to upgrade analysis techniques. Last was the publication of an "annual report" on these activities as a means of communicating with local officials and citizens (US Dept. of Transportation, 1968).

Extensive training and technical assistance was provided by the FHWA to shift urban transportation planning into a continuing mode of operation.

Intergovernmental Cooperation Act of 1968

Section 204 of the Demonstration Cities and Metropolitan Act was the forerunner of much more extensive legislation, adopted in 1968, designed to coordinate federal grant-in-aid programs at federal and state levels. The Intergovernmental Cooperation Act of 1968 required that federal agencies notify the governors or legislatures of the purpose and amounts of any grants-in-aid to their states. The purpose of this requirement was to make it possible for states to plan more effectively for their overall development (Washington Center, 1970).

The act required that the area-wide planning agency be established under state enabling legislation. It provided that in the absence of substantial reasons to the contrary, federal grants shall be made to general purpose units of government rather than special purpose agencies. The act also transferred administration of these intergovernmental coordination requirements from HUD to the Bureau of the Budget.

Bureau of the Budget's Circular No. A-95

To implement the 1968 Intergovernmental Cooperation Act, the Bureau of the Budget issued Circular No. A-95, "Evaluation, Review, and Coordination of Federal Assistance Programs and Projects," in July 1969 (Bureau of the Budget,

1969), superseded Circular No. A-82 (Bureau of the Budget, 1967). This circular required that the governor of each state designate a "clearinghouse" at the state level and for each metropolitan area. The function of these clearinghouses was to review and comment on projects proposed for federal-aid in terms of their compatibility with comprehensive plans and to coordinate among agencies having plans and programs that might be affected by the projects. These clearinghouses had to be empowered under state or local laws to perform comprehensive planning in an area (Washington Center, 1970).

The circular established a project notification and review system (PNRS) that specified how the review and coordination process would be carried out and the amount of time for each step in the process (Fig. 5.3). The PNRS contained an "early warning" feature that required that a local applicant for a federal grant or loan notify the state and local clearinghouses at the time it decided to seek assistance. The clearinghouse had 30 days to indicate further interest in the project or to arrange to provide project coordination. This regulation was designed to alleviate the problem many review agencies had of learning of an application only after it had been prepared, and thereby having little opportunity to help shape it (Washington Center, 1970).

Circular No. A-95 provided the most definitive federal statement of the process through which planning for urban areas should be accomplished. Its emphasis was not on substance but on process and on the intergovernmental linkages required to carry out the process.

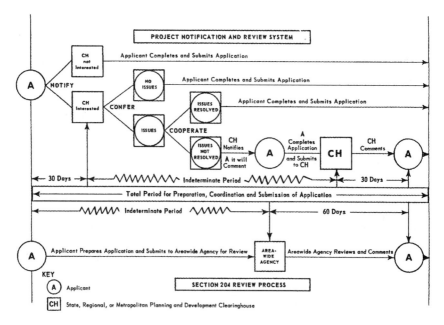

Fig. 5.3 Comparison of 204 review process and project notification and review system (Source: Bureau of the Budget, 1967)

The various acts and regulations to improve intergovernmental program coordination accelerated the creation of broader multifunctional agencies. At the state level, 39 Departments of Transportation had been created by 1977. Most of the departments had multimodal planning, programming, and coordinating functions. At the local level, there was a growing trend for transportation planning to be performed by comprehensive planning agencies, generally those designated as the A-95 clearinghouse (Advisory Commission, 1974).

Chapter 6
Rising Concern for the Environment and Citizen Involvement

During the decade of the 1960s, the growing concern for environmental quality put considerable pressure on the planning process and its ability to adapt to change. Public attention became focused on the issues of air and water pollution; dislocation of homes and businesses; preservation of parkland, wildlife refuges, and historic sites; and the overall ecological balance in communities and their capacity to absorb disruption. Moreover, citizens were concerned that changes were being made to their communities without their views being considered. The federal role in these matters, which had begun modestly in previous years, broadened and deepened during this period.

Citizen Participation and the Two-Hearing Process for Highways

Citizen reaction to highway projects usually was mostly vocal at public hearings. It became clear that citizens could not effectively contribute to a highway decision by the time the project had already been designed. Many of the concerns related to the basic issue of whether to build the highway project at all and the consideration of alternative modes of transportation. Consequently, in early 1969, the Federal Highway Administration (FHWA) revised Policy and Procedure Memorandum (PPM) 20–8, "Public Hearings and Location Approval" (US Department of Transportation, 1969a).

It established a two-hearing process for highway projects, replacing the previous single hearing, which occurred late in the project development process. The first "corridor public hearing" was to be held before the route location decision was made and was designed to afford citizens the opportunity to comment on the need for and location of the highway project. The second "highway design public hearing" was to focus on the specific location and design features. This PPM also required the consideration of social, economic, and environmental effects prior to submission of a project for federal aid (U.S. Dept. of Transportation, 1970b).

It was recognized that even a two-hearing process did not provide adequate opportunity for citizen involvement and, worse, provided a difficult atmosphere for

E. Weiner, *Urban Transportation Planning in the United States, Third Edition*,
doi:10.1007/978-0-387-77152-6, © Springer Science+Business Media, LLC 2008

dialogue. In late 1969, the basic guidelines for the 3C planning process were amended to require citizen participation in all phases of the planning process from the setting of goals through the analysis of alternatives. Consequently, it became the responsibility of the planning agency to seek out public views.

National Environmental Policy Act of 1969

The federal government's concern for environmental issues dated back to the passage of the Air Quality Control Act of 1955, which directed the Surgeon General to conduct research to abate air pollution. Through a series of acts since that time, the federal government's involvement in environmental matters broadened and deepened.

In 1969, a singularly important piece of environmental legislation was passed, the National Environmental Policy Act of 1969 (NEPA). This act presented a significant departure from prior legislation in that it enunciated for the first time a broad national policy to prevent or eliminate damage to the environment. The act stated that it was national policy to "encourage productive and enjoyable harmony between man and his environment."

Federal agencies were required under the act to use a systematic interdisciplinary approach to the planning and decision-making that affected the environment. It also required that an environmental impact statement (EIS) be prepared for all legislation and major federal actions that would affect the environment significantly. The EIS was to contain information on the environmental impacts of the proposed action, unavoidable impacts, alternatives to the action, the relationship between short-term and long-term impacts, and irretrievable commitments of resources. The federal agency was to seek comments on the action and its impacts from affected jurisdictions and make all information public.

The act also created the Council on Environmental Quality to implement the policy and advise the President on environmental matters.

Environmental Quality Improvement Act of 1970

The Environmental Quality Improvement Act of 1970 was passed as a companion to the NEPA. It established the Office of Environmental Quality under the Council of Environmental Quality. The office was charged with assisting federal agencies in evaluating present and proposed programs, and with promoting research on the environment.

These two acts dealing with the environment marked the first reversal in over a decade of the trend to decentralize decision-making to the state and local levels of government. It required the federal government to make the final determination on the trade-off between facility improvements and environmental quality. Further, it created a complicated and expensive process by requiring the preparation of an EIS and the seeking of comments from all concerned agencies. In this manner, the acts actually created a new planning process in parallel with the existing urban transportation planning process.

Nationwide Personal Transportation Study

Earlier national surveys of travel were limited to automobile and truck use. Between 1935 and 1940, and again during the 1950s, a number of states conducted motor vehicle use studies on the characteristics of motor vehicle ownership, users, and travel (Bostick et al., 1954; Bostick, 1963). During 1961, the US Bureau of the Census conducted the National Automobile Use Study of 5,000 households for BPR. The survey covered characteristics of motor vehicle ownership and use, and the journey to work. Income and other household data were available to relate to the travel and automobile information (Bostick, 1966).

The Nationwide Personal Transportation Study (NPTS) grew out these efforts and was designed to obtain current information on national patterns of passenger travel. The NPTS surveyed households covering all person trips by all modes and for all trip purposes. The NPTS was first conducted in 1969 (US Dept. of Transportation, 1972–1974) and was repeated at approximately 7-year intervals in 1977 (US Dept. of Transportation, 1980–83), in 1983 (Klinger and Kuzmyak, 1985–86), in 1990 (Hu and Young, 1992), in 1995 (MultiConsultant Assoc., 1999), and in 2001 (Hu and Reuscher, 2004). The first three surveys were conducted by the US Bureau of the Census for DOT using home interviews. The later surveys were conducted by private contractors using computer-assisted telephone interviewing (CATI) and random digit dialing to allow for unlisted telephone numbers as well as travel diaries in the 1995 survey.

In 2001, the survey was expanded by integrating the NPTS and the American Travel Survey (ATS). The survey was renamed to the National Household Travel Survey (NHTS). The 2001 NHTS was an inventory of the nation's daily and long-distance travel. The survey included demographic characteristics of households, people, vehicles, and detailed information on daily and longer-distance travel for all purposes by all modes. NHTS survey data were collected from a sample of US households and expanded to provide national estimates of trips and miles by travel mode, trip purpose, and a host of household attributes. When combined with historical data from 1969 through 1995, the 2001 NHTS survey data provided detailed information on personal travel patterns over time.

The sample size for the 2001 NHTS was 69,817 households comprising a national sample of 26,038 completed households, and 43,779 additional households collected for the use of and funded by 9 add-on areas. Respondents were asked to report in considerable detail on all trips made by household members. The survey collected household data on the relationship of household members, education level, income, housing characteristics, and other demographic information;

information on each household vehicle, including year, make, model, and estimates of annual miles traveled and fuel costs; data about drivers, including information on travel as part of work; data about one-way trips taken during a designated 24-h period (the household's designated travel day), including the time the trip began and ended, length of the trip, composition of the travel party, mode of transportation, purpose of the trip, and the specific vehicle used (if a household vehicle); and data describing round-trips taken during a 4-week period (the household's designated travel period) where the farthest point of the trip was at least 50 miles from home, including the farthest destination, access and egress stops, and overnight stays on the way to and from the farthest destination, mode, purpose, and travel party information. Data on walk and bike trips were included for the first time (Hu and Reuscher, 2004).

The NPTS provided national statistics on person travel with some disaggregation by Standard Metropolitan Statistical Areas (SMSA) size groupings. It summarized information on average daily travel by household members including trip purpose, mode, trip length, vehicle occupancy, time of day, and day of the week. By comparing successive surveys, the NPTS quantified a number of important national trends including (Table 6.1):

Table 6.1 Nationwide personal transportation study

Household and travel indicators (1969–2001)			
Summary statistic	1969	2001	1969–2001 (% change)
Total population	197.2 million	277.2 million	40.6
Total households	62.5 million	107.4 million	71.8
Total workers	75.8 million	148.3 million	95.6
Total personal vehicles	72.5 million	202.6 million	179.4
Annual personal vehicle trips	87.3 million	233.0 million	166.9
Annual household VMT	775.9 million	2,275.0 million	193.2
Annual person trips	145.1 million	407.3 million	165.0
Annual person miles	1,404.1 million	3,972.7 million	182.9
Indicator			
Persons per household	3.20	2.58	
Vehicles per household	1.20	1.89	
Vehicles per driver	0.70	1.06	
Percent of households with			
No vehicles	20.6	8.1	
One vehicle	48.4	31.4	
Two vehicles	26.4	37.2	
3+ Vehicles	4.6	23.2	
Annual VMT per household	12,423	21,187	70.5
% Work vehicle trips	31.9	22.1	
% Nonwork vehicle trips	68.1	77.9	
% Transit trips	3.4	1.6	
Automobile occupancy	1.90	1.63	

Source: Hu and Reuscher, 2004

- the significant increase in automobile ownership
- large increase in workers
- huge increases in personal and vehicle travel
- declining household size
- rise in multi-vehicle households and decline of zero-car households
- growth in VMT per household
- decline in the work trip fraction of travel
- increasing modal share of travel by private vehicle
- declining vehicle occupancy.

The NPTS became a unique and valuable data resource for analyzing the nation's travel patterns. It allowed the tracking of changes in key household travel characteristics and was used at the federal as well as state and local levels.

Clean Air Act Amendments of 1970

The Clean Air Act Amendments of 1970 reinforced the central position of the federal government to make final decisions affecting the environment. This act created the Environmental Protection Agency (EPA) and empowered it to set ambient air quality standards. Required reductions in new automobile emissions were also specified in the act. The act authorized the EPA to require states to formulate implementation plans describing how they would achieve and maintain the ambient air quality standards. In 1971, the EPA promulgated national ambient air quality standards and proposed regulations on state implementation plans (SIPs) to meet these standards (US Dept. of Transportation, 1975b).

The preparation, submission, and review of the SIPs occurred outside the traditional urban transportation planning process and, in many instances, did not involve the planning agencies developing transportation plans. This problem became particularly difficult for urban areas that could not meet the air quality standards even with new automobiles that met the air pollution emission standards. In these instances, transportation control plans (TCPs) were required that contained changes in urban transportation systems and their operation to effect the reduction in emissions. Rarely were these TCPs developed jointly with those agencies developing urban transportation plans. It took several years of dialogue between these air pollution and transportation planning agencies to mediate joint plans and policies for urban transportation and air quality.

Another impact of the environmental legislation, particularly the Clean Air Act, was the increased emphasis on short-term changes in transportation systems. In that the deadline for meeting the ambient air quality standards was fairly short, EPA was primarily concerned with actions that could affect air quality in that time frame. The actions precluded major construction and generally focused on low capital and traffic management measures. Up to that time, urban transportation planning had been focused on long-range (20 years or more) planning (US Dept. of Transportation, 1975b).

Boston Transportation Planning Review

The results of many urban transportation planning studies called for major expansions of the area's freeway system along with other highway improvements. Public transportation was often projected to have a minimal role in the area's future. In these urban transportation plans, many of the highway improvements were to be located in built-up areas where they would cause major disruptions and dislocations. As public awareness to social and environmental concerns grew in many urban areas, so too did the opposition to transportation plans that contained recommendations for major expansions of the highway system. When faced with these circumstances, urban areas were forced to reevaluate their plans. The prototype for these reevaluations was the Boston Transportation Planning Review (BTPR).

The long-range plan for the Boston region published in 1969 contained recommendations for a comprehensive network of radial and circumferential highways and substantial improvements to the existing mass transportation system. Much of the freeway portion of the plan was included as part of the Interstate highway system. Many of the recommended highways were contained in the earlier 1948 plan, which was typical of urban transportation plans of this period. Opposition to the 1969 plan developed even before it was published, especially from the affected communities (Humphrey, 1974).

Governor Francis Sargent ordered a moratorium on major highway construction in February 1970 shortly after the Boston City Council had already done so. He announced a major reevaluation of transportation policy for the Boston area and created the BTPR as an independent entity reporting directly to the governor to address the area's transportation issues.

The BTPR lasted about 18 months, during which time numerous transportation alternatives were identified and evaluated by an interdisciplinary team of professionals. The work was accomplished in an atmosphere of open and participatory interaction among planners, citizens, and elected officials. The BTPR led to the decision made by the governor not to build additional freeways within the Boston core. Instead, the major emphasis was on a mix of arterials, special-purpose highways, and major improvements in the mass transportation system (Humphrey, 1974).

There were several hallmarks of this new form of the urban transportation planning process, termed by Alan Altshuler, who chaired the BTPR, the "open study." First and foremost was the extensive involvement of professionals, citizens, interest groups, and decision-makers in all aspects of the restudy. Second, transit options were evaluated on an equal footing with highway options. Third, the restudy focused on both the broader region-wide scale and the finer community level scale. Fourth, there was less reliance on computer models for analysis and a more open attitude toward explaining the analytical methodology to the nontechnical participants. Fifth, the study used a wider range of evaluation criteria that accounted for more social and environmental factors. Sixth, decision-makers were willing to step in and make decisions at points where the process had reached a stalemate (Gakenheimer, 1976; Allen, 1985).

The BTPR occurred at the height of the citizen participation movement in a highly charged atmosphere outside the mainstream of decision-making in Boston.

Although it is unlikely that such a study will be repeated elsewhere in the same manner, the BTPR has left a permanent impact on urban transportation. The legacy of the BTPR has been to demonstrate a more open form of planning and decision-making that has greater concern for social and environmental impacts and the opinions of those affected by transportation improvements.

Urban Corridor Demonstration Program

In January 1970, the DOT initiated the Urban Corridor Demonstration Program to test and demonstrate the concerted use of available highway traffic engineering and transit operations techniques for relieving traffic congestion in radial corridors serving major urban corridors. The program emphasized low-capital intensive improvements rather than new major construction to demonstrate whether relatively inexpensive projects that could be implemented rapidly could play an effective role in relieving urban traffic congestion (Alan M. Voorhees and Assoc., 1974).

The program was focused on urbanized areas over 200,000 in population. It utilized existing federal programs for transit facilities and equipment, demonstrations, research and technical studies, and for highway construction, TOPICS, and fringe parking. The demonstration projects use various improvement techniques that were funded under these programs in a coordinated fashion to reduce peak-hour congestion.

In July 1970, 11 areas were selected to conduct planning for demonstration projects. An evaluation manual was developed to assist the participating urban areas in developing the experimental design, hypotheses to be tested, and overall evaluation strategy (Texas Transportation Institute, 1972). Based on the evaluation plans from these areas, eight areas were selected to carry out demonstrations, and seven actually conducted them. The projects tested line-haul improvements such as transit priority schemes, traffic engineering techniques, and bus service improvements; low-density collection–distribution improvements such as park and ride facilities, demand responsive buses, and shelters; and CBD collection–distribution system improvements such as bus shuttle service and improved transportation terminals.

This early attempt to integrate low-capital intensive transit and highway improvement techniques in a concerted manner to improve urban transportation pointed the way to the extensive use of transportation system management approaches in later years. Further experimentation on low-capital techniques continued with the establishment of the Service and Methods Demonstration Program in 1974.

Census Journey-to-Work Surveys

The decennial census, which is required by the Constitution, is the longest time series of US demographic data. The census was first taken in 1790 and broadened in 1810 to include other subjects. Interest in the census by transportation planners began in the late 1950s with the advent of comprehensive urban transportation studies and the need for data on socio-demographic characteristics. At that time, the HRB launched the Committee on Transportation Information Systems and Data Requirements to persuade the Bureau of the Census to include questions on place of work and automobile ownership in the 1960 census. In 1960, the format of the census was changed so that the majority of the population had to only answer a limited set of questions (short form), and a sample of the population had to answer a more detailed set of questions (long form). Journey-to-work and other transportation-related questions were included in the long form.

In the 1960s, the Bureau of the Census established a Small Area Data Advisory Committee, which included a number of transportation planners, to assist them in the planning for the 1970 census. Transportation planners recognized that the data from the decennial census could be used more broadly for transportation studies because it included most of the traditional variables used in the studies, and the journey-to-work question was similar to traditional origin–destination questions. In late 1966, the Bureau of the Census conducted a Census Use Study in New Haven, Connecticut. The purpose of the study was to examine the methods and procedures they had developed to facilitate the use of census data by local agencies. FHWA became involved because of their interest in an efficient method of maintaining current urban transportation planning data. A critical problem of the incompatibility of census tracts and traffic analysis zones was solved with the development of geographic coding systems. This permitted residence and work place addresses to be geographically coded to individual city blocks that allowed the census data to be summarized by traffic analysis zone (Sword and Fleet, 1973).

As a result of the pretest, the FHWA funded the Bureau of the Census to develop the capability to provide special summary tabulations, as the proposed 1970 tabulations would not have satisfied urban transportation study needs. The result was the Urban Transportation Planning Package that integrated journey-to-work and work place data along with socio-demographic data into an urban areas specific database that could be used by local planning agencies (Sword and Fleet, 1973).

During the 1970s, the use of the Urban Transportation Planning Package in transportation planning was evaluated in preparation for the 1980 census (Highway Research Board, 1971c; Transportation Research Board, 1974c). Many of the recommendations were incorporated by the Census Bureau. These included finer levels of stratification for vehicle ownership, modes and geographic detail, and the addition of travel times to work.

By the 1980s, the census journey-to-work survey had become a significant source of data for urban transportation planning. First, since the 1960s rising costs and diminished financial resources forced most urban transportation agencies to forgo large-scale data collection. Second, planning agencies were being faced with pressures from decision-makers for up-to-date information on which to base their analyses and recommendations. Third, improvements in data-based modeling reduced the need for locally conducted surveys, such as home-interview origin–destination studies. Fourth, improvements in both the transportation-related questions, and detail and accuracy of geographic coding of data from the 1980 census afforded planners a database that at least partially filled the void left by the lack of locally collected data (Transportation Research Board, 1985b).

The DOT provided technical assistance and training in the use of the 1980 census as they had with the 1970 census (Sousslau, 1983). By the early 1980s, over 200 MPOs had purchased Urban Transportation Planning Package tabulations.

Evaluation of the experience with the package continued (Transportation Research Board, 1984c). A conference on 9–12 December 1984 in Orlando, Florida, was organized by the TRB and sponsored by the DOT to review the progress to date and make recommendations for the 1990 census (Transportation Research Board, 1985b). The conference demonstrated the central role that census data has achieved in urban transportation planning.

FHWA analyzed the nation-wide changes in population, journey-to-work patterns, mode of travel to work, and vehicle availability occurring among the 1960, 1970, and 1980 censuses (Briggs et al., 1986). Further analyses were conducted under the National Commuting Study that was sponsored by a number of organizations led by AASHTO (Pisarski, 1987a, 1996).

The census journey-to-work became a significant source of travel data at the national level, and for State and local planning. At the national level, this data set increased in value with each addition to the series. At the local level, census data became more important as changes were made to improve its usefulness for urban transportation planning, and as cost constraints precluded collection of new data.

The Case of Overton Park

Section 4(f) of the Department of Transportation Act of 1966 prohibited the construction of any highway project that required the use of land from a public park, recreation area, or wildlife and waterfowl refuge of national, states, or local significance or any land from an historic site of national, state, or local significance unless there was no feasible and prudent alternative. An alternative may be considered not feasible and prudent if: it did not meet the project purpose and needed excessive cost of construction; there were severe operational or safety problems; there were unacceptable impacts (social, economic, or environmental); it caused serious community disruption; or a combination of any of these reasons. Given a range of alternatives, a transportation agency must select an avoidance alternative if it was feasible and prudent. By contrast, an alternative may be rejected if it was not feasible and prudent.

This provision was tested in the Overton Park case. Overton Park was a 342-acre city park located near the center of Memphis, Tennessee. A six-lane, high-speed expressway was proposed that would sever the zoo from the rest of the park. Although the roadway would be depressed below ground level except where it crossed a small creek, 26 acres of the park would be destroyed. The highway was to be a segment of Interstate Highway I-40. I-40 would provide Memphis with a major east–west expressway. This would allow easier access to downtown Memphis from the residential areas on the eastern edge of the city. The route was approved by the Bureau of Public Roads in 1956 and by the Federal Highway Administrator in 1966.

However, the enactment of Section 4(f) prevented distribution of federal funds for the section of highway designated to go through Overton Park. The Secretary of Transportation had to first determine whether the requirements of Section 4(f) had been met. Federal funding for the rest of the project was available and the State acquired a right-of-way on both sides of the park. In April 1968, the secretary announced that he agreed with the judgment of local officials that I-40 should be built through the park. In September 1969, the State acquired the right-of-way inside Overton Park from the city. Final approval for the project was not announced until November 1969. Upon approval of the route and design, the secretary did not indicate why he believed there were no feasible and prudent alternative routes. Nor did he indicate why design changes could not be made to reduce harm to the park.

A month later, a conservation group filed a lawsuit in federal court to halt construction. The petitioners contended that the secretary's action was invalid without a formal finding. They believed that the secretary did not make an independent determination but merely relied on the judgment of the Memphis City Council. Respondents argued that it was unnecessary for the secretary to make formal findings. They also argued that he did, in fact, exercise his own independent judgment, which was supported by the facts. Respondents introduced affidavits, which indicated that the secretary had made the decision and that the decision was supportable. These affidavits were contradicted by affidavits introduced by petitioners. The petitioners also sought to take the deposition of a former federal highway administrator who had participated in the decision to route I-40 through Overton Park.

The District Court and the Court of Appeals found that formal findings by the secretary were not necessary. They also refused to order the deposition of the former Federal Highway Administrator. In addition, the courts held that the affidavits contained no basis for a determination that the secretary had exceeded his authority.

The Supreme Court in the Overton Park case (*Citizens to Preserve Overton Park v. Volpe*, 401 US 402 (1971)) reversed the ruling of the District Court. The court ruled that determinations on no feasible and prudent alternative must find that there are unique problems or unusual factors involved in the use of alternatives or that the cost, environmental impacts, or community disruption resulting from such alternatives reach extraordinary magnitudes.

Interstate 40 was left incomplete and instead of crossing through downtown Memphis directly, as planned, Interstate 240 had been taken around downtown Memphis. This decision became a precedent for similar cases and the interpretation of the "prudent and feasible alternative" requirement of Section 4(f) of the DOT Act. This decision has defined Section 4(f) jurisprudence and practice for the last 35 years.

Chapter 7
Beginnings of Multimodal Urban Transportation Planning

By 1970, there were 273 urbanized areas actively engaged in continuing urban transportation planning (Fig. 7.1). By then, however, the urban transportation planning process was receiving criticism on a number of issues. It was criticized for inadequate treatment of the social and environmental impacts of transportation facilities and services. The planning process had still not become multimodal and was not adequately evaluating a wide range of alternatives. Planning was focused almost exclusively on long-range time horizons, ignoring more immediate problems. And, the technical procedures to carry out planning were criticized for being too cumbersome, time consuming, and rigid to adapt to new issues quickly. There was also concern expressed about their theoretical validity.

During the early 1970s, actions were taken to address these criticisms. Legislation was passed that increased the capital funds available for mass transportation and provided federal assistance for operating costs. Greater flexibility was permitted in the use of some highway funds including their use on transit projects. These provisions placed transit on a more equal footing with highways and considerably strengthened multimodal planning and implementation.

In addition, the federal government took steps to better integrate urban transportation planning at the local level, and to require shorter-range capital improvement programs along with long-range plans. Emphasis was placed on noncapital intensive measures to reduce traffic congestion as alternatives to major construction projects. And, state highway agencies were required to develop procedures for addressing social, economic, and environmental impacts of highways.

Urban Mass Transportation Assistance Act of 1970

The Urban Mass Transportation Assistance Act of 1970 was another landmark in federal financing for mass transportation. It provided the first long-term commitment of federal funds. Until the passage of this act, federal funds for mass transportation had been limited. It was difficult to plan and implement a program of mass transportation projects over several years because of the uncertainty of future funding.

E. Weiner, *Urban Transportation Planning in the United States, Third Edition*, doi:10.1007/978-0-387-77152-6, © Springer Science+Business Media, LLC 2008

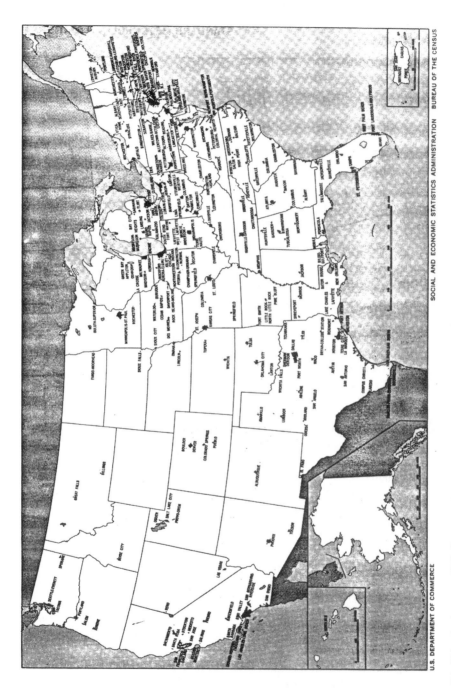

Fig. 7.1 Urbanized areas – 1970 (Source: US Dept. of Commerce, Bureau of Public Roads, Directory of Urbanized Areas, 1970)

The 1970 act implied a federal commitment for the expenditure of at least $10 billion over a 12-year period to permit confident and continuing local planning and greater flexibility in program administration. The act authorized $3.1 billion to finance urban mass transportation beginning in fiscal year 1971. It permitted the use of "contract authority" whereby the Secretary of Transportation was authorized to incur obligations on behalf of the USA with Congress pledged to appropriate the funds required to liquidate the obligations. This provision allowed long-term commitments of funds to be made.

This act also established a strong federal policy on transportation for elderly and handicapped persons:

> ...elderly and handicapped persons have the same right as other persons to utilize mass transportation facilities and services; that special efforts shall be made in the planning and design of mass transportation facilities and services so that the availability to elderly and handicapped persons to mass transportation which they can effectively utilize will be assured.... (US Dept. of Transportation, 1979b)

The act authorized that 2% of the capital grant and 1.5% of the research funds might be set aside and used to finance programs to aid elderly and handicapped persons.

The act also added requirements for public hearings on the economic, social, and environmental impacts of a proposed project and on its consistency with the comprehensive plan for the area. It also required an analysis of the environmental impacts of the proposed project and for the Secretary of Transportation to determine whether there was or not any feasible or prudent alternative to any adverse impact that might result.

Federal-Aid Highway Act of 1970

The Federal-Aid Highway Act of 1970 established the federal-aid urban highway system. The system in each urban area was to be designed to serve as major centers of activity and to serve local goals and objectives. Routes on the system were to be selected by local officials and state departments cooperatively. This provision significantly increased the influence of local jurisdictions in urban highway decisions. The influence of local officials in urban areas was further strengthened by an amendment to Section 134 on urban transportation planning:

> No highway project may be constructed in any urban area of 50,000 population or more unless the responsible local officials of such urban area...have been consulted and their views considered with respect to the corridor, the location and the design of the project. (US Dept. of Transportation, 1980a)

Funds for the federal-aid Urban system were to be allocated to the states on the basis of total urban population within the state. The act also authorized the expenditure of highway funds on exclusive or preferential bus lanes and related facilities. This could only be done if the bus project reduced the need for additional highway construction or if no other highway project could provide the person-carrying capacity of the bus project. There had to be assurances, as well, that the transit operator would utilize the facility. An additional provision of the act authorized expenditures of highway funds on fringe and corridor parking facilities adjacent to the federal-aid Urban system that were designed in conjunction with public transportation services.

This act also incorporated a number of requirements related to the environment. One required the issuance of guidelines for full consideration of economic, social, and environmental impacts of highway projects. A second related to the promulgation of guidelines for assuring that highway projects were consistent with SIPs developed under the Clean Air Act.

As a result of the 1970 highway and transit acts, projects for both modes would have to meet similar criteria related to impact assessment and public hearings. The highway act also increased the federal matching share to 70% for all non-Interstate highways, making it comparable to the 66 % federal share for mass transportation capital projects. In addition, the highway act legally required consistency between SIPs and urban highway plans.

Conference on Urban Commodity Flow

The urban transportation planning processes and methodologies that had been developed through the decade of the 1960s emphasized passenger movement. Little attention was given to the problems of commodity movements in urban areas. The majority of studies of urban goods movement had been limited to those related to trucks. Data on commodity movements were seldom collected because of the difficulty in tracking the movements and the lack of available methods (Chappell and Smith, 1971).

In recognition of the need for more information and better planning concerning the movement of goods in urban areas, a Conference on Urban Commodity Flow was convened at Airlie House in Warrentown, Virginia on 6–9 December 1970. Initially, the conference was to focus on information and techniques to forecast urban commodity movement. But, as planning for the conference progressed, there emerged a need for a more fundamental understanding of commodity movements and the economic, social, political, and technological forces that affected them (Highway Research Board, 1971a).

The conference revealed the lack of information on urban goods movement and the need for such information to make informed policy decisions on investment and regulation. The various viewpoints on the problems of urban commodity flow were explored. Planners, shippers, government agencies, freight carrier, and citizens saw the problems and consequences differently. With so many actors, the institutional issues were considered to be too complex to mount effective strategies to address the problems (Highway Research Board, 1971a).

The conferees concluded that goods movement needed more emphasis in the urban transportation planning process and that techniques for forecasting goods movement needed to be developed. The regulations and programs of federal, state, and local agencies needed to be coordinated to avoid conflicting effects on the goods movement industry that were not in the best interest of the public. Greater efforts were called for to explore means of reducing the economic, social, and environmental costs of goods movement in urban areas (Highway Research Board, 1971b).

This conference directed attention to the neglect of goods movement in the urban transportation planning process, and the complexity of the goods movement issue. It generated more interest and research in the subject and focused on the opportunity to develop strategies to deal with urban goods movement problems.

Discrete Choice Models

Travel demand forecasting through the 1950s and 1960s was carried out in a relatively aggregate manner. Although data were collected on the characteristics and travel behavior of individuals, this information was aggregated into travel analysis zones (TAZs) for the purposes of analysis and forecasting. The models that performed the analysis and forecasting used zonal averages or simple distributions of characteristics.

By the mid-1960s, many researchers recognized the limitations of the aggregate approach to travel analysis. They recognized that travel choices were discrete. You either go or you do not, you go either by car or by bus, you go either to Safeway or to another grocery. Further, populations were heterogeneous with regard to demographic characteristics, tastes, and personal circumstances. And, they would face transportation attributes of different alternatives on a trip by trip basis, such as time and costs, which would determine their travel choices (McFadden, 2002). These individual variations were not captured by the "averaging" approach used in conventional travel forecasting models.

Travel demand models based on the observed choices of individual tripmakers were first developed in academic research based on work in the fields of econometrics and psychometrics. These "disaggregate behavioral demand models" as they came to be known, were used to evaluate the relative importance of certain transportation variables in tripmaking decisions, or to derive values of time for cost-benefit analyses. Mode choice was the most frequently modeled travel decision. It was not until the early 1970's that transportation planners became aware of these models and their potential use in travel demand forecasting (Spear, 1977).

Disaggregate behavioral demand models predict the probability that an individual will make a particular choice. The estimate is a value ranging between0 and 1. There were a number of mathematical functions that were used to express this distribution. They were usually characterized by S-shaped curves, as shown in Fig. 7.2. The two functions that were most commonly used in individual choice modeling were the cumulative normal or probit function, and the logit function

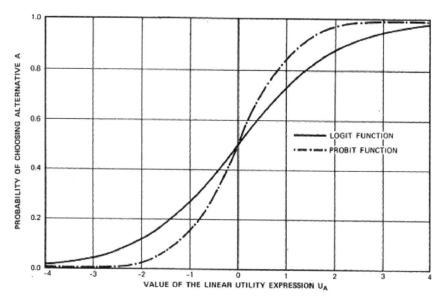

Fig. 7.2 Graph of logit and probit functions (Source: Spear, 1977)

(Spear, 1977). Eventually, the multinomial logit became the function most frequently used in these models.

Since the early developments in disaggregate demand models, a substantial amount of research was devoted to making these models responsive to the needs of transportation planners. Specifically, research focused on developing a theory of individual choice behavior; simplifying the computational requirements of model building; identifying new and more powerful explanatory variables; resolving some of the issues that limited the application of disaggregate demand choice models to other travel demand decisions; and demonstrating the capabilities of these models in solving practical planning problems (Spear, 1977).

Mt. Pocono Conference on Urban Transportation Planning

In recognition of the widespread awareness that urban transportation planning had not kept pace with changing conditions, a conference on Organization for Continuing Urban Transportation Planning was held at Mt. Pocono, Pennsylvania, in 1971. The focus of this conference was on multimodal transportation planning evolving from the earlier conferences that had focused on highway planning and the separation between planning and implementation (Highway Research Board, 1973a).

The conference recommended close coordination of planning efforts as a means of achieving orderly development of urban areas and relating the planning process more closely to decision-making processes at all levels of the government. It urged that urban planning be strengthened through state enabling legislation and bolstered by equitable local representation. Further, citizen participation should occur continually throughout the planning process but should not be considered as a substitute for decision-making by elected officials (Advisory Commission, 1974).

All comprehensive and functional planning, including multimodal transportation planning, should be integrated, including the environmental impact assessment process. The planning process should continually refine the long-range regional transportation plan at the subarea scale and focus on a 5- to 15-year time frame so that planning would be more relevant to programming and project implementation. Transportation planning should consider service levels consistent with local goals, and a wide range of alternatives should be evaluated. The impact of changes in the transportation system should be monitored to improve future decision-making and planning efforts (Advisory Commission, 1974).

The conference report went on to urge that this more inclusive kind of planning be supported by flexible funding from the federal government. This was to be done to avoid a preference for any mode so as not to unbalance specific urban transportation decisions contrary to local goals and priorities. The conference also supported additional resources for planning, research, and training.

DOT Initiatives Toward Planning Unification

The US Department of Transportation had been working for several years on integrating the individual modal planning programs. In 1971, the DOT established a trial program of intermodal planning in the field. The overall objective of the program was to integrate the modal planning programs at the urban-area level rather than at the federal level. With the successful completion of the trial program, the DOT implemented the program on a permanent basis by establishing intermodal planning groups (IPGs) in each of the ten DOT regions. The IPGs were charged with responsibility for obtaining and reviewing an annual unified work program for all transportation planning activities in an urban area; for obtaining agreement on a single recipient agency for area-wide transportation planning grants in each urban area; and for obtaining a short-term (3- to 5-year) transportation capital improvement program, updated annually, from each recipient agency (US Dept. of Transportation and US Dept. of Housing and Urban Development, 1974).

Also in 1971, a DOT transportation planning committee was established to promote a coordinated department-wide process for urban area- and state-wide transportation planning and for unified funding of such planning. As a result of the efforts of the committee, a DOT order was issued in 1973 that required that all urbanized areas submit annual unified work programs for all transportation planning activities as a condition for receiving any DOT planning funds. These work programs had to include all transportation-related planning activities, identification of the agency responsible for each activity, and the proposed funding sources. The work programs were used to rationalize planning activities and joint funding under the DOT planning assistance programs (US Dept. of Transportation and US Dept. of Housing and Urban Development, 1974).

Process Guidelines for Highway Projects

The Federal-Aid Highway Act of 1970 required that guidelines be issued to assure that possible adverse economic, social, and environmental effects were considered in developing highway projects and that decisions on these projects were made in the best overall public interest. Initially, guidelines were developed specifying requirements and procedures for evaluating the effects in each of the impact areas. These guidelines were presented and discussed at a Highway Research Board Workshop during July 1971 in Washington, DC. The primary conclusion of the workshop was that full consideration of adverse impacts and of decisions in the best overall public interest could not be assured by extensive technical standards. It would depend upon the attitudes, capabilities, organization, and procedures of the highway agencies responsible for developing the projects (US Congress, 1972a).

Based on the workshop recommendations and other comments, the emphasis of the guidelines was shifted to the process used in developing highway projects. In September 1972, FHWA issued PPM 90-4, "Process Guidelines (Economic, Social, and Environmental Effects of Highway Projects)" (US Dept. of Transportation, 1972a). These guidelines required each state to prepare an action plan spelling out the organizational arrangement, the assignment of responsibilities, and the procedures to be followed in developing projects in conformance with the law. The action plan had to address the process for the identification of social, economic, and environmental impacts, considerations of alternative courses of action, use of a systematic interdisciplinary approach, and the involvement of other agencies and the public. Flexibility was provided to the states to develop procedures that were adjusted to their own needs and conditions (U.S. Dept. of Transportation, 1974a).

The use of process guidelines was a further evolution of the manner in which highway projects were developed. The staffs of highway agencies were exposed to the views of other agencies and the public. Professionals with skills in the social and environmental areas were brought into the process. Gradually, the project development process became more open and embraced a broader range of criteria in reaching decisions.

UMTA's External Operating Manual

With the passage of the Urban Mass Transportation Assistance Act of 1970, the federal transit grant program substantially increased from less than $150 million annually before 1970 to over $500 million by 1972 (US Dept. of Transportation, 1977b). It was anticipated that both the level of funding and the number of projects to be administered would further increase. In August 1972, UMTA issued its first consolidated guidance for project management in its External Operating Manual (US Dept. of Transportation, 1972c).

The External Operating Manual contained general information on UMTA's organization and programs. It provided potential applicants with information on preparing an application for federal assistance, and the statutory criteria and program analysis guidelines UMTA would use in evaluating the applications. It also contained policies and procedures for administering projects.

The manual stated that the near-term objectives that UMTA sought to achieve with the federal transit program were increasing the mobility of nondrivers, relief of traffic congestion, and improving the quality of the urban environment. These objectives were related to urban areas of three size groups small areas under 250,000 in population, medium areas between 250,000 and 1,000,000 in population, and large areas over 1 million in population. For small areas, the primary objective was for the mobility of the transit dependent. In addition, for medium areas the use of noncapital intensive (i.e., transportation system management) strategies to reduce traffic congestion was emphasized. Additionally, for large areas, analysis of alternative transportation schemes including noncapital intensive strategies and new technologies was emphasized to support land development patterns (US Dept. of Transportation, 1972c).

Included as Appendix 2 of the Manual was the Urban Mass Transportation Planning Requirements Guide, which set forth the area-wide planning requirements for the transit program. These requirements were certified by HUD designed to be consistent with the 3C planning requirements of the FHWA. An urban area needed to have a legally established planning agency representing local units of government; a comprehensive, continuing area-wide planning process; and a land use plan to serve as the basis for determining travel demand.

The transportation planning requirements, which were certified by UMTA, included a long-range transportation planning process, a 5- to 10-year transit development program, and a short-range program. The agency conducting the transportation planning was to be, wherever possible, the agency carrying out the comprehensive planning. An area could meet the planning requirements on an interim basis, until 1 July 1972, if it had a planning process underway, but received only a 50% federal share for its transit project instead of the two-thirds share if the requirement was fully met.

The External Operating Manual was revised through 1974 but was updated and supplemented in later years with UMTA Circulars, Notices, and regulations (Kret and Mundle, 1982). The planning requirements contained in the manual were superseded by the joint FHWA/UMTA Urban Transportation Planning regulations (US Dept. of Transportation, 1975a).

Williamsburg Conference on Urban Travel Forecasting

By the latter part of the 1960s, use of the conventional urban travel forecasting procedures pioneered in the late 1950s and early 1960s was widespread but criticism of them was growing. Critics argued that conventional procedures were time consuming and expensive to operate and required too much data. The procedures had been designed for long-range planning of major facilities and were not suitable for evaluation of the wider range of options that were of interest, such as low-capital options, demand-responsive systems, pricing alternatives, and vehicle restraint schemes. Policy issues and options had changed, but travel demand forecasting techniques had not.

These issues were addressed at a conference on Urban Travel Demand Forecasting held at Williamsburg, Virginia, in December 1972, sponsored by the Highway Research Board and the US Department of Transportation. The conference concluded that there was a need for travel forecasting procedures that were sensitive to the wide range of policy issues and alternatives to be considered, quicker and less costly than conventional methods, more informative and useful to decision-makers, and in a form that nontechnical people could understand. Further, improvements in methodology were urgently needed, and significant improvements in capabilities could be achieved within 3 years based on the results of available research (Brand and Manheim, 1973).

The conference recommended several simultaneous paths to improve travel forecasting capabilities. First, the existing methodology was to be upgraded with the results of recent research. Second, emerging procedures in several urban areas were to be pilot tested. Third, research was to improve the understanding of travel behavior including before/after studies, consumer theory, psychological theory, and location behavior. Fourth, research was needed to transform the results of travel behavior research into practical forecasting techniques. Fifth, a two-way dissemination program was necessary to get new methods into the field and for the results of these applications to flow back to the researchers to improve the methods (Brand and Manheim, 1973).

The conferees were optimistic that the conversion to new, improved behavioral methods was soon to be at hand. They did recognize that a substantial amount of research was going to be necessary. And, in fact, the Williamsburg conference did launch a decade of extensive research and activity in disaggregate urban travel demand forecasting.

Federal-Aid Highway Act of 1973

The Federal-Aid Highway Act of 1973 contained two provisions that increased the flexibility in the use of highway funds for urban mass transportation in the spirit of the Mt. Pocono conference. First, federal-aid Urban system funds could be used for capital expenditures on urban mass transportation projects. This provision took effect gradually, but was unrestricted starting in fiscal year 1976. Second, funds for interstate highway projects could be relinquished and replaced by an equivalent amount from the general fund and spent on mass transportation projects in a particular state. The relinquished funds reverted back to the Highway Trust Fund.

This opening up of the Highway Trust Fund for urban mass transportation was a significant breakthrough sought for many years by transit supporters.

These changes provided completely new avenues of federal assistance for funding urban mass transportation.

The 1973 act had other provisions related to urban mass transportation. First, it raised the federal matching share for urban mass transportation capital projects from 66 $^2/_3$% to 80%, except for urban system substitutions, which remain at 70%. Second, it raised the level of funds under the UMTA capital grant program by $3 billion to $6.1 billion. Third, it permitted expenditure of highway funds for bus-related public transportation facilities, including fringe parking on all federal-aid highway systems.

The act called for realigning all federal-aid systems based on functional usage. It authorized expenditures on the new federal-aid urban system and modified several provisions related to it. "Urban" was defined as any area of 5,000 or more in population. Apportioned funds for the system were earmarked for urban areas of 200,000 or more in population. Most important, it changed the relationship between the state and the local officials in designating routes for the system. It authorized local officials in urbanized areas to choose routes with the concurrence of state highway departments (Parker, 1977).

Two additional provisions related directly to planning. For the first time, urban transportation planning was funded separately: 1/2 of 1% of all federal-aid funds were designated for this purpose and apportioned to the states on the basis of urbanized area population. These funds were to be made available to the metropolitan planning organizations (MPOs) that were designated by the states as being responsible for comprehensive transportation planning in urban areas.

The 1973 Federal-Aid Highway Act took a significant step toward integrating and balancing the highway and mass transportation programs. It also increased the role of local officials in the selection of urban highway projects and broadened the scope of transportation planning by MPOs.

Endangered Species Act of 1973

The Endangered Species Act of 1973 was enacted to prevent any animal or plant from becoming extinct in the USA. The act prevented the taking of endangered and threatened species of fish, wildlife, and plants, and the critical habitats where they live. The act applied to the loss of, or injury to, endangered species either directly or indirectly through activities that would interfere with their life support system (Alan M. Voorhees & Assoc., 1979).

Section 4 of the act required the determination of which species were endangered by the Secretary of Interior with regard to wildlife and plants, and the Secretary of Commerce with regard to fish. Section 7 of the act established a consultative process between any federal agency seeking to carry out a project or action and the appropriate department (either interior or commerce) to determine if there would be an adverse impact on any endangered species. The determination was to be made in the form of a biological opinion based on the best scientific and commercial data available. If the biological opinion found that an endangered species or its habitat was in jeopardy, the act required that reasonable and prudent alternatives be proposed by the Department of Commerce or Interior, respectively. Where the federal agency could not comply with the proposed alternatives, the project or action could not proceed (Ryan and Emerson, 1986).

The 1978 Amendments to the act established the Endangered Species Committee, which was authorized to grant exemptions from requirements of the act. This provision was a response to the decision by the US Supreme Court to uphold blockage of the completion of the Tennessee Valley Authority's Tellico Dam because it endangered a small fish called the snail darter (Salvesen, 1990).

In 1982, the act was again amended to allow for incidental takings of wildlife under certain conditions. For example, development could occur in the habitat of an endangered species if the development mitigated any adverse impacts of the species. This mitigation typically took the form of setting aside part of the site for a wildlife preserve, and by a finding that the development would not appreciably reduce the likelihood of the survival and recovery of the species in the wild (Salvesen, 1990).

The Endangered Species Act has been called the most powerful land use law in the nation. By 1990, there were about 500 plant and animal species listed as endangered or threatened in the USA, with more being added to the list each year. In the future, the act will affect many more development activities.

AASHTO Policy on Geometric Design of Urban Highways

By 1966, the 1957 edition of A Policy on Arterial Highways in Urban Areas had become partially obsolete as a result of the changing demands placed upon the urban transportation system (American Association of State Highway Officials, 1957). The American Association of State Highway and Transportation Officials (AASHTO) (the name was changed in 1973) began a 7-year effort to update and considerably expand this policy. The new edition was reissued as A Policy on Design of Urban Highways and Arterial Streets – 1973 (American Association of State Highway and Transportation Officials, 1973).

In addition to updated material on highway design, the policy contained two new sections on transportation planning and highway location not previously included in AASHTO policies. The material on transportation planning included a brief review of alternative organizational approaches, elements of a planning process, and steps in the process including data collection, forecasting, evaluation, surveillance, and reappraisal. The information closely paralleled the guidance provided by FHWA in PPM 50-9 and IM 50-4-68, and the technical guidance documented in their various manuals on the 3C planning process.

The section on highway location covered social and environmental effects of urban highway developments, community participation, and economic and environmental evaluation. The new material on highway design included design guidance for mass transit especially for buses on arterial streets and freeways.

The A Policy on Design of Urban Highways and Arterial Streets – 1973 attempted to show that the planning, location, and design of a highway were not three distinct independent processes but rather a coordinated effort by planners, locators, and designers.

In 1984, AASHTO issued A Policy on Geometric Design of Highways and Streets – 1984 which combined updated, and replaced the 1973 urban policy and 1965 rural policy in addition to several others (American Association of State Highway and Transportation Officials, 1984). This 1984 edition did not include the material from the 1973 urban policy on transportation planning and highway location but instead referenced it.

A Policy on Geometric Design of Highways and Streets was updated in 1990 and 2004. The more recent edition included the latest design practices in universal use as the standard for highway geometric design and was updated to reflect the latest research on super elevation and side friction factors. The policy was published in dual units (metric and US customary) and was made available on CD-ROM (AASHTO Policy of Geometric Design of Urban Highways, 1990, 2004).

1972 and 1974 National Transportation Studies

Although urban transportation planning had been legislatively required for over a decade, the results had not been used in the development of national transportation policy. Beyond that, a composite national picture of these urban transportation plans did not exist even though they were the basis for capital expenditure decisions by the federal government. In the early 1970s, the Department of Transportation conducted two national transportation studies to inventory and assess the current and planned transportation system as viewed by the states and urban areas.

The two studies differed in their emphasis. The 1972 National Transportation Study obtained information on the existing transportation system as of 1970, the transportation needs for the 1970–1990 period, and short-range (1974–1978) and long-range (1979–1990) capital improvement programs under three federal funding assumption (US Dept. of Transportation, 1972b). The study showed that the total transportation needs of the states and urban areas exceeded the financial resources of the nation to implement them and discussed the use of low-capital alternatives to improve the productivity of the existing transportation system, particularly in urban areas.

The 1974 National Transportation Study related more closely to the ongoing urban transportation planning processes (US Dept. of Transportation, 1975b). It obtained information on the 1972 inventories, long-range plans (1972–1990), and short-range programs (1972–1980) for the transportation system in a more comprehensive manner than did the 1972 study. The transportation system for all three periods was described in terms of the supply of facilities, equipment, and services, travel demand, system performance, social and environmental impacts, and capital and operating costs. Information on low-capital alternatives and new technological systems was also included. The 1972–1980 program was based on a forecast of federal funds that could reasonably be expected to be available and an estimate of state and local funds for the period (Weiner, 1974). This study again demonstrated that the long-range plans were overly ambitious in terms of the financial resources that might be available for transportation. Further, it showed that even after the expenditure of vast amounts of money for urban transportation, urban transportation systems would differ little in character in the foreseeable future (Weiner, 1975b).

The National Transportation Study process introduced the concept of tying state and urban transportation planning into national transportation planning and policy formulation. It stressed multimodal analysis, assessment of a wide range of measures of the transportation system, realistic budget limitations on plans and programs, and increasing the productivity of the existing transportation system. Although these concepts were not new, the National Transportation studies marked the first time that they had been incorporated into such a vast national planning effort (Weiner, 1976a).

National Mass Transportation Assistance Act of 1974

The National Mass Transportation Assistance Act of 1974 authorized for the first time the use of federal funds for transit operating assistance. It thereby continued the trend to broaden the use of federal urban transportation funds and provide state and local officials more flexibility. This act was the culmination of a major lobbying effort by the transit industry and urban interests to secure federal operating assistance for transit.

The act authorized $11.8 billion over a 6-year period. Under the Section 5 Formula Grant program, almost $4 billion was to be allocated to urban areas by a formula based on population and population density. The funds could be used for either capital projects or operating assistance. The funds for areas over 200,000 in population were attributable to those areas. The funds were to be distributed to "designated recipients" jointly agreed to by the governor, local elected officials, and operators of publicly owned mass transportation services. For areas under 200,000 in population, the governor was designated to allocate the funds.

Of the remaining $7.8 billion, $7.3 billion was made available for capital assistance at the discretion of the Secretary of Transportation, under the Section 3 Discretionary Grant program, and the remainder was for rural mass transportation. Funds used for capital projects were to have an 80% federal matching share. Operating assistance was to be matched 50% by the federal government.

Section 105(g) of the act required applicants for transit projects to meet the same planning statute as Section 134 of the highway act. Finally, highway and transit projects were subject to the same long-range planning requirement. Although many urbanized areas already had a joint highway/transit planning process, this section formalized the requirement for multimodal transportation planning.

The act also required transit systems to charge elderly and handicapped persons fares that were half regular fares when they traveled in off-peak hours. This was a further condition to receiving federal funds.

The act created a new Section 15 that required the Department of Transportation to establish a data reporting system for financial and operating information and a uniform system of accounts and records. After July 1978, no grant could be made to any applicant unless they were reporting data under both systems.

PLANPAC and UTPS Batteries of Computer Programs

The computer programs developed and maintained by BPR during the 1960s were essential to most urban transportation planning studies that generally did not have the time and resources to develop their own programs. The battery had been written for most part by the US Bureau of Standards and consisted of 60 single purpose computer programs. Toward the end of the decade of the 1960s, new batteries of computer programs were being developed for transportation planning for the recently introduced third generation of computers, the IBM 360 (US Dept. of Transportation, 1977a).

The new package of urban transportation planning computer programs, known as PLANPAC, was written to take advantage of the new capabilities of these computers. Most highway agencies were acquiring IBM 360s for their own computer installations and would soon be able to use the new computers. PLANPAC included computer programs to analyze survey data, develop and apply trip generation relationships, calibrate and apply trip distribution models, perform traffic assignment, evaluate networks, and plotting and utility programs to handle data sets (US Dept. of Transportation, 1977a).

New programs continued to be written and added to PLANPAC. In 1974, the FHWA completed a reorientation of the package. Many of the programs in PLANPAC that were not associated with the traditional four-step urban travel forecasting process were shifted to BACKPAC, a back-up package of additional computer programs for urban transportation planning. These included computer programs for traffic signal optimization, parking studies, highway capacity analysis, carpool matching, micro traffic analysis, land use forecasting, and freeway management. This resulted in 59 programs being retained in PLANPAC and 244 programs being included in BACKPAC.

A battery of computer programs for transit system planning was also developed during the mid-1960s by the US Department of Housing, and Urban Development that administered the federal transit program at that time. The battery was first written for the IBM 7090/94 computers and consisted of 11 multipurpose programs. Around 1973, UMTA assumed responsibility for the HUD transit planning package and released an enhanced version for the IBM 360 as the UMTA Transportation Planning System (UTPS). The programs were designed for network analysis, travel demand estimation, sketch planning, and data manipulation. The programs were compatible and communicated through a common data base.

In 1976, the FHWA decided not to perform any further developments for PLANPAC but instead join with UMTA to support the UTPS package whose name was changed to Urban Transportation Planning System. FHWA did make a commitment to maintain and support PLANPAC as long as users needed it. The first release of the UMTA/FHWA multimodal UTPS was in 1976. A 1979/80 release provided additional capabilities and contained 20 programs.

The development and support of computer programs by FHWA and UMTA substantially assisted urban transportation planning studies in performing their various analytical and planning functions. These computer batteries facilitated the use of conventional planning techniques and furthered this style of urban transportation planning.

Chapter 8
Transition to Short-Term Planning

As planning for the Interstate Highway System was being completed, attention turned to increasing the productivity and efficiency of existing facilities. In planning for major new regional transportation facilities, many urban areas had neglected maintaining and upgrading other facilities. However, environmental concerns, the difficulty of building inner city freeways, renewed interest in urban mass transit, and the energy crisis gave added impetus to the focus on more immediate problems. Signs were becoming evident of the changing emphasis to shorter-term time horizons and the corridor level in transportation planning. Gradually, planning shifted toward maximizing the use of the existing system with a minimum of new construction. Further, the connection was strengthened between long-term planning and the programming of projects (Weiner, 1982).

Emergency Energy Legislation

In October 1973, the Organization of Petroleum Exporting Countries (OPEC) embargoed oil shipments to the USA and, in doing so, began a new era in transportation planning. The importance of oil was so paramount to the economy and, in particular, the transportation sector in which oil shortages and price increases gradually became one of the major issues in transportation planning (Fig. 8.1).

The immediate reaction to the oil embargo was to address the specific emergency. President Nixon signed the Emergency Petroleum Allocation Act of 1973 in November of that year, which established an official government allocation plan for gasoline and home heating fuel. It regulated the distribution of refined petroleum products by freezing the supplier–purchaser relationships and specifying a set of priority users. The act also established price controls on petroleum. It gave the president authority to set petroleum prices, not to exceed $7.66 a barrel. This authority was to terminate on 30 September 1981.

The Emergency Highway Energy Conservation Act, signed on 2 January 1974, established a national 55 mile per h speed limit to reduce gasoline consumption. It was extended indefinitely on 4 January 1975 (US Dept. of Transportation, 1979c).

E. Weiner, *Urban Transportation Planning in the United States, Third Edition,*
doi:10.1007/978-0-387-77152-6, © Springer Science+Business Media, LLC 2008

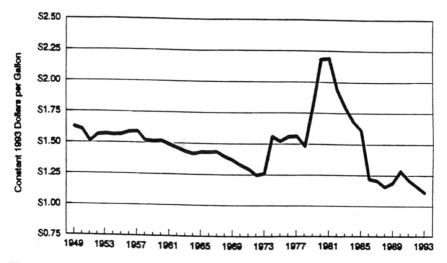

Fig. 8.1 Real gasoline prices (1949–1993) (Source: US Department of Energy, Energy Information Agency)

It also provided that Federal-aid highway funds could be used for ridesharing demonstration programs.

As the immediate crisis abated, the focus shifted to longer-term actions and policies to reduce the nation's dependence on oil, especially imported oil. The Energy Policy and Conservation Act of 1975 was passed by Congress to ensure that automobile gasoline consumption would be reduced to the lowest level possible and to promote energy conservation plans. As directed, the US Department of Transportation through the National Highway Traffic Safety Administration (NHTSA) promulgated regulations that required the corporate average fuel economy (CAFE) be raised from 18.0 miles per gallon in 1978 to 27.5 miles per gallon in 1985 and beyond (US Dept. of Transportation, 1979c).

Reaction to the energy crisis of 1973/1974 evolved slowly at the local level as information and analysis tools gradually appeared. Most local planning agencies knew little about energy consumption and conservation and needed to learn about this new issue that had been thrust upon them. It was not until the second crisis in 1979 with fuel shortages and sharply increasing prices that energy issues were thoroughly integrated into urban transportation planning.

Service and Methods Demonstration Program

The focus on transportation planning and development was shifting to shorter-term, low-capital improvements in the early 1970s. Many of these improvements, which were grouped under the term "transportation system management" (TSM) techniques, were only in the conceptual stage or in limited applications in the USA and other countries. There was a need to perform the final steps of evaluation and development, where necessary, to bring these new improvement strategies into operational practice.

The Service and Methods Demonstration (SMD) Program was established in 1974 to promote the development, demonstration, evaluation, and widespread adoption of innovative transit services and transportation management techniques throughout the USA. The program focused on concepts that used existing technology to create improvements that require relatively low levels of capital investment and that can be implemented within a short time frame. The concepts were demonstrated in real-world operational environments and evaluated to determine their costs, impacts, and implementation characteristics. Evaluation findings were widely disseminated to transportation planners, policy makers, and transit operators (Spear, 1979).

The SMD Program began with six demonstrations involving specialized transportation for the elderly and handicapped, double-deck buses, and priority lanes for highway occupancy vehicles. By 1978, the program was sponsoring 59 ongoing demonstrations, evaluating 31 special case study projects, and had begun a cooperative program with the FHWA to evaluate another 17 projects in the National Ridesharing Demonstration Program.

Projects were divided into four program areas. First, under conventional service improvements, projects concentrated on improving productivity, reliability, and effectiveness with such techniques as priority treatment for buses and other high occupancy vehicles, route restructuring, auto restricted zones, and articulated buses. In the second category of pricing and service innovation were projects on fare payment strategies, fare integration, fare change strategies, service changes, and parking pricing. The third category of paratransit services contained projects on ridesharing, brokerage, and taxicabs. Fourth, transportation services for special user groups focused on accessible bus services, user-side subsidies, coordination of social service agency transportation, and rural public transportation (Spear, 1981).

The Service and Methods Demonstration Program made a major contribution to the identification, evaluation, and dissemination of transportation system management techniques. This effort accelerated the introduction and adoption of innovative approaches to the provision of public transportation service. It also spurred experimentation with new public transportation service concepts by other agencies at the state and local levels.

Taxicabs

With the growing interest in demand responsive types of urban public transportation services, there was renewed interest on taxicab transportation. Taxicab transportation had been a significant segment of urban transportation for many years but had received little attention by transportation planners. Taxicabs provided service with characteristics between the automobile and mass transportation. They were capable of accessing any point in an urban area, could respond on demand by hailing or telephone, and provided personal transportation service. In these regards they were more similar to personal vehicles. Conversely, a fare had been required, vehicle parking was eliminated, some wait was required, and they could carry groups of passengers. In these regards, they were similar to mass transportation. In that taxicab services had been more tailored to demands, their fares have been higher than mass transportation (Weiner, 1975c).

In 1974, the taxicab industry was composed of 7,200 fleet operations in addition to several thousand individual operators. These fleets were franchised to operate in 3,300 communities and, in many instances, were the only form of public transportation. Taxicab companies and operators were private enterprises operating under government regulations. They operated in a highly competitive environment. Most large communities allowed limited or free entry into the taxicab business or required bids for exclusive franchises. It was not uncommon to have several operators in the same community.

In 1970, the taxicab industry operated about three times as many vehicles and twice as many vehicle miles, and collected more passenger revenue as the nation's transit industry (Wells et al., 1974). Employment was stable from 1967 to 1970 at about 111,000 persons. This figure represented average annual employment. However, the turnover rate for employees was high. The industry provided employment for many unemployed, part-time, and temporary workers, which varied with economic conditions (Webster et al., 1974).

Taxicabs were used by travelers with a wide range of trip purposes by having varied socio-economic characteristics. They generally fell into two general categories: those without alternative means of travel and those who chose taxicabs for their high level of service. In the first group were senior citizens, disabled persons, persons with low incomes, those without personal vehicles or driver's licenses, and housewives. In the second group were higher-income individuals, managers, and executives (Weiner, 1975c).

Work and work-related trips represented 38% of taxicabs trips compared to 31% of trips for all modes in 1970. Most taxicab work trips occurred during regular peak hours. But, there was a concentration of work trips at night when mass transportation services were minimal or when it may have been unsafe to walk or wait at transit stops. Family business trips accounted for another 45% compared with 30% for all modes. Medical and dental trips represented 16 percentage points of family business trips compared to 2% by all modes. Over 10% of these trips were taken at night, which was probably trips for emergency services.

Taxicab transportation had been a flexible mode of transportation. Consequently, taxicabs had been well suited for a number of special purposes. Taxicab transportation was most attractive for serving lower density area and off-peak travel particularly where there is only minimal mass transit service. In this regard, taxicabs have been a supplement to conventional mass transit. The use of taxicabs for collection and distribution functions for both passengers and freight was gradually being realized. Group riding in taxicabs offered advantages of increasing taxicab productivity and reducing individual trip costs.

Taxicabs continued to be an important element in urban transportation systems. Efforts were being made to reduce the regulatory and institutional barriers to greater use of taxicabs for a wider array of functions and increased productivity.

OTA's Report on Automated Guideway Transit

By the time the report Tomorrow's Transportation: New Systems for the Urban Future (Cole, 1968) was published in 1968, UMTA barely had a research program in the area of new urban transit technologies. A small grant had been made for development of Westinghouse's Transit Expressway and several new system feasibility studies were begun in 1967. By 1970, decisions had been reached to proceed with funding of three major automated guideway transit (AGT) demonstration projects – the Transpo 72 exhibition and two other demonstrations (US Congress, Office of Technology Assessment, 1975).

Transpo 72 was held at the Dulles International Airport near Washington, DC, in the spring of 1972. Four companies built and operated prototype AGT systems for public demonstration. In 1971, UMTA awarded a grant to the Vought Corporation to build a group rapid transit (GRT) system, Airtrans, as the internal circulation system for the Dallas–Ft. Worth Airport. Service began in 1974. The third GRT demonstration connected three separate campuses of West Virginia University at Morgantown. Boeing Aerospace Company became the manager of the project which was largely based on a proposal by Alden Self-Transit Systems Corporation. Public service began in October 1975. The system was expanded with an UMTA grant and operations began in July 1979 (US Dept. of Transportation, 1983b).

By the end of 1975, another 18 systems were in operation or under construction. They were all simple shuttle loop transit (SLT) systems at airports, amusement parks, and shopping centers. All were funded with private funds (US Dept. of Transportation, 1983b).

In September 1974, the US Senate Transportation Appropriations Committee directed the Congressional Office of Technology Assessment (OTA) to assess the potential for AGT systems. The report, produced in June 1975, was a comprehensive assessment of AGT systems and contained five reports from panels of specialists. Overall, the report concluded that the $95 million spent on AGT research and development up to that time by UMTA had not produced the direct results expected in the form of fully developed systems in urban settings. The OTA went further in concluding that insufficient funding was directed at new systems research and that the program needed restructuring with a clarification of objectives (US Congress, Office of Technology Assessment, 1975).

The OTA found that SLT systems were promising for specialized urban transportation problems. With regard to the more sophisticated GRT systems, the OTA found that a number of cities had shown interest but that there were serious technical problems. As to the small vehicle personal rapid transit (PRT) systems, only preliminary studies were recommended. A major conclusion was that the program emphasized hardware development, but further research was needed on social, economic, and environmental impacts. Also UMTA had not developed a mechanism for qualifying new technological systems for capital grants (US Congress, Office of Technology Assessment, 1975).

In response to the study, UMTA launched the AGT Socio-Economic Research Program in 1976. It consisted of assessments of existing AGT installations, studies of capital and operating costs, travel market analyses, and an assessment of AGT technology compared with other alternatives in urban area application (US Dept. of Transportation, 1983b).

A review of local planning studies conducted under this program found that more than 20 cities had considered AGT systems. The conclusion reached was that there was considerable uncertainty with regard to costs, public acceptance, reliability, crime, and land use impacts (Lee et al., 1978). Planning procedures and data were not available to adequately assess new technological systems as an alternative to conventional urban technologies.

Also in 1976, UMTA initiated the Downtown People Mover (DPM) program. It was designed to demonstrate the application of an SLT type system in an urban environment. Impact studies were to be conducted to assess the systems with regard to patronage, community acceptance, reliability, maintainability, safety, and economics. Four cities were selected for these demonstrations: Cleveland, Houston, Los Angeles, and St. Paul. Three other cities were approved for participation using their existing commitments of federal funds: Detroit, Miami, and Baltimore (Mabee and Zumwalt, 1977). Detroit and Miami have constructed DPMs.

Model 13(c) Labor Protection Agreement for Operating Assistance

Section 13(c) was included in the Urban Mass Transportation Act of 1964 to protect employees in the transit industry from potential adverse effects of federal transit assistance. At the time, federal assistance was in the form of capital grants and loans that could be used for public acquisition of private operations. A major concern was the loss of collective bargaining rights when employees entered the public sector.

Section 13(c) required an applicant for federal assistance to make arrangements to protect the interests of employees. Employee protection arrangements under Section 13(c) included: (1) preservation of rights under existing contracts; (2) continuation of collective bargaining rights; (3) protection of employees against a worsening of their positions; (4) assurances of employment or reemployment for existing employees; and (5) paid training or retraining programs.

The Secretary of Labor was responsible for determining whether these arrangements were fair and equitable. There had been an evolution in the administration of Section 13(c) since it was enacted. Originally the Department of Labor (DOL) only required a statement that the interests of employees would not be adversely affected by the Federal grant. By 1966, however, there had evolved detailed 13(c) agreements that were the result of collective bargaining between grant applicants and the employee representatives. These 13(c) agreements were subject to renegotiation with each new grant.

With the passage of the National Mass Transportation Assistance Act of 1974, federal funds became available for operating assistance under the Section 5 Formula Grant program. Grants for operating assistance were also required to comply with the Section 13(c) provisions. To facilitate processing of these operating assistance applications, organized labor, the American Public Transit Association (APTA), and the DOL developed a national model 13(c) agreement pertaining to such agreements. The model agreement was signed in July 1975 by APTA, the Amalgamated Transit Union, and the Transport Workers Union of America. APTA established a procedure under which individual transit properties could affiliate themselves with the agreement and, thereby, become eligible for coverage by it for operating assistance applications (Lieb, 1976).

The model Section 13(c) agreement for transit operating assistance reduced the time and effort of individual transit properties and labor representatives to negotiate agreement and accelerated the use of federal funds for operating assistance.

Joint Highway/Transit Planning Regulations

The UMTA and FHWA had worked for several years on joint regulations to guide urban transportation planning. Final regulations were issued to take effect in October 1975 (US Dept. of Transportation, 1975a). They superseded all previous guidelines, policies, and regulations issued on urban transportation planning by the UMTA and FHWA.

The regulations provided for the designation of MPOs by the Governors and local elected officials, and, to the maximum extent feasible, that the MPOs be established under state legislation. The MPO was to be the forum of cooperative decision-making by principal elected officials. Principal elected officials of the local jurisdictions were to have adequate representation on the MPO. The MPO, together with the state, was responsible for carrying out the urban transportation planning process. The regulations also required agreements on the division of responsibility where the MPOs and A-95 agencies were different. A multiyear prospectus and annual unified work program had to be submitted specifying all transportation-related planning activities for an urban area as a condition for receiving federal planning funds (Fig. 8.2).

The urban transportation planning process was required to produce a long-range transportation plan, which had to be reviewed annually to confirm its validity. The transportation plan had to contain a long-range element and a shorter-range "transportation systems management element" (TSME) for improving the operation of existing transportation systems without new facilities. An appendix to the regulations

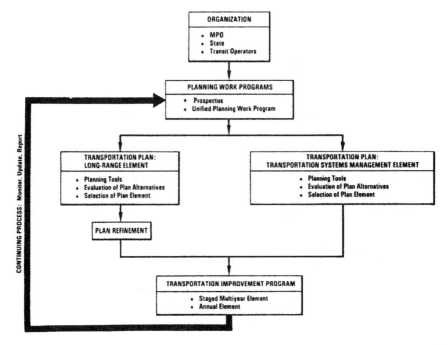

Fig. 8.2 Joint FHWA/UMTA urban transportation planning process (Source: US Dept. of Transportation, 1975a)

Table 8.1 Approximate start dates for early US traffic calming initiatives

Community	Year
Austin, TX	1986
Bellevue, WA	1985
Charlotte, NC	1978
Eugene, OR	1974
Gainesville, FL	1984
Montgomery County, MD	1978
Portland, OR	1984
San Jose, CA	1978

Source: Ewing, 1999

contained a list of major categories of actions to be considered for inclusion in the TSME (Table 8.1). The appendix stated that the feasibility and need for the individual actions differed with the size of the urbanized area, but that some actions in each of the categories would be appropriate for any urbanized area.

A multiyear "transportation improvement program" (TIP) also had to be developed consistent with the transportation plan. The TIP had to include all highway and transit projects to be implemented within the following 5 years. It thereby became the linkage between the planning and programming of urban transportation projects. It also brought together all highway and transit projects into a single document that could be reviewed and approved by decision-makers. The TIP had to contain an "annual element" that would be the basis for the federal funding decisions on projects for the coming year.

The regulations provided for a joint FHWA/UMTA annual certification of the planning process. This certification was required as a condition for receiving federal funds for projects. The regulations incorporated previously legislated requirements related to social, economic, and environmental impact analysis, air quality planning, and the elderly and handicapped.

These joint regulations applied to all urban highway and transit programs including those for transit operating assistance. They represented the most important action up to that time to bring about multimodal urban transportation planning and programming of projects. They changed the emphasis from long-term planning to shorter range transportation system management, and provided a stronger linkage between planning and programming. These regulations were another turning point in the evolution of urban transportation planning that set the tone for the next several years.

Traffic Calming

The concept of "traffic calming" began as a grassroots movement in the late 1960s when angry residents of the Dutch city of Delft fought cut-through routes for vehicles by turning their streets into "woonerven" or "living yards." What were once channels for the movement of cars became shared areas, outfitted with tables, benches, sand boxes, and parking bays jutting into the street. The effect was to turn the street into an obstacle course for motor vehicles and an extension of home for residents. Woonerven were officially endorsed by the Dutch government in 1976. Over the next decade, the idea spread to many other countries (Ewing, 1999).

Berkeley, California, was probably first to city in the USA to establish a full-blown program of traffic calming, when it adopted a city-wide traffic management plan in 1975. Seattle, Washington, may have been first to do area-wide planning, when it conducted neighborhood-wide demonstrations in the early 1970s. Seattle has had more experience implementing more traffic calming measures than any other community in the USA. Other cities followed the examples of Berkeley and Seattle, as shown in Table 8.1 (Ewing, 1999).

Traffic calming was the combination of mainly physical measures that reduce the negative effects of motor vehicle use, altered driver behavior, and improved conditions for nonmotorized street users. The immediate purpose of traffic calming was to reduce the speed and volume of traffic to acceptable levels ("acceptable" for the functional class of a street and the nature of bordering activity). Reductions in traffic speed and volume, however, were just means to other ends such as traffic safety and active street life. Different localities undertook traffic calming for different reasons. Traffic calming goals included

- Increasing the quality of life
- Incorporating the preferences and requirements of the people using the area (e.g., working, playing, residing) along the street(s) or at intersection(s)
- Creating safe and attractive streets
- Helping to reduce the negative effects of motor vehicles on the environment (e.g., pollution, sprawl)
- Promoting pedestrian, cycle, and transit use (Lookwood, 1997)

Traffic calming practice has evolved over time. Table 8.2 shows the use of one or more engineering measures used in 153 cities and counties. Others had educational and enforcement activities that would fall under a broader definition of traffic calming.

There has been resistance from some transportation professionals (those who emphasize vehicle traffic flow over other street design objectives), and from the financial costs for implementing traffic calming projects. There has sometimes been opposition from residents to traffic calming, although this usually related to specific traffic calming devices (such as speed humps) rather than the overall concept of traffic calming. Opposition often declined significantly within a few months after traffic calming was implemented. Traffic calming critics have raised a number of concerns related to delay to emergency vehicles, civil rights violations (if traffic restrictions limit access to some neighborhoods), increased air pollution (from speed humps), discomfort to people with disabilities (from speed humps), problems for cyclists, liability and lawsuits, neighborhood conflict (Calongne, 2003).

Traffic calming programs have usually been implemented by local engineering departments. These programs have involved educating planners and traffic engineers about traffic calming strategies, establishing policies and guidelines for implementing traffic calming projects, and developing funding sources. Specific traffic calming projects have been initiated by neighborhood requests, traffic safety programs, or as part of community redevelopment. Traffic calming strategies have evolved into context-sensitive design practices that allow planners and engineers to use flexible standards that can accommodate community values and balanced objectives. These strategies have also been incorporated the design of new developments and urban redevelopment.

Table 8.2 Prevalence of selected traffic calming measures in 153 cities and counties

Measure	Number of jurisdictions
Speed humps	79
Diverters/closures	67
Traffic circles	46
Chokers	35
Engineering measures (any kind)	110

Source: Ewing, 1999

Policy on Major Urban Mass Transportation Investments

The level of federal funds for urban mass transportation had increased dramatically since 1970. However, the requests for federal funds from urban areas outpaced that increase. In particular, there was a resurgence of the conviction that rail transit systems could largely solve the problems of congestion and petroleum dependence while promoting efficient development patterns. Consequently, the need to assure that these funds were used effectively and productively became apparent.

The UMTA set forth its views on this issue in the document, Preliminary Guidelines and Background Analysis (Transportation Research Board, 1975a). It was prepared for review at a conference on the Evaluation of Urban Transportation Alternatives held at Airlie House, Virginia, in February 1975. The conference was attended by a broad spectrum of persons from all levels of government, the transit industry, consultants, universities, and private citizens. The conference report indicated a number of concerns with the guidelines, which were transmitted to the UMTA (Transportation Research Board, 1977).

With the assistance of the conference findings, the UMTA developed a draft policy statement to guide future decisions regarding federal assistance in the funding of major mass transportation projects. This Proposed Policy on Major Urban Mass Transportation Investments was published in August 1975 (US Dept. of Transportation, 1975c). It embodied a number of principles.

First, area-wide transportation improvement plans should be multimodal and include region-wide and community-level transit services (Table 8.3). Second, major mass transportation investment projects should be planned and implemented in stages to avoid premature investment in costly fixed facilities and to preserve maximum flexibility to respond to future unknowns. Third, full consideration should be given to improving the management and operation of existing transportation systems. Fourth, the analysis of alternatives should include a determination of which alternative meets the local area's social, environmental, and transportation goals in a cost-effective manner. And fifth, full opportunity should be provided for involvement of the public and local officials in all phases of the planning and evaluation process (Transportation Research Board, 1977).

The UMTA stated that the level of federal funding would be based on a cost-effective alternative that would meet urban area needs and goals in a 5- to 15-year time frame and that was consistent with the long-range transportation plan.

A second Conference on Urban Transportation Alternative Analysis was held in March/April 1976 at Hunt Valley, Maryland. This conference, too, was attended by a broad spectrum of the professional community. There was considerable discussion on several issues including the criteria to be used to measure cost effectiveness, where the cost-effectiveness analysis fit in the overall planning process and the differences in the project development process between transit and highways (Transportation Research Board, 1977).

Using the recommendations from the second conference, the UMTA prepared and published a final policy statement in September 1976 (US Dept. of

Table 8.3 Actions to be considered for inclusion in the transportation system management element

Actions to ensure the efficient use of existing road space
- Traffic operations improvements
- Preferential treatment of transit and high occupancy vehicles
- Provision for pedestrians and bicycles
- Management and control of parking
- Changes in work schedules, fare structures, and automobile tools

Actions to reduce vehicle use in congested areas
- Encouragement of carpooling and other forms of ridesharing
- Diversion, exclusion, and metering of automobile access to specific areas
- Area licenses, parking surcharges, and other forms of congestion pricing
- Establishment of car-free zones and closure of selected streets
- Restrictions of downtown truck deliveries during peak hours

Actions to improve transit service
- Provision of better collection, distribution, and internal collection service within low-density areas
- Greater responsiveness and flexibility in routing, scheduling, and dispatching of transit vehicles
- Provision of Express Services
- Provision of Extensive Park and Ride Services From Fringe Parking Areas
- Provision of Shuttle Transit Services From CBD Fringe Parking Areas
- Encouragement of Jitneys and Other Flexible Paratransit Services and Their Integration in the Transit System
- Simplified fare collection systems and policies
- Better passenger information systems and services

Actions to increase transit management efficiency
- Improve marketing
- Develop cost accounting and other management tools to improve decision-making
- Establish maintenance policies that ensure greater equipment reliability
- Using surveillance and communications technology to develop real-time monitoring and control capability

Source: US Dept. of Transportation, 1975a

Transportation, 1976b). Although changes in the proposed policy were made, the principles remained basically unchanged. In February 1978, the UMTA provided further elaboration in its Policy Toward Rail Transit (US Dept. of Transportation, 1978a). It stated that new rail transit lines or extensions would be funded in areas where population densities, travel volumes, and growth patterns indicated the need. Preference would be given to corridors serving densely populated urban centers. It reaffirmed the principles of analysis of alternatives, including TSM measures, incremental implementation, and cost effectiveness. The policy added the requirement that the local area had to commit itself to a program of supportive actions designed to improve the cost effectiveness, patronage, and prospect for economic viability of the investment. This included automobile management policies; feeder service; plans, policies, and incentives to stimulate high density private development near stations; and other measures to. revitalize nearby older neighborhoods and the central business district. With this policy supplement, rail transit was to become a tool for urban redevelopment.

Characteristics of Urban Transportation Systems

Urban transportation planning in the mid-1970s was a more diverse and complex activity compared to the rather uniform process that existed during the mid-1960s. This change was caused by the need to address an expanded list of issues, and was fostered by the issuance of the Joint FHWA/UMTA Planning Regulations and UMTA's Policy on Major Urban Mass Transportation Investments (US Dept. of Transportation, 1975a, 1976b). The range of alternatives that had to be evaluated widened to include a fuller consideration of transit system options, transportation system management measures, and traffic engineering improvements. A more thorough assessment of social, economic, environmental, and energy impacts was required. Consequently, urban areas were conducting transportation systems evaluations with increasing sophistication that consumed more time and resources.

Even though there were many sources of information on the characteristics of urban transportation systems and their impacts to facilitate this evaluation process, they were difficult to locate, conflicting, often out of date, and generally local in nature. There was a need to synthesis and codify this data and information so that it would be more accessible. An earlier effort in the 1960s by the Institute of Traffic Engineers, Capacities and Limitations of Urban Transportation Modes was more narrowly focused and reflected the range of issues at that time (Institute of Traffic Engineers, 1965).

To fill this gap, a handbook was prepared and published in early 1974 under the title, Characteristics of Urban Transportation Systems (CUTS) (Sanders and Reynen, 1974). CUTS was designed as a single reference source containing information of the performance characteristics of urban transportation systems for use in the evaluation of transportation alternatives. The first edition contained data on rail transit, bus transit, the automobile/highway system, and pedestrian assistance systems. The seven supply parameters selected were speed, capacity, operating cost, energy consumption, air pollution and noise, capital cost, and accident frequency. The CUTS handbook was periodically updated and expanded. Later editions included data on activity center systems as well as the original four modes. Labor inputs were added to the supply parameters in later editions of the handbook (Reno and Bixby, 1985). The seventh edition of the handbook was published in 1992 (Cambridge Systematics et al., 1992).

CUTS was supplemented with two additional handbooks that provided data on the demand characteristics of urban transportation systems. The first, released in 1977, was Traveler Response to Transportation System Changes (Pratt, Pedersen and Mather, 1977). It summarized and synthesized information, primarily from existing literature, on the traveler behavior changes for a wide variety of changes in the transportation system. The initial edition distilled and interpreted data on seven types of transportation changes including high occupancy vehicle priority facilities, variable working hours, van and buspools, transit scheduling frequency changes, routing changes, transit fare changes, and transit marketing. Parking and express transit were added in the second edition (Pratt and Copple, 1981). The third edition was developed under the Transit Cooperative Research Program. It was to cover 17 topics that included eight new topics. An Interim Handbook was published with the first seven topics while research way underway for the remaining topics (Pratt et al., 2000).

The second handbook was Characteristics of Urban Transportation Demand (CUTD) along with a later issued appendix (Levinson, 1978, 1979). The CUTD handbook contained data on area-wide travel characteristics and typical usage information for rail, bus, and highways systems. The data was designed as inputs and cross checks for urban travel forecasting. The appendix contained more detailed city-specific and site-specific data on travel. The revision to CUTD reorganized, integrated, and updated the information included in the earlier edition (Charles River Associates, 1988). CUTD was again updated using travel surveys from various MPOs, Federal survey data, and other surveys of travel activity (Reno et al., 2002).

These efforts sought to capitalize on the large body of data and experience on urban transportation systems that had been accumulated in the previous two decades and make it more available and accessible to the transportation planning community. It came at a time when the range of information needed for transportation system evaluation had greatly broadened but the resources for collecting new data were narrowing.

Light Rail Transit

In the late 1960s and early 1970s, many urban areas were seeking alternatives to the construction of freeways. San Francisco and Washington, DC, had decided to construct heavy rail systems, but many areas did not have the density or potential travel demand to justify such systems. Moreover, heavy rail systems had high construction costs and disrupted the areas through which they passed during construction. Busways and preferential treatment for buses were being considered as alternatives to high-cost fixed guideway systems, particularly in the USA. In Europe, especially West Germany, light rail transit was the preferred alternative. This European experience renewed interest in light rail systems in the USA (Diamant et al., 1976).

In 1971, the San Francisco Municipal Railway (Muni) requested bids on 78 new light rail vehicles to replace its deteriorating PCC car fleet. The two bids that were received were rejected as being too costly. About this time, the Massachusetts Bay Transportation Authority (MBTA) and the Southeastern Pennsylvania Transportation Authority (SEPTA) decided to preserve and upgrade their light rail systems. These events provided the opportunity to develop a standard design for common use. The UMTA authorized a grant to the MBTA to develop specifications for a new US Standard Light Rail Vehicle (SLRV). The first SLRVs were built by Boeing Vertol and tested in 1974 at the UMTA's test track in Pueblo, Colorado (Silken and Mora, 1975).

In December 1975, the UMTA expressed its concern that urban areas should give adequate consideration to light rail transit (LRT) in a Policy Statement on

Light Rail Transit. The UMTA stated that while it had no modal favorites, the increasing demand for transit capital assistance combined with escalating transit construction costs made it essential that cost-effective approaches be fully explored. UMTA considered LRT as a potentially attractive option for many urban areas and would assist in its deployment in areas where proper conditions existed (Transportation Systems Center, 1977).

As interest in LRT grew, a series of conferences was organized to exchange information and explore the technical aspects and applications of LRT. The first conference, held in Philadelphia in 1975, had as its objective the reintroduction of LRT to a wide spectrum of decision-makers in government, industry, and academia (Transportation Research Board, 1975b). In 1977, a second conference in Boston addressed the need for a more detailed focus on the theme of planning and technology (Transportation Research Board, 1978). Several years later, in 1982, a third conference occurred in San Diego with the theme of planning, design, and implementation of LRT in existing urban environments (Transportation Research Board, 1982a). The fourth conference in Pittsburgh in 1985 focused on cost-effective approaches in the deployment of LRT systems that capitalized on the flexibility of this mode of transit (Transportation Research Board, 1985a).

By the 1990s, LRT had achieved a substantial resurgence in the USA. Boston, Cleveland, Newark, New Orleans, Philadelphia, Pittsburgh, and San Francisco had renovated existing lines or replaced their existing vehicle fleets or both (Table 8.4).

Table 8.4 US light rail systems

Metropolitan area	Year built	Year modernized	Directional route (miles)
Baltimore, MD	1992		57.6
Boston, MA	1897	1975–1989	51.0
Buffalo, NY	1985		12.4
Cleveland, PH	1913	1980s	30.4
Dallas, TX	1996		87.7
Denver, CO	1994		31.6
Houston, TX	2004		14.8
Los Angeles, CA	1990		109.7
Memphis, TN	1993		10.0
Minneapolis, MN	2004		24.4
New Jersey Transit, NJ	1935	1980s	99.9
New Orleans, LA	1835	1980s	25.3
Philadelphia, PA	1892	1981	66.3
Pittsburgh, PA	1891	1987	45.3
Portland, OR	1986		97.7
Sacramento, CA	1987		58.4
St. Louis, MO	1993		75.8
Salt Lake City, UT	1999		37.3
San Diego, CA	1981		96.6
San Francisco, CA	1912	1981	72.9
San Jose, CA	1988		58.4
Seattle, WA	2003		3.6
Tampa, FL	2002		4.8

Source: US Dept of Transportation, Federal Transit Administration, National Transit Database

Baltimore, Buffalo, Dallas, Los Angeles, Portland, Sacramento, St. Louis, San Diego, and San Jose, had opened new LRT lines, and new LRT lines were under construction in Bayonne, Northern New Jersey, and Salt Lake City.

Federal-Aid Highway Act of 1976

The Federal-Aid Highway Act of 1976 broadened the use of funds from trade-ins of nonessential Interstate routes. The process of increasing flexibility in the use of interstate funds began with the Section 103(e)(2), referred to as the Howard-Cramer Amendment, of the Federal-Aid Highway Act of 1968. It allowed withdrawal of a nonessential Interstate route and the use of the funds on another interstate route in the state.

In the Federal-Aid Highway Act of 1973, Section 103(e)(4) allowed urbanized areas to withdraw a nonessential interstate segment within an area upon joint request of local elected officials and the governor. An equivalent amount of funds could be spent then from general revenues for mass transportation capital projects at an 80% federal matching share. The 1976 act allowed the funds from the interstate substitution to be used also for other highways and busways serving those urbanized areas (Bloch et al., 1982).

The 1976 act also changed the definition of construction to allow federal funds to be expended on resurfacing, restoration, and rehabilitation (3R) of highways. This was done in recognition of the growing problem of highway deterioration. The completion date for the Interstate system was extended to 30 September 1990. Finally, the act expanded the transferability of federal funds among different federal aid systems, thereby increasing flexibility in the use of these funds.

ITE Trip Generation Report

In 1972, the Technical Council of the Institute of Transportation Engineers (ITE) formed the Trip Generation Committee to develop a report on trip generation rates. The purpose of the Committee was to collect trip generation rate data already measured by others and to compile these data into one common source. The first edition of Trip Generation, An Informational Report, was published in 1976 and contained data collected between 1965 and 1973 from nearly 80 different sources (Institute of Transportation Engineers, 1976). Revised and updated editions were published in 1979, 1982, 1987, and 2003). (Institute of Transportation Engineers, 1979, 1982, 1987, 1991, 1996).

The seventh edition of Trip Generation represented the most comprehensive database then available on trip generation rates (Institute of Transportation Engineers, 2003). These data were collected through volunteer efforts and did not represent ITE's recommendations on individual rates or preferred application of the data. The seventh edition of Trip Generation included numerous updates to the statistics and plots published in the sixth edition. A significant amount of new data were collected and several new land uses were added. Data from more than 500 new studies were added to the database for a combined total of more than 4,250 individual trip generation studies. New land uses included assisted living, continuing care retirement community, batting cages, adult cabaret, multiplex movie theater, soccer fields, athletic club, private school (kindergarten to grade 8), baby superstore, pet supply superstore, office supply superstore, book superstore, discount home furnishing superstore, arts and craft store, automobile parts and service center, and automated car wash. Many categories, however, contained a limited number of studies. Rates were given for several different variables of a project including floor area, employment, and acreage, as well as for several time periods. In earlier editions of the report, trip rates were given in the form of cells of a series of matrices. Starting with the fourth edition, rates were calculated using regression equations.

The ITE Trip Generation reports became the most widely used reference for trip generation data by traffic engineers and transportation planners for site level planning and analysis. At times, the Trip Generation report was used as an expedient when a site-specific analysis would be more appropriate.

Urban System Study

The joint highway/transit planning regulations were controversial during their preparation and after their issuance. The states contended that the federal requirement to create metropolitan planning organizations (MPOs) with the responsibility to program funds preempted the states' right of self-determination. In essence, they argued that MPOs were another level of government. Those at the local level of government were more supportive of the regulations, especially the greater authority to select projects and program funds. But, there was widespread concern that the planning and programming process had become too inflexible and cumbersome (US Dept. of Transportation, 1976a).

Consequently, the Federal-Aid Highway Act of 1976 required a study of the various factors involved in the planning, programming, and implementation of routes on the urban system. The study was conducted jointly by the FHWA and UMTA and submitted to Congress in January 1977 (US Dept. of Transportation, 1976a). It was a major undertaking involving a liaison group of 12 organizations representing state and local interests, site visits to 30 urbanized area, and field data on the remaining areas.

The study concluded that the planning requirements were being carried out responsibly by all participants. This was true in spite of the controversy over the responsibilities of the MPO. They also found that the flexibility in the use of urban system funds for transit was not widely used. Only 6.4% of the funds were being used for transit projects. It was concluded that overall the complexity of federal requirements deterred many local governments from using their federal urban system funds (Heanue, 1977). The study recommended that no changes should be made at that time, the process was new and participants had not had sufficient time to adjust, and that even though there was some confusion and controversy, the process was working properly (US Dept. of Transportation, 1976a).

Road Pricing Demonstration Program

Road pricing had long been discussed as a means to manage traffic demand as was used in many other industries to manage demand for services. The basic approach was to increase prices for the use of facilities and service when demand was highest so that those users would either pay the higher cost to be served during the peak or divert to lower demand periods or alternative modes (Vickrey, 1959). An extensive research program on the feasibility of road pricing was conducted by the Urban Institute (Kulash, 1974).

In an attempt to stimulate the use of road pricing, the US Department of Transportation began a demonstration program in 1976. Secretary of Transportation, William T. Coleman, wrote to the mayors of 11 cities about the availability of a road pricing demonstration and offering Federal funding for administration enforcement and evaluation of a vehicle licensing scheme inviting their participation (Arrillaga, 1978). This approach to road pricing was based on the successful application in the city state of Singapore (Watson and Holland, 1978).

Of the cities that responded, three were most promising: Madison, Wisconsin, Berkeley, California, and Honolulu, Hawaii. These cities seemed most committed to reducing automobile use and to using the resulting revenue to finance transit expansion (Higgins, 1986). Preliminary studies were conducted for each of the cities. Based on these preliminary analyses, all three cities declined to pursue the demonstrations any further. A number of reasons were cited in opposition to the schemes including harm to business, coercive interference with travel rights, regressive impacts on the poor, and inadequate information dissemination and promotion.

More than a decade would pass before there was renewed interest in trying road pricing schemes. This would come under the stimulus of the Clean Air Act and the difficulty some urbanized areas had in meeting national ambient air quality standards.

National Transportation Trends and Choices

Ten years after it was established, the US Department of Transportation, under Secretary William T. Coleman, completed its first multimodal national transportation planning study. The report, National Transportation Trends and Choices – To The Year 2000, described DOT's views regarding the future evolution of transportation, set forth the decisions that needed to be made, and described the changes that would best serve national objectives (US Dept. of Transportation, 1977c).

National Transportation Trends and Choices elaborated upon a key policy theme of Secretary Coleman's statement of national transportation policy:

> Underlying comprehensive transportation policy is the recognition that diversity and inter-modal competition are essential to an effective transportation system. Government policy must move in the direction of increasing equal competitive opportunity among the transportation modes, minimizing the inequitable distortions of government intervention and enabling each mode to realize its inherent advantages. (US Dept. of Transportation, 1977c)

National Transportation Trends and Choices was designed to show the Congress and the public that the DOT was making both substantive and resource allocation decisions effectively and coherently in light of long-range consequences, intermodal trade-offs, and broader national goals and objectives. In addition, the planning effort was designed to facilitate decision-making within the federal government and to encourage consistency by state and local agencies and the private sector. This study was intended to initiate a continuing national planning process based on common time horizons and planning assumptions.

The needs estimates in National Transportation Trends and Choices were developed for the 15-year period 1976–1990. For highways and public transportation, the estimates were based on updates of the data from the 1974 National Transportation Report (US Dept. of Transportation, 1975d), which were submitted by only 15 states. The aviation needs estimate were developed by updating the 1976 National Airport System Plan plus additional analyses. Railroad and pipeline needs were estimated based on assumptions developed by the study staff.

National Transportation Trends and Choices was received by the Congress with little fanfare. However, the thrust of the report toward greater competition and reduced federal regulation was reflected in actions taken in later years. The study did not become the beginning of a longer-term national planning effort.

Transit Uniform System of Accounts and Records

Transit operating and financial data had been collected by the American Public Transit Association (APTA) and its predecessor, the American Transit Association, since 1942 (American Public Transit Association, 1989). This data had been the primary source of comparative transit information for operators, researchers, and governmental agencies. It had been recognized for some time, however, that this data had limitations in terms of uniformity of data definitions, consistency of reporting, and accuracy. As the involvement of federal, state, and local governments increased in funding urban public transportation, particularly operating assistance, the need for a uniform system of accounts and records was recognized (US Dept. of Transportation, 1977d).

In 1972, the American Transit Association (ATA) and Institute for Rapid Transit (IRT), predecessors of APTA, began Project FARE, Uniform Financial Accounting and Reporting Elements, to develop a uniform industry data reporting system. Project FARE developed and pilot tested a new system of accounts and records to meet the needs of the industry and government agencies to monitor operating performance (Arthur Andersen & Co., 1973).

Shortly thereafter, the Urban Mass Transportation Act of 1974 created a new Section 15 that required the Department of Transportation to establish a data reporting system for financial and operating information and a uniform system of accounts and records. UMTA continued to work with an Industry Control Board to modify and adapt the FARE system to accommodate the requirements of Section 15. The resulting system was required to be instituted by all recipients of UMTA Section 5 Formula Grant funds (US Dept. of Transportation, 1977e).

The Section 15 Transit Data Reporting System was first applied for the fiscal year 1979 (US Dept. of Transportation, 1981d). Over 400 transit systems reported under the system. Data items included those covering revenues, government subsidies, capital and operating costs, organizational structure, vehicles, employees, service provided, ridership, safety, energy consumption, and operating performance. Over the period of years, the system underwent a number of modifications to its content, structure, and procedures to adjust to changing data requirements. This included broadening the data base to include commuter rail, vanpools, and purchased (contracted) services.

Starting with fiscal year 1999, the transit data were incorporated into the National Transit Database (NTDB). This searchable computer database provided access to transit operating and financial data by federal, state, and local officials, and the private sector.

Clean Air Act Amendments of 1977

The Clean Air Act Amendments of 1977 increased the flexibility and local responsibility in the administration of the Clean Air Act. The amendments required state and local governments to develop revisions to state implementation plans (SIPs) for all areas where the national ambient air quality standards had not been attained. The revised SIPs were to be submitted to the EPA by 1 January 1979, and approved by 1 May 1979.

The revised plans had to provide for attainment of national ambient air quality standards by 1982, or in the case of areas with severe photochemical oxidant or carbon monoxide problems, no later than 1987. In the latter case, a state must demonstrate that the standards cannot be met with all reasonable stationary and transportation control measures. The plans also had to provide for incremental reductions in emissions (reasonable further progress) between the time the plans were submitted and the attainment deadline. If a state failed to submit a SIP or if EPA disapproved the SIP and the state failed to revise it in a satisfactory manner, EPA was required to promulgate regulations establishing a SIP by 1 July 1979. If, after 1 July 1979, EPA determined that a state was not fulfilling the requirements under the act, it was to impose sanctions. This would include stopping federal aid for highways (Cooper and Hidinger, 1980).

In many major urbanized areas the revised SIPs required the development of transportation control plans (TCPs) that included strategies to reduce emissions from transportation-related sources by means of structural or operational changes in the transportation system. Since state and local governments implement changes in the transportation system, the act strongly encouraged the preparation of transportation elements of the SIP by metropolitan planning organizations. These local planning organizations were responsible for developing the transportation control measure element of the SIP (Cooper and Hidinger, 1980).

From 1978 to 1980, the DOT and EPA, after long negotiations, jointly issued several policy documents to implement the Clean Air Act's transportation requirements. One of these, signed in June 1978, was a "Memorandum of Understanding" that established the means by which the DOT and the EPA would assure the integration of transportation and air quality planning. A second one, issued also in June 1978, "Transportation Air Quality Planning Guidelines" described the acceptable planning process to satisfy the requirements. Another, in March 1980, was a notice containing guidelines for receiving air quality planning grants under Section 175 of the act (Cooper and Hidinger, 1980).

In January 1981 DOT issued regulations on air quality conformance and priority procedures for use in federal highway and transit programs. The regulations required that transportation plans, programs, and projects conform with the approved SIPs in areas that had not met ambient air quality standards, termed "nonattainment areas." In those areas, priority for transportation funds was to be given to "transportation control measures" (TCMs) that contributed to reducing air pollution emissions from transportation sources. Where an area's transportation plan or program was not in conformance with the SIP, "sanctions" were to be applied that prohibited the use of federal funds on major transportation projects (US Dept. of Transportation, 1981b).

The 1977 Clean Air Act Amendments certainly gave impetus to short-range planning and transportation system management strategies. They also added a new dimension to the institutional and analytical complexity of the planning process.

Chapter 9
Emphasizing Urban Economic Revitalization

In the mid-1970s, the country was feeling the effects of structural changes in the economy, high unemployment, inflation, and rising energy prices. Many of the problems had been developing for a number of years. The economy was in a transition from a predominantly manufacturing base to one that had a larger share concentrated in service, communication, and high technology industries. Jobs in the manufacturing sector were declining and new jobs were growing in the new sectors of the economy. People were moving to those areas of the country where new jobs were being created, especially the south and the west. The older urban areas in the northeast and Mid-west were being affected most severely by these changes. But older central cities in all sections of the country were in decline as jobs and people migrated first to the suburbs and then to the newer urban areas where the economies were growing.

These older communities and central cities were severely distressed economically and limited in their ability to address these problems themselves. It was recognized that the federal government had contributed to these problems with programs that had unintended consequences. However, many of the decisions that affected changes in urban areas were outside the control of even the federal government and often any level of government. The federal, state, and local levels of government would, therefore, have to cooperate among themselves and with the private sector in order to alleviate these problems.

1978 National Urban Policy Report

In Title VII of the Housing and Urban Development Act of 1970, the Congress required preparation of biennial reports on national growth and development. Congress recognized the need to analyze the many aspects of the nation's growth in a systematic manner with the objective of formulating a national urban growth policy. The first report, transmitted to Congress in 1972, discussed the broad subject of national growth, including both rural and urban areas (Domestic Council, 1972). The 1974 report focused on the dominant role of the private sector in determining growth and the ways in which the public

E. Weiner, *Urban Transportation Planning in the United States, Third Edition*,
doi:10.1007/978-0-387-77152-6, © Springer Science+Business Media, LLC 2008

and private sectors could influence development patterns. The 1976 report discussed the decline of older northeastern cities, the constraints of energy, environmental resources, and the need to conserve and rehabilitate existing housing and public facilities (Domestic Council, 1976).

The National Urban Policy and New Community Development Act of 1977 amended the 1970 Act to designate the report the "National Urban Policy Report" rather than the more general "Report on Urban Growth" (Domestic Council, 1976). Less than a year later, on 27 March 1978, President Carter presented his Message to Congress on National Urban Policy. The policy was designed to build a new Partnership to Conserve America's Communities involving all levels of government, the private sector, and neighborhood and voluntary organizations. It contained a number of proposals to improve existing programs and for new initiatives with the purpose of revitalizing distressed central cities and older suburbs (US Dept. of Housing and Urban Development, 1978b).

The President's Message was followed in August by the President's 1978 National Urban Policy Report (US Dept. of Housing and Urban Development, 1978b). Like its predecessors, the report discussed the demographic, social, and economic trends in the nation's urban areas. But, it was the first report to recommend a national urban policy. The recommendations in the Report and the President's Message were developed by an inter-departmental committee called the Urban and Regional Policy Group. The group worked for a year with extensive public involvement to formulate its analysis of the problems and recommendations (US Department of Housing and Urban Development, 1978a).

The urban policy consisted of nine objectives. The first urban policy objective was to, "encourage and support efforts to improve local planning and management capacity and the effectiveness of existing federal programs by coordinating these programs, simplifying planning requirements, reorienting resources, and reducing paperwork." Other objectives called for greater state, private sector, and voluntary involvement to assist urban areas. Several objectives were for fiscal relief for distressed communities and assistance to disadvantaged persons. The last objective was for an improved physical environment and reduced urban sprawl (US Dept. of Housing and Urban Development, 1978b).

A wide range of legislative and administrative actions were taken to implement the national urban policy (US Dept. of Housing and Urban Development, 1980). The Department of Transportation, FHWA, and UMTA issued guidance for evaluating the impact on urban centers of major transportation projects and investments. The guidance required an analysis of the impacts of improvements in highways and transit on central cities' development, tax base, employment, accessibility, and environment. In addition, impacts on energy conservation, and on minorities and neighborhoods were to be analyzed. Furthermore, the guidance required that improvements to existing facilities be considered first, including the repair and rehabilitation of transportation facilities and TSM measures to increase the effectiveness of those facilities. In this manner, the guidance sought to assure that the new investments in transportation facilities would be cost effective (US Dept. of Transportation, 1979e).

The new national urban policy gave added impetus to the shift from constructing new facilities to managing, maintaining, and replacing existing facilities. It was rooted in the belief that mobility could be assured despite energy, environmental, and financial constraints. The key was to manage the use of the automobile in the city better. The challenge was for the urban transportation planning process to maintain and enhance mobility while meeting these other objectives (Heanue, 1980).

Surface Transportation Assistance Act of 1978

The Surface Transportation Assistance Act of 1978 was the first act that combined highway, public transportation, and highway safety authorizations in one piece of legislation. It provided $51.4 billion for the fiscal years 1979 through 1982, with $30.6 billion for highways, $13.6 billion for public transportation, and $7.2 billion for highway safety. It was the first time that authorizations for the highway program were made for a 4-year period. Highway Trust Fund user charges were extended 5 years to 1984 and the fund itself to 1985 (U.S. Dept. of Transportation, 1979d).

Title I, the Federal-Aid Highway Act of 1978, accelerated completion of the National System of Interstate and Defense Highways. It concentrated funds on projects that were ready to be constructed by changing the availability of a state's apportionment from 4 to 2 years. If the funds were not used, they could be reallocated to states with projects ready to go. The act withdrew authority to replace one interstate route with another. It placed a deadline of 30 September 1983, on substituting public transportation or other highway projects for withdrawn Interstate routes. The federal share for both highway and transit substitute projects was increased to 85%. The act required that environmental impact statements for Interstate projects be submitted by 30 September 1983, and that they be under contract or construction by 30 September 1986, if sufficient federal funds were available. If the deadlines were not met, the interstate route or substitute project was to be eliminated.

The act also raised the federal share for noninterstate highways from 70 to 75%. It further increased the allowable amount of funds that could be transferred among federal aid systems to 50%. The eligibility of federal funds for carpools and vanpools was made permanent. The amount of $20 million annually for fiscal years 1979 through 1982 was authorized for bicycle projects. The act substantially increased the funding for bridge replacement and rehabilitation to $1 billion annually.

Title III, the Federal Public Transportation Act of 1978, expanded the Section 5 Formula Grant program. The basic program of operating and capital assistance was retained with the same population and population density formula at higher authorization levels. The "second tier" program was authorized with the same project eligibility and apportionment formula. However, the funds were to be initially split so that 85% went to urbanized areas over 750,000 in population and the remaining 15% to smaller areas. The third tier was established for routine purchases of buses and related facilities and equipment. A new fourth tier replaced the Sections 17 and 18 commuter rail programs. The funds could be used for commuter rail or rail transit capital or operating expenses. The funds were apportioned two-thirds based on commuter rail vehicle miles and route miles and one-third on rail transit route miles.

The act changed the availability of funds for transit from 2 to 4 years. It formalized the "letter of intent" process whereby the federal government committed funds for a transit project in the Section 3 Discretionary Grant program. Public hearings were required for all general increases in fares or substantial changes in service. A small formula grant program for nonurbanized areas (Section 18) was established for capital and operating assistance. Apportioned on nonurbanized area population, it authorized an 80% federal share for capital projects and 50% for operating assistance. The act also established an intercity bus terminal development program, intercity bus service operating subsidy program, and human resources program for urban transit systems.

The urban transportation planning requirement was changed in an identical fashion in the highway and transit titles. Energy conservation was included as a new goal in the planning process and alternative transportation system management strategies to make more efficient use of existing facilities that were required to be evaluated. The designation of metropolitan planning organizations was to be by agreement among general purpose units of local government and in cooperation with the governors. Within 1 year after enactment, local government representing at least 75% of all local governmental units and at least 90% of the population in the area may redesignate the MPO in cooperation with the governor. For the transit program, it was further required that plans and programs encourage to the maximum extent feasible the participation of private enterprise. Funding for transit planning grants was set at 5.5% of Section 3 appropriations.

A "Buy America" provision was included to apply to all contracts over $500,000. The provision could be waived if its application was inconsistent with the public interest, domestic supplies were not available or of unsatisfactory quality, or if the use of domestic products would increase the cost by over 10%.

Quick Response Urban Travel Forecasting Techniques

Most urban travel forecasting techniques were developed to evaluate regional transportation systems and to produce traffic volumes for the design of facilities. These procedures were geared to long-range planning studies that often took several years to carry out and had extensive data requirements. Urban transportation planning, however, was transitioning to a shorter-term time horizon and issues were refocusing on low-capital improvements and environmental impacts. In light of these trends, there was a need for simplified analytical procedures that were easy to understand, relatively inexpensive and less time consuming to apply, and responsive to the policy issues of the day (Sousslau et al., 1978a).

To address this issue, the National Cooperative Highway Research Program (NCHRP) launched a research project on quick response urban travel forecasting techniques (Sousslau et al., 1978b). The study found that no existing travel estimation technique was adequate to respond to the many new policy issues being faced by decision-makers.

To fill the gap, the project developed a set of manual urban travel estimation techniques based upon the four-step conventional urban travel forecasting process. The techniques covered trip generation, trip distribution, mode choice, auto occupancy, time-of-day distribution, traffic assignment, capacity analysis, and development density/highway spacing relationships. The approach minimized the need for data by supplying tables and graphs that could use "default" values to substitute for local information. A User's Guide was produced as part of the project that allowed the estimation of travel demand using charts, tables, and nomographs (Sousslau et al., 1978c).

The original Quick Response System (QRS) was principally used for planning problems that were too small to warrant use of the full regional scale urban travel forecasting procedures. To increase the usefulness and applicability of QRS, a microcomputer version was developed (COMSIS Corp., 1984). The microcomputer programs contained all of the functions originally developed in manual form and an additional mode choice estimation technique.

The microcomputer version of QRS increased the size of the transportation planning that could be analyzed. But, the analysis became disproportionately more difficult to handle as the size of the analysis area increased. A more sophisticated version of QRS was developed to expand its utility. The new QRS II departed from QRS by requiring that transportation networks be drawn and analyzed as part of the analytical process. Consequently, QRS II could be used for routine calculations of the manual techniques as QRS allowed, as well as perform detailed analyses comparable to those that could be performed with conventional urban travel forecasting procedures (Horowitz, 1989).

QRS II became widely used for sketch planning, small area analysis, and in a number of instances was used as replacement for the conventional urban travel forecasting process using UTPS.

National Energy Act of 1978

In 1979, Iran cut off crude oil shipments to Western nations, resulting in shortage of oil products, especially gasoline, and price increases. Most of the regulations implemented in 1973 and 1974 were still in effect and basically unchanged (diesel fuel prices had been deregulated in 1976). During the intervening years, other legislation had been passed to stimulate oil production and foster conservation (Schueftan and Ellis, 1981). The Department of Energy Organization Act of 1977 brought together most federal energy functions under a single cabinet level department.

In October 1978, the Congress passed the National Energy Act that was composed of five bills. The National Energy Conservation Policy Act of 1978 extended two state energy conservation programs that required states to undertake specific conservation actions including the promotion of carpools and vanpools. The Powerplant and Industrial Fuel Use Act of 1978 required Federal agencies to conserve natural gas and petroleum in the programs that they administered (US Dept. of Energy, 1978). To implement Section 403(b) of the act, President Carter signed Executive Order 12185 in December 1979 extending existing efforts to promote energy conservation through federal aid programs.

The DOT issued final regulations in August 1980 in compliance with the Executive Order. These regulations required that all phases of transportation projects from planning to construction and operations be conducted in a manner that conserves fuel. It incorporated energy conservation as a goal into the urban transportation planning process and required an analysis of alternative TSM improvements to reduce energy consumption (US Dept. of Transportation, 1980c).

Other actions affected urban transportation and planning. President Carter signed an Executive Order in April 1979 that began the phased decontrol of petroleum prices. By 30 September 1981, petroleum prices were to be determined by the free market. This process was accelerated by President Reagan through an Executive Order in January 1981, which immediately terminated all price and allocation controls (Cabot Consulting Group, 1982).

The Emergency Energy Conservation Act of 1979, which was signed in November 1979, required the president to establish national and state conservation targets. States were to submit state emergency conservation plans that would meet the targets. The act expired in July 1983 with neither targets being set nor plans being prepared. However, many states became active in contingency planning for a potential future energy emergency (Cabot Consulting Group, 1982).

Energy conservation had become integrated into the urban transportation planning process as a result of federal and state legislation and regulation. It gave further impetus to reducing the use of automobiles and for emphasis on transportation system management. Energy contingency planning became more widespread by planning organizations, transit authorities, and highway departments.

Council on Environmental Quality's Regulations

The Council on Environmental Quality (CEQ) issued final regulations on 29 November 1978, establishing uniform procedures for implementing the procedural provisions of the National Environmental Policy Act of 1969. They applied to all federal agencies and took effect on 30 July 1979. They were issued because the 1973 CEQ Guidelines for preparing environmental impact statements (EISs) were not viewed consistently by all agencies leading to differences in interpretations (Council on Environmental Quality, 1978).

The regulations embodied several new concepts designed to make the EIS more useful to decision-makers and the public, and to reduce paperwork and delays. First, the regulations created a "scoping" process to provide for the early identification of significant impacts and issues. It also provided for allocating responsibility for the EIS among the lead agency and cooperating agencies. The scoping process was to be integrated with other planning activities (Council on Environmental Quality, 1978).

Second, the regulations permitted "tiering" of the EIS process. This provided that environmental analyses completed at a broad scale (e.g., region) need not be duplicated for site-specific projects; the broader analyses could be summarized and incorporated by reference. The purpose of "tiering" was to eliminate repetition and allow discussion of issues at the appropriate level of detail (Council on Environmental Quality, 1978).

Third, in addition to the previously required EIS, which discussed the alternatives being considered, a "record of decision" document was required. It had to identify the "environmentally preferable" alternative, the other alternatives considered, and the factors used in reaching the decision. Until this document was issued, no action could be taken on an alternative that would adversely affect the environment or limit the choice of alternatives (Council on Environmental Quality, 1978).

The regulations generally sought to reduce the paperwork in the EIS process by such techniques as limiting the length of the document to 150 pages (300 in complex situations), specifying a standard format, emphasizing that the process focus on real alternatives, allowing incorporation of material by reference, and using summaries for circulation instead of the entire EIS. Agencies were encouraged to set time limits on the process and to integrate other statutory and analysis requirements into a single process.

In October 1980, the FHWA and UMTA published supplemental implementing procedures. They established a single set of environmental procedures for highway and urban transit projects. They also integrated the UMTA's procedures for alternatives analysis under its major investment policy with the new EIS procedures. This permitted the preparation of a single draft EIS/alternatives analysis document. These regulations were an important step toward integrating highway and transit planning and reducing duplicative documentation (US Dept. of Transportation, 1980b).

BART Impact Program

The San Francisco Bay Area Rapid Transit (BART) system was the first regional rail transit system to be built in the USA since World War II. It provided a unique opportunity for studying the impacts of such a system on the urban environment. The BART Impact Program was organized to evaluate the effects of BART on the economy, environment, and people of the Bay Area. It began in 1972 with the start of BART system operation and lasted for 6 years.

The study addressed a broad range of potential rail transit impacts, including impacts on the transportation system and travel behavior, land use and urban development, the environment, public policy, the regional economy, and social institutions and lifestyles. The incidence of these impacts on population groups, local areas, and economic sectors was also measured and analyzed (Metropolitan Transportation Commission, 1979a,b).

The BART system included 71 miles of track with 34 stations of which 23 had parking lots (Fig. 9.1). The four lines had stations spaced one-third to one-half mile apart in the cities of San Francisco and Oakland, and 2–4 miles apart in the suburbs. In 1975 BART served a population of about 1 million residing in three counties. Fares ranged from $0.25 to $1.45, with discounts for the elderly, handicapped, and children. BART cost $1.6 billion to build of which 80% was locally funded (Metropolitan Transportation Commission, 1979a,b).

The program produced a considerable amount of information on the impacts of BART and by implication the impacts of rail systems on urban areas. Its major findings included

- BART provided a significant increase in the capacities of the major regional travel corridors, particularly approaching the cities of San Francisco and Oakland. However, it had not provided a long-term solution for traffic congestion because the additional capacity had been filled by new trips that had previously been deterred by traffic congestion. It most effectively served suburbanites commuting to work in San Francisco.
- BART had been integrated into the Bay Area with a minimum of environmental and social disruption because of its careful planning and design.
- To date, BART had not had a major impact on Bay Area land use. Some land use changes were evident where BART provides travel time advantages, where communities had acted to support and enhance the system's impacts through zoning and development plans, and where market demand for new development was strong, as in downtown San Francisco. It was likely that many potential impacts had not yet had time to develop.
- The $1.2 billion expended in the Bay Area for BART construction generated local expenditures totaling $3.1 billion during a 12-year period. However, over the long term, BART had not induced economic growth in the Bay Area; that is, the system had not measurably enhanced the competitive advantage of the region in relation to other metropolitan areas in the country (Metropolitan Transportation Commission, 1979a,b).

An important implication of the BART Impact Program's findings was that by itself rail transit could be expected to have only a limited impact on the various aspects of the urban environment. Existing local conditions and the enactment of supportive policies were more important in determining the influence of a rail system on an urban area. For example, neither BART nor any other similar rail system was likely to cause high-density residential development nor discourage urban sprawl in

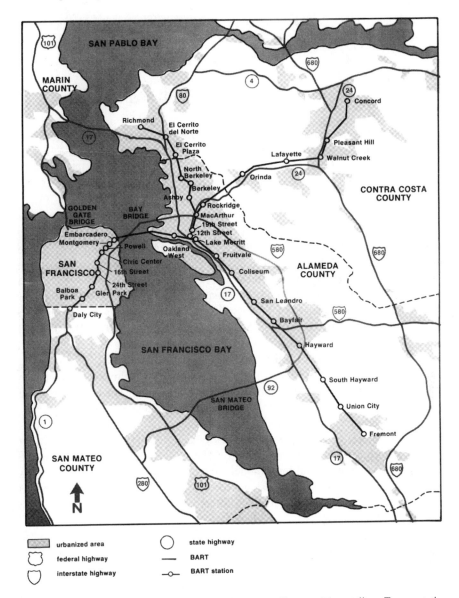

Fig. 9.1 San Francisco bay area rapid transit system (Source: Metropolitan Transportation Commission, 1979b)

an established urban area unless strong regionally coordinated land use controls were implemented.

Partly as a result of the BART experience, the Urban Mass Transportation Administration began to require localities building or planning to build new rail lines with federal assistance to commit themselves to a program of local supportive actions to enhance the project's cost effectiveness and patronage.

International Conferences on Behavioral Travel Demand

The Williamsburg Urban Travel Forecasting Conference gave widespread recognition to disaggregate behavioral demand models. The momentum created by this conference caused an upsurge in research in behavioral travel demand. The research was so extensive and widespread that the need arose for better interchange of ideas and developments.

To fill this void, the Transportation Research Board Committee on Traveler Behavior and Values began organizing a series of International Conferences on Behavioral Travel Demand. Later, the organizing role was performed by the International Association for Travel Behavior, which was established in April 1985. The conferences brought together those involved in travel demand research from many countries. The first one occurred in South Berwick, Maine, in 1973 (Stopher and Meyburg, 1974). Later conferences were held in Asheville, North Carolina, in 1975 (Stopher and Meyburg, 1976); Melbourne, Australia, in 1977 (Hensher and Stopher, 1979); Grainau, Germany, in 1979 (Stopher, Meyburg and Brog, 1981); Easton, Maryland, in 1982 (Transportation Research Board, 1984b); Noordwijk, The Netherlands, in 1985 (Dutch Ministry, 1986); Aix-En-Provence, France, in 1987 (International Association for Travel Behavior, 1989); Quebec, Canada, in 1991 (Stopher and Lee-Gosselin, 1996); and Santiago, Chile, in 1994.

The proceedings of these conferences provide a comprehensive documentation of the progress in behavioral travel demand research and the important issues concerning the research community. The subject areas expanded from the development of multinomial logit models and attitudinal methods to encompass noncompensatory models, trip chaining, life cycle and adaptation, activity-based analysis, and new approaches to data collection for travel behavior research (Kitamura, 1987).

Table 9.1 shows the workshop themes for the first six conferences. Disaggregate choice analyses and attitudinal methods were recurring themes at all of the conferences and were the main threads connecting the conferences. Their subthemes were also selected as workshop topics including aggregation issues, noncompensatory models, market segmentation, disaggregate trip distribution models, errors and uncertainty, and transferability. Various planning applications were addressed at the 1982 Easton conference. The themes of longitudinal analysis and stated preference methods were introduced at the 1985 Noordwijk conference (Kitamura, 1987).

Research recommendations from the conferences often served as the agenda for further work in the following years. The focus of these discussions was to gain a better understanding of travel behavior and to develop travel demand models with stronger theoretical bases. Using this approach, travel forecasting would become

Table 9.1 International conferences on behavioral travel demand

Workshop Theme	1973	1975	1977	1979	1982	1985
Mathematics of disaggregate models	X	X	X	X	X	X
Attitudinal measurements and models	X	X	X	X		X
Policy issues, policy relevance	X		X	X		
Travel time values	X	X	X			
Extension of present methodology	X					
Aggregation problems	X					
Implementing disaggregate models		X		X		
Application of behavioral models		X		X		
Disaggregate trip distribution models		X				
Household structure and adaptation		X		X		X
Supply-demand equilibrium		X	X			
Market segmentation		X	X			
Activity analysis and trip chaining			X	X		X
Accessibility and mobility			X	X		
Freight transportation			X			
Impact assessment			X			
Transferability				X		X
Survey methods, data needs				X	X	
Errors and uncertainty				X		
Noncompensatory and discontinuous models				X		
New transportation technology				X		
Strategic planning					X	
Long-range urban systems planning					X	
Project planning					X	
Micro-scale planning					X	
Systems operations					X	
Travel behavior characteristics and synthesis					X	
Quick-response and sketch-planning techniques					X	
Investment and financial analysis					X	
Longitudinal analysis						X
Stated preference methods						X

Source: Kitamura, 1987

more sensitive to relevant policy issues, require less data to estimate, and be less costly and time consuming to use.

Great strides were made in achieving these ends. But in doing so, a class of models was produced that was substantially different from conventional forecasting techniques. As a result, progress in diffusing these techniques into practice was slow. This gap in progress between application and research then became the major issue of concern in the field of travel forecasting. This issue was the focus of the 1982 conference in Easton (Transportation Research Board, 1984b).

National Ridesharing Demonstration Program

The oil embargo of 1973–1974 spurred government efforts to encourage commuter ridesharing. Ridesharing was considered to be a highly desirable approach to reducing drive-alone commuting, and thereby reducing congestion, air pollution, and energy consumption. Moreover, ridesharing could be expanded at little or no cost in comparison to constructing or expanding highway facilities.

With the passage of the Emergency Highway Conservation Act of 1974, which authorized the use of federal aid highway funds for carpool demonstrations, the federal government actively promoted and supported the development of ridesharing (US Dept. of Transportation, 1980d). From 1974 and 1977, FHWA funded 106 carpool demonstration projects in 34 states and 96 urbanizes areas at a total cost of $16.2 million with the vast majority having a Federal matching share of 90% (Wagner, 1978).

The Department of Energy Organization Act of 1977 transferred to DOT responsibilities for transportation energy conservation programs and ridesharing education. Partly, as a result of these new responsibilities, DOT set a goal to increase ridesharing by 5%. To accomplish this goal, DOT established the National Ridesharing Demonstration Program in March, 1979. The 2-year national program consisted of four major elements: a national competition to stimulate innovative and comprehensive approaches to ridesharing, an evaluation of those projects, technical assistance and training, and an expanded public information campaign (US Dept. of Transportation, 1980d).

The National Ridesharing Demonstration Program funded projects at 17 sites for $3.5 million. Demonstration elements included employer-based marketing, park-and-ride lots, vanpools, regional marketing, shuttle bus service, flextime, and legislative initiatives. An evaluation of these projects found the primary market for ridesharing to be multiworker households with one car living far from the work site. Between 2 and 5% of the carpoolers surveyed indicated that the program affected their decision to form or maintain a carpool. Most commuter carpools were found to consist of informal arrangements among household members or fellow workers. The proportion of employees ridesharing and the size of carpools were found to increase with firm size. Flextime arrangements did not seem to affect ridesharing (Booth and Waksman, 1985).

Ridesharing continued to be a major alternative to driving alone. Gradually, it became integrated with other measures into more comprehensive congestion relief programs.

Urban Initiatives Program

The National Mass Transportation Assistance Act of 1974 authorized the use of federal funds for joint development purposes through the Young Amendment. The Young Amendment allowed local agencies to use federal funds to improve those facilities within the zone affected by the construction and operation of mass transit improvements that were needed to be compatible with land use development. Assistance was available for establishing public or quasi-public corridor development corporations to accomplish this (Gortmaker, 1980).

The Urban Initiatives program, however, was not implemented until it was authorized in Section 3(a)(l)(D) of the Surface Transportation Assistance Act of 1978. This section of the act authorized federal grants for land acquisition and the provision of utilities on land that was physically or functionally related to transit facilities for the purpose of stimulating economic development.

The Urban Initiatives program was one element of the DOT effort to implement President Carter's Urban Policy. The guidelines for the program were issued in April 1979 (US Dept. of Transportation, 1979g). The program allowed expenditures for preconstruction activities (e.g., design and engineering studies, land acquisition and write-down, and real estate packaging) and items that connect transportation with land developments (e.g., pedestrian connections, parking, and street furniture). Preference was to be given to projects that demonstrated that they advanced Urban Policy objectives.

During the 3 years of the program, 47 projects were funded in 43 urban areas. They integrated transportation projects with economic development activities. Many of these projects were transit malls or intermodal terminals. The program extended the traditional funding beyond direct transit projects to the related development tied to transit service (Rice Center, 1981).

The practice of setting aside federal funds for Urban Initiatives' projects was discontinued in March 1981. However, these types of activities continued to be eligible for funding under the regular transit programs.

Section 504 Regulations on Accessibility for the Handicapped

Section 504 of the Rehabilitation Act of 1973 provided that no person who is otherwise qualified should be discriminated against due to handicap in any program or activity receiving federal financial assistance. In 1976, the UMTA issued regulations that required "special efforts" in planning public mass transportation facilities that can be utilized by elderly and handicapped persons. It also required that new transit vehicles and facilities be accessible to handicapped. Handicapped groups thought the regulations were too vague and difficult to enforce (US Dept. of Transportation, 1976c).

More stringent regulations were published in May 1979. They required all existing bus and rail systems to become fully accessible to handicapped persons within 3 years. This included 50% of the buses in fixed route service to be accessible to wheelchair users. For extraordinarily expensive facilities, the time limit could be extended to 10 years for bus facilities, to 30 years for rail facilities, and to 5 years for rail cars. Steady progress to achieve accessibility was required. New facilities and equipment were still required to be accessible to receive federal assistance (US Dept. of Transportation, 1979f).

Transit authorities complained that the requirements were far too costly and sued the DOT for exceeding its authority. The US Court of Appeals in a decision in 1981 said that the 1979 regulations went beyond the DOT's authority under Section 504. Following the decision, the DOT issued regulations on an interim basis and indicated that there would be new rulemaking leading to a final rule. The interim regulations required applicants to certify that "special efforts" were being made to provide transportation that was accessible to handicapped persons (US Dept. of Transportation, 1981a).

Section 317(c) of the Surface Transportation Assistance Act of 1982 required the DOT to publish a proposed rule that would include (1) minimum criteria for the provision of transportation services to handicapped and elderly individuals, (2) a public participation mechanism, and (3) procedures for the UMTA to monitor transit authorities' performance. A NPRM was issued in September 1983 (US Dept. of Transportation, 1983f), and final regulations in May 1986 (US Dept. of Transportation, 1986b).

The 1986 regulations established six service criteria that applied to urban mass transportation for persons with disabilities: (1) anyone who is physically unable to use the bus system for the general public must be treated as eligible for the service; (2) the service must operate during the same days and hours as the general service; (3) the service must operate in the same geographic area; (4) fares for trips on the two services must be comparable; (5) service must be provided within 24 h of a request; and (6) restrictions or priorities for service may not be imposed based on trip purpose. The regulations did not require existing, inaccessible rail systems to be made accessible.

The amount of money transit authorities were required to spend in the service was limited to 3% of their operating expenditures to avoid undue financial burden on them. Transit authorities were given 1 year to plan the services and up to 6 years to phase them in. The planning process was required to involve disabled and other interested persons.

DOT's Section 504 regulations had long been controversial. The DOT was faced with the difficult job of accommodating both the concerns of the handicapped community for adequate public transportation and the concerns of transit authorities and local governments for avoiding costly or rigid requirements. This rulemaking process was the most complex and protracted in urban transportation. It engendered a fierce debate between those who felt that handicapped persons should have the right to be mainstreamed into society, and those who believed that there were more cost-effective means of providing transportation for those persons using paratransit-type services.

National Transportation Policy Study Commission

The National Transportation Policy Study Commission was created by the Federal-Aid Highway Act of 1976 to study the transportation needs through the year 2000, and the resources, requirements, and policies to meet those needs. The Commission was composed of 19 members; 6 senators, 6 representatives, and 7 public members appointed by the president.

The commission and its technical staff completed more than 2 years of analysis, consultant studies and public hearings, and published its final reports, National Transportation Policies Through The Year 2000, and the Executive Summary in June of 1979 (National Transportation Policy Study Commission, 1979a,b).

The report concluded that the existing level of investment was insufficient to meet growing transportation needs, and that a capital investment of over $4 trillion was required for the 15-year period 1976–2000. It further concluded that government overregulation was inhibiting capital investment, and that the maze of federal agencies, congressional committees, and conflicting policies were driving up costs and retarding innovation.

The report contained over 80 specific recommendations, reflecting several themes:

1. National transportation policy should be uniform across modes.
2. Federal involvement should be substantially reduced (greater reliance on the private sector and state and local governments).
3. Federal actions should be subjected to economic analysis of benefits and costs.
4. The use of the transportation system to pursue nontransportation goals should be done in a cost-effective manner.
5. Transportation research and safety required federal involvement and financial assistance.
6. Users and those who benefit from federal actions should pay.

The National Transportation Policy Study Commission was unique because of the extent of Congressional involvement. Congress created the commission, staffed it, chaired it with its own members, and determined the policy conclusions (Allen-Schult and Hazard, 1982).

Interstate Substitutions

The urban routes of the interstate highway system were the most difficult and expensive to be built. The development of these urban interstate highway projects caused substantial controversy in a number of urban areas. Critics complained that the provision of 90% funding for Interstate highway projects distorted the planning process, putting transit and local highway projects at a disadvantage.

The Congress addressed these controversies by passing the so-called Howard-Cramer amendment (Section 103(e)(2)) to the Federal-Aid Highway Act of 1968 which allowed an interstate highway route to be traded in for another Interstate highway route so long as the initial route was not essential to a unified and connected Interstate and that a toll road world not be built in its place. During the 10-year existence of the Howard-Cramer amendment (which ended in November 1978) 9 states withdrew 16 separate sections (Polytechnic Institute of New York, 1982).

The Howard-Cramer provisions did not satisfy critics who wanted Interstate monies to be available for transit projects. The result was the Interstate Substitute program, which was established by the 1973 Federal-Aid Highway Act and amended by subsequent legislation. Section 103(e)(4) of the act permitted the governor and local elected officials jointly to withdraw planned interstate routes or segments that were within or which connect urbanized areas, and to use the equivalent funds for substitute mass transit or noninterstate highway projects. Withdrawal requests were reviewed and approved jointly by Federal Transit Administration and the Federal Highway Administration. Substitute projects were funded from general revenue not the Highway Trust Fund, at 80/20 Federal/local matching ratio, equivalent to the transit capital grant matching ratio (Polytechnic Institute of New York, 1982).

The Interstate substitution provisions were amended four times, generally expanding the eligibility of substitutable projects and the use of trade in funds. These amendments made more segment types eligible for trade-in, increased the value of withdrawn segments, expanded the use of traded in funds, increased the federal matching share to 85/15, and extended the date that substitutions could occur. Detailed regulations for this process were issued in October 1980 (US Dept. of Transportation, 1980e).

Over the life of the program, roughly 80% of the funds were used for transit projects and the remainder of various noninterstate highway projects. Substitute funds were used for a wide variety of highway and public mass transit projects. Interstate grants for transit projects financed the construction and improvements of transit facilities, the purchase of rolling stock, and other transportation equipment. As the interstate highway system itself drew to completion, substitute projects of either highway or transit nature were largely completed. Fiscal year 1995 was the last year in which interstate substitute funds were appropriated.

Aspen Conference on Future Urban Transportation

As the decade drew to a close, the assault on the automobile never seemed so widespread. Energy conservation and environmental protection were national priorities. Fiscal resources were constrained and cost effectiveness was the major criterion in urban transportation evaluations. Reversing central city decline was emerging as a key concern. And mobility for the transportation disadvantaged still required attention (Hassell, 1982). What was the future for urban personal mobility in the USA? Had the dominance of the automobile in the US economy and society peaked?

To address these issues, the Transportation Planning Division of the American Planning Association sponsored the Aspen Conference on Future Urban Transportation in June 1979. The conference was supported and attended by representatives of both the public and private sectors. The conferees could not reach a consensus on an image of the future but agreed on a range of factors that would be influential. Incremental planning was seen as the only feasible and desirable approach to the future (American Planning Association, 1979).

The conferees did conclude that there are "...no panaceas; no substantial increases in mobility due to new techniques...no quick or cheap energy solutions, and none without major environmental risks and costs...no promise of breakthrough in environmental technology...no major solutions through changes in living patterns or economic structure...no simple mechanism for restructuring urban form so as to reduce urban travel..." (American Planning Association, 1979). The conferees did make certain general recommendations for approaches to energy, mobility and accessibility, environmental, social, safety, and economic issues. They concluded that, at least for the rest of this century, the automobile would continue to be the principal and preferred mode of urban transportation for the majority of the American people. Public transportation would become increasingly important in supplying mobility. Both would require increased public investment from all levels of government (American Planning Association, 1979).

Land Use Impacts of Beltways

The new national urban policy focused on the preservation of existing urban centers and in particular central business districts (CBDs). The policy raised concern regarding the impacts of urban beltways on urban centers. The issue was whether beltways would undermine central city revitalization efforts and attempts to achieve compact, energy-efficient, and environmentally beneficial land use patterns.

Complete or partially complete beltways existed in 35–40 urban areas. They were mostly planned during the 1940s and 1950s as part of the development of the interstate highway system. By 1979, there were another 30 proposals to build beltways around US urban areas. Beltways were originally designed to allow intercity traffic to bypass developed urban areas. But, as development moved outward into the suburbs, beltways became more heavily used by local traffic. Little thought had been given to how beltways would influence development when they were originally designed. But once they were built, people became concerned about their effects on the economic health of central cities (Payne-Maxie and Blayney-Dyett, 1980; Dtett, 1984).

The US Department of Transportation and the US Department of Housing and Urban Development jointly sponsored a study of beltways in the 1970s to test the widespread assumption that beltway construction was undermining other federal efforts to support central cities. The beltway study used a statistical comparison of 27 cities with beltways and 27 cities without them and detailed case studies of eight beltway regions. The study found little support for the hypothesis of suburban gains at the expense of central cities. The study found no statistically significant differences between beltway and nonbeltway cities in regional economic growth, rate of suburbanization, CBD retail sales, and residential development locations. Some differences between the two types of regions were detected, but the differences were small. The impacts of beltways included the following:

- A small impact on employment, supporting a shift in jobs to the suburbs.
- A "one-time" effect on office location, drawing some offices out of CBDs.
- A change in the location and timing of regional shopping malls, office parks, and industrial parks, but not the feasibility of these projects. Feasibility depended more on market conditions, land availability, and labor force locations.

The study further found that central cities could counter the negative effects of beltways with CBD revitalization and economic development programs. In addition, in some cities, beltways supported the development of suburban centers at interchanges and thereby lessened the amount of strip development (PayneMaxie and Blayney-Dyett, 1980; Dyett, 1984).

However, other researchers believed that the primary impact of beltways was in the 1980s, after most Interstate highways had been completed (Muller, 1995). In the 1980s, high rise/high technology growth was spurred by a rapidly expanding computer industry, which preferred suburban locations, and an expansion of the service industry. Suburban downtowns with high-rise office buildings were developed. Hughes and Sternlieb (1988) suggested that it took a whole generation of living with interstate highways before developers realized that the intersections of beltways and radial interstate highways afforded the same regional accessibility advantages as the CBD. This situation weakened the economic position of the CBD and encouraged the development of suburban activity centers at the most accessible sites, frequently the intersection of two interstate highways.

The concern regarding the land development impacts of beltways on central cities and their economic viability of CBDs still continues. The connection between transportation improvements and land development patterns became a more important focus for the transportation planning process.

Highway Performance Monitoring System

During the mid-1970s, the FHWA shifted its approach to the biennial reporting of highway needs as required by Senate Joint Resolution 81 (P.L. 89–139). The earlier reports on highway needs contained estimates of the 20-year costs to remove all highway deficiencies throughout the nation (US Congress, 1972b,c). But, it had become apparent that, as highway travel and needs grew and national priorities changed, there would be insufficient funds to remove all highway deficiencies in the foreseeable future. Later reports, therefore, introduced the idea that "performance" could be used to measure the effectiveness of past highway investments and to analyze future investment alternatives (US Congress, 1975).

To obtain continuous information on the performance of the national highway system, FHWA, in cooperation with the states, developed the Highway Performance Monitoring System (HPMS). The first use of this system was in the 1976 National

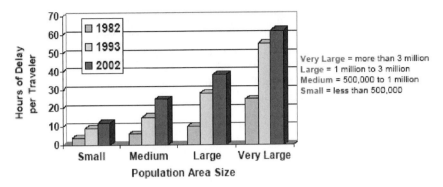

Fig. 9.2 Change in congestion levels by urban area size 1982–2002 (Source: Schrank and Lomax, 2005)

Highway Inventory and Performance Study (US Dept. of Transportation, 1975e). Data were collected on the highway system by functional class according to the functional realignment of federal aid systems that was required by the Federal-Aid Highway Act of 1973 to be accomplished by 30 June 1976.

FHWA collected HPMS data annually from the states on a sample of highway sections. In selecting the sample, the highway system was first stratified into urbanized area, small urban, and rural categories. Urbanized area data could be reported either individually or combined for an entire state. Within each category, highway sections were divided by functional class and traffic volume group using average annual daily traffic. A sampling rate was determined for each group of highway sections, with higher sampling rates for the higher functionally classified highway sections. For each sampled highway section, detailed information was collected on such items as length, functional classification, geometric characteristics, traffic and capacity, pavement type and condition, structures, traffic signals, and parking (US Dept. of Transportation, 1984e).

The first national highway needs report to use the HPMS data to describe the conditions and performance of the nation's highways was submitted to the Congress in 1981 (US Congress, 1981). It showed the deterioration in highway system performance and rising congestion. Subsequent national highway needs reports used the HPMS data to monitor the changing performance of highway system (US Congress, 1989).

The Federal Highway Administration also developed an analytical methodology that used the HPMS data to test national highway policy alternatives. Using this methodology, FHWA forecasted future highway investment requirements under various assumptions such as different highway travel growth rates, various highway conditions and performance levels, and the diversion of highway perk period travel to transit, alternative routes, and off-peak periods (US Congress, 1989). In addition, the analytical methodology was adapted so that the states could perform the same types of analyses on the HPMS data for their individual data as was performed on the national data (US Dept. of Transportation, 1987d).

Since the HPMS was the only comprehensive and continuous source of highway performance data that was available at the national and state levels, it was also used to monitor the growth in urban highway congestion (Lindley, 1987, 1989; Lomax et al., 1988; Hanks and Lomax, 1989; Schrank et al., 1993). Figure 9.2 shows the change in the congestion levels by urban area population from 1982 to 2002 (Schrank and Lomax, 2005).

Chapter 10
Decentralization of Decision-making

Through the decade of the 1970s there was a sharp increase in the range and complexity of issues required to be addressed in the urban transportation planning process. The combination of requirements and regulations had become burdensome and counter-productive. Organizations and techniques seemed unable to adapt with sufficient speed. It was becoming impossible to analyze all of the trade-offs that were required. This problem was not confined to urban transportation but to most activities in which the federal government was involved. It ushered in a new mood in the nation to decentralize control and authority, and to reduce federal intrusion into local decision-making (Weiner, 1983).

President Reagan's Memorandum on Regulations

On 29 January 1981, President Reagan sent a memorandum to all major domestic agencies to postpone the implementation of all regulations that were to take effect within the coming 60 days (Reagan, 1981b). This was to provide time for the newly appointed Task Force on Regulatory Relief to develop regulatory review procedures.

The Executive Order 12291 on Federal Regulation was issued on 17 February 1981 (Reagan, 1981a). It established procedures for reviewing existing regulations and evaluating new ones. It required that a regulation have greater benefits to society than costs and that the approach used must maximize those benefits. All regulatory actions were to be based on a regulatory impact analysis that assessed the benefits and the costs.

The order set in motion a major effort at the federal level to eliminate and simplify regulations and limit the issuance of new regulations. The impact on federal agencies was quickly felt.

Conferences on Goods Transportation in Urban Areas

The movement of goods in urban areas continued to be an important issue for planners, researchers, and decision-makers after the Conference on Urban Commodity Flow in December 1970 had concluded that goods movement needed

E. Weiner, *Urban Transportation Planning in the United States, Third Edition*,
doi:10.1007/978-0-387-77152-6, © Springer Science+Business Media, LLC 2008

more emphasis in the urban transportation planning process. Considerable progress was made in the ensuing years in gaining a better understanding of goods movement issues and problems, and in development of courses of action to lead to their resolution.

To facilitate an exchange of experiences and ideas among those concerned about urban goods movement, a series of conferences sponsored by the Engineering Foundation was held under the title of Goods Transportation in Urban Areas: in August 1973 at South Berwick, Maine (Fisher, 1974); in September 1975 at Santa Barbara, California (Fisher, 1976); in December 1977 at Sea Island, Georgia (Fisher, 1978); and in June 1981 at Easton, Maryland (Fisher and Meyburg, 1982).

The conferences highlighted the progress that had been made in identifying problems and analysis techniques, and discussed changes in institutional arrangements, regulations, and physical facilities to improve the movement of goods. Yet, even after all of this work, most urban transportation planning processes gave little attention to the movement of goods. There still was no generally accepted methodology for urban goods movement planning; no urban areas had collected the necessary data to analyze commodity (as opposed the vehicle) flows; and a consensus had not been reached on the data items to be collected. Attempts at system-level goods movement models and demand forecasting techniques had not been successful (Hedges, 1985).

The fourth conference on goods transportation occurred at a time when the pace of deregulation was increasing. In this deregulated environment, barriers to entry were being removed, limitations on rates and rate structures reduced, and the role of the public sector lessened. The emphasis shifted to transportation system management approaches that sought to make more efficient use of existing facilities and equipment. These strategies had short implementation periods, addressed specific site problems, could be carried out in an incremental manner, and did not require extensive institutional coordination. Such approaches were appropriate for the deregulated environment that was emerging in which there was only limited interaction between the public and the private sectors.

There remained after these conferences the need for a better understanding of the issues, more complete measurement of the phenomena, more thorough documentation of the accomplishments, and wider dissemination of the information. The creation of effective cooperation among those concerned about goods movement problem, particularly the public and the private sectors, was still being called for to improve the productivity of goods movement in urban areas (Fisher and Meyburg, 1982).

Airlie House Conference on Urban Transportation Planning in the 1980s

Concern had been growing in the planning community about the future of urban transportation planning. On the one hand planning requirements had become more complex, new planning techniques had not found their way into practice, and future changes in social, demographic, energy, environmental, and technological factors were unclear. On the other hand, fiscal constraints were tight and the federal government was shifting the burden of decision-making to state and local governments and the private sector. The future of planning was in doubt.

To address these concerns, a conference was held at Airlie House, in Virginia, on 9–12 November 1981, on Urban Transportation Planning in the 1980s. The conference reaffirmed the need for systematic urban transportation planning, especially to maximize the effectiveness of limited public funds. But the planning process needed to be adjusted to the nature and scope of an area's problems. It might not be the same for growing and for declining areas, nor for corridor- and for regional-level problems (Transportation Research Board, 1982b).

The conferees also concluded that the federal government had been overly restrictive in its regulations, making the planning process costly, time consuming, and difficult to administer. It was concluded that the regulations should be streamlined, specifying goals to be achieved and leaving the decisions on how to meet them to the states and local governments. The conferees called for a recognition of the need for different levels of 3C planning by urbanized areas of various sizes. Additionally, greater flexibility in the requirements for MPOs was recommended, with more responsibility given to the agencies that implement transportation projects; and finally, less frequent federal certification was recommended (Transportation Research Board, 1982b).

Increased attention to system management and fiscal issues was needed, but long-range planning needed to also identify shifts in the major longer-term trends that would affect the future of urban areas. This strategic planning process should be flexible to fit local concerns (Transportation Research Board, 1982b).

The conference recommendations reflected the new mood that the federal government had overregulated and was too specific in its requirements. The planning process was straining under this burden, finding it difficult to plan to meet local needs. The burden had to be lifted for the planning process to be viable.

Federal-Aid Highway Act of 1981

The Federal-Aid Highway Act of 1981 established early completion and preservation of the interstate system as the highest priority highway program. To ensure early completion, the act reduced the cost to complete the system by nearly $14 billion, from $53 billion to $39 billion, by limiting eligible construction items to those that provided a minimum level of acceptable service. This included full access control, a pavement design to accommodate 20-year forecasted travel, meeting essential environmental requirements, a maximum design of six lanes in areas under 400,000 in population and eight lanes in larger areas, and any high occupancy lanes previously approved in the 1981 Interstate Cost Estimate (ICE).

The act expanded the interstate resurfacing, restoration, and rehabilitation (3R) program by added reconstruction as an eligible category. This new category of the new 4R program included the addition of travel lanes, construction and reconstruction of interchanges, and the acquisition of right of way. Construction items that were removed from the interstate construction program were eligible for 4R funding. The federal share was increased from 75% under the 3R program to 90% under the 4R program. Funds were to be allocated to states 55% based on interstate lane miles and 45% on vehicle miles of travel. Every state with Interstate mileage had to receive a minimum of 1/2 of 1% of the funds for the program.

This act marked a shift in focus in the federal highway program toward finally completing the interstate system and moving ahead with rehabilitating it.

E.O. 12372, Intergovernmental Review of Federal Programs

Office of Management and Budget's Circular A-95 (which replaced Bureau of the Budget Circular A-95) had governed the consultation process on federal grant programs with state and local governments since its issuance in July 1969. Although the A-95 process had served a useful function in assuring intergovernmental cooperation on federal grant programs, there were concerns that the process had become too rigid and cumbersome and caused unnecessary paperwork. To respond to these concerns and to delegate more responsibility and authority to state and local governments, the president signed Executive Order 12372, "Intergovernmental Review of Federal Programs," on 14 July 1982 (Reagan, 1982).

The objectives of the Executive Order were to foster an intergovernmental partnership and strengthen federalism by relying on state and local processes for intergovernmental coordination and review of federal financial assistance and direct federal development. The Executive Order had several purposes. First, it allowed states, after consultation with local officials, to establish their own process for review and comment on proposed federal financial assistance and direct federal development. Second, it increased federal responsiveness to state and local officials by requiring federal agencies to "accommodate" or "explain" when considering certain state and local views. Third, it allowed states to simplify, consolidate, or substitute state plans for federal planning requirements. The order also revoked OMB Circular A-95, although regulations implementing this circular remained in effect until 30 September 1983.

There were three major elements that comprised the process under the Executive Order. These were establishing a state process, the single point of contact, and the federal agency's "accommodate" or "explain" response to state and local comments submitted in the form of a recommendation. First, a state could choose which programs and activities are being included under that state process after consulting with local governments. The elements of the process were to be determined by the state. A state was not required to establish a state process; however, if no process was established, the provisions of the Executive Order did not apply. Existing consultation requirements of other statutes or regulations would continue in effect, including those of the Inter-governmental Cooperation Act of 1968 and the Demonstration Cities and Metropolitan Development Act of 1966.

Second, a single point of contact had to be designated by the state for dealing with the federal government. The single point of contact was the only official contact for state and local views to be sent to the federal government and to receive the response.

Third, when a single point of contact transmitted a state process recommendation, the federal agency receiving the recommendation had to either (1) accept the recommendation (accommodate); (2) reach a mutually agreeable solution with the parties preparing the recommendation; or (3) provide the single point of contact with a written explanation for not accepting the recommendation or reaching a mutually agreeable solution. If there was nonaccommodation, the department was generally required to wait 15 days after sending an explanation of the nonaccommodation to the single point of contact before taking final action.

The regulations implementing Executive Order 12372 for transportation programs were published on 24 June 1983 (US Dept. of Transportation, 1983a). They applied to all federal aid highway and urban public transportation programs.

Woods Hole Conference on Future Directions of Urban Public Transportation

The transit industry was growing restless as the demands for and requirements on transit services were changing. Older cities were concerned about rehabilitation while newer ones were focused on expansion. Future changes in the economic base, land use, energy, and sociodemographic characteristics were uncertain. The transit industry was coming out of a period in which federal priorities and requirements had changed too frequently. Transit deficits had risen sharply over the previous decade and the federal government had declared that it planned to phase out operating subsidies. And many were calling for the private sector to provide an increased share of transit services because they were more efficient.

A diverse group of conferees met at the Woods Hole Study Center in Massachusetts, 26–29 September 1982, to discuss Future Directions of Urban Public Transportation (Transportation Research Board, 1984a). The conference addressed the role of public transportation, present and future, the context within which public transportation functioned, and strategies for the future. Attendees included leaders of the transit industry and government, academics, researchers, and consultants. There were wide differences of opinion that had not disappeared when the conference concluded.

The conferees did agree that, "Strategic planning for public transportation should be conducted at both the local and national levels." The transit industry should be more aggressive in working with developers and local governments in growing parts of metropolitan areas to capitalize on opportunities to integrate transit facilities into major new developments. The industry needed to improve its relationship with highway and public works agencies as well as state and local decision-makers. Financing transit had become more complex and difficult but had created new opportunities (Transportation Research Board, 1984a).

The conferees called for reductions in federal requirements and avoidance of rapid shifts in policy in the future. The federal government should have a more positive federal urban policy and the UMTA should be transit's advocate within the federal government (Transportation Research Board, 1984a).

Agreement could not be reached on the future role of urban transit. Some felt that the transit industry should only concern itself with conventional rail and bus systems. Others argued that transit agencies should broaden the range of services provided to include various forms of paratransit and ridesharing so as to attract a larger share of the travel market. Nevertheless, the conference was considered to be the first small step in a strategic planning process for the transit industry.

Easton Conference on Travel Analysis Methods for the 1980s

The Airlie House Conference on Urban Transportation Planning in the 1980s highlighted the shifts in planning that were occurring and were likely to continue (Transportation Research Board, 1982b). State and local governments would assume a greater role as the federal government disengaged, finances would be tighter, system rehabilitation would become more important, and traffic growth would be slower.

A conference was held at Easton, Maryland, in November 1982 to discuss how well travel analysis methods were adapted to the issues and problems of the 1980s. This Conference on Travel Analysis Methods for the 1980s focused on defining the state of the art versus the state of practice, describing how the methods have been and can be applied, and identifying gaps between art and practice that needed more dissemination of current knowledge, research, or development. The conference extended the discussions of the International Travel Demand Conferences but concentrated on the application of travel analysis methods and on improving the interaction between researchers and practitioners (Transportation Research Board, 1984b).

The conference reviewed the state of the art and practice and how they applied to the various levels of planning. There were extensive discussions on how capable travel analysis procedures were in dealing with major transportation issues and why they were not being extensively applied in practice (Transportation Research Board, 1984b).

The conferees found that in an era of scarce resources, sound analysis of alternatives would continue to be important. Travel analysis methods that were currently available were suitable for issues that could be foreseen in the 1980s. These disaggregate techniques, which had been developed during the 1970s, had been tested in limited applications and were now ready for wide-scale use. Their use in the analysis of small-scale projects, however, might not be justified because of their complexity (Transportation Research Board, 1984b).

It was clear, however, that new disaggregate travel analysis techniques were not being used extensively in practice. The gap between research and practice was wider than it had ever been. The new mathematical techniques and theoretical bases from econometrics and psychometrics had been difficult for practitioners to learn. Moreover, the new techniques were not easily integrated into conventional planning practices. Neither researchers nor practitioners had made the necessary effort to bridge the gap. Researchers had been unwilling to package and disseminate the new travel analysis methods in a form usable to practitioners. Practitioners had been unwilling to undergo retraining to be able to use these new techniques. Neither group had subjected these methods to rigorous tests to determine how well they performed or for what problems they were best suited (Transportation Research Board, 1984b).

The conferees concluded that the travel demand community should concentrate on transferring the new travel analysis methods into practice. A wide range of technology transfer approaches was suggested. The federal government and Transportation Research Board were recommended to lead in this endeavor (Transportation Research Board, 1984b).

Surface Transportation Assistance Act of 1982

Through the decade of the 1970s there was mounting evidence of deterioration in the nation's highway and transit infrastructure. Money during that period had been concentrated on building new capacity and the transition to funding rehabilitation of the infrastructure had been slow. By the time the problem had been faced, the cost estimate to refurbish the highways, bridges, and transit systems had reached hundreds of billions of dollars (Weiner, 1983).

The Surface Transportation Assistance Act of 1982 was passed to address this infrastructure problem. The act extended authorizations for the highway, safety, and transit programs by 4 years, from 1983 to 1986 (US Dept. of Transportation, 1983g) (Table 10.1). In addition, the act raised the highway user charges by 5 cents (in addition to the existing 4 cents) a gallon on fuel effective 1 April 1983. Other taxes were changed including a substantial increase in the truck user fees, which were changed from a fixed rate to a graduated rate by weight. Of the revenues raised from the 5-cent increase in user fees (about $5.5 billion annually), the equivalent of a 4-cent raise in fuel user charges was to increase highway programs, and the remaining 1 cent was for transit programs (Weiner, 1983).

The additional highway funds were for accelerating completion of the interstate highway system (to be completed by 1991), an increased 4R (interstate resurfacing, restoration, rehabilitation, and reconstruction) program, a substantially expanded bridge replacement and rehabilitation program, and greater funding for primary, secondary, and interstate projects (Weiner, 1983).

The act authorized the administration of highway planning and research (HP&R) funds as a single fund and made them available to the states for a 4-year period.

Table 10.1 Surface transportation assistance act of 1982

	Authorization levels by fiscal year ($ millions)			
	1983	1984	1985	1986
Highway construction				
Interstate construction	4,000.0	4,000.0	4,000.0	4,000.0
Interstate 4R	1,950.0	2,400.0	2,800.0	3,150.0
Interstate highway substitutions	257.0	700.0	700.0	725.0
Primary system	1,890.3	2,147.2	2,351.8	2,505.1
Secondary system	650.0	650.0	650.0	650.0
Urban system	800.0	800.0	800.0	800.0
Other highway programs	1,178.2	1,120.0	1,154.0	1,106.0
Subtotal – highway	10,724.0	11,817.2	12,455.8	12,936.1
Highway safety				
Bridge replacement and rehabilitation	1,600.0	1,650.0	1,750.0	2,050.0
Safety construction	390.0	390.0	390.0	390.0
Other safety programs	199.5	205.3	205.6	155.6
Subtotal – safety	2,189.5	2,245.3	2,345.6	2,595.6
Urban mass transportation				
Discretionary capital grants	779.0	1,250.0	1,100.0	1,100.0
Formula grants	–	2,750.0	2,950.0	3,050.0
Interstate transit substitutions	365.0	380.0	390.0	400.0
R&D, admin., and misc.	86.3	91.0	100.0	100.0
Subtotal – urban transit	1,230.3	4,471.0	4,540.0	4,650.0
Total	14,143.8	18,533.5	19,341.4	20,181.7

Source: US Dept. of Transportation, 1983g

A standard federal matching ratio for the HP&R program was set at 85%. A 1½% share of bridge funds was authorized for HP&R purposes. As a result of the large expansion in the construction program, the level of funding increased substantially for the HP&R program and urban transportation planning (PL) purposes.

The act restructured federal urban transit programs. No new authorizations were made for the Section 5 formula grant program. Instead, a new formula grant program was created that allowed expenditures on planning, capital, and operating items. Substantial discretion was given to state and local governments in selecting projects to be funded using formula grants with minimal federal interference. However, there were limitations on the use of the funds for operating expenses. The act provided for a distribution of funds into areas of different sizes by population; over 1 million, between 1 million and 200,000, under 200,000, and rural. Within these population groups, the funds were to be apportioned by several formulas using such factors as population, density, vehicle miles, and route miles (Weiner, 1983).

The revenue from the 1-cent increase in highway user charges was to be placed into a Mass Transit Account of the Highway Trust Fund. The funds could only be used for capital projects. They were to be allocated by a formula in fiscal year 1983, but were discretionary in later years. The definition of capital was changed to include associated capital maintenance items. The act also required that a substantial number of federal requirements be self-certified by the applicants and that other requirements be consolidated to reduce paperwork (Weiner, 1983).

A requirement was also included for a biennial report on transit performance and needs, with the first report due in January 1984. In addition, the act provided that regulations be published that set minimum criteria on transportation services for the handicapped and elderly.

The Surface Transportation Assistance Act of 1982 was passed under considerable controversy about the future federal role in transportation, particularly the Administration's position to phase out of federal transit operating subsidies. Debates on later appropriations bills demonstrated that the issue remained controversial.

Advent of Microcomputers

By the early 1980s, there was a surge in interest and use of microcomputers in urban transportation planning. The FHWA and UMTA had increasingly focused their computer-related research and development activities on the application of small computers. These technical support activities were directed at gaining a better understanding of the potential and applicability of microcomputers, promoting the development and exchange of information and programs, and evaluating and testing programs. Some software development was carried out, but most software were produced commercially.

A user support structure was developed to assist state and local agencies. This included the establishment of two user support centers; one at Rensselaer Polytechnic Institute for the transit industry and another at the DOT's Transportation Systems Center (TSC) for transportation planning, transportation system management (TSM), and traffic engineering applications. Three user groups were formed under DOT sponsorship; transit operations, transportation planning and TSM, and traffic engineering. These groups exchanged information and software, developed and promoted standards, and identified research and development needs. Assistance was provided through the user support centers. A newsletter, MicroScoop, was published periodically to aid in the communication process.

The FHWA and UMTA developed a 1-day seminar entitled, "Microcomputers For Transportation" to acquaint users with the capabilities and uses of microcomputers. They also published reports on available software and sources of information (US Dept. of Transportation, 1983d,e). As the capabilities of microcomputers increased, they offered the opportunity of greater analytical capacity to a larger number of organizations. As a result, their use became more widespread.

New Urban Transportation Planning Regulations

The joint FHWA/UMTA urban transportation planning regulations had served as the key federal guidance since 1975 (US Dept. of Transportation, 1975a). In 1980, there was an intensive effort to amend these regulations to ensure more citizen involvement, to increase the emphasis on urban revitalization, and to integrate corridor planning into the urban transportation planning process (Paparella, 1982). Proposed amendments were published in October 1980. Final amendments were published in January 1981, to take effect in February.

These amendments were postponed as a result of President Reagan's January 1981 memorandum to delay the effective day of all pending regulations by 60 days. During this period, the amendments were reviewed based on the criteria in the President's memorandum and Executive Order 12291. Consequently, the amendments were withdrawn and interim final regulations were issued in August 1981. These regulations included minimal changes to streamline the planning process in areas under 200,000 in population, to clarify transportation system management, and to incorporate legislative changes (US Dept. of Transportation, 1983c).

To obtain public comment on further changes in the regulations, FHWA and UMTA published an issues and options paper in December 1981, entitled Solicitation of Public Comment on the Appropriate Federal Role in Urban Transportation Planning. The comments clearly indicated the preference for fewer federal requirements and greater flexibility. Further indication of these views resulted from the Airlie House Conference on Urban Transportation Planning in the 1980s (Transportation Research Board, 1982b).

Based on the comments, the joint urban transportation planning regulations were rewritten to remove items that were not actually required. The changes in the regulations responded to the call for reducing the role of the federal government in urban transportation planning. The revised regulations, issued on 30 June 1983, contained new statutory requirements and retained the requirements for a transportation plan, a transportation improvement program (TIP) including an annual element (or biennial element), and a unified planning work program (UPWP), the latter only for areas of 200,000 or more in population. The planning process was to be self-certified by the states and MPOs as to its conformance with all requirements when submitting the TIP (US Dept. of Transportation, 1983c).

The regulations drew a distinction between federal requirements and good planning practice. They stated the product or end that was required but left the details of the process to the state and local agencies, so that the regulations no longer contained the elements of the process nor factors to consider in conducting the process (US Dept. of Transportation, 1983c).

The MPO was to be designated by the governor and units of general-purpose local government. The urban transportation planning process was still the mutual responsibility of the MPO, state, and public transit operators. But, the nature of the urban transportation planning process was to be the determination of governor and local governments without any federal prescription. Governors were also given the option of administering the UMTA's planning funds for urban areas with populations under 200,000.

The revised regulations marked a major shift in the evolution of urban transportation planning. Up to that time, the response to new issues and problems was to create additional federal requirements. These regulations changed the focus of responsibility and control to the state and local governments. The federal government remained committed to urban planning by requiring that projects be based on a 3C planning process and by continuing to provide funding for planning activities. But it would no longer specify how the process was to be performed.

Chapter 11
Promoting Private Sector Participation

As the decade of the 1980s progressed, there was a growing awareness that the public sector did not have the resources to continue providing all of the programs to which it had become committed. This was particularly true at the federal level of government. Moreover, by continuing these programs, governmental bodies were preempting areas that could be better served by the private sector. Governments and public agencies began to seek opportunities for greater participation of the private sector in the provision and financing of urban transportation facilities and services. In addition, the federal government sought to foster increased competition in the provision of transportation services as a means to increase efficiency and reduce costs. Changes in the transportation system were intended to be the outcome of competition in the marketplace rather than of public regulation. This necessitated eliminating practices whereby unsubsidized private transportation service providers competed on an unequal basis with subsidized public agencies (Weiner, 1984).

Paratransit Policy

The range of public transportation services options known as "paratransit" was brought to national attention in a report by The Urban Institute (Kirby et al., 1975). Paratransit-type services had already been receiving growing interest (Highway Research Board, 1971a, 1973b; Transportation Research Board, 1974a,b; Rosenbloom, 1975; Scott, 1975). Paratransit was seen as a supplement to conventional transit that would serve special population groups and markets that were otherwise poorly served. It was also seen as an alternative, in certain circumstances, to conventional transit. It fit well into the tenor of the times which sought low-cost alternatives to the automobile that could capture a larger share of the travel market. Paratransit could serve low-density, dispersed travel patterns and thereby compete with the automobile.

The UMTA struggled for many years to develop a policy position on paratransit. The transit industry expressed concern about paratransit alternatives to conventional transit. Paratransit supporters saw it as the key option to compete against the automobile in low-density markets. It was the same debate that surfaced at the

E. Weiner, *Urban Transportation Planning in the United States, Third Edition*,
doi:10.1007/978-0-387-77152-6, © Springer Science+Business Media, LLC 2008

Woods Hole Conference on Future Directions of Urban Public Transportation (Transportation Research Board, 1984a).

Finally, in October 1982, the UMTA published the Paratransit Policy. Paratransit was portrayed as a supplement to conventional transit services that could increase transportation capacity at low cost. It could provide service in markets that were not viable for mass transit. Paratransit could also serve specialized markets (e.g., elderly and handicapped) and be an alternative to the private automobile. Its potential in rural areas was emphasized as well (US Dept. of Transportation, 1982a).

The Paratransit Policy encouraged local areas to give full consideration to paratransit options. It supported the use of paratransit provided by private operators, particularly where they were not subsidized. The policy fostered reducing regulatory barriers to private operators, timely consultation with the private sector, matching services to travel needs, and integration of paratransit and conventional transit services (US Dept. of Transportation, 1982a).

It was stated that UMTA funds were available for planning, equipment purchase, facility acquisition, capital, administrative, and research expenses. The UMTA preferred unsubsidized, privately provided paratransit, but would provide financial support where justified (US Dept. of Transportation, 1982a).

Transportation Management Associations

The aftermath of two energy crises in 1973 and 1979 and the rise in traffic congestion, especially in suburban areas, prompted many employers to become involved in commuting issues. Employers used a number of approaches including subsidizing transit passes, ridesharing matching services, preferential treatment for pooling vehicles, flexible work schedules, and payroll deductions for transit passes and pooling activities (Schreffler, 1986).

These activities led to the establishment of a number of transportation management associations (TMAs) starting in the early 1980s. TMAs were generally nonprofit associations formed by local employers, businesses, and developers to cooperatively address community transportation problems (Orski, 1982). TMAs were funded by membership fees, based on a voluntary assessment. Some TMAs were formed to specifically deal with transportation concerns, and others were elements of larger multipurpose organizations. Most TMAs served employment centers, usually in the suburbs, while others focused on downtown centers, and still others were regional in scope.

TMAs varied in the types of support that they provided to employees, customers, and tenants. These functions included the management of ridesharing programs, administration of parking management strategies, operation of internal circulation service, contracting for subscription bus services, administration of flexible work hours programs, management of local traffic flow improvements, and technical assistance and education. TMAs also served as the coordinating mechanism with public agencies to represent business interest, organize private sector support for projects, and sponsor special studies.

The number of TMAs grew slowly through the 1980s and, by 1989, there were about 70 in operation or forming. Their support broadened as public agencies fostered the formation of TMAs through start-up funding, technical assistance, and participating directly in the association. TMAs were considered to be a promising approach for involving the private sector in addressing commuting problems and maintaining mobility (Dunphy and Lin, 1990).

Revised Major Transit Capital Investment Policy

By the early 1980s, there had been a huge upsurge of interest in building new urban rail transit systems and extensions to existing ones. Beginning in 1972, new urban rail systems had begun revenue service in San Francisco, Washington, DC, Atlanta, Baltimore, San Diego, Miami, and Buffalo. Construction was underway for new systems in Portland, Oregon, Detroit, Sacramento, and San Jose. A total of 32 urban areas were conducting studies for major new transit investments in 46 corridors. It was estimated that if all of those projects were carried out, the cost to the federal government would have been at least $19 billion (US Dept. of Transportation, 1984a).

The federal funds for rail projects came, for the most part, from the Section 3 Discretionary Grant program. This program was funded by the revenue from 1 cent of the 5-cent increase in the user charge on motor fuels that was included in the Surface Transportation Assistance Act of 1982, and amounted to $1.1 billion annually. UMTA, however, was giving priority to projects for rehabilitation of existing rail and bus systems. Only $400 million annually was targeted for use on new urban rail projects. The resulting gap between the demand for federal funds for major transit projects and those available was, therefore, very large.

In an attempt to manage the demand for federal funds, UMTA issued a revised Urban Mass Transportation Major Capital Investment Policy on 18 May 1984 (US Dept. of Transportation, 1984b). It was a further refinement of the evaluation process for major transit projects that had been evolving over a number of years. Under the policy, the UMTA would use the results of local planning studies to calculate the cost effectiveness and local financial support for each project. These criteria would be used to rate the projects. The UMTA would fund only those projects that ranked high on both criteria to the extent that they did not exceed the available funds. The lower-ranked projects were still eligible for funding if additional money became available.

The project development process involved a number of stages after which the UMTA would make a decision on whether to proceed to the next stage (Fig. 11.1). The most critical decision was taken after the alternatives analysis and draft environmental impact statement (AA/DEIS) was completed. During this stage, the cost effectiveness of new fixed guideway projects was compared to a base system called

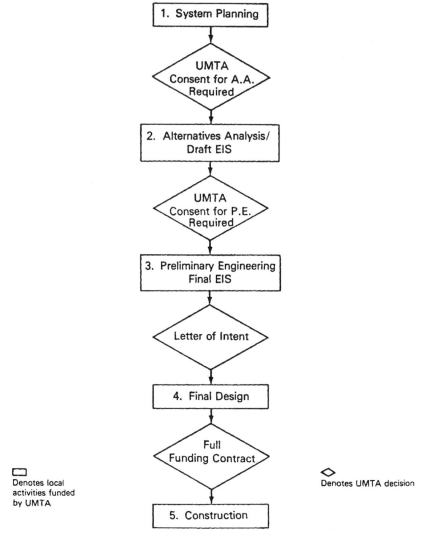

Fig. 11.1 UMTA project development process for major investments. (Source: US Dept. of Transportation, 1984b)

the "transportation system management" alternative. This TSM alternative consisted of an upgraded bus system plus other actions that would improve mobility with a minimal capital investment, such as parking management techniques, carpool and vanpool programs, traffic engineering improvements, and paratransit services. Often, the marginal improvement in mobility of a fixed guideway proposal over the TSM was found to be not worth the cost to construct and operate it.

Projects were rated on cost effectiveness and local fiscal effort after the AA/ DEIS was completed. Local fiscal effort consisted of the level of funding from state, local, and private sources. In addition, the projects had to meet several threshold criteria. First, the fixed guideway project had to generate more patronage than the TSM alternative. Second, the cost per additional rider of the fixed guideway project could not exceed a preset value that UMTA was to determine. Third, the project had to meet all statutory and regulatory requirements.

The pressure for federal funds for new urban rail projects was so great, however, that the matter was often settled politically. Starting in fiscal year 1981, the Congress began to earmark Section 3 Discretionary Grant funds for specific projects, thereby preempting UMTA from making the selection. UMTA continued to rate the projects and make the information available to Congressional committees.

In 1987, the Surface Transportation and Uniform Relocation Assistance Act established grant criteria for new fixed guideway projects along the lines that UMTA had been using. The projects had to be based on alternatives analysis and preliminary engineering, be cost effective, and be supported by an acceptable degree of local financial commitment.

Transportation Demand Management

Suburban congestion became a growing phenomenon during the 1980s and had reached severe proportions by the early 1990s in many urban areas. Approaches used to serve downtown-oriented travel were less applicable to the more diverse, automobile-dominated suburban travel patterns (Higgins, 1990). Moreover, building new highway capacity had become considerably more difficult in an era of tight budgets and heightened environmental awareness. New strategies were developed to mitigate suburban congestion under the general category of transportation demand management (TDM).

Transportation demand management was a process designed to modify transportation demand. It differed from transportation system management (TSM) in that it focused on travel demand rather than on transportation supply, and often involved the private sector in implementing the strategies. TDM aimed to reduce peak period automobile trips by either eliminating the trip, shifting it to a less congested destination or route, diverting it to a higher occupancy mode, or time shifting it to a less congested period of the day. TDM strategies often worked in conjunction with TSM measures. TDM had the additional attraction of increasing the efficiency of the transportation system at little or no cost (Ferguson, 1990).

Transportation demand management most often focused on a suburban activity center but was also used for CBDs and radial corridors (COMSIS, 1990). TDM strategies required the cooperation of many agencies and organizations including developers, land owners, employers, business associations, and state and local governments (Ferguson, 1990). In some instances, legal support was provided in the form of a trip reduction ordinance (TRO) to strengthen compliance with the

TDM measures. The first area-wide TRO was adopted in Pleasanton, California, in 1984. A TRO provided some assurance that consistent standards and requirements would be applied to all businesses in the area and gave these businesses the legal backing to implement automobile reduction strategies. Although the main goal of most TROs was to mitigate traffic congestion, improvement in air quality was an important goal as well (Peat Marwick Main & Co., 1989).

Transportation demand management measures included improved alternatives to driving alone, such as pooling and biking; incentives to shift modes, such as subsidizing transit fares and vanpooling costs; disincentives to driving, such as higher parking fees and reduced parking supply; and work hours management, such as flexible work hours and compressed work weeks (COMSIS, 1990). TROs required businesses and employers to establish a TDM plan, implement a TDM program, monitor progress, update the plan periodically, have a professionally trained coordinator, and, in some instances, achieve a specified level of trip reduction with fines and penalties for violations.

Transportation demand management became more important in addressing suburban traffic congestion as urban areas found increasing difficulties to highway expansion and air quality problems became more widespread.

Private Participation in the Transit Program

The Reagan Administration was committed to a greater private sector role in addressing the needs of communities. They believed that governments at all levels should not provide services that the private sector was willing and able to provide, and that there would be increased efficiencies in an operating environment in which there was competition. Consequently, the Department of Transportation sought to remove barriers to greater involvement of the private sector in the provision of urban transportation services and in the financing of these services.

The instances of private provision of urban public transportation services and in public/private cooperative ventures had been increasing slowly. Transit agencies were having difficulty thinking in terms of private involvement in what they viewed as their business. Private transportation operators had voiced concerns that, in spite of statutory requirements, they were not being fully or fairly considered for the provision of public transportation service. But large, operating deficits were creating pressure to find cheaper means to provide service, and private providers were increasingly being considered. Some transit agencies were beginning to contract out services that they found too expensive to provide themselves.

To promote increased involvement of the private sector in the provision of public transportation services, the UMTA issued a Policy on Private Participation in the Urban Mass Transportation Program (US Dept. of Transportation, 1984c). It provided guidance for achieving compliance with several sections of the Urban Mass Transportation Act. Section 3(e) prohibited unfair competition with private providers by publicly subsidized operators. Section 8(e) required maximum participation of the private sector in the planning of public transportation services. Section 9(f), which was added by the Surface Transportation Assistance Act of 1982, established procedures for involving the private sector in the development of Transportation Improvement Program as a condition for federal funding.

The Policy on Private Participation in the Urban Mass Transportation Program called for early involvement of private providers in the development of new transit services and for their maximum feasible participation in providing those services. The policy identified the principal factors that the UMTA would consider in determining whether recipients complied with the statutes. It indicated that private transportation providers must be consulted in the development of plans for new and restructured services. Moreover, private carriers must be considered where new or restructured public transportation services were to be provided. A true comparison of costs was to be used when comparing publicly provided service with private providers. An independent local dispute resolution mechanism was to be established to assure fairness in administering the policy.

This policy represented a major departure from past federal policy toward public transportation operators. Where public operators had had a virtual monopoly on federal funds for transit facilities, equipment, and service, now they needed to consider private sector operators as competitors for providing those services.

National Transit Performance Reports

Assessments of the nation's public transportation systems and estimates of future needs to improve those systems had been made intermittently over the years. Several estimates had been made as part of multimodal national transportation studies (US Dept. of Transportation, 1972b, 1975b, 1977c). Occasionally, Congress required that estimates of public transportation facility needs be made (US Dept. of Transportation, 1972d, 1974b; Weiner, 1976b). Also, APTA and AASHTO made several estimates over the years of transit needs and submitted them to the Congress (American Public Transportation Association, 1994).

With the Surface Transportation Assistance Act of 1982, the Congress placed such reporting on a regular periodic basis. Section 310 of that act required biennial reports in January of even years on the condition and performance of public mass transportation systems, and any necessary administrative of legislative revisions. That section also required an assessment of public transportation facilities, and future needs for capital, operation, and maintenance for three time periods: 1, 5, and 10 years.

The first transit performance report was designed as the prototype for future reports. It focused entirely on current conditions and performance of the nation's public transportation systems but did not contain projections of future facility needs or costs. The report concluded that the transit industry was in transition, and traditional markets were shifting. The industry continued to respond in a conventional manner by expanding service and focusing on peak-period demand. In addition, operating costs had increased dramatically while fares had not kept pace with inflation. Consequently, operating deficits and government subsidies had been increasing (US Dept. of Transportation, 1984d).

The report indicated that the future federal role in mass transportation needed to consider the program's efficiency, transit's infrastructure needs compared to other needs, opportunities for private sector involvement, and the state and local financial outlook (US Dept. of Transportation, 1984d).

The second and third transit performance reports continued the focus on current performance and conditions of the nation's transit systems. They concluded that the transit industry had adequate funding in the form of public subsidies, but that it faced problems with efficiency and productivity. These problems resulted from a lack of competitive pressure on transit management and labor. They called for local reconsideration of the level of mass transportation provided, and the manner in which it was delivered and priced (US Dept. of Transportation, 1987a, 1988a).

The reports recommended that state and local decision-makers be given more responsibility in meeting local mobility needs, increased competition in the provision of transit services, more efficient use of financial resources, and targeting cost recovery to beneficiaries, and greater involvement of the private sector in the provision and financing of transit service (US Dept. of Transportation, 1987a, 1988a).

Charter Bus Regulations

The Urban Mass Transportation Act of 1964 defined mass transportation to specifically exclude charter services. Federal assistance for mass transportation was, therefore, not to be used to provide such services. The federal government had thereby declared at the outset of the transit program that it confined its role to assisting only regular mass transit services. The Comptroller General ruled, however, in a 1966 case that buses purchased with federal funds could provide charter service if the service was incidental, and did not interfere with the provision of regular transit services for which the buses were purchased.

As public transit agencies engaged in charter bus operations, there was a concern, generally raised by private bus operators, that public agencies were competing unfairly. The argument was that public agencies were using federal subsidies to allow them to underprice their services and thereby foreclose private operators from charter service markets. The Federal-Aid Highway Act of 1973 sought to clarify the charter bus prohibition. It required all recipients of federal transit funds or highway funds used for transit to enter into an agreement with the Secretary of Transportation that they would not operate any charter service outside of their mass transportation service area in competition with private operators (US Dept. of Transportation, 1982a).

The Housing and Community Development Act of 1974 gave the Secretary of Transportation the flexibility to tailor solutions to this problem to the individual situation. The agreements negotiated with recipients were to provide fair and equitable arrangements to assure that publicly and privately owned operators for public bodies did not foreclose private operators from the intercity charter bus industry where such operators were willing and able to provide such service. The National Mass Transportation Assistance Act of 1974 extended these charter bus provisions to federal financial assistance for operating expenses, which was a new category of federal assistance established by that act (US Dept. of Transportation, 1982a).

Regulations to implement these charter bus provisions were published in April 1976 (US Dept. of Transportation, 1976d). Under the regulations, a public transit operator could not provide intercity or intracity charter bus service unless it was incidental to the provision of mass transportation service. A service was considered incidental if it did not (a) occur during peak hours, (b) require a trip more than 50 miles beyond the recipient's service area, or (c) require a particular bus for more than 6 h. If a public operator provided intercity charter service, the charter revenues had to cover its total costs and the rates charged could not foreclose competition from private operators. Some 79 separate costs had to be accounted for in the public operator's certification.

Both public and private operators found the regulation unsatisfactory. Public operators supported easing the restrictions on their provision of charter bus service as a means to provide supplemental revenue and improve their financial condition. Private operators preferred tightening the restrictions and strengthening enforcement, which they felt was inadequate. Moreover, it was clear that the recordkeeping and certification requirements on grant recipients were unnecessarily burdensome.

Finding a balance between the views of public and private operators was extremely difficult, and UMTA struggled with the problem for a number of years. Shortly after issuing the regulation in 1976, the UMTA published an Advanced Notice of Proposed Rulemaking (ANRPM) requesting views on several issues and suggestions on how to make the regulation more effective. A public hearing was held in January 1977 to solicit additional comments. Afterwards, UMTA issued two additional ANRPMs in an attempt to obtain the views of interested parties on a number of issues and possible options for modifying the regulation (US Dept. of Transportation, 1981c, 1982b).

Finally, a NORM was published in March 1986 (US Dept. of Transportation, 1986a), and a final rule in April 1987 (US Dept. of Transportation, 1987b). It prohibited any UMTA recipient from providing charter bus service using UMTA assistance if there was a private charter bus operator willing and able to provide the service. A recipient could provide vehicles to a private operator if the operator had insufficient vehicles, or lacked vehicles accessible to handicapped persons. An exception could be granted to a recipient for special events, or to small urban areas that could document cases of hardship.

Surface Transportation and Uniform Relocation Assistance Act of 1987

With 5 titles and 149 sections, the Surface Transportation and Uniform Relocation Assistance Act of 1987 (STURAA) was the most complicated piece of legislation up to that time on surface transportation matters. It was passed on 2 April 1987, over President Reagan's veto. The STURAA authorized $87.6 billion for the 5-year period from fiscal year 1987 to 1991 for the federal aid highway, safety, and mass transportation programs (Table 11.1). It also updated the rules for compensating persons and businesses displaced by federal development, and extended the Highway Trust Fund through 30 June 1994 (US Dept. of Transportation, 1987c).

Title I, the Federal-Aid Highway Act of 1987, authorized $67.1 billion for highway and bridge programs over a 5-year period. The basic features of the highway programs were extended at levels 10–25% below those in the Surface Transportation Assistance Act of 1982 (STAA).

Some $17.0 billion was authorized through 1993 for completion of all remaining segments of the Interstate system. A minimum of one-half percent apportionment

Table 11.1 Surface transportation and uniform relocation assistance act 1987

	Authorization levels by fiscal year ($ Millions)				
	1987	1988	1989	1990	1991
Highway construction					
Interstate construction	3,000.0	3,150.0	3,150.0	3,150.0	3,150.0
Interstate 4R	2,815.0	2,815.0	2,815.0	2,815.0	2,815.0
Interstate highway Substitutions	740.0	740.0	740.0	740.0	740.0
Primary system	2,373.0	2,373.0	2,373.0	2,373.0	2,325.0
Secondary system	600.0	600.0	600.0	600.0	600.0
Urban system	750.0	750.0	750.0	750.0	750.0
Bridge replacement and rehabilitation	1,630.0	1,630.0	1,630.0	1,630.0	1,630.0
Safety construction	126.0	330.0	330.0	330.0	330.0
Other programs	1,315.7	1,329.5	1,329.0	1,329.0	1,329.0
Subtotal – highway	13,574.6	13,737.4	13,736.9	13,886.0	13,886.0
Highway safety					
State/community grants	126.0	126.0	126.0	126.0	126.0
R&D grants	33.0	33.0	33.0	33.0	33.0
Subtotal – safety	159.0	159.0	159.0	159.0	159.0
Urban mass transportation					
Discretionary grants	1,097.2	1,208.0	1,255.0	1,305.0	1,405.0
Formula grants	2,000.0	2,350.0	2,350.0	2,350.0	2,350.0
Interstate transit Substitutions	200.0	200.0	200.0	200.0	200.0
R&D, admin., and misc.	–	50.0	50.0	50.0	50.0
Subtotal – transit	3,297.2	3,558.0	3,605.0	3,655.0	3,755.0
Total	17,161.6	17,561.0	17,760.0	17,860.0	17,504.5

Source: US Dept. of Transportation, 1987c

for each state for interstate construction was continued. The act authorized $1.78 billion over 5 years to fund 152 specifically cited projects outside of the regular federal aid highway programs. Each state was guaranteed a minimum of one-half percent of the newly authorized funds. This was considerably more than the 10 projects specifically cited in the STAA.

The act permitted states to raise the speed limit on interstate routes outside urbanized areas from 55 to 65 m.p.h. With regard to bridge tolls, the act required that they be "just and reasonable" and removed any federal review and regulation. It provided for seven pilot projects using federal aid funds that were not to exceed 35% of the costs, in conjunction with tolls for new or expanded noninterstate highway toll projects. Up to that time, federal aid highway funds could not be spent on any public highway that had tolls on it, and the tolls had to be removed after the costs were paid off.

An allocation of one-quarter percent of major highway authorizations was set aside for a new cooperative research program directed at highway construction materials, pavements, and procedures. This Strategic Highway Research Program (SHARP) was to be carried out with the cooperation of the National Academy of Sciences and AASHTO.

Title II, the Highway Safety Act of 1987, authorized $795 million over 5 years for safety programs in addition to the $1.75 billion for safety construction programs in the Federal-Aid Highway Act of 1987. It required the identification of those programs that are the most effective in reducing accidents, injuries, and deaths. Only those programs would be eligible for federal aid funds under the Section 402 State and Community Grant program. Safety "standards" that States must meet to comply with this program were redefined as "guidelines."

Title III, the Federal Mass Transportation Act of 1987, authorized $17.8 billion for federal mass transit assistance for fiscal years 1987 through 1991. The act continued the Section 3 Discretionary Grant program at graduated authorization levels of $1.097 billion in FY 1987 rising to $1.2 billion in FY 1991 funded from the Mass Transit Account of the Highway Trust Fund. The program was to be split as 40% for new rail starts and extensions, 40% for rail modernization grants, 10% for major bus projects, and 10% on a discretionary basis.

Grant criteria were established for new fixed guideway systems and extensions. The projects had to be based on alternatives analysis and preliminary engineering, cost effective, and supported by an acceptable degree of local financial commitment. A plan for the expenditure of Section 3 funds was required to be submitted to the Congress annually.

The act authorized $2.0 billion for FY 1987, and $2.1 billion annually for FYs 1988 through 1991 from the General Fund for the Section 9 and 18 Formula Grant programs. The cap on operating assistance for urbanized areas under 200,000 in population was increased by 32.2% starting with FY 1987 with additional increases tied to rises in the Consumer Price Index. It was unchanged from the Surface Transportation Assistance Act of 1982 for larger urbanized. Newly urbanized areas (1980 Census or later) were allowed to use up to two-thirds of their first year Section 9 apportionment for operating assistance. Revenues from advertising and concessions beyond FY 1985 levels no longer had to be included in net project cost.

Unobligated Section 9 funds remaining in the last 90 days of the availability period were allowed to be used by the Governor anywhere in the state. Advanced construction approval was authorized for projects under the Section 3 and 9 programs. The provision permitting three-for-two trade-in of capital assistance for operating assistance was repealed. The definition of eligible associated capital items was broadened to include tires and tubes, and the eligible threshold for such items was reduced from 1% to one-half percent of the fair market value of rolling stock. Section 9 funds were allowed to be used for leasing arrangements if it was more cost effective than acquisition or construction.

A new Section 9B formula grant program was established funded by a portion of the revenues from the Mass Transit Account of the Highway Trust Fund. The program funds, authorized at $575 million over 4 years from 1988 to 1991, were to be apportioned using the Section 9 program formula and could only be used for capital projects. The act also authorized $200 million annually for transit interstate substitute projects.

A bus testing facility was authorized to be established and the testing of all new bus models required. A new University Centers program was authorized for the establishment of regional transportation centers in each of the ten federal regions. The Buy America threshold for rolling stock was increased from 50 to 55% domestic content on 1 October 1989, and to 60% on 1 October 1991. The project cost differential was increased from 10 to 25%.

With regard to planning, the act required development of long-term financial plans for regional urban mass transit improvements and the revenue available from current and potential sources to implement such improvements.

Title IV, the Uniform Relocation Act Amendments of 1987, revised and updated some of the provisions Uniform Relocation Assistance and Real Property Act of 1970. The act generally increased payments for residences and businesses displaced by construction of transportation projects and broadened eligibility for payments under the program. FHWA was designated as the lead federal agency to develop regulations to implement the act.

Title V, the Highway Revenue Act of 1987, extended the Highway Trust Fund to 30 June 1993, and extended taxes and exemptions to 30 September 1993.

National Conferences on Transportation Planning Applications

By the mid-1980s, there was a broader range of issues than ever for urban transportation planners to deal with. State and local planning agencies had to be resourceful in adapting existing planning procedures to fit individual needs. Often planning methods or data had not been available when needed to adequately support planning and project decisions. Compromises between accuracy, practicality, simplifying assumptions, quicker responses, and judgment often resulted in innovative analysis methods and applications.

To share experiences, and highlight new and effective applications of planning techniques, a National Conference on Transportation Planning Applications was held in Orlando, Florida on 20–24 April 1987. The conference was dominated by practicing planners from state and local agencies, and the consulting community who described the application of planning techniques to actual transportation problems and issues (Brown and Weiner, 1987).

The conference surfaced several important issues. First, the realm of urban transportation planning was no longer solely long term at the regional scale. The conference gave equal emphasis to both the corridor and site level scale of planning in addition to the regional level. Many issues at the local level occurred at finer scales, and planners were spending considerably more effort at these scales than at the regional scale. The time horizon too had shifted to short term with many planning agencies concentrating on rehabilitating infrastructure and managing traffic on the existing system.

Second, the microcomputer revolution had arrived. Microcomputers were no longer curiosities but essential tools used by planners. There were many presentations of microcomputer applications of planning techniques at the conference.

Third, with tighter budgets and the increasing demands being placed on them, transportation planning agencies found it increasingly difficult to collect large-scale regional data sets such as home interview, origin–destination surveys. Consequently, there was considerable discussion on approaches to obtain new data at minimal cost. Approaches ranged from expanded use of secondary data sources, such as census data, to small stratified sample surveys, to extended use of traffic counts. However, low-cost approaches to updating land use data bases were not available.

Fourth, there was concern about the quality of demographic and economic forecasts, and their effects on travel demand forecasts. It was observed that errors in demographic and economic forecasts could be more significant than errors in the specification and calibration of the travel demand models. With this in mind, there was discussion about appropriate techniques for demographic forecasting during periods of economic uncertainty.

Fifth, a clear need to develop integrated analysis tools that could bridge between planning and project development was identified. The outputs for regional scale forecasting procedures could not be used directly as inputs for project development but there were no standard procedures or rationales for performing the adjustments. Without standard procedures, each agency had to develop their own approaches to this problem.

This conference demonstrated that there was considerable planning activity at the state and local levels. Much of this activity showed that planning agencies were adapting new ideas to local transportation problems within the constraints of time and money available to them.

The conference was the first in a series that occurred in a 2-year cycle. The series focused on planning applications of traditional techniques adapted for new situations, innovative techniques, and research needs to improve planning practice

(Second Conference on Application of Transportation Planning Methods, 1989; Third National Conference on Transportation Planning Applications, 1991; Faris, 1993; Engelke, 1995).

Smuggler's Notch Conference on Highway Finance

Highway revenue had been increased during the early 1980s with a 4-cent raise in the federal highway user charge by the Surface Transportation Assistance Act of 1982, and by raises in many state user fees. Yet, even with these raises, highway needs were forecasted to increase faster than revenue. With the federal funding commitment defined in legislation to increase modestly, the financial burden for constructing and maintaining the nation's highways would fall more heavily on state and local governments. State and local officials were, therefore, looking for additional funding resources.

In response to this issue, the American Association of State Highway and Transportation Officials sponsored a National Conference on State Highway Finance entitled "Understanding the Highway Finance Evolution/Revolution" at Smuggler's Notch, Vermont, on 16–19 August 1987. The conference was organized to discuss the response to growing highway needs and potential funding sources. Five major funding techniques were addressed user fees, nonuser fees, special benefit fees, private financing, and debt financing (American Association of State Highway and Transportation Officials, 1987a).

The conferees concluded that highway officials would need to develop a clear vision of the public's real need, a thorough understanding of the authorizing environment, and the organizational capacity to implement the plans that were envisioned. Further, it was concluded that user fees remained the most promising and among the most equitable sources of highway funding. Nontraditional funding sources were found to be supplements to, not replacements for, traditional sources.

Moreover, highway programs could be more successful if they were presented as products of a process that combined sound fiscal planning with sound engineering. These programs would, also, be better received if they were related to key policy issues such as economic development and tourism (American Association of State Highway and Transportation Officials, 1987a).

Revised FHWA/UMTA Environmental Regulation

In August 1987, after more than 4 years of work, the FHWA and UMTA published changes to their joint environmental regulation as part of the overall DOT effort to streamline federal regulations and time-consuming procedures. The regulation provided more flexibility to field offices to decide whether projects required comprehensive environmental assessments (US Dept. of Transportation, 1987e).

The new regulation changed the manner in which categorical exclusions were handled. These categories of actions were considered to have no significant environmental impacts. Previously, a project had to fall into one of the specified categorical exclusions to allow a FHWA or UMTA field office to process it without requiring an comprehensive environmental assessment. The new regulation allowed field offices to review projects that meet the criteria for categorical exclusion and determine if a comprehensive environmental assessment was required based on a review of the project documentation.

The new regulation also clarified that a supplemental environmental impact statement (EIS) would only be required for changes in highway or transit projects where those changes would cause additional significant environmental impact, not evaluated in the original EIS.

The regulation clarified and consolidated the requirements for public involvement in the FHWA and UMTA project development processes. With regard to the FHWA requirements, the earlier regulation specified the various elements in an acceptable public involvement process including such items as the procedure for public hearings, content of notices, timing of the process, and those to invite to the public hearings. The revised regulation required the states to develop their own public involvement procedures and eliminated the FHWA requirement for state action plans. These state procedures were to have public involvement integrated into the project development process, and to begin public involvement early and maintain it continuously throughout. The public involvement procedures had to be fully coordinated with the NEPA process and cover such issues as public hearings, information to be presented at hearings, and transcripts of hearings. At least one public hearing was required after the draft EIS (DEIS) was completed and circulated for review. This was also the case for UMTA projects. States were given 1 year after publication of the regulation to develop their procedures.

Other changes were made to update the regulation to bring it into conformance with changes in other areas. This included removing references to A-95 clearinghouse to conform with E.O. 12372 "Intergovernmental Review of Federal Programs," as well as those references to MPOs which were covered under the new joint FHWA/UMTA urban transportation planning regulation.

Los Angeles' Regulation XV

As part of a long-range plan to achieve the National Ambient Air Quality Standards by 2010, the Los Angeles Southern California Air Quality Management District (SCAQMD) issued Regulation XV. Under Regulation XV, each employer of 100 or more employees had to ensure that its workforce achieved a certain "average vehicle ridership" (AVR) for journeys to work which occur between 6:00 a.m. and 10:00 a.m. The AVR was calculated by dividing the number of employees arriving at the work site by the number of autos arriving at the work site during those hours. Regulation XV went into effect on 1 July 1988, and applied to all or part of six counties in Southern California. The regulation affected almost 7,000 firms, agencies, and institutions employing about 3.8 million workers (Giuliano and Wachs, 1991).

The regulation specified a different AVR depending on the location. Central business district employers had to achieve a AVR of 1.75 persons per vehicle while employers in outlying areas had to meet a AVR of 1.3 or 1.5 persons per vehicle. All of the targets were above the existing AVR of 1.1 persons per vehicle. Employers had to submit plans to the SCAQMD for achieving their specified AVR within 1 year using measures such as subsidized ridesharing, free and preferential parking for carpools and vanpools, monthly transit passes, and provision for bicycle parking. At the end of the year, if the company had not implemented the plan it was subject to a fine. If the company had implemented the plan but fell short of the required AVR, it had to revise the plan and implement it the next year. This result was not considered a violation, and a fine was not assessed (Wachs, 1990).

The AVR goal established for the region was quire ambitious, resulting in more than a 20% increase, but the result was more modest. The AVR increased 2.7%, from 1.226 to 1.259 during the first year of the program. The percentage of workers driving to work decreased from 75.8 to 70.9%, with the shift going primarily to carpools.

Chapter 12
The Need for Strategic Planning

By the early 1990s, there were major changes underway that would have significant effects on urban transportation and urban transportation planning. The era of major new highway construction was over in most urban areas. On a selective basis, gaps in the highway system would be closed and a few new routes would be constructed, but the basic highway system was in place. However, the growth in urban travel was continuing unabated. With only limited highway expansion possible new approaches needed to be found to serve this travel demand. Moreover, this growth in traffic congestion was contributing to degradation of the urban environment and urban life and needed to be abated. Previous attempts at the selected application of transportation system management measures (TSM) had proven to have limited impacts on congestion, providing the need for mor comprehensive and integrated strategies. In addition, a number of new technologies were reaching the point of application, including intelligent vehicle highway systems (IVHS) and magnetically levitated trains.

Many transportation agencies entered into strategic management and planning processes to identify the scope and nature of these changes, to develop strategies to address these issues, and to better orient their organization to function in this new environment. They shifted their focus toward longer-term time horizons, more integrated transportation management strategies, wider geographic application of these strategies, and a renewed interest in technological alternatives.

The shortage of financial resources was still a serious concern. In the debate over the reauthorization of the Intermodal Surface Transportation Efficiency Act of 1991, there was considerable discussion over the level of funding, the amount of flexibility in using those funds, and the degree of authority that local agencies would be given in programming the funds.

National Council on Public Works Improvement

Concern for the nation's deteriorating infrastructure prompted the Congress to enact The Public Works Improvement Act of 1984. The act created the National Council on Public Works Improvement to provide an objective and comprehensive overview of the state of the nation's infrastructure. The council carried out a broad research program.

E. Weiner, *Urban Transportation Planning in the United States, Third Edition*, doi:10.1007/978-0-387-77152-6, © Springer Science+Business Media, LLC 2008

The Council's first report provided an overview of available knowledge, explored the definition of needs, and reviewed key issues including the importance of transportation to the economy, management and decision-making practices, technological innovation, government roles, and finance and expenditure trends (National Council on Public Works Improvement, 1986). The second report was a series of study papers assessing the main issues in nine categories of public works facilities and services, including highways and bridges (Pisarski, 1987b), and mass transit (Kirby and Reno, 1987).

The final report of the council concluded that most categories of public works were performing at only passable levels, and that this infrastructure was inadequate to meet the demands of future economic growth and development. Highways were given a grade of C+ with the council concluding that although the decline of pavement conditions had been halted, overall service continued to decline. Spending for system expansion had fallen short of need in high-growth suburban and urban areas, and many highways and bridges still needed to be replaced. Mass transit was graded at C−, and the council concluded that transit productivity had declined significantly, and that is was overcapitalized in many smaller cities and inadequate in large older cities. Mass transit faced increasing difficulty in diverting persons from automobiles, and was rarely linked to land use planning and broader transportation goals (National Council on Public Works Improvement, 1988).

Part of the problem was found to be financial with investment in public works having declined as a percent of the gross national product from 1960 to 1985. The council recommended that all levels of government increase their expenditures by as much as 100%. It endorsed the principle that users and other beneficiaries should pay a greater share of the cost of infrastructure service. The council also recommended clarification of government roles to focus responsibility, improvement in system performance, capital budgeting at all levels of government, incentives to improve maintenance, and more widespread use of low-capital techniques such as demand management and land use planning. The council called for additional support for research and development to accelerate technological innovation, and for training of public works professionals.

Transportation 2020

With the completion of the National Interstate and Defense Highway System provided for in the Surface Transportation and Uniform Relocation Assistance Act of 1987, there was a need for a new focus for the nation's surface transportation program in the postinterstate era. Debates accompanying the passage of the 1982 and 1987 surface transportation acts demonstrated the lack of consensus on future surface transportation legislation which could, potentially, manifest itself in the form of a reduced federal surface transportation program.

To address this concern, AASHTO created the Task Force on the Transportation 2020 Consensus Program in February 1987. The purposes of the task force were to: assess the nation's surface transportation requirements through the year 2020;

develop options for meeting those requirements at the federal, state, and local levels; and achieve a consensus on how to meet those requirements (American Association of State Highway and Transportation Officials, 1987b). The Task Force involved the participation of more than 100 state and local government groups, highway-user organizations, and trade and industry associations.

As a part of the fact-finding stage of the program, 65 public forums were held throughout the USA under the leadership of the Highway Users Federation for Safety and Mobility in cooperation with state transportation agencies to obtain information on transportation needs and problems (Highway Users Federation, 1988).

In addition, a conference on the Long-Range Trends and Requirements for the Nation's Highway and Public Transit Systems was held in June 1988, in Washington, DC (Transportation Research Board, 1988). The conference objective was to identify the nature and level of demand for future highway and public transit services and their future role. The conference addressed economic growth, demographics and life style, energy and environment, development patterns and personal mobility, commercial freight transportation, new technology and communications, and resources and institutional arrangements.

The conference concluded that as the year 2020 approached, there will continue to be modest economic growth; population increases will be concentrated in the nonwhite groups, particularly in the south and west; there will be further decentralization of residences and work places into suburban areas; the automobile will remain the predominant mode of transportation; the reduction in air pollution and energy use will pose a greater challenge; new technologies will not be realized unless there is a concerted effort by the public and private sectors; states and localities will need to play a greater role in funding and planning.

In September 1988, the Transportation 2020 group published The Bottom Line, which summarized their estimates of surface transportation investment requirements through the year 2020 (American Association of State Highway and Transportation Officials, 1988). They reported that $80 billion annually was needed for highways and $15 billion annually was needed for public transportation from all sources, including federal, state, and local governments just to maintain the transportation infrastructure. To maintain the current level of service in the face of increased travel in the future, more than 40% increase over existing funding levels would be required.

To analyze information from the 2020 process and formulate national strategies 12 key associations of Transportation 2020 formed a Transportation Alternatives Group (TAG). The recommendations of TAG were directed toward increasing the level of funding for the preservation and expansion of nation's surface transportation system, greater flexibility, increased emphasis on safety, assurance of equitable cost allocation, greater regulatory uniformity in freight transportation, improvement in air quality, attention to intermodal access, support for intercity and rural public transportation, and renewal of surface transportation research, especially for intelligent vehicle highway systems (Transportation Alternatives Group, 1990). These recommendations were used to develop and consolidate support for a new broad national surface transportation program.

Williamsburg Conference on Transportation and Economic Development

As public funds for transportation investment became more constrained, there was a growing interest in demonstrating the benefit of these investments on economic development. Transportation planners and policy makers sought to justify transportation investment not just as another expenditure but as a factor that would increase economic productivity and international competitiveness. Some research at the macro economic level showed that a strong relationship existed between public capital investment and private sector productivity, profitability, and investment (Aschauer, 1989).

The primary difficulty for transportation planners in addressing this issue was isolating the economic consequences of the transportation investments and comparing them with the consequences of other public and private investments. A further problem was the establishment of causal relationships between specific transportation investments and subsequent economic events.

To address these issues, an international conference on "Transportation and Economic Development," was held in Williamsburg, Virginia, on 5–8 November 1989. The conference focused on evaluating the methods and modeling techniques for relating transportation investment to economic development. A series of case studies was examined to assess this relationship at the state and regional levels (Transportation Research Board, 1990a).

The conference concluded that the primary benefits of a transportation investment accrued to the user in terms of savings in travel time, cost, and accident reduction. Economic impacts measured the secondary benefits that affected income, employment, production, resource consumption, pollution generation, and tax revenues. Existing economic impact models were found to be limited in their ability to duplicate the complex reality of a dynamic economy, lacking in empirical data, and often unreliable in practice.

The conference also concluded that a good transportation system was a necessary but not a sufficient condition for development. The correlation between the level of infrastructure investment and the income found in prior studies had not been shown to be a causal relationship. The conference stressed that there was still a need for research to develop causal-based methodologies.

National Transportation Strategic Planning Study

With the start of the decade of the 1990s fast approaching and a new century not far off, there was concern about the future of the nation's transportation system. The concern was expressed in the House Report on the 1988 DOT Appropriations Report:

> With the scheduled completion of the Interstate highway system in 1992, the growing constraints on expansion of airport capacity, and the projected doubling of traffic by the

year 2000 in many of our large urban areas, the federal government will be faced with major decisions in the early 1990s about its role, responsibility, and choice of options to continue the development and improvement of our future transportation network. The Committee believes it is a major national economic, social, and defense priority to ensure that this country continues to have the best transportation network in the world.

To address these issues, the 1988 Department of Transportation Appropriations Act called for a long-range, multimodal study to the year 2015 for transportation facilities and services to carry persons and goods. The National Transportation Strategic Planning Study (NTSPS) was completed in March 1990 (US Dept. of Transportation, 1990a). It was the first national transportation assessment to be conducted by DOT in 15 years, and the first to analyze all modes of transportation to the same level of detail.

The NTSPS report provided an overview of the Nation's transportation system and identified future investments required to maintain and develop the infrastructure. The report analyzed the trends and key factors expected to influence transportation demand and supply over the next 25–30 years, including demographics, the economy, energy, and the environment. It examined important issues including trends in passenger and freight movements, international comparisons of infrastructure, usage and policies; economic deregulation; safety, security, and accessibility; and new technology.

The report included an analysis of each of the six individual transportation modes: aviation, highway, public transportation, railroads, pipelines and water-borne, and defense transportation. The modes were analyzed in terms of current conditions and performance, forecast future travel demand, funding sources, key issues, and future investment requirements. Finally, the report synthesizes the results of five urban areas studies that were conducted by local planning agencies.

The National Transportation Strategic Planning Study was used as background for and to provide support to A Statement of National Transportation Policy issued by Secretary Samuel K. Skinner in February 1990 (US Dept. of Transportation, 1990b). It was the first comprehensive policy statement issued by DOT in over a decade. In preparing the policy, DOT engaged in an extensive outreach program through public hearings, focus group sessions, seminars with transportation experts, informal discussions, and correspondence. DOT launched the program by issuing an overview of the nation's transportation system and an identification of issues (US Dept. of Transportation, 1989a). A conference was held in Washington, DC, at National Academy of Sciences in July 1989, to open the public debate on national transportation policy (US Dept. of Transportation, 1989b).

At the end of the 1-year process, the policy was published. It set forth new directions for national transportation policy which were grouped under six themes:

1. maintain and expand the Nation's transportation system;
2. foster a sound financial base for transportation;
3. keep the transportation industry strong and competitive;
4. ensure that the transportation system supports public
5. safety and national security;
6. protect the environment and the quality of life;
7. advance US transportation technology and expertise.

The policy also set out the strategies and actions to accomplish the various objectives encompassed by the six themes.

Intelligent Vehicle Highway Systems

As highway congestion grew, with its concomitant air pollution, accidents, and economic losses, new approaches were being sought to improve mobility and alleviate these problems. One approach was the development and application of intelligent vehicle highway systems (IVHS), often referred to as "smart cars" and "smart highways."

IVHS technologies developed from advances in electronics, communications, and information processing. They incorporated advanced communications technology, computers, electronic displays, warning systems, and vehicle/traffic control systems, and allowed for two-way communications between highways and drivers. Although the USA had taken the early lead in the late 1960s and early 1970s in researching these technologies through the programs such as Electronic Route Guidance System (ERGS) and Urban Traffic Control Systems (UTCS), further development lagged in the USA while the Japanese and Europeans mounted aggressive, well-funded research and development programs in the 1980s.

Concerned about the loss of US leadership, the Congress directed the Secretary of Transportation to assess ongoing European, Japanese, and US IVHS research initiatives; analyze the potential impacts of foreign IVHS programs on the introduction of advanced technology for the benefit of US highway users and on US vehicle manufacturers and related industries; and make appropriate legislative and/or programmatic recommendations.

The report, completed in March 1990, described IVHS technologies in terms of advanced traffic management systems, advanced driver information systems, freight and fleet control systems, and automated vehicle control systems (US Dept. of Transportation, 1990c). The report concluded that the use of IVHS technologies had the potential to reduce congestion, promote safety, and improve personal mobility. There would, however, need to be extensive testing to determine which IVHS technologies were most cost effective. US industry and the public would have to become more involved in IVHS or the European and Japanese manufacturers could gain a competitive advantage from their extensive research and development programs.

The report recommended the establishment of a national cooperative effort to foster the development, demonstration, and implementation of IVHS technologies. The federal role would be in the areas of coordination and facilitation of research and development, planning and conducting demonstrations and evaluations, coordination of standards and protocols, and participating in research related to DOT's operating and regulatory responsibilities. Developing and marketing IVHS technologies would be the responsibility of the private sector, and state and local governments would still be responsible for highway operations and traffic management. Parallel development in both the highway infrastructure and the vehicle would be required in order for these technologies to be successful.

In April 1990, a national leadership conference in Orlando, Florida, "Implementing Intelligent Vehicle Highway Systems," brought together senior executives from the private sector. The conference recommended the establishment of a new organization to guide the development and coordination of IVHS activities (Highway Users Federation, 1990). As a result, in July 1990, IVHS America was established by the Highway Users Federation and the American Association of State Highway and Transportation Officials (AASHTO) to bring together private companies, state and local governments, and the research community.

The advent of IVHS technologies had opened a new chapter in surface transportation. IVHS had quickly become an accepted concept and generated wide ranging research and development projects. Demonstrations began in Los Angeles, California, in July 1990, with the Pathfinder project, and the next year in Orlando, Florida, with the TravTek project, both designed to evaluate the usefulness of advanced traffic information systems.

Lawsuit against the Metropolitan Transportation Commission's Travel Models

In June 1989, two environmental organizations, the Sierra Club Legal Defense Fund and the Citizens for a Better Environment, filed lawsuits in the Federal District Court of Northern California claiming that the State of California, the Metropolitan Transportation Commission (MTC) of San Francisco, and other regional agencies had violated the provisions of the Clean Air Act Amendments of 1977 by not doing enough to meet the clean air standards (Garrett and Wachs, 1996).

The subject of the litigation was a nonattainment element included as part of the Bay Area's 1982 SIP for meeting the CO and ozone air quality standards by 1987. That element was to consider delaying any proposed highway projects that would worsen emissions. The case focused on the general issue of the effects of increased highway capacity on reducing transit usage, discouraging infill and densification, increasing highway speeds, inducing highway travel, promoting population growth and economic development, and enabling the spread of urban sprawl, all of which would contribute to greater air pollution emissions (Harvey and Deakin, 1991).

The role of transportation in the SIP was estimated through the air quality and transportation conformity analyses. The transportation plan was required to contribute to meeting the air quality standards by a specified date. The MTC undertook a conventional "state of the practice" analysis to determine the emission impacts of the transportation plan. The environmental groups argued that conventional regional travel forecasting models overstated the emissions benefits of highway investments by fully reflecting speed improvements on reducing emissions but showing little or none of the induced travel resulting from faster times (Harvey and Deakin, 1992).

Table 12.1 shows the possible responses to highway capacity increases argued by the environmental organizations (Stopher, 1991). The environmental organizations argued that the MTC travel models did not take account of all of these travel responses. Consequently, MTC proposed an analysis procedure with feedback to

Table 12.1 Travel responses to highway capacity increases

- *Foregone trips.* Trips that have been foregone because of congestion will now be made. This will result in an absolute increase in numbers of trips using the facility that has been expanded.
- *Peak spreading.* There will be a reduction in peak spreading from people no longer delaying trips or start in early to avoid congestion. This will result in a shift of trips between the traditional off-peak periods to the peak periods and is likely to restore the precapacity increase level of congestion in the peak.
- *Route changes.* Trips that may have used parallel or nearby alternative routes, in order to avoid congestion, may now divert and take the new facility, if the capacity increase boosts travel speeds above those of competing routes.
- *Chained trips.* Trips that have been made part of an existing trip through trip chaining may now be "unchained," effectively adding more trips to the total. In particular, home-to-work trips that may have been used for side trips to shopping, banking, other personal errands, etc., may now be replaced by several "out-and-back" trips from home for the same purposes.
- *Destination changes.* Trips made to nearby, but less-desired locations, may now be made to further-away, more-desired locations leading to an increase in trip lengths and therefore lengthening the distances that are made on the expanded facility.
- *Mode changes.* People who have chosen to use transit or carpools will now return to using solo drive. This will also result in an absolute increase in auto trips on the expanded facility.
- *Auto ownership.* If auto uses increases, auto ownership will eventually exhibit increases, also, provided that the shift away from transit and carpool is maintained.
- *New development.* In the longer term, if congestion levels are lowered for sufficient time, developers can be expected to seek additional development that will increase the number of residents and jobs in the vicinity of the and jobs in the vicinity of the expanded facility.

Source: Stopher, 1991

trip generation, auto ownership, residential location, and employment location. MTC argued that practical models of regional growth as a function of infrastructure investments were not available. The Court accepted the proposed conformity analysis procedure. However, the Judge qualified the decision noting that nothing in his reading of the 1990 Clean Air Act Amendments of 1990 would preclude EPA from requiring a growth analysis in future guidance. In May 1992, after 3 years of effort, the Court ruled that MTC was making reasonable progress in cleaning the region's air. All parties agreed that there were no technical issues remaining (Harvey and Deakin, 1992).

This lawsuit masked a turning point in urban transportation planning and analysis. The dispute centered on the differences of the two sides on the role and purpose of planning. Throughout the 1950s and 1960s, transportation plans were used as a general set of guidelines to assist decision-makers to formulate policy and not always available to the public. More recently, transportation plans were seen as providing guidance for solving specific problems. With extensive public participation, plans were considered to be programs of actions, and in some instances, a "contract" between the various concerned groups and the government. Plans were to respond to changing conditions and binding on those who proposed them (Garrett and Wachs, 1996).

Geographic Information Systems

After years of development, geographic information systems (GIS) were beginning to be used by planning agencies to support analysis and decision-making. GIS was a computerized data management system designed to capture, store, retrieve, analyze, and display spatially referenced data. Databases that were geographically coded were accessible more quickly and cheaper than would otherwise be the case. Moreover, GIS allowed the use of information from different databases that would be too difficult or too expensive to use together had they not been geographically coded. Geographic information systems also facilitated moving between different scales of planning where data had to be aggregated or disaggregated between different zone systems and networks with different levels of detail (Weiner, 1989).

A number of transportation planning agencies made extensive commitments of time and money to develop GIS capability for their urban areas. GIS was used to manage land use, population, and employment data for input to the Urban Transportation Planning System (UTPS) to estimate trip generation rates. GIS was also used to generate plots of output files including volumes, bandwidths, facility types, and other link attributes. In addition, the GIS thematic mapping capabilities were used to analyze and present data from the Census Bureau's Urban Transportation Planning Package (UTPP). GIS capability allowed areas to merge land use data from field surveys with existing databases.

The Census Bureau developed a digital map database that automated the mapping and related geographic activities to support its survey programs. This system, known as Topologically Integrated Geographic Encoding and Reference (TIGER), was available as the base map for a local GIS. In an early demonstration, TIGER, in conjunction with a GIS, was used to produce base maps and data files for transportation planning and analysis. It facilitated the integration of the Census UTPP and local databases. The TIGER file was finally developed for the entire country.

Most states were developing GIS capabilities and applications as well (Vonderohe et al., 1991). Computer software was generally acquired from private vendors. Applications included highway inventories, pavement management, accident analysis, bridge management, project tracking, environmental impact analysis, and executive information systems.

Transit agencies were also adapting GIS to performing their planning functions (Schreiber, 1991). These functions included ridership forecasting, service planning, map design and publishing, facilities management, customer information services, and scheduling and run-cutting. Most transit agencies obtained their software from commercial sources.

The development of GIS capabilities and applications required a major commitment by an entire organization of staff and money. It was an evolving phenomenon with new applications and products continuously being developed (Moyer and Larson, 1991). In addition, computer and information resources were also improving. Nevertheless, GIS expanded the capability of agencies to conduct analyses and support decision-makers.

National Maglev Initiative

As the expense and difficulty in expanding or building new airports and highways in crowded intercity travel corridors grew, other forms of transportation were being considered to relieve congestion and to provide more efficient service. Among these alternatives was the expansion of high-speed rail service in the USA. High-speed passenger rail was already operating in Europe and Japan, and magnetically levitated trains were being actively developed by the Germans and the Japanese.

The earliest involvement of the USA with high-speed rail (defined as traveling 125 m.p.h. or faster) predated the creation of the Department of Transportation. Under the High Speed Ground Transportation Act of 1965, the Federal Railroad Administration (FRA) ran a research program in high-speed ground transportation and a demonstration program involving the Metroliner and Turbo Train. The demonstrations showed that improved railroad trip times between cities in the Boston–Washington Corridor would attract passengers to the railroad.

Under the same act, the department undertook a planning program to determine the best form of transportation to emphasize for passenger movement in the Northeast Corridor. This eventually led to the Northeast Corridor Improvement Project in 1976, which invested over $2.3 billion in improved rail transportation. That project resulted in 2-h and 30-min, 125-m.p.h. Metroliner service from Washington to New York.

In the 1970s, the department's research and development program funded studies of two types of maglev vehicles with the intention of selecting the most desirable system for testing. FRA's Office High Speed Ground Transportation expended over $2.3 million on maglev research between 1971 and 1976. Much of the research was done through contracts with Ford Motor Company, The Stanford Research Institute, and the Mitre Corporation. In 1974, a prototype linear induction motor research vehicle produced from this research set a world speed record of 255 m.p.h. By the time that the program was terminated in 1976, the research had produced a scale model demonstration (US Dept. of Transportation, 1990d).

Following the termination of US government-funded research, companies in Japan and Germany continued the development of maglev systems with substantial support from their governments. In the USA, private industry virtually abandoned its interest in high-speed maglev systems. However, UMTA supported research on low-speed urban maglev systems with Boeing Company until 1986.

During the 1980s, through its emerging corridors program, FRA funded market feasibility studies for the development of high-speed rail systems in several dense corridors. Under this program, grants for ten corridor studies were made totaling $3.8 million. Then, after years of little interest or activity in magnetic levitation technology, the National Maglev Initiative (NMI) was launched in January 1990, to assess the potential of maglev transportation in the USA. This initiative was a joint undertaking of FRA, the US Army Corps of Engineers, and the Department of Energy in partnership with the private sector and state governments. The goal of the cooperative effort was to improve intercity transportation in the twenty-first century through the development and implementation of commercially viable, advanced maglev systems.

The NMI included a review of the safety, engineering, economic, and environmental aspects of maglev systems. Projects under the NMI analyzed maglev subsystems and components to improve performance, reduce costs, and lower risks. System concept development projects evaluated new approaches for maglev that could be used as the basis for an advanced maglev system.

A preliminary assessment of the potential for maglev implementation in the USA concluded that as many as 2,600 route-miles might be economically feasible, depending on the assumptions used (US Dept. of Transportation, 1990d) (Fig. 12.1). This assessment of financial feasibility would be refined as the NMI developed additional information and the analyses became more sophisticated.

In November 1990, the TRB completed a Study of High-Speed Transportation in High-Density Corridors in the United States (Transportation Research Board, 1990b). The study assessed the applicability of a wide range of technology options for serving the major high-density travel corridors in the USA over the intermediate to long term. The study concluded that there were a number of available high-speed rail technologies that could operate at speeds up to 200 m.p.h., and that systems under development would be able to exceed this speed. Higher speed, however, would come at an additional cost and energy penalties.

The major cost of these systems was in the acquisition of the right of way and construction of the guideway, stations, and supporting structures. The most important factor in determining financial viability of these systems, whether public or private, was ridership. The primary market for these systems was in the 150–500-mile trip range and in competition with air travel. It was unlikely that any US corridor could support a high-speed rail system to the degree that it would cover capital and operating costs. Furthermore, there were no institutional arrangements to support the development of high-speed rail systems in the USA.

The TRB report recommended that maglev offered a better research opportunity because of its potential for higher speeds and lower costs than conventional technology. Further research under the NMI should be conducted and the results reviewed to determine the need for additional research and development.

Clean Air Act Amendments of 1990

In the years after the passage of the Clean Air Act Amendments of 1970, considerable progress was made in reducing air pollution in the nation's urban areas. Average automobile emissions dropped from 85 g per mile of carbon monoxide (CO) in 1970 to 25 g per mile in 1988. Lead usage in gasoline dropped by 99% between 1975 and 1988. From 1978 to 1988, transportation-related emissions decreased 38% for CO, 36% for hydrocarbons, and 15% for nitrogen oxides (NOX). The reduction occurred despite a 24% increase in vehicle miles of travel during the same period. Nevertheless, by 1988, 101 urban areas failed to meet

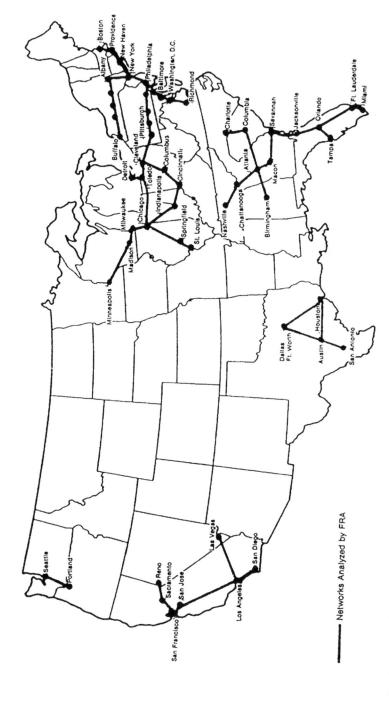

Fig. 12.1 Potential maglev corridors (Source: US Dept. of Transportation, 1990d)

national ambient air quality standards (NAAQS) for ozone, and 44 areas failed to meet the NAAQS for CO (US Dept. of Transportation, 1990a).

In June 1989, President Bush proposed major revisions to the Clean Air Act. In the Congress, the bill was extensively debated and revised before it was passed. On 15 November 1990, the President signed the Clean Air Act Amendments of 1990.

Of the 11 titles in the act, 2 in particular directly pertained to transportation. Title 1 addressed the attainment and maintenance of NAAQS. Nonattainment areas were classified for ozone, CO, and particulate matter in accordance with the severity of the air pollution problem. Depending upon the degree to which an area exceeded the standard, that area was required to implement various control programs and to achieve attainment of the NAAQS within a specified period of time. The areas that were farthest out of compliance were given the longest length of time to achieve the standards (Table 12.2).

Those urban areas that were classified as "Non-attainment areas" had to undertake a series of transportation actions that accumulated with the degree of severity. Urban areas classified as "marginal" for ozone compliance had to complete an emissions inventory within 2 years of enactment and every 3 years thereafter. In addition, these areas had to correct their existing inspection/maintenance (I/M) programs. "Moderate" areas had to submit revised State Implementation Plans (SIPs) that reduced volatile organic compounds (VOC) emissions by 15% from 1990 baseline emissions over the 6 years following enactment. In addition to the 15% reduction, emissions arising from growth in VMT had to be offset. Reductions from other federal programs including tailpipe emission standards, evaporative controls, and fuel volatility could not be credited toward the 15% reduction. These areas also had to adopt a basic I/M program (Hawthorn, 1991).

"Serious" areas, in addition to meeting the requirements for moderate areas, had to show "reasonable further progress." These areas had to submit SIP revisions

Table 12.2 Classification of areas under the clean air act amendments of 1990

Class	No. of areas	Attainment date	Transportation provisions
Ozone (NAAQS = .12 parts per million)			
Marginal	39	3 years	Emissions inventory
Moderate	32	6 years	Emissions reduction of 15% in 6 years (2.5% per year)
Serious	16	9 years	After 6 years, 3% per year. VMT reduction
Severe	7	15 years	After 2 years, TCMs to offset travel growth and employer trip reductions
Extreme	1	20 years	Possible heavy-duty vehicle restrictions
Carbon monoxide (NAAQS = 9 parts per million)			
Moderate	38	31 December 1995	VMT forecasts in SIPs and automatic contingency measures
Serious	3	31 December 2000	After 2 years, TCMs to offset travel growth, oxygenated fuel, and economic disincentives

Source: US Environmental Protection Agency, 1990

within 4 years of enactment that included all feasible measures to achieve VOC emission reductions of 3% annually for each consecutive 3-year period beginning 6 years after enactment. For areas with 1980 populations of 250,000 or more, a clean-fuel program had to be established, which required fleets of 10 vehicles or more to use nonpolluting fuels. Areas exceeding 200,000 in population had to adopt an enhanced I/M program within 2 years of enactment. After 6 years, and for each third year after that, areas had to demonstrate that vehicle emissions, congestion levels, VMT, and other relevant parameters were consistent with those used in the SIP. If not, an SIP revision was required within 18 months that included transportation control measures (TCMs) to reduce emission levels consistent with the levels forecasted in the SIP (US Environmental Protection Agency, 1990).

Urban areas that were classified as "severe" had to meet the requirements for "serious" areas and also submit SIP revisions within 2 years of enactment, which identified and adopted TCMs to offset the growth in emission and the growth in trips or VMT. This offset was, in addition to the 2.5% annual reduction, required for "moderate" areas. The SIP had to include a requirement for employers of 100 or more to increase average work trip passenger occupancy by not less than 25% above the average for all work trips in the area. Employers had to submit compliance plans within 2 years of SIP submission demonstrating compliance 4 years after submittal of the SIP.

"Extreme" areas, those which exceeded the standard by more than 133%, had to meet the requirements for "severe" areas. In addition, the SIP could contain measures to reduce high-polluting or heavy-duty vehicles during peak traffic hours.

Similar provisions were established for the two categories of CO nonattainment areas. Areas classified as "moderate" had to submit an emissions inventory within 2 years of enactment and every 3 years thereafter. For some areas, fuel with a 2.7% oxygen content was required during winter months. Within 2 years of enactment, moderate CO areas had to revise their SIPs to contain VMT forecasts until attainment using EPA guidance for the forecasting. Some of these areas had to adopt an enhanced I/M program within 2 years of enactment. For the most severe of the moderate areas with 1980 populations of 250,000 or more, a clean-fuel program had to be established, which required fleets of 10 vehicles or more to use nonpolluting fuels. All SIP revisions had to include contingency measures to be automatically implemented if VMT levels exceed projections or if attainment by the deadline was missed.

In addition to meeting the requirements for moderate areas, "serious" CO areas had to submit SIP revisions within 2 years of enactment that included TCMs to reduce CO emissions and offset emission increases from VMT growth and the seasonal use of oxygenated fuel. The oxygen content of the fuel had to be sufficient in combination with other measures to provide for the attainment of the CO standard by the applicable date. If the area failed to meet the standard, a program of TCMs and economic incentives had to be implemented.

The "conformity" provisions in the 1990 act were expanded from the Clean Air Act Amendments of 1977. A conformity determination was required to assure that federally approved or financially assisted projects or actions conform to a SIP. The 1990 provisions shifted the emphasis from conforming to a SIP to conforming to a

SIP's purpose of eliminating and reducing the severity and number of violations of the NAAQS and achieving expeditious attainment of the standards. In addition, no activity could cause or contribute to new NAAQS violations, nor increase the frequency or severity of any existing violations of any standard, nor delay the timely attainment of any required NAAQS. The new provisions still required the DOT and MPOs to make conformity determinations but they were to be much more dependent on quantitative analyses (Shrouds, 1991).

The process recognized that transportation-related air quality issues had to be analyzed on a system-wide basis and be controlled through regional strategies to be effective. Consequently, projects had to be analyzed in the aggregate rather than on a project basis as previously required. At the project level, three conditions had to be met in order to make a conformity determination. One was that the project came from a conforming plan and program. The second was that the design concept and scope of the project had not changed once the plan and program were found to conform. Third was that the design concept and scope of the project at the time of the conformity determination for the program was adequate to determine emissions. If the project had changed, it had to be reanalyzed with the other projects in the conforming plan and program to determine that it would not increase emissions or otherwise interfere with meeting the deadlines (Shrouds, 1991).

The Clean Air Act Amendments of 1990 expanded the "sanctions" where states failed to carry out requirements of the act. Previously, sanctions were only applied for failing to submit a SIP. Under the new provisions, sanctions could additionally be triggered when EPA disapproved a SIP or a state or MPO failed to implement any SIP provision. Moreover, sanctions could be imposed for failures unrelated to transportation or mobile sources, for example, for failures related to stationary sources.

Under the 1990 provisions, there were two mandatory sanctions. They were withholding approval of federal-aid highway projects and a two-for-one emissions offset for new or modified stationary sources. Areas had 18 months to correct the deficiency before the sanctions took effect. Previously, sanctions could only be applied to the nonattainment area. The 1990 provisions expanded the application of sanctions to any portion of the state that EPA determined reasonable and appropriate. The 1990 act also expanded the list of projects that were exempt from the sanctions. These project types included safety demonstrations, transit capital, HOV lanes and other HOV incentives, traffic flow improvements which would reduce emissions, fringe parking, single occupant vehicle disincentives including pricing, and incident management.

The planning procedures of the 1990 act required state and local agencies to review and update, if necessary, the SIP planning, implementation, enforcement, and funding responsibilities. It also required the certification of the Lead Planning Organization (LPO) to prepare the SIP, which was to include local elected officials, representatives of the state and local air agency, MPO, and state DOT. The 1990 act expanded the boundaries for nonattainment areas to the metropolitan statistical area (MSA), unless the governor requested the exclusion of certain unaffected portions.

The 1990 act called for the development of implementation guidance on various aspects of the process. EPA, in consultation with DOT, was to issue guidance for forecasting VMT within 6 months of enactment. Transportation planning guidance was to be issued within 9 months by EPA in consultation with DOT and state and local officials. EPA, with concurrence of DOT, was to issue criteria and procedures for conformity determinations within 12 months of enactment. Also, within 12 months of enactment, EPA was to issue guidance on the formulation and emission reduction potential of 16 TCMs including public transit, trip reduction ordinances, HOV lanes, and traffic flow improvements.

Title 2 of the Clean Air Act Amendments of 1990 contained provisions related to mobile sources. The act set more stringent emission standards for automobiles and light duty trucks to be met between model years 1996 and 2003; beginning with 40% of vehicles in 1994 and increasing to 100% by 1998. An additional 50% reduction was to be required after 2003 if EPA found that it was necessary and technologically feasible. Emission control equipment need to be warranted for 10 years and 100,000 miles.

A pilot program was set up for the sale of clean fuel vehicles in California. Other cities could opt-in to the program. The act also required government and private fleets in polluted areas to purchase 30% of the vehicles to be clean fueled. The act required the sale of "reformulated gasoline" with specified oxygen content in the nine cities with the most severe ozone problems. It also required the sale of gasoline with higher oxygen content to reduce winter CO pollution. As of 1 January 1996, lead was banned from use in motor fuel.

Particulate matter standards for buses were set at .10 g per brake horsepower hour in model year 1993. EPA was directed to set bus emission standards and could by regulation require the purchase of alternate fueled buses in urban areas over 750,000 population.

The Clean Air Act Amendments of 1990 created a major challenge to transportation planners to continue to provide urban mobility while meeting the requirements to improve air quality under tight time deadlines.

Strategic Planning and Management

Planning in many transportation agencies evolved through the 1970s from a long-range multiyear process directed at developing projects for implementation to attempts that considered possible future events and planned strategically to influence them. A 1983 review of strategic planning in transportation agencies found that some form of strategic planning existed in a few state transportation and port authority organizations (Meyer, 1983). The main problem with these early efforts was that there was little connection between these plans and the day-to-day operations of the agency. Consequently, few of these strategic plans were implemented (Tyndall et al., 1990).

In 1982, the Pennsylvania Department of Transportation began a process that marked a fundamental change in strategic planning, which became known as "strategic management." The department established an iterative process that linked its strategic planning to day-to-day management and operations as a means to deal effectively with the continually changing internal and external environments in which they had to function.

An NCHRP project, "Strategic Planning and Management Guidelines for Transportation Agencies," reviewed the status of strategic planning in transportation agencies and developed guidelines for successfully institutionalizing it (Tyndall et al., 1990). The project found 25 transportation agencies nation wide that were actively engaged in some form of strategic planning and management. It also found that many other agencies had little interest in or understanding of strategic management and focused instead on day-to-day operations that they deemed more important.

Although there was no consensus on the definition of strategic management, an operating definition was adopted for the project. "Strategic management is an interactive and ongoing process consisting minimally of the following fundamental components: mission statement (including goals and objectives), environmental scan, strategy development, action plan development, resource allocation, and performance measurement" (Tyndall et al., 1990).

The project developed guidelines for transportation agencies to evolve their current management system into a strategic management system. It recognized that there were many approaches to effective strategic management. The essential ingredients were a future vision, involvement of all managers, top-level commitment, integration of existing management systems and processes, and focused planning of activities.

Strategic planning and management was gradually adopted by more transportation agencies in coming to grips with the many changes that they faced and to improve their organization's effectiveness.

Americans with Disabilities Act of 1990

The Americans With Disabilities Act (ADA) was signed by President Bush in July 1990, after passage by the Congress with an overwhelming majority. The ADA prohibited discrimination on the basis of disability in both the public and the private sectors. Its primary purpose was to make it easier for persons with disabilities to become part of the American mainstream.

In April 1991, DOT issued a proposed regulation to implement the ADA. The new regulation incorporated and amended those regulation governing Section 504 of the Rehabilitation Act of 1973. The new regulation applied to all providers whether they received federal funds or not, whereas the earlier regulation only applied to federal fund recipients. The Department of Transportation had previously issued a regulation on 4 October 1990, which required transit authorities to only buy or lease accessible transit vehicles. A plan to implement the new regulation had to be submitted by 26 January 1992, and implemented by 26 July 1992, 1 year after the ADA was signed into law (US Dept. of Transportation, 1991a).

A major feature of the new regulation was the requirement that any operator of a fixed route transit system provide paratransit or other special services to persons with disabilities. The paratransit service had to be comparable to the level of service provided to individuals without disabilities who use the fixed route system.

The regulation required that the paratransit services be provided to all origins and destinations within a corridor of a given width on each side of any fixed transit route. The service area width varied depending upon the population density. The service had to be operated the same days and hours as the fixed route service. A 24-h advanced reservation system was required where service had to be provided if requested on the previous day. The fare had to be comparable with the base fare of the fixed route service. Each transit system had to establish a system to determine eligibility for the new paratransit service. A waiver provision was included if the transit system could demonstrate that providing full-blown paratransit service would cause an undue financial burden. The system was still required to provide service to the extent that it could.

Under the regulation, transit systems with inaccessible commuter, rapid and light rail stations would be required to identify "key" stations, following a public participation process, and make them accessible to persons with disabilities within 3 years. "Key" stations were those with high volumes, transfer points, ends of lines, and stations that served major activity centers. Some extensions were available for "key" stations, up to 20–30 years, as long as certain progress was made in making other stations accessible.

The regulation also incorporated the proposed standards by the Architectural and Transportation Compliance Board for accessible vehicles and facilities, issued in April 1990.

DOT estimated the average annual cost for providing paratransit service. These costs ranged from $28.7 million for the ten largest urban areas, $10 million for other areas over 1 million in population, to $750,000 for areas under 250,000 in population. DOT indicated that there would not be additional federal funds to implement this regulation.

Intermodal Surface Transportation Efficiency Act of 1991

With the completion of the National Interstate and Defense Highway System provided for in the Surface Transportation Assistance Act of 1982, the debate on the reauthorization of the surface transportation legislation focused on the nature and size of the postinterstate program. Clearly, the shortage of financial resources was still a serious concern, as well as the issues of an increase in the federal gas tax, the level of funding for the program, the amount of flexibility in using those funds for other than highway purposes, the federal matching share, and the degree of authority that local agencies would be given in programming the funds. Other issues were also in dispute relating to the continuance of federal transit operating assistance, criteria for new rail transit systems, and the earmarking of funds for specific highway and transit projects.

The bill that was finally signed into law by President Bush on 18 December 1991, opened a new era in surface transportation. The Intermodal Surface Transportation Efficiency Act of 1991 (ISTEA) authorized $151 billion over 6 years for highways, mass transit, and safety programs (Table 12.3). In a major

Table 12.3 Intermodal surface transportation efficiency act of 1991. Authorization levels by fiscal year ($ millions)

	1992	1993	1994	1995	1996	1997	Total
Surface Transportation							
NHS	3,003	3,599	3,599	3,599	3,600	3,600	21,000
Construction	1,800	1,800	1,800	1,800	0	0	7,200
Maintenance	2,431	2,913	2,914	2,914	2,914	2,914	17,000
Substitutions	240	240	240	240	0	0	960
STP	3,418	4,096	4,096	4,096	4,097	4,097	23,900
Bridge replacement and rehabilitation	2,288	2,762	2,762	2,762	2,763	2,763	16,100
Demo projects	543	1,225	1,159	1,101	1,101	1,101	6,230
Congestion and air quality	858	1,028	1,028	1,028	1,029	1,029	6,000
Other programs	1,875	761	816	801	828	828	5,910
Equity adjust	2,236	2,055	2,055	2,055	4,055	4,055	16,512
Subtotal	18,692	20,479	20,469	20,396	20,387	20,389	120,812
Highway safety							
State/community	126	171	171	171	171	171	981
Safety R&D	44	44	44	44	44	44	264
Traffic and vehicle safety	69	71	74	77	0	0	291
Other programs	39	11	11	11	4	4	80
Subtotal	278	297	300	303	219	219	1,616
Mass transit							
Discretionary	1,342	2,030	2,050	2,050	2,050	2,900	12,422
Formula	1,823	2,604	2,643	2,643	2,643	3,741	16,096
Rural	106	152	154	154	154	218	937
Substitutions	160	165	0	0	0	0	325
Elderly and disabled	55	70	69	69	69	97	428
Plan and research	120	164	161	161	161	224	987
Administration	37	50	49	49	49	70	304
Subtotal	3,643	5,235	5,125	5,125	5,125	7,250	31,499
Motor carrier safety							
Safety grants	65	76	80	83	85	90	479
Safety functions	49	0	0	0	0	0	49
Other	7	1	1	0	0	0	9
Subtotal	121	77	81	83	85	90	537
Research							
BTS	5	10	15	15	20	25	90
Bus testing	4	0	0	0	0	0	4
University centers	5	6	6	6	6	6	35
Research institutes	11	9	9	6	6	6	47
IVHS	94	113	113	113	113	113	659
Subtotal	119	138	143	140	145	150	836
Total	22,850	26,226	26,118	26,047	25,961	28,098	155,300

Source: US Dept. of Transportation, 1991b

breakthrough, the act created a surface transportation program with flexible funding that opened the door to new opportunities to address state-wide and urban transportation problems (US Dept. of Transportation, 1991b).

The purpose of the act was set forth in its statement of policy:

It is the policy of the United States to develop a National Intermodal Transportation System that is economically efficient and environmentally sound, provides the foundation for the Nation to compete in the global economy, and will move people and goods in an energy efficient manner.

Title I, Surface Transportation, established a new National Highway System (NHS) consisting of 155,000 miles (plus or minus 15%) of Interstate highways, urban and rural principal arterials, and other strategic highways. The final system was to be proposed by the by the Department of Transportation, after consultation with the states, and be designated by law by 30 September 1995. In the interim, the NHS was to consist of highways classified as principal highways. The NHS was funded at $21 billion over 6 years at a 80% federal matching share. States could transfer up to 50% of their funds to the Surface Transportation Program, and up to 100% in states with nonattainment areas with approval of the US Department of Transportation.

The interstate system retained its identity even though it became part of the NHS. It was renamed the "Dwight D. Eisenhower National System of Interstate and Defense Highways." Funding was provided for completion of the remaining links and for continuation of the interstate maintenance and interstate transfer programs. ISTEA created a new block grant program, the Surface Transportation Program (STP), which made funds available for a broad range of highway, mass transit, safety, and environmental purposes. STP funds could be used for highway construction and 4R; bridge projects; transit capital projects; carpool, parking, bicycle, and pedestrian facilities; highway and transit safety improvements; traffic monitoring, management, and control facilities; transportation control measures; and wetland mitigation efforts.

The STP was authorized at $23.9 billion over 6 years at a 80% federal matching share. Additional funds could be transferred to the program from the so-called equity adjustments. Each state was required to set aside 10% of the funds for safety construction activities and another 10% for transportation enhancements, which included bicycle and pedestrian facilities; acquisition of scenic easements or scenic or historic sites; landscaping and beautification; preservation or rehabilitation of historic sites; preservation of abandoned rail corridors including conversion to bicycle or pedestrian trails; control of outdoor advertising; archaeological research; and mitigation of water pollution from highway runoff. The remaining 80% had to be allocated state wide, as shown in Fig. 12.2. (US Dept. of Transportation, 1992a).

The Bridge Replacement and Rehabilitation program was continued with minor changes. Up to 40% of a State's funds could be transferred to the NHS or STP. In addition, 539 special projects were Congressionally designated at a total cost of $6.2 billion.

A new Congestion Mitigation and Air Quality Improvement Program was established, with a 80% federal matching rate, for transportation projects in ozone and carbon monoxide nonattainment areas. These projects must contribute to an area meeting the NAAQS. If a state does not have any of these areas, it could use the

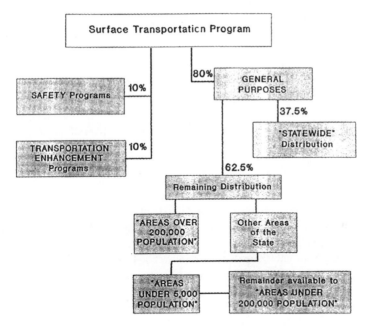

Fig. 12.2 Allocation of surface transportation funds (Source: US Dept. of Transportation, 1992a)

funds as if they were STP funds. The funds were to be distributed based on each state's share of population in nonattainment areas weighted by the degree of air pollution. A minimum apportionment of 1/2 percent was guaranteed to each state.

The were a number of equity adjustment provisions in the ISTEA that were designed to achieve equity in funding levels among the states.

The 90 Percent Minimum Allocation and Donor State Bonus addressed equity between contributions to the Highway Trust Fund and allocations for major program categories. A sum of $2 billion annually was set aside to reimburse states for highway segments constructed with state funds that were later incorporated into the interstate system. Another equity account was established to ensure that annual state shares would not be reduced from prior year amounts. The 90% of payment guarantees assured that states would receive 90% of their contributions to the Highway Trust Fund for all highway programs except special projects.

Special projects and programs were created is several areas. The National Magnetic Levitation Prototype Development Program was authorized at $725 million to develop a prototype maglev system selected from applicants from across the nation. A Maglev Project Office was to be established jointly between the Department of Transportation and Cops of Engineers. A separately funded $25 million High Speed Ground Technology Development Program was created to demonstrate and promote new high-speed ground technologies already under construction or in operation. Another provision of the act allowed the use of federal aid highway rights of way for commuter or high-speed rail, maglev systems, and mass transit facilities, where there was sufficient land or space and that would not adversely affect automobile safety.

Tolls were permitted on federal aid highway facilities to a much greater degree than that in the past. Projects that would become eligible for federal funding was expanded to include initial construction of toll facilities, 4R work on toll facilities, and reconstruction or replacement of free highways (except interstate facilities), bridges and tunnels, and conversion to toll facilities. The federal matching share for highway projects was 50% and 50 or 80% for bridges and tunnels depending on the nature of the work.

A Congestion Pricing Pilot Program was established for five congestion pricing pilot projects with up to three of them on interstate highways. The program was funded at $25 million annually with a 50% federal matching share. In addition, the ISTEA created a program to fund state planning, design, and development activities of Scenic Byways.

The Symms National Recreational Trails Act of 1991, in Title IB, provided $180 million over 6 years for the creation and maintenance of recreational trails for motorized and nonmotorized vehicles. A new trust fund was created in Title VIII to finance the program, drawing 0.3% of the revenues to the Highway Trust Fund. Funds were to be allocated to the states based in part on the amount of nonhighway recreational fuel used and could be used for land acquisition, construction, maintenance, restoration, and education.

ISTEA strengthened the metropolitan planning process and expanded the role of MPOs in project selection and transportation decision-making. MPOs continued to be required in all urbanized areas with population of 50,000 or greater. Existing MPO designations remained valid unless revoked by the governor and local units of government representing 75% of the affected population in the metropolitan area or as otherwise provided under state or local procedures. New MPO designations or redesignations could be made by agreement between the governor and local units of government representing 75% of the affected population in the metropolitan area or in accordance with applicable state or local law. More than one MPO could be designated for an urbanized area if the governor determines that the size and complexity of the area warrant it. Where more than one MPO existed in an urban area, they were to consult with each other and the state to coordinate plans and programs (Highway Users Federation, 1991).

Metropolitan area boundaries were defined for carrying out the metropolitan transportation planning process and for expenditure of STP funds suballocated to areas over 200,000 in population. The boundaries were to be established by agreement between the governor and the MPO, and were to encompass the current urbanized area and the area to be urbanized during a 20-year forecast period, and could extend to the MSA or CMSA boundary. In nonattainment areas, the boundary had to encompass the nonattainment area unless the MPO and the governor decided to exclude a portion.

Large urbanized areas over 200,000 in population were designated as transportation management areas (TMAs). These areas had additional requirements related to congestion management, project selection, and certification. The governor and MPOs could request additional designations as TMAs.

Each metropolitan area had to prepare a long-range plan, updated periodically, which identified transportation facilities that functioned as an integrated transportation system, including a financial plan, assess capital investment, and other measures to preserve the existing transportation system, and make the most efficient use of existing transportation facilities to relieve congestion, and indicated appropriate enhancement activities. A reasonable opportunity for public comment was required before the long-range plan was approved. In nonattainment areas, development of the long-range plan had to be coordinated with the development of transportation control measures for the state implementation plan required under the Clean Air Act.

ISTEA required MPO's to include consideration of 15 interrelated factors in the development of their 20-year metropolitan transportation plan (Table 12.4). One important factor was the effect of transportation decisions on land use and development and consistency with land use and development plans. Abbreviated planning procedures could be prescribed for areas not designated as TMAs based on the complexity of the transportation problems, however, not in nonattainment areas for ozone and carbon monoxide.

Table 12.4 Metropolitan transportation planning factors

1. Preservation of existing transportation facilities and, where practical, ways to meet transportation needs by using existing transportation facilities more efficiently
2. The consistency of transportation planning with applicable federal, state, and local energy conservation programs, goals, and objectives
3. The need to relieve congestion and prevent congestion from occurring where it has not yet occurred
4. The likely effect of transportation policy decisions on land use and development and the consistency of transportation plans and programs with the provisions of all applicable short- and long-term land use and development plans
5. The programming of expenditures on transportation enhancement activities as required in Section 133
6. The effects of all transportation projects to be undertaken in the metropolitan area, without regard to whether such projects are publicly funded
7. International border crossings and access to ports, airports, intermodal transportation facilities, major freight distribution routes, national parks, recreation areas, monuments, historic sites, and military installations
8. The need for connectivity of roads within the metropolitan area with roads outside the metropolitan area
9. The transportation needs identified through use of the management systems required by Section 303 of this title
10. Preservation of rights-of-way for construction of future transportation projects, including identification of unused rights-of-way that may be needed for future transportation corridors and identification of those corridors for which action is most needed to prevent destruction or loss
11. Methods to enhance the efficient movement of freight
12. The use of life-cycle costs in the design and engineering of bridges, tunnels, or pavement
13. Methods to expand and enhance transit services and to increase the use of such services

14. Capital investments that would result in increased security in transit systems

Source: US Dept. of Transportation, 1992a

In TMAs, the transportation planning process had to include a congestion management system (CMS) for the effective management of new and existing transportation facilities through the use of travel demand reduction and operational strategies.

A Transportation Improvement Program (TIP) was required to be developed by the MPO in cooperation with the state and transit operators. The TIP has to be updated at least every 2 years and approved by the MPO and the governor, with a reasonable opportunity for public comment prior to approval. The TIP had to include a priority list of projects and a financial plan consistent with the funding that could be reasonably be expected to be available.

In TMAs, all projects, except those on the NHS, and projects under the Bridge and I-maintenance programs, were to be selected by the MPO in consultation with the state from the approved TIP in accordance with the priorities established in the TIP. The other projects were to be selected by the state in cooperation with the MPO from the approved TIP. In all other metropolitan areas, projects were to be selected by the state in cooperation with the MPO from the approved TIP.

Federal certification of the transportation planning process was required for TMAs at least every 3 years. TMAs that were not certified were subject to funding sanctions. One percent of highway funds, except those for Interstate construction and substitution, were authorized for metropolitan transportation planning (PL). Additional funds could be spent from the NHS and STP programs. States were required to develop formulas for distributing PL funds using, based on population, status of planning, and metropolitan transportation needs, attainment of air quality standards and other factors necessary to carry out applicable federal laws.

ISTEA created a new requirement for states to undertake a continuous state-wide transportation planning process modeled on the metropolitan transportation planning process. States were required to develop a long-range plan covering all modes of transportation, coordinated with the transportation planning carried out in metropolitan areas, with opportunity for public comment. The state plans and programs were to provide for the development of transportation facilities that functioned as an intermodal state transportation system. Twenty factors were specified to be considered in the process (Table 12.5).

A state-wide transportation improvement program (STIP) was required to be developed and federally approved at least every 2 years. The STIP was to be consistent with the long-range state-wide and metropolitan transportation plans and expected funding, and there had to be opportunity for public comment. In nonattainment areas, the STIP had to conform to the SIP. Two percent of federal aid highway funds were made available for planning and research programs. Not less that 25% of these funds had to be used for research, development, and technology transfer activities, unless the state certified that planning expenditures would exceed 75% of the funds. State-wide planning activities were also eligible under the NHS and STP programs.

One of the factors that had to be considered in both the metropolitan and state-wide planning processes was the results of the management systems. This refers to the requirement that states and metropolitan areas develop, establish, and implement

Table 12.5 State-wide transportation planning factors

1. The transportation needs identified through the management systems
2. Any federal, state, or local energy use goals, objectives, programs, or requirements
3. Strategies for incorporating bicycle transportation facilities and pedestrian walkways in appropriate projects throughout the state
4. International border crossings and access to ports, airports, intermodal transportation facilities, major freight distribution routes, national parks, recreation and scenic areas, monuments and historic sites, and military installations
5. The transportation needs of nonmetropolitan areas through a process that includes consultation with local elected officials with jurisdiction over transportation
6. Any metropolitan area plan developed pursuant to 23 U.S.C. 134 and Section 8 of the Federal Transit Act, 49 U.S.C
7. Connectivity between metropolitan planning areas within the state and with metropolitan planning areas in other states
8. Recreational travel and tourism
9. Any state plan developed pursuant to the Federal Water Pollution Control Act
10. Transportation system management and investment strategies designed to make the most efficient use of existing transportation facilities
11. The overall social, economic, energy, and environmental effects of transportation decisions (including housing and community development effects and effects on the human, natural, and manmade environments)
12. Methods to reduce traffic congestion including methods that reduce motor vehicle travel, particularly single-occupant motor vehicle travel
13. Methods to expand and enhance appropriate transit services and to increase the use of such services
14. The effect of transportation decisions on land use and land development, including the need for consistency between transportation decision-making and the provisions of all applicable short-range and long-range land use and development plans
15. Strategies for identifying and implementing transportation enhancements where appropriate throughout the state
16. The use of innovative mechanisms for financing projects, including value capture pricing, tolls, and congestion pricing
17. Preservation of rights-of-way for construction of future transportation projects
18. Long-range needs of the state transportation system for movement of persons and goods
19. Methods to enhance the efficient movement of commercial motor vehicles
20. The use of life-cycle costs in the design and engineering of bridges, tunnels, or pavements

Source: US Dept. of Transportation, 1992a

six management systems for highway pavement, bridges, highway safety, traffic congestion, public transportation facilities and equipment, and intermodal transportation facilities and systems. These management systems were to be designed to obtain the optimum yield from the transportation system.

Title II, the Highway Safety Act of 1991, continued the nonconstruction highway safety programs at $1.6 billion for the 6-year period. The act expanded the list of uniform guidelines for the State and Community Highway Safety Grant Program. Amounts from this program were made available for specific purposes to encourage the use of safety belts, motorcycle helmets, alcohol countermeasures, and National Driver Register. The act reauthorized the Highway Safety R&D program and regular NHTSA activities. It also made permanent the law allowing a 65 m.p.h. speed limit on rural sections of noninterstate highways constructed to appropriate standards.

Title III, the Federal Transit Act Amendments of 1991, authorized $31.5 billion for the 6-year period. The act renamed the Urban Mass Transportation Administration to be the Federal Transit Administration (FTA) to reflect the broader responsibility of the agency. The Section 3 Discretionary and Formula Capital Grant program was reauthorized with minor changes. The funds were split 40% for new starts, 40% for rail modernization, and 20% of bus and other projects. The federal matching share was increased from 75 to 80%.

New fixed guideway projects had to be based on the results of alternatives analysis and preliminary engineering, justified by expected mobility improvements, environmental benefits, cost effectiveness, and operating efficiency, and supported by an acceptable degree of local financial commitment. These criteria could be waived if the project was in an extreme or severe nonattainment area and is included in the SIP, if the project requires less that $25 million in Section 3 funds, if the federal share is less than one-third, or the project if the project is funded entirely with FHWA funds.

The act established a three-tier formula for distributing rail modernization funds. The first $455 million was to be distributed to nine urbanized areas using statutory percentages. The next $45 million was to be allocated to six urbanized areas using specified percentages in the statute. Tier three distributed the next $70 million 50% to the urbanized areas mentioned in the previous two tiers, and 50% to the other urbanized areas with fixed guideway systems 7 or more years in operations according to the Section 9 rail formula. Any remaining funds were to be distributed according to the Section 9 rail formula. Authorization for bus and other projects totaled $2.5 million. At least 5.5% were to be spent in nonurbanized areas.

The Section 9 Formula program was authorized at $16.1 billion for the 6-year period. There were few changes in the program structure. The funds could be used for highway projects in TMAs if the requirements of ADA were met, and if the MPO approved, and if there was a balanced local approach to highway and transit funding. Operating assistance caps became subject to an annual inflation adjustment.

Funding for the Section 18 Small Urban and Rural Transit program was raised from 2.93 to 5.5% of the Section 9 program. Funds could be used for a new category of intercity bus service. The Section 16(b)(2) program, which provides transportation services for elderly and disabled, was authorized at 1.34% of the Section 9 program. Funds could be used for service contracts and could go to nonprofit groups.

A new Transit Planning and Research program was established and funded by a 3% set aside from the entire transit program. This program replaced the Section 6 Research, Section 8 Planning, Section 10 Managerial Training, Section 11(a) University Research, Section 8(h) Rural Transportation Assistance Program (RTAP), and Section 20 Human Resources programs. Of these funds, 45% was for MPOs for Metropolitan Transportation Planning, 5% for RTAP, 10% for states for planning, research, and training, 10% for a new Transit Cooperative Research Program (TCRP) to be administered by the TRB, and 30% for a National Planning and Research program. The metropolitan transportation planning requirements paralleled those in Title I. An additional amount was made available for the University Centers program.

Title IV, the Motor Carrier Act of 1991, reauthorized the Motor Carrier Safety Assistance Program (MCSAP) and required state uniformity in vehicle registration and fuel tax reporting. MCSAP funds could be used for state enforcement of federal truck and bus safety requirements, drug interdiction, vehicle weight and traffic enforcement, uniform accident reporting, research and development, and public education. The act required that states join the International Registration Plan and the International Fuel Tax Agreement. The act limited the use of longer combination vehicles to those states and routes where they were lawful on 1 June 1991.

Title V, Intermodal Transportation, established a national policy to encourage and promote development of a national intermodal transportation system. It created an Intermodal Advisory Board and an Office of Intermodalism in the Office of the Secretary to coordinate policies to promote intermodal transportation, maintain and disseminate intermodal transportation data, and coordinate intermodal research. The act authorized a program to develop model state intermodal transportation plans, including systems for collecting intermodal data, at $3 million with no more than $500,000 to any one state. The act also established a National Commission on Intermodal Transportation to report to the Congress by 3 September 1993.

Title VI, Research, provided major increases in funding for research and applied technology. The act authorized $108 million to implement the results of the Strategic Highway Research Program (SHRP) and for the Long Term Pavement Performance Program. The responsibilities of the National Highway Institute were expanded and they were allowed to charge fees to defray the costs of their programs. The act authorized the federal government to engage in collaborative research and development with other private and public organizations with up to a 50% federal share. A new International Highway Transportation Outreach Program was established to inform the US highway community of foreign innovations and promote US expertise and technology internationally.

The act established a Bureau of Transportation Statistics to compile transportation statistics, implement a long-term data collection program, issue guidelines for data collection, make statistics accessible, and identify information needs.

The transit bus testing program was expanded to include emissions and fuel economy. A new National Transit Institute was established to develop and administer training programs for those involved in federal-aid transit activities. Five new University Transportation Centers were added to the original ten to be funded by FHWA and FTA. In addition, five University Research Institutes were established.

Part B of this Title, Intelligent Vehicle-Highway Systems (IVHS) Act, established a 6-year program with funding of $659 million with $501 for the IVHS Corridors program and $158 for IVHS research and development. The act required the promotion of compatible standards and protocols to promote the widespread use of IVHS technologies, the establishment of evaluation guidelines for operational tests, and the establishment of an IVHS clearinghouse.

The act also called for the development of a completely automated highway and vehicle system that would serve as the prototype for future fully automated IVHS systems. The fully automated roadway or test track was to be in operation by the end of 1997. The IVHS Corridors program was designed to provide operational

tests under real world conditions. Corridors that meet certain criteria could participate in the development and implementation of IVHS technologies.

Part C, Advanced Transportation Systems and Electric Vehicles, established a
program for advanced mass transportation systems including electric trolley buses,
alternative fuel buses, or other systems that employ advanced technology to operate
cleanly and efficiently. The federal government could pay a 50% share for at least
three consortia to acquire plant sites, convert the plant facilities, and acquire equipment for developing or manufacturing these systems.

Title VII addressed air transportation. Title VIII, the Surface Transportation
Revenue Act of 1991, extended the Highway Trust Fund through fiscal year 1999.
The act reduced the motor fuel tax rate by 2.5 cents after 30 September 1995, to
11.5 cents for gasoline and 17.5 cents for diesel fuel. At that time, the Mass Transit
Account would be credited with 1.5 cents per gallon of the tax with the remainder
going to the Highway Account.

Manual of Regional Transportation Modeling Practice
for Air Quality Analysis

Passage of the Clean Air Act Amendments of 1990 and the Intermodal Surface
Transportation Efficiency Act of 1991 heightened concerns regarding the quality of
regional transportation analysis methods used to estimate travel and air quality.
In response to these concerns, the National Association of Regional Councils
(NARC) launched the Clean Air Project with the goal of developing guidance for
use by MPOs to review and, where necessary, upgrade their travel forecasting models to meet the requirements of the two acts (Harvey and Deakin, 1991).

NARC sponsored a conference to identify problems with current travel forecasting practice, develop guidance on best practices for a manual, and identify modeling research to respond to the new transportation/air quality analysis process
(Hawthorn and Deakin, 1991). The key shortcomings of current practice that were
identified included

- politically determined land use forecasts;
- omission of key variables for predicting travel behavior (household income,
  parking and auto operating costs, and number of workers per household);
- no trip generation variables beyond auto ownership and income (e.g., household
  size would be a good predictor);
- inadequate representation of trip attractions;
- omission of transit and walking accessibility in trip distribution models;
- lack of peaking information by trip type and market segment;
- simplistic representation of socioeconomic variables affecting travel behavior;
- simplistic characterization and modeling of nonwork travel;
- inaccurate travel speeds.

The Manual of Regional Transportation Modeling Practice for Air Quality Analysis was published in 1993 (Harvey and Deakin, 1993). While the manual suggested methods and procedures for the conduct of transportation–air quality modeling under the 1990 Clean Air Act Amendments, it did not set standards for modeling, describe a single modeling approach for all MPOs, or recommend specific pieces of software. Instead, the emphasis was on identifying potential problem areas that MPOs should consider in reviewing their models, and on recommending sound options for addressing such problems. The manual was based on the premise that good practice should be designed to respond to the key issues facing the area for which the analysis is being done. Since such issues varied from place to place and over time, modeling practice also should be expected to vary. Furthermore, the modeling practice for a particular area should constitute a realistic use of available resources, and hence would tend to vary with the size of the region and with the severity of the air quality problem, among other factors – including local concerns about transportation and its social, economic, and environmental impacts.

The Manual was designed to

- explain the purposes for which regional travel models are likely to be used in the next decade, with an emphasis on the requirements of transportation – air quality planning;
- suggest a set of criteria by which model performance is likely to be judged in key applications;
- list the principal technical and procedural characteristics necessary to ensure acceptable model performance in each type of application;
- provide examples of good practice for each major element of the modeling process, recognizing the ways in which practice must vary to suit local conditions (e.g., regional size, resource availability, air pollution severity);
- provide examples of advanced practice;
- discuss the likely direction of change in the state-of-the-art, to help MPOs anticipate new analytical requirements over the coming decade.

Harvey and Deakin noted that the quality of models in practical use at the time varied significantly and merely bringing all MPOs up to current standard practice would be quite an improvement. Harvey and Deakin also noted that many MPOs were not gathering the data they needed to develop and maintain adequate travel models. They recommended regular collection of land use, land use regulations, travel behavior surveys, network, and monitoring data. They also recommended additional staffing to maintain and operate the models.

Chapter 13
The Growth of Sustainable Development

As the concern for the effects of transportation on living quality and the environment grew, broader approaches to transportation planning were being developed. This concern was being expressed not only in the USA but worldwide. The term "sustainable development" became popularized in 1987 when the World Commission on Environment used it to describe a process of economic growth with "the ability to ensure the needs of the present without compromising the ability of future generations to meet their own needs." The global impact of transportation on the environment was reemphasized at the United Nations Conference on the Environment in Rio de Janeiro, Brazil, in 1992, which focused on global climate change.

To respond to those concerns, the Administration developed The Global Climate Action Plan which contained nearly 50 initiatives designed to return US greenhouse emissions to their 1990 levels by the year 2000 (Clinton and Gore, 1993). In addition, President Clinton appointed a Council on Sustainable Development which completed the report Sustainable Development: A New Consensus for Prosperity, Opportunity, and a Healthy Environment for the Future (The President's Council on Sustainable Development, 1996).

Passage of the Intermodal Surface Transportation Efficiency Act of 1991 and the Clean Air Act Amendments of 1990 demonstrated the concern for the air pollution effects of increased motor vehicle travel. The acts created the "conformity" process to assure that transportation plans and projects contribute to the NAAQS. This process had a major impact on the urban transportation planning process – increasing its complexity and requiring greater accuracy and precision in the results.

The concern for environmental quality and sustainable development brought renewed interest in the relationship between land use development patterns and transportation demand. Neo-traditional town planning was advanced as one approach to promoting increased use of transit, more walking and biking trips, and fewer automobile trips. This was to be achieved with higher densities, mixed use development, and infill projects designed to improve the overall living environment.

The conformity process and the potential effects of transportation on development focused attention on the ability of transportation and air quality models to forecast travel demand and air pollution accurately. To address these concerns, the federal government established the Travel Model Improvement program to develop new and improved travel forecasting techniques for use by states and MPOs.

E. Weiner, *Urban Transportation Planning in the United States, Third Edition*, doi:10.1007/978-0-387-77152-6, © Springer Science+Business Media, LLC 2008

Charlotte Conference on Moving Urban America

Passage of the Intermodal Surface Transportation Assistance Act of 1991 and the Clean Air Act Amendments of 1990 opened a new era in planning and decision-making concerning urban transportation projects. The acts provided greater flexibility while mandating new institutional arrangements and stronger environmental constraints. A conference was held in Charlotte, North Carolina, on 6–9 May 1992, to provide initial guidance under these acts on the appropriate planning and decision-making process needed to develop projects that would improve urban mobility with emphasis on efficiency, concern for the environment, and recognizing the shared responsibilities among responsible agencies, and affected groups (Transportation Research Board, 1993).

The conference's five workshops covered state transportation plans, state implementation plans (SIPs), management systems, transportation improvement programs (TIPs), and metropolitan long-range plans. The findings of the conference address a broad range of issues. The success of flexible funding depends on decisions that are made cooperatively by state and local officials. Inclusion of the EPA without compromising its regulatory function is critical to successfully blending air quality and transportation planning into a single integrated function. States and MPOs must expand participation to involve the full range of community interests if the new scope of planning is to be meaningful. Federal guidance should be general and flexible; federal agencies should support local initiatives undertaken in advance of regulation and encourage experimentation. Federal agencies should be clearing-houses to provide timely exchange of ideas and should provide technical assistance to upgrade analytical tools and training needed by the planning profession.

The multiple factors that must be considered in adopting state and regional transportation plans should be expanded to include quality of life issues. The transportation–land use connection demands special attention. The complexity of the combined transportation and air quality planning must be simplified.

The conferees agreed that ISTEA had appropriately moved the planning process into a broader institutional context involving more stakeholders and had increased the flexibility for state and local agencies to fashion solutions suited to local needs and priorities.

Travel Model Improvement Program

Passage of the Intermodal Surface Transportation Efficiency Act of 1991 and the Clean Air Act Amendments of 1990 brought increased concern about the limitations of travel forecasting procedures to meet the requirement of these acts. Current travel forecasting procedures had been in use for almost 30 years, and although some improvements had been made over the years, these procedures were basically the same as those originally developed in the early 1960s (Weiner, 1993a,b).

Current procedures were limited in terms of their ability to analyze the types of alternatives envisioned by these acts and in their ability to accurately estimate the impacts of these alternatives. Further, many changes had occurred in the demographic diversity and development patterns of the nation, in transportation and telecommunications technologies, and in computer hardware and software capabilities, such as GIS techniques, that needed to be incorporated into these procedures.

The Travel Model Improvement Program (TMIP) was established by the DOT and EPA in the Fall of 1991 to address these needs. TMIP was directed at upgrading travel analysis and forecasting techniques for application by state and local agencies – both for passenger and freight (Weiner and Ducca, 1996). The program consisted of five tracks of activity.

Track A, Outreach, was designed to improve the state of practice in state and local transportation agencies using technical assistance, training, manuals of practice, newsletters, conferences, and clearinghouse functions.

Track B, Near Term Improvements, was directed at capturing the best new techniques and approaches used in the traditional travel forecasting process and make them generally available to local planning agencies. It focused on making immediate improvements to the existing procedure to meet the new legislative requirements in a timely manner.

Track C, Long Term Improvements, was intended to develop a new generation of travel forecasting procedures. A new approach, termed TRansportation ANalysis and SIMulation System (TRANSIMS), was developed by Los Alamos National Laboratory. TRANSIMS, a region-wide microsimulation procedure, was a complete redesign of the entire forecasting process, simulating the behavior of households, individuals, and the operation of vehicles on the transportation network.

Track D, Data, addressed data needs both to support upgrading current methods and to develop new techniques, eventually leading to guidance on changing data collection programs. The new procedures were expected to alter data needs and usage, eliminating the need for some data elements and requiring other new data elements.

Track E, Land Use, was designed to improve the quality of land use forecasting techniques, including both the need for regional forecasting models and the need to understand the effects of urban design on travel.

TMIP evolved from defining user needs, to product development and testing, to product delivery and implementation. The program provided useful techniques and assistance to the user community to upgrade their travel analysis techniques. It stimulated a renewed interest improving the quality travel analysis procedures.

Livable Communities Initiative

The Livable Communities Initiative (LCI) was created by the Federal Transit Administration to promote transit as the means to strengthen the link between transportation and communities. The LCI was intended to provide an alternative to low-density sprawl development patterns served primarily by automobiles with higher density, mixed use development reinforced with travel demand and parking management policies (US Dept. of Transportation, 1996a,b). The LCI was designed to promote and support transit-oriented design (TOD) or neo-traditional urban design (Beimborn et al., 1991; Rabinowitz et al., 1991).

The objectives of the LCI were to (1) strengthen the link between transit and community planning including supportive land use policies and urban design; (2) stimulate active and diverse participation by the community in the decision-making process; (3) increase access to employment, education, and other community facilities an services; (4) leverage resources from other federal, state, and local programs.

Under the LCI, 16 projects were funded for a total cost of $68.9 million, with $35.0 million covered by FTA. These projects included a wide range of facilities as part of transit projects such as a child care center, police station, community center, bus shelters, information kiosks, improved safety enhancements, bus and bicycle access, transit plaza, Head Start facility, health care clinic, and library.

Energy Policy Act of 1992

The Energy Policy Act of 1992 passed after extensive debate. The act was wide ranging covering matters of energy production, conservation, waste disposal, alternative fuels, and taxes and tax incentives. Several provisions directly related to transportation.

The act increased the limit on tax-exempt transit benefits to $60 per month for those transit riders receiving the benefits. It made parking benefits over $155 per month taxable to the automobile users. These two provisions moved toward leveling the playing field on subsidies to automobiles and transit.

A phase in schedule was established for alternative fuel vehicles for certain vehicle fleets. Alternative fuels included compressed natural gas, ethanol, methanol, propane, electricity, and hydrogen. The phase in was to reach 75% of federal fleet vehicle acquisitions by 1999, 75% of state fleet vehicle acquisitions by 2000, and 90% of acquisitions for certain company vehicle fleets by 1999.

The act authorized $50 million a year for 10 years for electric motor vehicle demonstration programs, and $40 million for a 5-year period for electric motor vehicle infrastructure and support systems development program. It authorized $35 million annually for 3 years to demonstrate alternative fuel urban transit buses.

Transportation Implication of Telecommuting

The 1992 DOT Appropriations Act required the Department of Transportation to conduct a study of the potential for telecommuting to reduce traffic congestion and the resulting air pollution, energy consumption, accidents, and construction of new transportation facilities (US Dept. of Transportation, 1993a).

The study reviewed the trends in telecommunications and the factors affecting telecommuting. Telecommuting was defined as a worker making an electronic trip instead of a physical trip in a vehicle. Telecommuting could be from a home, a telework center, or from some other remote location. It could occur only 1 day a week, or for the majority of the week.

The study concluded that telecommuting was being practiced on a substantial and rapidly increasing scale. The number of telecommuters was forecasted to grow from 2 million in 1992 to between 7.5 and 15.0 million by 2002. It also suggested that over the next decade telecommuting had the potential to provide substantial public benefits in reducing congestion, air pollution, traffic accidents, and energy consumption. The study cautioned that the emergence of latent travel demand could diminish congestion and air quality benefits. Telecommunication services and equipment were considered to be adequate for most existing applications of telecommuting, but high-bandwidth communication capabilities would be useful currently, and would be needed in the future.

The study made a number of recommendations, some of which had already been implemented. First, the DOT should actively promote telecommuting as a traffic demand measure to reduce the use of automobiles. Second, under ISTEA, telecommuting projects should be eligible for federal funding to develop telecommuting programs that could include planning, management, organization, promotion, marketing, training, and public awareness campaigns, but not the acquisition and equipping of facilities such as telework centers. These telecommuting programs had to be part of a transportation plan and program developed by state and local agencies. The Intermodal Surface Transportation Efficiency Act of 1991 authorized federal funding of transportation projects or programs having air quality benefits under the Clean Air Act, which would include a wide range of telecommuting activities (Weiner, 1994).

The DOT proposed to work with state and local governments and the private sector to monitor telecommuting activities and to disseminate relevant information on telecommuting as a travel demand management measures (COMSIS et al., 1993).

Metropolitan and State-Wide Planning Regulations

Regulation implementing the state-wide and metropolitan transportation planning provisions of the Intermodal Surface Transportation Efficiency Act of 1991 was issued in October 1993 (US Dept. of Transportation, 1993b). These regulations closely followed the legislative requirements.

The metropolitan transportation planning regulations addressed the major elements of the process required to produce the long-range transportation plan and the shorter-term transportation improvement program (TIP). The regulations emphasized a formal proactive and inclusive public involvement process that provided ample opportunity for community participation. It required explicit consideration of the 15 planning factors cited in ISTEA. The regulations provided guidance on the conduct of Major Investment Studies (MIS) for the analysis of new transportation facilities or substantial increase in facility capacity (US Dept. of Transportation, 1995).

The regulations addressed the integration of the management systems into the overall planning process, and the linkage between transportation and air quality planning in the conformity requirements (Figure 13.1). It set forth the financial planning requirements to assure that financial resources were reasonably available to implement all elements of the transportation plan. The metropolitan transportation planning process was required to be self-certified annually by the states and MPOs, and to be reviewed at least every 3 years by FHWA and FTA to determine if the process meets the requirements in the regulations.

The state-wide transportation planning requirements closely paralleled the metropolitan planning requirements. States were required to prepare a long-range state-wide intermodal transportation plan that considered the 23 factors cited in ISTEA. These plans had to be linked to the metropolitan plans developed by the MPOs. The state-wide transportation planning process had to give sufficient opportunity to provide input from users, transportation providers, and the public (US Dept. of Transportation, 1996c).

States were also required to prepare a short-term state-wide transportation improvement program (STIP) that included all capital and operating projects to be funded by the federal government or requiring federal action. The STIP had to include the metropolitan TIPS verbatim and be consistent with the state-wide plan. The STIP had to be financially constrained by year to those projects for which the sources of funding could be identified. The state-wide transportation planning

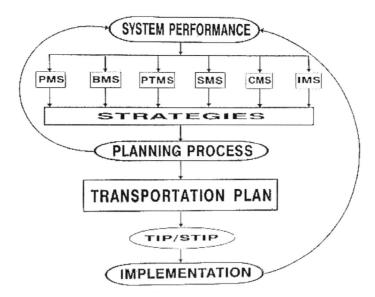

Fig. 13.1 Planning and management systems (Source: US Dept. of Transportation, 1993b)

process was required to incorporated the results of the management systems that were focused on performance improvement and asset management (US Dept. of Transportation, 1996c).

Transportation – Air Quality Conformity Regulations

The US Environmental Protection Agency issued regulations for the transportation conformity provisions of Section 176 of the Clean Air Act Amendments of 1990 (CAAA) in November 1993, after 2 years of heated discussions between transportation and environmental groups (US Environmental Protection Agency, 1993). "Conformity" was defined in the CAAA as the assurance that transportation plans and programs aim to meet the same goals set forth for air quality improvements in state Implementation Plans (SIPs) for cleaner air. Transportation conformity was in the 1977 amendments to the Clean Air Act but was not clearly defined. The CAAA corrected that problem.

The regulations established the procedures and criteria for conformity determinations on transportation plans, programs, and projects (Figure 13.2). Conformity determinations must be made in nonattainment areas and maintenance areas (areas previously in nonattainment but now in attainment). To achieve conformity, plans must be analyzed to assure that the resulting air quality emissions would be within the level established by the SIP. The conformity analysis must include all regionally significant transportation projects. The STIP and TIP were also subject to conformity determinations, as well as individual transportation projects. The transportation plans, STIPs and TIPs, and individual transportation projects must also seek to implement the transportation control measures (TCMs) called for in the SIP (Shrouds, 1995).

The conformity requirements significantly changed the process for developing transportation plans, programs, and projects, and increased the emphasis on demand management strategies and operational improvements to the existing transportation infrastructure. The conformity requirements increased the demands on travel and air quality forecasting procedures to be more accurate and more sensitive to travel demand management strategies. They also caused a greater level of cooperation between the transportation and air quality agencies.

Making the Land Use, Transportation, Air Quality Connection (LUTRAQ)

In 1990, the 1,000 Friends of Oregon created the Making the Land Use, Transportation, Air Quality Connection (LUTRAQ) project in response to a proposal to build a bypass around the southwest side of Portland, Oregon. The project analyzed the use of transit oriented development (TOD) in conjunction with a light rail system as an alternative to a proposed highway bypass with more traditional

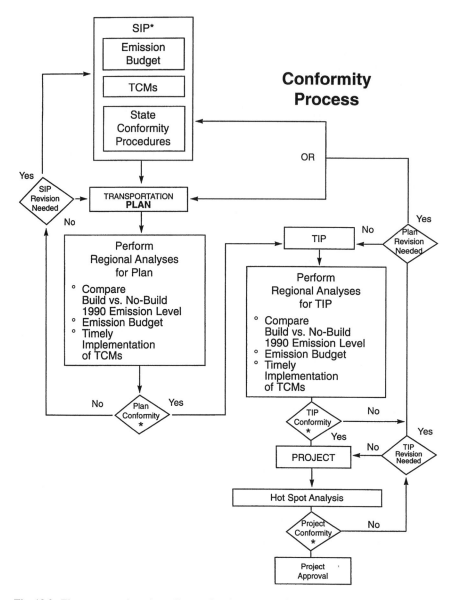

Fig. 13.2 The transportation-air quality conformity process (Source: US Dept. of Transportation, 1995)

low-density suburban development patterns. The land use development using neo-traditional town planning principles was designed to encourage more walking, biking, and transit use as an alternative to the increased use of automobiles (Bartholomew, 1995; 1,000 Friends of Oregon, 1997).

LUTRAQ reviewed current land use–transportation models, implemented improvements to the modeling capability, developed a land use–transportation alternative around a light rail line and TOD, analyzed the highway bypass and light rail alternatives, and developed a series of implementation actions for the light rail/TOD alternative.

The study concluded that the light rail/TOD strategy could significantly reduce congestion, automobile trips, VMT, and air pollution emissions over the highway bypass alternative. It was the only alternative to satisfy the Clean Air Act requirements. The Portland area regional government endorsed the LUTRAQ plan and incorporated its components into the region's 50-year land use and transportation plan.

Transportation Management Systems

The Intermodal Surface Transportation Efficiency Act of 1991 required states and metropolitan areas to develop and implement six systems for managing: highway pavement (PMS), bridges (BMS), highway safety (SMS), traffic congestion (CMS), public transportation facilities and equipment (PTMS), and intermodal transportation facilities and systems (IMS). These management systems were intended to be tools that provided information to assist state and local decision-makers in selecting cost-effective policies, programs, and projects to protect and improve the nation's transportation infrastructure.

ISTEA required that the states establish these transportation management systems in fiscal year 1995 and certify that they had done so by 1 January 1995. Failure to do so could result in 10% of the funds apportioned to the state be withheld. States and MPOs were to cooperate in the development and implementation of the management systems. Transportation needs identified through the management systems had to be considered in the metropolitan and state-wide planning process. In TMAs, CMSs had to provide for effective management of new and existing transportation facilities through the use of travel demand reduction and operational management strategies.

Interim final regulations were issued in December 1993, to implement the management systems provisions of ISTEA (US Dept. of Transportation, 1993c). They addressed procedures for systematically collecting and analyzing information as well as integration of the management systems into the overall planning process. Definitions of the management systems are shown in Table 13.1 (US General Accounting Office, 1997).

However, there was concern that the management systems had substantially increased the data collection and reporting burden of the states and MPOs. Consequently, the requirement for these transportation management systems was eliminated and made optional at the discretion of the states by the National Highway System Designation Act of 1995. Nevertheless, many states continued the development and implementation of these management systems often customized to their own needs (US General Accounting Office, 1997).

Table 13.1 Definition of Management Systems

Management system	Definition
Pavement management system	This system provides information for use in implementing cost-effective reconstruction, rehabilitation, and preventative maintenance programs and results in pavements designed to accommodate current and forecasted traffic in a safe, durable, and cost-effective manner
Bridge management system	This system, among other things, includes procedures for collecting, processing, and updating bridge inventory data; predicts bridge deterioration; identifies projects to improve bridge conditions, safety, and serviceability; estimates costs; and determines least-cost strategies for bridge maintenance, repair, and rehabilitation
Safety management system	This system is a systematic process for reducing the number and severity of traffic accidents by incorporating opportunities to improve highway safety in all phases of highway planning, design, construction, and maintenance. It includes collecting and analyzing highway safety data; disseminating public information and providing educational activities; and ensuring coordination among the agencies responsible for different safety elements (such as vehicle, roadway, and human factors)
Congestion management system	This system is a systematic process that provides information on a transportation system's performance and alternative strategies to alleviate congestion and enhance the mobility of persons and goods. The system includes monitoring and evaluating transportation system performance, identifying alternative strategies to alleviate congestion, assessing and implementing cost-effective strategies, and evaluating the effectiveness of the implemented actions
Public transportation management system	This system is a systematic process for collecting and analyzing information on the condition and cost of transit assets (e.g., maintenance facilities, stations, terminals, equipment, and rolling stock) on a continual basis, identifying needs, and enabling decision-makers to select cost-effective strategies for providing and maintaining transit assets in serviceable condition
Intermodal management system	This system is a systematic process for identifying linkages between modes of transportation, defining strategies for improving the effectiveness of modal interactions, and evaluating and implementing these strategies

Source: US General Accounting Office, 1997

E.O. 12893 Principles for Federal Infrastructure Investment

Executive Order 12893, issued on 26 January 1994, set forth the Principles for Federal Infrastructure Investment, which applied to all Federal agencies with infrastructure responsibilities (Clinton, 1994a). It required that all investments be based on a systematic analysis of benefits and costs, including both qualitative and quantitative measures. These analyses had to compare a comprehensive set of options including managing demand, repairing facilities, and expanding facilities.

The order called for the efficient management of infrastructure including a focus on improving the operation and maintenance of facilities, as well as the use of pricing to manage demand. The order required agencies to seek private sector participation in investment and management of infrastructure. Federal agencies were to encourage state and local recipients to implement planning and management systems that support these principles.

E.O. 12898 on Environmental Justice

President Clinton issued Executive Order 12898, "Federal Actions to Address Environmental Justice in Minority Populations and Low-Income Populations," on 11 February 1994 (Clinton, 1994b,c). The order was designed to focus attention on the environmental and human health conditions in minority communities and low-income communities to ensure that all federal programs and activities do not use criteria, methods, or practices that discriminate on the basis of race, color, or national origin.

The Executive Order required that environmental impact process under NEPA be used to address environmental justice issues. Under that process, federal actions and projects have to be analyzed to include the human health, economic, and social effects on minority communities and low-income communities. Mitigation measures had to address the significant and adverse environmental effects on minority communities and low-income communities. The affected communities must have opportunities to provide input in the identification of impacts and mitigation measures.

In May 1995, DOT sponsored a Conference on Environmental Justice and Transportation: Building Model Partnerships to develop strategies and build workable partnerships to address the concerns related to environmental justice. The conferees made a number of major recommendations: (1) ensuring greater stakeholder participation and public involvement in transportation decision-making; (2) directing resources to identify and address discriminatory outcomes, disproportionate impacts, and inequitable distribution of transportation investments and their civil rights implications; (3)improving research, data collection, and assessment techniques; (4) promoting interagency cooperation in transportation planning, development, and program implementation to achieve livable, healthy, and sustainable communities (Environmental Justice Resource Center, 1996). In April 1997, DOT issued an order that established procedures to achieve environmental justices as part of its mission (US Dept. of Transportation, 1997a).

National Bicycling and Walking Study

In 1990, bicycling and walking were described as "the forgotten modes" of transportation. For most of the preceding decades, these two nonmotorized transportation options had been largely overlooked by federal, state, and local transportation agencies.

Several national surveys confirmed that bicycling and walking were popular activities among Americans of all ages. An estimated 131 million Americans regularly bicycled or walked for exercise, sport, recreation, or simply for relaxation and enjoyment of the outdoors. However, as modes of transportation, bicycling and walking had not yet realized their potential. An average of just $2 million of federal transportation funds were spent each year on bicycle and pedestrian projects, and the percentage of commuting trips made by bicycling and walking fell from a combined 10.6% in 1960 to 3.9% in 1990. In 1991, the US Congress requested a report on how the US DOT proposed to increase bicycling and walking while improving the safety of the two modes.

In response to this request, a series of 24 case studies was commissioned to investigate different aspects of the bicycling and walking issue. These reports, in addition to other information, gathered a wealth of information on bicycling and walking and provided a snapshot of the state of bicycling and walking in the USA. The studies also highlighted information gaps, identified common obstacles and challenges to improving conditions for the nonmotorized traveler, and suggested possible activities and a leadership role for the department.

The final report of the National Bicycling and Walking Study contained two overall goals (US Department of Transportation, 1994):

1. Double the percentage of total trips made by bicycling and walking in the USA from 7.9 to 15.8% of all travel trips.
2. Simultaneously reduce by 10% the number of bicyclists and pedestrians killed or injured in traffic crashes.

In addition to these goals, the *Study* identified a nine-point Federal Action Plan as well as a five-point State and Local Action Plan with a range of suggested activities for state and local agencies.

Ten years later, a report was completed updating the progress in achieving the goals and elements of the action plans (US Department of Transportation, 2004a). Most importantly, there had been increased funding for bicycling and walking projects with the enactment of ISTEA in 1991 and TEA-21 in 1998. Federal aid funding was made available under a number of highway programs. Planning requirements for bicycling and walking were established for states and metropolitan planning organizations. Other provisions included the requirements that states establish and fund a bicycle and pedestrian coordinator in their Department of Transportation and that bicyclist and pedestrian safety continue as priority areas for highway safety program funding. In addition, actions taken by the US DOT, such as the issuance of the "Design Guidance" language in 2000, contributed to continuing record levels of spending on bicycling and walking initiatives. Further, with more information and technical resources available about pedestrian and bicycle facilities and programs, states and local governments increasingly used their own funds for projects and programs benefiting bicyclists and pedestrians. By 2003, $422 million had been spent nation wide on pedestrian and bicycle improvements.

Actions taken in response to the Federal Action Plan, as well as the nation-wide emergence of pedestrian advocacy organizations, substantially boosted the level of attention paid to walking issues by both the department and state and local agencies. Through a range of activities such as the development of a Pedestrian Safety Road show, support for Safe Routes to School and annual Walk to School Day events, and collaboration with the health promotion and injury prevention communities, the awareness of pedestrian issues became higher than that at any previous time. There was also an increased emphasis on issues affecting access to the transportation system for people with disabilities.

By 2004, all state DOTs had designated a bicycle and pedestrian coordinator, and 29 of the 50 states had adopted state-wide bicycle or bicycle and pedestrian plans. Approximately half the states reported that bicycle and pedestrian facilities were included in some or most highway projects; the remaining states usually developed bicycle and pedestrian facilities as separate or independent projects. Most states had an overall long-range transportation plan that integrated bicycling and walking; one-third had a separate long-range plan for bicycling and walking.

Some states and localities had revised their vehicle codes and/or drivers' manuals since 1994 to better address bicycling and walking issues, others had passed child helmet laws for bicyclists. As March 2004, 20 states had enacted age-specific bicycle helmet laws and more than 131 localities had enacted some type of bicycle helmet legislation.

Bicyclists and pedestrians represented more than 16% of all traffic fatalities in 1993, and then dropped to 12.3% in 2003. At the same time, there was an increase in overall traffic fatalities of more than 7%. The declines between 1993 and 2003 in pedestrian fatalities (17.3%), pedestrian injuries (27.7%), bicyclist fatalities (23.3%), and bicyclist injuries (35.3%) have exceeded the target set by the National Bicycling and Walking Study.

States and local areas, where successful bicycling and walking programs are in place, are characterized by a higher level of integration of bicyclist and pedestrian needs throughout the programs, policies, and procedures of various government agencies. This integration, also known as institutionalization, results in comprehensive programs with stable funding and bicycling- and walking-compatible environments.

The National Bicycling and Walking Study established the target of doubling the percentage of trips made by bicycling and walking from 7.9 to 15.8%. In 1990, a total of 18 billion walking trips and 1.7 billion bicycling trips were reported representing 7.2 and 0.7%, respectively, of all trips counted by the study. In 2001, the total number of reported walking and bicycling trips nearly doubled to 38.6 billion, although it was only 9.5% of all reported trips.

Curbing Gridlock: Peak-Period Fees to Relieve Traffic Congestion

Traffic congestion had been steadily increasing for a number of years. The delay and wasted fuel from being stuck in traffic was estimated to cost over $40 billion a year. Traffic congestion also increased air pollution. With travel demand far outpacing the provision of highway capacity, there was little prospect that metropolitan areas cold build their way out of congestion. Transportation policy increasingly focused on managing the demand for transportation to alleviate adding capacity on new highways for use by solo drivers. Economists had long argued that some direct pricing mechanism for highway use would help allocate demand on existing facilities more efficiently by shifting some road users to off-peak hours and alternative modes of transportation. This shift in policy, combined with environmental goals for cleaner air, and rapid advances in electronic toll collection renewed interest in an old idea – congestion pricing. To assess the potential of congestion pricing as a tool for congestion management, the National Research Council conducted a study of this approach (National Research Council, 1994).

The National Research Council concluded that congestion pricing had great promise to reduce congestion significantly while helping to meet air quality and energy conservation goals. Moreover, by relying on a market mechanism, it would accomplish these ends while providing net benefits to the society. Congestion pricing, however, had long been an unattractive option for travel demand management. Economists had promised for decades that congestion pricing would work if governments would only try it. Transportation officials had consistently thought the policy impractical. Politicians had feared that motorists would pay the fees but hate them, and would then retaliate against the officials who allowed it to occur.

The study found that in the private sector, peak demand was managed through pricing. However, proposals for peak-period pricing of road use had been dismissed as impractical because of the difficulty of charging users efficiently. But, developments in electronic toll collection had made it possible to charge users varying prices with considerable efficiency without invading privacy. The study found that as variable pricing of road use had become technically feasible, the debate had shifted to questions of effectiveness and political acceptability.

Economic theory and analytical modeling predicted that variable pricing would reduce congestion. The reduction of only a few percentage points in the number of motorists in the traffic stream could return traffic to free flow. However, empirical information was not available for some important potential behavioral responses. Sufficient experience with pricing transportation services indicated that congestion pricing would reduce demand, but the magnitude of that change was not known. In addition, little specifically was known about how motorists might shift the timing of trips; choose alternate routes; choose among solo driving, carpools, and transit options; or simply forgo trips. Lack of understanding about the ability of motorists to adapt to congestion pricing also made it difficult to estimate the potential hardship on some individuals. The economic effects on commuters of different income levels showed that all income groups could benefit from congestion pricing if some of the funds collected were redistributed in ways specifically designed to achieve this goal. Motorists with substantially longer-than-average commutes could be disadvantaged even after revenues were redistributed if they continued to drive alone. Those who did not have better alternatives would drive alone and be made worse off. Those who did have better alternatives than driving alone (who could shift to a carpool or to transit with an acceptable trade-off between lower out-of-pocket costs and time losses) might be made better off because of more attractive carpooling and transit alternatives or higher speeds and, perhaps, more frequent transit service.

The substantial revenues that could be raised were appealing in an era of financial stringencies in many states and regions; Past efforts to resolve congestion through capacity enhancement had not worked because latent demand filled up any added capacity in areas experiencing population or employment growth. And advances in technology had made it possible to charge users at low cost and with minimal inconvenience or intrusion on privacy. These reasons why congestion pricing appears more appealing to some did not mean that the political barriers to this policy had disappeared. The political and administrative challenges faced by congestion pricing were as significant as before. The lack of existing institutions to manage regional congestion pricing in the USA remained a significant barrier.

Because of the controversy about congestion pricing proposals, careful analyses of how the policy would work at the local level, who would benefit, and how to compensate those disadvantaged by the policy are essential to informing the public deliberations about this policy. Assuming that these early congestion pricing projects were implemented, careful and extensive evaluation was essential. These projects will remain controversial. The quality of the debates about these efforts would be substantially enhanced by reliable information about how traffic flows change, by careful analyses of winners and losers, and by survey research regarding motorist perceptions before and after the change.

Whether congestion pricing will prove politically feasible in more than one or two places remains to be seen. Public and political concerns about fairness and motorist resistance to direct charges for highway use continue to be significant obstacles. The uses of the substantial revenues that congestion pricing can generate provide an opportunity to improve the efficiency of the transportation system, ameliorate the negative impact on adversely affected groups, and result in a net benefit for society. Some individuals would still be hurt, however, and whether they would be more motivated to resist congestion pricing than the majority who would benefit would be demonstrated only in actual practice.

Conference on Institutional Aspects of Metropolitan Transportation Planning

After several years under ISTEA, the DOT and TRB sponsored a conference to assess the progress in implementing the metropolitan transportation planning provisions of the act, and the capacity of MPOs to carry out the provisions of the act (Transportation Research Board, 1995a). The conference brought together officials from federal and state agencies, MPOs, universities, consulting firms, and community activist groups to discuss a wide ranges of issues regarding the metropolitan transportation planning regulations.

As background for the conference, the US Advisory Commission on Intergovernmental Relations (ACIR) prepared the report, MPO Capacity: Improving the Capacity of Metropolitan Planning Organizations to Help Implement National Transportation Policies (Advisory Commission on Intergovernmental Relations, 1995). This study reviewed the progress of the transportation planning process in a number of metropolitan areas. The study found that MPOs experienced several changes resulting from ISTEA including increased public participation, improved air quality analysis procedures, enhanced intergovernmental coordination, and consideration of intermodal issues. Conversely, MPOs raised concerns with regard to increased regulatory burden and workload levels, uncoordinated deadlines, unachievable expectations, disrupted relationships within the MPO, and strained relationships with the state departments of transportation. The report recommended several actions directed at developing a capacity building program for MPOs and supporting regulatory relief.

The conferees discussed issues that related to roles and responsibilities, public participation, fiscal reality, technical linkages, decision-making, and integrating related activities into the process. The general consensus of the conference participants was that ISTEA had provided numerous opportunities to enhance the metropolitan transportation planning process. Although areas of concern were noted, along with items that needed further research and possible changes, the overall sentiment supported the basic concepts of ISTEA. The recommendations from the conference were consistent with and complementary to those in the ACIR report. They focused on improved technical assistance, procedural development, development of training programs and case studies of good practice, and better communication among those involved in the metropolitan transportation planning process around the country. There was also a call to simplify many aspects of the process.

Implications of Expanding Metropolitan Highway Capacity

The Clean Air Act Amendments of 1990 and the Intermodal Surface Transportation Efficiency Act of 1991 focused attention on the issue of the travel inducing effects of expanding highway capacity in metropolitan areas and the potential impacts on air quality and energy consumption. This issue of the effect of highway expansion on induced travel had been debated for many years resulting in much conjecture and no consensus. The Transportation Research Board undertook a study to evaluate the evidence regarding the impacts of highway capacity additions on traffic flow, travel demand, land use, vehicle emissions, air quality, and energy use (Transportation Research Board, 1995b). Of particular concern was the ability of current forecasting techniques to accurately estimate the impacts of expanded highway capacity on improving traffic flow and resulting air pollution effects.

The study included an extensive review of research and experience. It concluded that current analytical methods were inadequate for addressing federal regulatory requirements for estimating emissions and ambient air quality. Modeled estimates were imprecise and limited in their account of changes in traffic flow characteristics, tripmaking, and land use attributable to transportation investments. The accuracy implied in EPA's conformity regulations demanded a level of analytic precision beyond current modeling capabilities. The complex and indirect relationship between highway capacity additions, air quality, and energy use, which is heavily dependent upon local conditions, makes it impossible to generalize about the effects of added capacity on air quality and energy use even with improved models.

In the end, the study concluded that polices to curb the growth in motor vehicles would have a relatively small effect on air quality. Major highway capacity additions would likely have greater effects but could take a longer period to impact spatial patterns and induced travel, an eventually air quality. Improvements in vehicle technology would yield greater air quality benefits than the focus on curbing travel growth.

National Highway System Designation Act of 1995

The Intermodal Surface Transportation Efficiency Act of 1991 required the DOT to submit a proposed National Highway System to provide an interconnected system of principal arterial routes that will serve major population centers, international border crossings, ports, airports, public transportation facilities, and other intermodal transportation facilities and other major travel destinations, meet national defense requirements, and serve interstate and interregional travel.

The proposed NHS was developed by DOT in cooperation with the states, local officials, and metropolitan planning organizations and submitted to the Congress on 9 December 1993. The NHS was designated into law on 28 November 1995, when President Clinton signed the National Highway System Designation Act of 1995 (Figure 13.3). The system consisted of 160,00 miles which included the interstate system. The NHS represented 4% of the nation's roads and carried 40% of all highway traffic and 70% of all truck traffic. About 90% of the population lived within 5 miles of a NHS road.

In addition to designating the NHS, the 1995 Act repealed the national 55–miles-per-hour speed limit for cars and trucks, and removed the funding penalties for states that failed to enact motorcycle helmet laws (Bennett, 1996).

The Act created a State Infrastructure Bank (SIB) Pilot Program that could included up to 10 States. No new Federal-aid funds were provided to capitalize the banks. States could contribute up to 10 percent of several categories of their federal-aid highway and federal transit funds to capitalize their bank. States had to match 25 percent of the Federal contribution with funds from non-federal sources.

The act eliminated the requirement in ISTEA for management systems making them optional by the states. It added a sixteenth factor, recreational travel and tourism, to be considered by MPOs in developing transportation plans and programs. It also clarified that transportation conformity requirements of ISTEA and the Clean Air Act apply only to nonattainment areas or those areas subject to maintenance plans.

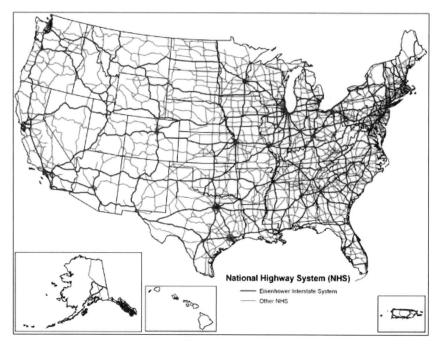

Fig. 13.3 National highway system (Source: Bennett, 1996)

Major Investment Studies

Prior to the Intermodal Surface Transportation Efficiency Act of 1991, the Federal Highway Administration (FHWA) and Federal Transit Administration (FTA) had different project development procedures for major projects, specifically FTA's Alternatives Analysis requirements and FHWA's highway corridor planning procedures (Cook, et al., 1996). These procedures were replaced by the requirements of Major Investment Studies (MIS) that were incorporated into the Metropolitan Planning regulations implementing the metropolitan planning requirements of ISTEA (US Dept. of Transportation, 1993b).

The MIS regulations required that for any major transportation investment a study evaluate all reasonable alternative multimodal transportation improvement strategies to address the problems within the corridor of subarea. The MIS was to be a cooperative process among the various agencies and stakeholders to establish a range of alternative investments or strategies, and evaluate the effectiveness and cost effectiveness of the alternatives in attaining local, state, and national goals and objectives. The process was to include consideration of direct and indirect costs of the alternatives and such factors as mobility improvements, social, economic and environmental costs, safety, operating efficiency, land use, economic development, financing, and energy consumption. The public involvement process had to be proactive to provide opportunities for various interest groups to participate. The analysis was to be consistent with Executive Order 12893 on Principles for Federal Infrastructure Investments.

A conference was held on 25–28 February 1996, in San Francisco, California, to determine how well the process was working after more than 2 years of experience. The conference focused on policy issues, the relation of MIS to the overall planning and project development process, management and institutional issues affecting MIS, and the decision process for the MIS. The conference concluded that MIS was a useful technique that focused on defining problems, then built a process to reach a consensus on appropriate solutions. It reflected the objectives of ISTEA of improved mobility, intermodalism, innovation, flexibility, improved air quality, using new technologies, involving the public in decision-making, coordination of transportation investment with land use, environment, and other community interests.

The guidance on MIS provided sufficient flexibility to adapt to local conditions. However, further improvements were needed in the areas of collaborative relationships among the various levels of government and across transportation modes as well as clarification between the MIS process and NEPA procedures. MIS needed to be more fully integrated into the metropolitan planning process, and financial planning should accompany alternatives analysis. The experience with MIS needed to be more generally disseminated. A continuing education process needed to be carried out for decision-makers, the public, and other stakeholders for an effective MIS process.

Chapter 14
Expanding Participatory Democracy

For most of the century, transportation decisions were made by engineers and planners in government organizations. With the passage of the Federal-Aid Highway Act of 1962 and its successors, pubic officials participating in MPOs gained some control of transportation decisions within their urban areas. With the passage of ISTEA, other stakeholders and private citizens had to be given a reasonable opportunity to comment on the long-range transportation plans and the shorter-term transportation improvement programs. The regulations implementing the legislation required a formal proactive and inclusive public involvement process that provided ample opportunity for community participation.

Reinforcing this expansion of participatory decision-making process, President Clinton issued an Executive Order entitled "Federal Actions to Address Environmental Justice in Minority Populations and Low-Income Populations." The order was designed to focus attention on the environmental and human health conditions in minority and low-income communities to ensure that all federal programs and activities did not use criteria, methods, or practices that discriminated on the basis of race, color, or national origin.

The Executive Order required that environmental impact process under the National Environmental Policy Act be used to address environmental justice issues. Under that process, federal actions and projects had to be analyzed to include the human health, economic, and social effects on minority communities and low-income communities. Mitigation measures had to be developed to address the significant and adverse environmental effects on minority and low-income communities. The affected communities had to have opportunities to provide input in the identification of impacts and mitigation measures.

As the public gained more influence over transportation decisions in their affected areas, public interest groups became more sophisticated in their participation in the transportation planning process. They built a nation-wide communication network that provided technical assistance and formed an integrated lobbying group. Some developed tools to conduct their own independent analyses.

There was also continuing efforts to expand the range of financing options as well as movement toward institutional change and new approaches to address the ever-widening range of issues that needed to be dealt with by transportation

E. Weiner, *Urban Transportation Planning in the United States, Third Edition*,
doi:10.1007/978-0-387-77152-6, © Springer Science+Business Media, LLC 2008

planning agencies. This was the tone of transportation planning and policy on the threshold of a new century.

Deployment of Intelligent Transportation Systems

The Intermodal Surface Transportation Efficiency Act of 1991 (ISTEA) established the Federal program to research, develop, and operationally test Intelligent Transportation Systems (ITS) and to promote their implementation. The program was designed to facilitate deployment of technology to enhance the efficiency, safety, and convenience of surface transportation, resulting in improved access, saved lives and time, and increased productivity (US Dept. of Transportation, 2000b).

In a 1996 speech, Secretary of Transportation, Federico Peña, established a broad vision for ITS deployment to create an intelligent transportation infrastructure across the USA that would save time and lives and improve the quality of life for Americans. As part of this speech, the secretary articulated an ITS deployment goal – to achieve a complete ITS infrastructure in the country's 75 largest metropolitan areas within 10 years. In addition, the secretary emphasized the importance of integration so that the different technologies could be used together. He described 9 components that should make up ITS in the 75 metropolitan areas including such systems as:

- traffic control systems;
- freeway management systems;
- transit management systems;
- incident management programs;
- electronic toll collection for roads and bridges;
- electronic fare payment systems for such things as the bus, train, and toll lanes;
- railroad-grade crossings;
- emergency response providers; and
- traveler information systems.

The secretary stated that the federal role in making this goal a reality included developing a national architecture and standards for ITS technologies to ensure that local ITS investments would be interoperable, investing in model deployment sites to serve as examples for the rest of the country, and investing in training to expand technical expertise for deploying ITS technologies. The secretary also emphasized the importance of strategic investment in ITS technologies and projected impacts of increasing infrastructure capacity, reducing Americans' travel time by at least 15%. He emphasized the cost effectiveness of ITS, saying that building the needed highway capacity for 50 cities in the next 10 years would cost $150 billion, while implementing an intelligent transportation infrastructure for these 50 cities would cost $10 billion and gain two-thirds of the capacity needed. He also included a commitment to upgrade technologies in 450 other communities and on rural roads and interstates.

At the 10-year point in this program, the US General Accountability Office (GAO) conducted a review of the progress that had been achieved (US General Accountability Office, 2005). The study focused on the goal for the 75 metropolitan areas. The GAO found that US DOT had undertaken several roles to facilitate states' ITS deployment, such as showcasing ITS benefits through a benefits database available on its website. US DOT also developed measures to track progress toward the ITS deployment goal. US DOT biennially surveyed the 75 metropolitan areas' transportation-related agencies and rated the areas' deployment levels according to its measures. Progress had been made toward achieving US DOT's deployment goal, but the goal and measures had limitations and fell short of capturing ITS's impact on congestion. Accordingly, 62 of the 75 metropolitan areas had met their goal of deploying integrated ITS infrastructure in 2004.

US DOT defined the goal of complete intelligent transportation infrastructure to include two elements – deployment, meaning the extent that certain technologies are installed over certain areas such as freeways, and integration, meaning the extent of coordination between different agencies that deploy ITS technologies. However, according to the criteria, metropolitan areas with relatively low thresholds of ITS infrastructure could still meet the goal. Among other things, the measures did not capture the extent to which deployed ITS technologies were effectively operated, and in some metropolitan areas, operations of ITS technologies were limited. In highly congested metropolitan areas, ITS infrastructure tended to be more complex because it typically consisted of a set of systems deployed by multiple agencies. A state transportation department, city traffic department, transit agency, and toll authority could each deploy different ITS technologies that addressed their transportation needs. Transportation agencies could integrate their ITS technologies by coordinating ITS information sharing and other operations.

Many of the ITS studies reviewed suggested that ITS deployment could have benefits of relieving congestion, increased traffic throughput, improved safety, and better air quality. Results from some studies suggest that ITS benefits depended upon effectively operating ITS technologies to meet local conditions. However, few studies provided information about cost effectiveness of the ITS deployments, which was essential for maximizing public investments. Barriers to ITS deployment and use included the limited public awareness of the impact of ITS, difficulty of funding ITS operations, limited technical expertise, and lack of technical standards.

Activity-Based Travel Forecasting Conference

The development of activity-based travel analysis grew out of the dissatisfaction with trip-based forecasting approaches. Concerns about aggregate phenomena such as congestion, emissions, and land use patterns led planners to consider policies aimed at controlling them. These included, for example, employer-based commute programs, travel demand management measures, peak-period road pricing, transportation control measures, intelligent transportation systems, and transit-oriented land development. But these policies did not affect the aggregate phenomena directly. Instead, they affected them indirectly through the behavior of individuals. Furthermore, individuals adjusted their behavior in complex ways, motivated by a desire to achieve their activity objectives.

The activity-based approach to travel demand analysis, which developed over a period of two decades, was founded on the long-accepted idea that travel was generally not undertaken for its own sake but rather to participate in an activity at a location that was separated from one's current location. The idea that travel was a derived demand had been accepted by travel demand modelers. However, traditional travel demand models paid only lip service to this fundamental idea by segmenting trips by trip purpose and modeling the trips for different purposes separately.

The development of the activity-based approach to travel demand analysis was characterized by a desire to understand the phenomenon of urban travel, not merely to develop predictive models that appeared to produce acceptable forecasts. Proponents of this approach believed that one needed to have a good understanding of the behavioral phenomenon being modeled in order to develop sound predictive models. Much of the early work on the activity-based approach to travel demand analysis used in-depth interviews, with small samples, in an attempt to gain a good understanding of urban travel behavior.

The activity-based approach to travel demand analysis was characterized by the following features: (1) treatment of travel as a demand derived from desires and demands to participate in other, nontravel activities; (2) focusing on the sequences or patterns of behavior, not discrete trips; (3) analysis of households as the decision-making units; (4) examination of detailed timing and duration of activities and travel; (5) incorporation of spatial, temporal, and interpersonal constraints; (6) recognition of the interdependence among events separated in space and time; (7) use of household and person classification schemes based on differences in activity needs, commitments, and constraints; and (8) recognition of the importance of dynamic analysis, the need to examine activities over as they adapt to changing conditions.

A conference was sponsored by the US Department of Transportation and the US Environmental Protection Agency to explore the progress of activity-based travel analysis. The principal goal of the conference was to promote the use of activity-based approaches for travel forecasting. Corollary purposes were to identify activity-based forecasting techniques that could be put into practice and to recommend actions to advance the state-of-the-art. Conclusions from the conference indicated that it was useful because it brought together researchers and practitioners to introduce and discuss the need and potential for new procedures. The practitioners were exposed to some new developments that might improve their practice in the future. However, there was disappointment that the state-of-the-art had not yet reached the point of providing tested techniques that the practitioners could use immediately. The researchers were apprised of the needs of practitioners as guidance for their future development efforts (Texas Transportation Institute, 1997).

Public Involvement

The expansion of public involvement, which occurred over many years, empowered groups and individual citizens to have a voice in policy decisions that affected them and their communities. The mandates for public involvement in transportation planning codified lessons learned in the 1970s and 1980s – lessons that many transportation agencies learned after the fact from project delays, lawsuits, and public outcry about transportation decisions made without citizen input (O'Connor et al., 2000).

The Intermodal Surface Transportation Efficiency Act of 1991 (ISTEA) mandated emphasis on early, proactive, and sustained citizen input into transportation decision-making – with special outreach efforts targeted at traditionally underserved populations. ISTEA's directive was reinforced by the passage of the Transportation Equity Act for the 21st Century (TEA-21). These acts focused and applied to the transportation planning and development process the intent of NEPA that agencies encourage and facilitate public involvement in decisions that affect the quality of the human environment. The Council on Environmental Quality (CEQ) regulations on implementing NEPA required that agencies make diligent effort to involve the public in preparing and implementing their NEPA procedures. They also required that agencies provide public notice of NEPA-related hearings, public meetings, and the availability of environmental documents so as to inform those persons and agencies who may be interested or affected (Council on Environmental Quality, 1978).

FHWA and FTA developed guidance for implementing public involvement processes. As the agency responsible for coordinating the regional transportation planning process, MPOs were required to actively involve all affected parties in an open, cooperative, and collaborative process that provided meaningful opportunities to influence transportation decisions. Decision-makers had to consider fully the social, economic, and environmental consequences of their actions, and assure the public that transportation programs support adopted land use plans and community values. FHWA and FTA published the guide Public Involvement Techniques for Transportation Decision-Making to provide agencies with access to a wide variety of tools to involve the public in developing specific plans, programs, or projects through their public involvement processes. MPOs had to develop effective involvement processes custom tailored to local conditions (Howard/Stein-Hudson, 1996).

Rather than establishing a set of uniform rules, the policies of FHWA and FTA established performance standards that included:

* early and continuous involvement;
* reasonable public availability of technical and other information;

- collaborative input on alternatives, evaluation criteria, and mitigation needs;
- open public meetings where matters related to transportation policies, programs, and projects are being considered; and
- open access to the decision-making process prior to closure (US Dept. of Transportation, 2004b).

States and MPOs adapted public participation guidelines to their local conditions. In varying ways, these agencies conducted their public participation processes. Many states and MPOs in major metropolitan updated their public involvement plans and procedures regularly using input from staff experience and the public.

The public participation requirements endeavored to make the transportation planning and development process more democratic. They required that all parties which might be affected by the transportation decision have an opportunity to understand the problems, the various options being considered, and the final decision. Moreover, the guidance sought to have these affected parties actively participate in identifying the transportation problems, offer options to be considered, and voice their opinion on the final decision.

National Transportation System

In late 1993, Secretary Peña unveiled the proposed National Highway System (NHS) and stated his intention to launch work on a National Transportation System (NTS) initiative. In doing so, he set in motion a process that would draw upon the National Performance Review (NPR) for direction, influence the development of a departmental proposal for the reauthorization of the surface transportation financial assistance programs, and begin to position the department to assess and analyze the performance of the transportation system from the customer's perspective. The NTS initiative was embodied in the first goal of Secretary Peña's Strategic Plan for the Department, "Tie America Together."

The secretary directed that extensive public hearings be held to involve the transportation community and interested citizens in the development of a comprehensive NTS. There was widespread concern and opposition to the initial idea of developing a map of a designated NTS. As a result, the department shelved the idea of developing a specific NTS map. The NTS initiative was refocused on the development of a process for evaluating the nation's transportation system. The NTS evolved to embody a number of ideas:

- A concept that recognizes the interaction between the nation's goals and objectives and the components of the nation's transportation system.
- A method of looking at the total transportation system and focusing on the social and economic outcomes that are ultimately what the customers use transportation to accomplish.
- An institutional framework for a cooperative partnership among the federal government, state and local agencies, the private sector, and the general public.

- A technical process bringing the user perspective to the forefront with analytical and measurement tools to build the capability to assess performance, identify issues and problems, evaluate policy options, and develop strategies.
- A strategic planning structure for the future development of the nation's transportation system.

A Progress Report on the National Transportation System Initiative was produced that described the development and use of a set of national transportation performance measures and a national transportation network analysis capability. These tools would be used in the assessment of the nation's transportation system, the identification and analysis of key issues affecting transportation, and the analysis of policy, program management, and regulatory options. The results of those efforts were intended for presentation in biennial reports on the state of the national transportation system (US Dept. of Transportation, 1996d).

State Infrastructure Banks

Section 350 of the National Highway System Designation Act of 1995 authorized the US DOT to establish the State Infrastructure Bank (SIB) Pilot Program. A SIB is a revolving fund mechanism for financing a wide variety of highway and transit projects through loans and credit enhancement. SIBs were designed to complement traditional federal aid highway and transit grants by providing the states increased flexibility for financing infrastructure investments by supporting certain projects that can be financed – in whole or in part – with loans, or that can benefit from the provision of credit enhancement. As loans were repaid, or the financial exposure implied by a credit enhancement expired, a SIB's initial capital was replenished, and it could support a new cycle of projects. In this way, SIBs represented an important new strategy for maximizing the purchasing power of federal surface transportation funds. Broadly speaking, this expansion of the level of investment that was associated with a strategic contribution of public capital can be termed "leverage" (US Dept. of Transportation, 1997b).

Under the initial SIB Pilot Program, ten states were authorized to establish SIBs. In 1996 Congress passed supplemental SIB legislation as part of the DOT Fiscal Year 1997 Appropriations Act that enabled additional qualified states to participate in the SIB pilot program. This legislation included a $150 million General Fund appropriation for SIB capitalization. The Transportation Equity Act for the 21st Century extended the pilot program for four states, California, Florida, Missouri, and Rhode Island, by allowing them to enter into cooperative agreements with the US DOT to capitalize their banks with federal aid funds provided in FY 1998 through FY 2003.

SIBs provided states significantly increased financing flexibility to meet transportation needs. The ability of SIBs to stretch both federal and state dollars to increase transportation infrastructure investment enabled projects to be built that might otherwise had been delayed or not funded due to budgetary constraints. Although authorizing federal legislation established basic requirements and the overall operating framework for a SIB, states had the flexibility to tailor the bank to meet state-specific transportation needs. As of September 2001, 32 states (including Puerto Rico) had entered into 245 loan agreements with a dollar value of over $2.8 billion (US Dept. of Transportation, 2002b).

Envision Utah

Population growth in the Salt Lake City region was growing at 2–4% annually and vehicle miles traveled was increasing at 2–3 times that rate. To accommodate such growth, a substantial amount of money would have had to be spent on the infrastructure of the transportation system to keep up with demand. The State of Utah had no regional governments, state land-use planning was rejected by a public vote, and a culture of local control and private property rights had been engrained in the political culture. To fill the void in long-range land use planning, Envision Utah was formed in 1997 as a nonprofit corporation to evaluate growth issues in Utah. Envision Utah initiated a process that created a clear civic view of transportation and growth in the area. Some of the agencies that they worked with on this effort included Utah Department of Transportation and Utah Transit Authority. Eighty-five percent of its funding came from private sources.

Envision Utah created an approach to developing its quality growth strategies based on the recognition that land use decisions were local decisions; hence, the process to develop a strategy needed to be bottom–up, emphasizing broad public participation, engaging all stakeholder interests and relying on education and persuasion. Envision Utah worked with local elected officials to involve a broad range of stakeholders in the development of growth scenarios.

Envision Utah developed received 17,000 responses to its public survey which resulted in the formation of six goals:

1. enhance air quality;
2. increase mobility and transportation choices;
3. preserve critical lands, including agriculture and sensitive and strategic open lands;
4. conserve and maintain available water resources;
5. provide housing opportunities for a range of family and income types; and,
6. maximize efficiency in public and infrastructure investments to promote other goals (Envisioin Utah, 2000).

Based on these goals, Envision Utah embarked on a process to identify where growth should occur and how it should be accommodated. Envision Utah considered four groups as part of the "Communication Pyramid" (Fig. 14.1) that should be involved in the planning process: regional stakeholders, local stakeholders (e.g., mayors, councilors), active citizens (people who sometimes come to meetings and

Fig. 14.1 Envision Utah's communication
pyramid (Source: Envisioin Utah, 2000)

always vote and take surveys), and the general public. Regional stakeholders should be people like large landowners who would be affected by and could implement the plan. This group should also be as diverse as possible. Business leaders were considered to be very valuable in that they wanted to see the larger picture – quality of life issues – and if they were sold on any given scenario, then the politicians would agree with them. To get active citizens and the general public involved, personalized, hand-signed invitations from the mayor of the citizens' home towns sent to residents to attend scenario planning workshops proved highly effective, even more so than regular advertising.

The plan that they created focused on sub-areas within the Wasatch Valley, and each local government adopted the plan as an addendum to their general plans. Over 2,000 people were involved in workshops that were held throughout the 10-county region. The workshops used sets of chips that represented various density possibilities (a compact and walkable set, a hybrid set with high infill, a set that represents the current trend with some compact development, and a low density set that represents the current trend – participants were shown images to represent what each type of chip would look like) to accommodate the growth that the region would see over the coming couple of decades. Each group's map was then put into GIS to create layers of density for maps of the region. These maps were then grouped to represent four different visions of growth for the region. Images and maps of these visions of growth were then generated and brought back to the public for their input via videos, mailings, inserts, and polling.

Presented with this information, most people preferred the scenarios that represented more infill, redevelopment, and growth on new land focused into walkable, transit-oriented communities. Once this civic view became clear, local officials were able to see what their citizens wanted. Because the scenario planning approach gathered up the vision from the grassroots and refined it, it was not necessary to defend it because it already have broad-based support. The sheer number of supporters who were part of a process overcame a small but loud opposition.

Context-Sensitive Design

By the mid-1990s, a great number of major highway projects around the country were being significantly delayed or stopped, not for lack of funding or even demonstrated transportation need, but for lack of satisfaction that the proposed solution met community and other nontransportation needs. The public and local officials had begun to question not only the design or physical features of projects, but also the basic premise or assumptions behind them as put forth by the many agencies. Out of this concern emerged a new approach to developing traditional highway projects called "context sensitive design."

This approach was built upon 30 years of history in national environmental policy making that had demonstrated a response to increasing public interest and concern about transportation projects' impacts. Beginning in 1969, NEPA required that agencies performing federally funded projects undergo a thorough analysis of their impacts to both natural and human environmental resources. In 1991, Congress emphasized the Federal commitment to preserve historic, scenic, and cultural resources as part of the ISTEA. Section 1016(a) of that act provided approval for transportation projects that affected historic facilities or were located in areas of historic or scenic value only if projects were designed to appropriate standards or if mitigation measures allowed for the preservation of these resources (Neuman et al., 2002).

In 1995, the National Highway System Designation Act emphasized flexibility in highway design to further promote preservation of historic, scenic, and aesthetic resources. This act provided funding for transportation enhancements and supported applications to modify design standards for the purpose of preserving important historic and scenic resources. Moreover, the act extended these considerations to federally funded transportation projects not on the National Highway System (Neuman et al., 2002).

In July 1997, FHWA, in cooperation with the AASHTO and several related interest groups, published Flexibility in Highway Design (US Dept. of Transportation, 1997c). This design guide illustrated how to make highway improvements while preserving and enhancing the adjacent land or community. It demonstrated how highway designers could develop roadway designs that fully considered aesthetic, historic, and scenic values along with considerations of safety and mobility in a manner beyond the most conservative use of A Policy on the Geometric Design of Highways and Streets (AASHTO Green Book).

In May 1998, the Maryland Department of Transportation hosted a workshop called "Thinking Beyond the Pavement," which brought together state and federal officials, academia, and the public to discuss ways to integrate highway development with communities and the environment while maintaining safety and performance. The conference also focused on ways to move environmentally sensitive design practices into the mainstream of transportation design (Maryland Department of Transportation, 1998).

Context-sensitive design emphasized four critical elements. It actively sought public involvement from the outset. It developed designs that met the needs of specific sites rather than trying to use centralized, standardized solutions, recognizing that different communities may have had different values and priorities. It engaged landscape architects, planners, and architects who contributed their skills to develop creative design solutions. And it used the flexibility contained in the current design guidelines to balance safety and capacity with environmental, cultural, and historical concerns (Moler, 2002).

Five pilot state DOTs (Connecticut, Kentucky, Maryland, Minnesota, and Utah) were selected to work with FHWA in defining and institutionalizing context-sensitive design principles and practices. Policy reviews, training, and other activities were conducted, with the results shared with other AASHTO members at national conferences and meetings.

Transportation Equity Act for the 21st Century

TEA-21, signed into law on 9 June 1998 by President Clinton, built and expanded upon the successful Intermodal Surface Transportation Efficiency Act of 1991 (ISTEA) policies and programs. TEA-21 authorized a record $198 billion in surface transportation investment for highways, highway safety, transit, and other surface transportation programs from fiscal years 1998 through 2003. It continued all the major ISTEA programs, and added a number of new programs to meet specific safety, economic, environmental, and community challenges.

In the flurry to get the bill to the floor, there were a number of technical errors, and a couple of key safety provisions were inadvertently dropped. Unlike the experience with ISTEA, where the technical corrections bill was never enacted, the Congress quickly passed a technical corrections bill on 22 July 1998, the TEA-21 Restoration Act, which is now a part of TEA-21.

Although TEA-21 retained the basic structure established by ISTEA, it did include some important changes. Two of the most significant achievements of TEA-21 were the guaranteed funding and the continuation and expansion of the environmental programs created by ISTEA. TEA-21 also strengthened the planning requirements, expanded the flexible funding provisions, and placed a stronger emphasis on safety. It included some new programs, such as funding for border crossing and trade corridor activities, to meet specific challenges. It continued special provisions for hiring women and minorities, the Disadvantaged Business Enterprise requirement, and labor protections such as the Davis-Bacon prevailing wage guarantee.

Title I, Federal-Aid Highways, continued and strengthened the intermodal aspects of ISTEA by providing greater flexibility to use funds for a wide array of surface transportation projects, including publicly owned intracity and intercity bus terminals and infrastructure-based intelligent transportation system capital improvements.

The planning process for metropolitan areas and states was strengthened, and freight shippers were given a voice in these planning processes. It continued the environmental programs created by ISTEA such as the transportation enhancements set aside and the Congestion Mitigation and Air Quality Improvement Program, made some additional items eligible for funding, such as natural habitat mitigation, and provided significant funding for maintenance of existing systems (US Dept. of Transportation, 1998).

TEA-21 substantially increased investment in a number of core programs. The National Highway System (NHS), the 163,000 miles of rural and urban roads serving major population centers, was authorized at $28.6 billion for fiscal years 1998 through 2003. Funds were to be distributed based on each state's lane-miles of principal arterials (excluding the Interstate), vehicle-miles traveled on those arterials, diesel fuel used on the state's highways, and per capita principal arterial lane-miles. TEA-21 required the inclusion of congressionally mandated high-priority corridors as soon as feasibility studies were completed. Project eligibility was expanded to include natural habitat mitigation, publicly owned intracity and intercity bus terminals, and infrastructure-based intelligent transportation system capital improvements. The 46,000 mile Interstate System retained its separate identify within the NHS.

The Interstate Maintenance program was retained and authorized at $23.8 billion for fiscal years 1998 through 2003. Reconstruction was restored as an eligible activity, but single occupancy vehicle (SOV) lanes continued to be ineligible. Funds were to be distributed based on each state's lane-miles of interstate routes open to traffic, vehicle-miles traveled on those interstate routes, and contributions to the Highway Account of the Highway Trust fund attributable to commercial vehicles.

The Surface Transportation Program (STP), authorized at $33.3 billion, provided flexible funding that may be used by states and localities for projects on any federal aid highway, including the NHS, bridge projects on any public road, transit capital projects, and public bus terminals and facilities. TEA-21 expanded and clarified eligible projects to include several environmental provisions such as natural habitat mitigation, programs to reduce extreme cold starts, and environmental restoration and pollution abatement projects, as well as modification of sidewalks to meet the Americans with Disabilities Act, infrastructure-based intelligent transportation systems capital improvements, and privately owned intercity bus terminals and facilities.

STP funds were to be distributed among the states based on each state's lane-miles of Federal-aid highways, total vehicle-miles traveled on those Federal-aid highways, and estimated contributions to the Highway Account of the HTF. TEA-21 retained the set aside for urbanized areas with populations over 200,000 which had to be made available (obligated) in two 3-year increments rather than one 6-year period as in ISTEA. Of the amount available to the states, the state was required to use a certain amount (based on fiscal year 1991 Federal-aid Secondary program funding) in areas with a population of less than 5,000. This amount was about $590 million per year, and 15% of the amount could be spent on rural minor collectors.

The 10% set-aside from the STP funds was continued for safety-related construction activities. Because of the substantial increase in the STP program, this set-aside would amount to close to $3.7 billion dollars over the 6-year period. These funds may be used for the railway–highway crossing program and hazard elimination projects. In addition, the hazard elimination program funds could be used for interstates, any public transportation facility, and any public bicycle or pedestrian pathway or trail, as well as traffic calming projects. Project eligibility was broadened to include off-roadway and bicycle safety improvements.

Another 10% set aside from STP funds was continued for transportation enhancements resulting in almost to $3.7 billion (including highway equity funds) to improve communities' cultural, aesthetic, and environmental qualities.

The Highway Bridge Replacement and Rehabilitation Program (HBRRP) was authorized at $20.4 billion for the 6-year period, to help states replace or rehabilitate deficient highway bridges and to seismic retrofit bridges located on any public road. The distribution formula and program requirements were basically unchanged, except eligibility was expanded to cover the application of anti-icing and deicing and the installation of scour countermeasures, both of which would extend the useful life of bridges. Of the total provided, $525 million was set aside for high-cost bridge projects, of which a portion was to be used for seismic retrofit. The set asides for timber bridges and for Indian Reservation Roads Bridges were, the requirement was continued that not less than 15% or more than 35% of a states' funds be used off-system. The act continued to allow the transfer of up to 50% of apportionments to other key surface transportation programs, but with a new provision that the amount transferred would be deducted from future apportionments.

The Congestion Mitigation and Air Quality Improvement Program was continued as a separate program, and funding was increased by about 35% to $8.1 billion for the 6-year period. This program assists communities meet national standards for healthy air.

The emergency relief grants to state and local governments were continued at $100 million annually for damage to roads as a result of natural disasters. TEA-21 authorized $4.1 billion for federal lands highways, $148 million for improvements to roads of scenic or historic value, and $270 million to create and maintain recreational trails. TEA-21 also provided $220 million for the construction of ferries and ferry terminals, most of which would go to the states of Alaska, New Jersey, and Washington.

TEA-21 expanded the provisions to make bicycling and walking safer and more viable ways of travel. Funding sources for construction of bicycle transportation facilities and pedestrian walkways and nonconstruction projects related to safe bicycle use included the National Highway System (NHS), Surface Transportation Program (STP) Funds, Transportation Enhancement Activities (10% of each State's annual STP funds), Congestion Mitigation and Air Quality Improvement (CMAQ) Program Funds, Hazard Elimination, Recreational Trails, Scenic Byways, and Federal Lands Highway Funds.

TEA-21 established two new programs that would help ensure the nation's continued transportation advantage and allow the USA to compete effectively in world markets. The border crossings and trade corridors programs would provide $700 million to support trade and improve security at borders and to design and construct corridors of national significance.

The general structure of the planning processes for metropolitan areas and states was retained as were the requirements for developing Transportation Improvement Programs (TIPs at the metropolitan level and STIPs at the state level) and long-range plans at the metropolitan and state levels. But, TEA-21 streamlined the metropolitan and state-wide transportation planning processes and specifically included freight shippers as stakeholders.

TEA-21 consolidated the long lists of planning factors required by ISTEA into seven broad areas that must be considered in the metropolitan and state-wide transportation planning processes:

1. Support the economic vitality of the metropolitan area (for state-wide plans, it says vitality of the USA, the states, and metropolitan areas) especially by enabling global competitiveness, productivity, and efficiency.
2. Increase the safety and security of the transportation system for motorized and nonmotorized users.
3. Increase the accessibility and mobility options available to people and for freight.
4. Protect and enhance the environment, promote energy conservation, and improve quality of life.
5. Enhance the integration and connectivity of the transportation system, across and between modes throughout the state, for people and freight.
6. Promote efficient system management and operation.
7. Emphasize the preservation of the existing transportation system.

Another change in the planning provisions was that failure to consider any factor shall not be reviewable by any court. Although hotly contested, the fiscal constraint provision was retained.

Section 1210, Advanced Travel Forecasting Procedures, provided funds for the completion of the core development of the Transportation Analysis and Simulation System (TRANSIMS), packaging it in a user friendly format, training and technical assistance for users. Beginning in the year 2000, the bill also provides financial support on a cost-sharing basis for a limited number of urban areas to convert from existing forecasting procedures to TRANSIMS. TEA-21 allocated $25 million to this effort.

A newly created magnetic levitation transportation technology deployment program, authorized at close to a billion dollars, was designed to encourage the construction of an operating transportation system employing magnetic levitation.

TEA-21 created a new program, the Transportation and Community and System Preservation Pilot Program, to help state and local governments plan environmentally friendly development. This program was created in response to the increasing interest in "smart growth" policies that encouraged investments in maintaining existing infrastructure rather than supporting new construction. The key purpose of this pilot program was to devise innovative neighborhood, local, metropolitan, state, or regional strategies that improve the efficiency of the transportation system, minimize environmental impacts, and reduce the need for costly public infrastructure investments.

In response to delays associated with environmental requirements, TEA-21 created an environmental streamlining pilot program to reduce red tape and paperwork in project reviews without compromising environmental protections. TEA-21 also eliminated the separate major investment study requirement and required the secretary to work with other agencies to streamline the environmental review process.

TEA-21 provided for more than 1,800 high-priority highway and surface transportation projects, priced at more than $9 billion as well, at another close to that amount in transit projects.

A new State Infrastructure Bank (SIB) pilot program was created under which four states – California, Florida, Missouri, and Rhode Island – were authorized to enter into cooperative agreements with the secretary to set up infrastructure revolving funds.

Subtitle E, the Transportation Infrastructure Finance and Innovation Act of 1998, created a new $530 million credit assistance program to help leverage $10.6 billion for construction of projects of national importance, such as intermodal facilities, border crossing infrastructure, and expansion of multi-state highway trade corridors.

Title II, Highway Safety, increased funding for safety, provided greater flexibility in using categories of funding for a wide variety of safety-related efforts, and created new programs directly specifically toward eliminating behavior, such as drunk driving and failure to use seat belts that is known to save lives. The highway safety programs focus on three key areas: driver behavior, road design, and vehicle standards.

TEA-21 consolidated the behavioral and roadway state and community highway safety formula programs and provided $932.5 million over the 6-year period. At least 40% of these funds were to be used by states and communities to address local traffic safety problems.

TEA-21 authorized $583 million in incentives to promote seat belt and child safety seat use. TEA-21 also included an ambitious timetable to develop and implement advanced air bag technologies that protect children and smaller adults while preserving the life-saving benefits for everyone else.

TEA-21 also created a $500 million incentive program to encourage states to adopt tough 0.08 blood alcohol concentration standards for drunk driving. Another $219 million in grants was made available to encourage graduated licensing and other alternative strategies. Tough new measures to target repeat drunk drivers and to ban open alcohol containers in cars were also enacted.

In addition, the act provided another $32 million for a new program to encourage states to improve their highway safety data.

Title III, Federal Transit Administration Programs, authorized $41 billion for transit. It continued and increased funding for new transit systems and extensions of existing systems, as well as the urbanized area formula grants program, the formula grants for other than urbanized areas, and the formula grants for elderly individuals and individuals with disabilities.

TEA-21 authorizes $19.97 billion for formula programs, which included set asides for the Rural Transportation Accessibility Incentive Program that provides funding to help public and private over-the-road bus operators comply with accessibility requirements, the Clean Fuels Program, and the Alaska Railroad. Of this total, $18 billion was for urban formula grants; 1% of that amount must be spent for newly created transit enhancement activities. The rural formula grant program was authorized at $1.2 billion. Although operating assistance was not longer an eligible activity for the larger urbanized areas (those over 200,000), the definition of a capital project was expanded to include preventive maintenance that would cover many projects formerly included under the operating assistance category. The formula grant program for the special needs of elderly individuals and individuals with disabilities was authorized at $456 million for the 6-year period.

TEA-21 continued the current program structure of the three major capital investment programs: new starts, fixed guideway modernization, and bus and bus-related facilities. More than $8 billion was authorized for new rail transit systems, $6.59 billion was made available for fixed guideway modernization, and a total of $3.55 billion was authorized for bus and bus-related facilities.

Transit projects were subject to the same metropolitan and state-wide planning requirements as for highways. Tax-free employer-paid transit benefits were increased from $65 to $100 per month, promoting transit ridership and putting it on a more equal footing with the benefits provided to those driving automobiles.

Under the Clean Fuels Formula Grant Program, TEA-21 authorized $500 million to help transit operators purchase low-emissions buses and related equipment and to modify garage facilities to accommodate clean-fuel vehicles. TEA-21 also included $250 million, matched by private funding, to develop clean, fuel-efficient trucks and other heavy vehicles.

TEA-21 created a $750 million Job Access and Reverse Commute program to help lower-income workers and those making the transition from welfare to work.

Title IV, Motor Carrier Safety, restructured the National Motor Carrier Safety Program to give states the ability to tailor solutions to their own needs and continued the Motor Carrier Safety Assistance Program, authorized at $579 million, to support state enforcement of commercial motor vehicle safety.

Title V, Transportation Research, established a strategic planning process to determine national research and technology development priorities for surface transportation and provided $592 million for transportation research, development, and technology transfer activities.

TEA-21 also authorized $250 million for the Technology Deployment Initiatives and Partnerships Program, designed to accelerate adoption of innovative technologies. Almost half of the total was targeted to the Innovative Bridge Research and Construction Program, which was to demonstrate the application of innovative materials technology in the construction of bridges.

The Bureau of Transportation Statistics, funded at $186 million, was continued and expanded. Among their new duties, BTS was to support activities such as commodity flow studies and transportation's role in supporting trade.

The University Transportation Centers were continued and expanded to include 10 regional centers, to be selected competitively, and 23 centers at universities named in the act.

In addition to clarifying that the major programs funds may be used for ITS capital improvements, $1.28 billion was authorized to develop and deploy advanced ITS technologies to improve safety, mobility, and freight shipping.

Title VI, Ozone and Particulate Matter Standards, authorized full federal funding of a monitoring network for fine particles for the revised standards for ozone and particulate matter, including a new fine particulate matter standard, promulgated by EPA under the Clean Air Act of 1997.

Title VII, Miscellaneous, reauthorized the existing high-speed rail development program, created in the Swift Rail Development Act of 1994, for a total of $40 million for corridor planning and $100 million for technology improvements.

A new Light Density Rail Line Pilot program was authorized at $105 million. In addition, a new Railroad Rehabilitation and Improvement Financing was created to provide credit assistance, through direct loans and loan guarantees, to public and private sponsors of intermodal and rail projects for railroad capital improvements. No direct federal funding was authorized, but the secretary was authorized to accept a commitment from a nonfederal source to fund the required credit risk premium. The aggregate unpaid principal amounts of obligations for direct loans and loan guarantees could not exceed $3.5 billion at any one time, of which not less than $1 billion had to be available solely for other than Class 1 carriers.

Title VIII, Transportation Discretionary Spending Guarantee and Budget Offsets, established new budget categories for highway and transit discretionary. Spending that effectively created a budgetary "firewall" between the highway and transit programs and all other domestic discretionary programs. Now, if highway or transit spending was to be reduced, spending for other domestic programs could not be increased accordingly, which removed the principal incentive to limit transportation spending. The firewall amount for highways was keyed to projected receipts to the Highway Account of the Highway Trust Fund, an estimated total of $157.5 billion for the 6-year period. Another $4.43 billion in highway funding was exempt from the obligation limitation, bringing the total guaranteed amount for highways to $161.95 billion. The guaranteed funding for transit had a single component, the firewall amount, which was set at just over $36 billion for the 6-year period. TEA-21 authorizes another $5 billion for transit and $15 billion for highways beyond the guaranteed funding levels.

Title IX, Amendments of Internal Revenue Code of 1986, extended the existing tax of 18.3 cents per gallon of gasoline through fiscal year 2005 with the share of the tax devoted to the Transit Account of the Highway Trust Fund set at 2.86 cents. The 4.3 cents per gallon, previously set aside for deficit reduction, was made available for transportation purposes.

Welfare to Work – Job Access and Reverse Commute Program

In August 1996, President Clinton signed the Personal Responsibility Work Opportunity Reconciliation Act, creating a new era in social welfare policy. Principal among the reforms was elimination of the Aid to Families with Dependent Children program, replaced with Temporary Assistance to Needy Families. The act provides states with annual block grants and wide latitude in program development and implementation. The act required welfare recipients to work as a condition of receiving public assistance. One of the most significant barriers to finding and maintaining employment was lack of transportation (US Dept. of Transportation, 2000c).

The Job Access and Reverse Commute Program (JARC) was created by Section 3037 of TEA-21 to address these needs. The purpose of the JARC program was to develop new transportation services designed to transport welfare recipients and low-income individuals to jobs, training, and child care, and to develop transportation services for residents of urban centers and rural and suburban areas to suburban employment opportunities. Emphasis was placed on projects that use mass transportation services.

JARC grants could be used to finance capital projects and operating costs of equipment, facilities, and associated capital maintenance items related to providing access to jobs; promote use of transit by workers with nontraditional work schedules; promote use by appropriate agencies of transit vouchers for welfare recipients and eligible low-income individuals; and promote use of employer-provided transportation including the transit pass benefit program. JARC funds were allocated on a discretionary basis as follows: 60% to areas over 200,000 population; 20% to areas of under 200,000 population; and 20% to nonurbanized areas. The federal/local share was 50/50.

JARC eligible recipients included local governmental authorities and agencies and nonprofit entities. MPOs, as the regional umbrella for transportation planning and other services, could improve coordination among local public and private agencies developing regional approaches to welfare to work transportation. DOT expected that the JARC grant program would be a catalyst for broadening the transportation planning process to better integrate employment and social equity considerations.

Georgia Regional Transportation Authority

The Georgia Regional Transportation Authority (GRTA) was created by the General Assembly in 1999 to address the problems caused by the explosive growth of the Atlanta region. As Atlanta grew, it become harder to get around the region. Atlantans drove almost 32 miles per day per capita, among the most of major cities in the nation. Development in the Atlanta region consumed about 50 acres of green space every day. From 1990 to 1996, the population of the region increased about 16% while the amount of developed land increased by 47%.

The problem reached crisis proportions when the use of federal funds for new highway projects was restricted in the 13-county metro area because of failure to meet the National Ambient Air Quality Standards. In 1998, alarmed by this restriction and national publicity about Atlanta's air pollution and traffic problems, the metro Atlanta Chamber of Commerce recommended that the state create a new authority with broad powers to deal with local governments (Georgia Regional Transportation Authority, 2003).

The authority was charged with combating air pollution, traffic congestion, and poorly planned development in the metropolitan Atlanta region. As other areas of the state fall out of attainment, they would also fall under the purview of GRTA. GRTA was formed to ensure that metropolitan Atlanta could sustain its economic growth, while maintaining the quality of life that made the area so attractive to businesses and workers.

Realizing that traffic and other growth-related problems must be addressed on a regional basis, the legislature granted GRTA broad powers, which allowed GRTA to use a "carrot and stick" in its dealings with local governments. GRTA could issue $1 billion in revenue bonds and $1 billion in general obligation bonds, the latter of which must be approved by the General Assembly. The authority could assist local governments in financing mass transit or other projects to alleviate air pollution. GRTA board approval was also required for land transportation plans in the region, and for use of federal or state funds for transportation projects associated with major developments such as large subdivisions or commercial buildings, that affect the transportation system in the metro Atlanta region. Local governments can override a GRTA veto of use of transportation funds for development project with three-fourths "supermajority." The 15 GRTA board members also sat as the Governor's Development Council, and in that capacity they were responsible for assuring that local governments meet state requirements for land use planning (Georgia Regional Transportation Authority, 2003).

In June of 1999, the State DOT settled a lawsuit that had been filed by the Georgia Conservancy, the Sierra Club, and Georgians for Alternative Transportation, challenging 61 road projects in the 13-county area. Under the terms of the settlement, only 17 of those projects could go forward until the region has a transportation plan that met air quality standards. The ARC adopted such a plan in March of 2000, the GRTA board subsequently approved the plan, and the lapse ended on 25 July 2000, when the federal government approved the region's transportation plans.

Congestion Management Systems

Growth in traffic out paced the ability of state and local governments' ability to implement capacity solutions to alleviate congestion. In order to "manage" the level of congestion within metropolitan areas, congestion management systems (CMS) were created as a way to address this traffic and person travel growth. CMS were one of the management systems required by ISTEA. Even though the rest of the management systems were made optional by the NHS Designation Act, a CMS was still required for those MPOs that had over 200,000 in population and were classified as Transportation Management Areas (TMAs).

A CMS was a systematic process for defining what levels of congestion were acceptable to a community; developing performance measures for congestion; identifying alternative strategies to manage congestion; prioritizing funding for those strategies; and assessing the effectiveness of those actions. A CMS included methods to monitor and evaluate performance, identify alternative actions, assess and implement cost-effective actions, and evaluate the effectiveness of implemented actions. At the core, a CMS included a system for data collection and performance monitoring, performance measures or criteria for identifying when action is needed, a range of strategies for addressing congestion, and a system for prioritizing which congestion management strategies would be most effective in alleviating congestion and enhancing mobility.

In TMAs designated as ozone or carbon monoxide nonattainment areas, Federal guidelines prohibited projects that increased capacity for single occupant vehicles (SOVs) unless the project came from a CMS. The CMS provided an appropriate analysis of all reasonable (including multimodal) travel demand reduction and operational management strategies for the corridor in which a project that would result in a significant increase in capacity for SOVs is proposed (Table 14.1). If the analysis demonstrated that travel demand reduction and operational management strategies could not fully satisfy the need for additional capacity in the corridor, the CMS was to identify all reasonable strategies to manage the SOV facility effectively. SOV projects that were part of the CMS had to include operational management and/or travel demand reduction strategies to effectively manage these facilities so system performance did not worsen after the facilities were constructed (US Dept. of Transportation, 1995).

The key to the CMS in metropolitan areas was monitoring and analysis of the entire transportation system's performance, in the broadest terms, not the performance

Table 14.1 Congestion management strategies

- Travel demand management measures
- Traffic operational improvements
- Measures to encourage use of high occupancy vehicle (HOV) lanes
- Public transit capital and operational improvements
- Measures to encourage use of nonmotorized modes
- Congestion pricing
- Growth management
- Access management techniques
- Incident management techniques
- Intelligent transportation systems applications
- Addition of general purpose lanes

Source: US Dept. of Transportation, 1995

of one mode or another as measured by narrowly defined mode specific criteria. Performance was measured in terms of congestion relief and other state- and- locally selected performance indicators. The strategies that resulted from the CMS were incorporated into the long-range transportation plans and TIPs. Although the CMS was the responsibility of the MPO, the expertise of transportation operations managers was vital to developing and evaluating congestion mitigation strategies. Because the CMS typically considered a diverse set of strategies, it was often accessible to a wide range of stakeholders.

States and MPOs adopted a variety of practices in implementing their CMS. Since the inception of CMS requirements, practice evolved along a number of dimensions. There was a migration away from volume-based measures toward ones that were based on travel time. Advances in technology also created opportunities to collect more data and do so more cost effectively, through use of tools such as GPS and GIS applications and coordination with state DOTs and traffic management centers that were collecting data for traffic operations using ITS infrastructure. Data being collected and strategies identified for the CMS helped address other regional goals, such as improving planning for nonmotorized modes, freight, safety, and emergency management. The extent of traffic congestion problems and the size of the MPO also affected the level of resources that were available and appropriate to devote to CMS activities (Grant and Fung, 2005).

However, for several reasons, the CMS process was marginalized in some regions. Intensive data collection activities turned some stakeholders away from the CMS process. The CMS functioned primarily as a routine analysis and data collection process, isolated from most planning and programming and from ongoing management and operations efforts.

Value Pricing Pilot Program

TEA-21 created the Value Pricing Pilot Program. This program replaced the Congestion Pricing Pilot Program that was authorized by the ISTEA. TEA-21 authorized US DOT to enter into cooperative agreements with up to 15 state or local governments or other public authorities, to establish, maintain, and monitor local value pricing pilot programs. Further, it permitted the use of tolls on the Interstate system in HOV lanes if the vehicles were part of a local value pricing pilot program under this section (US Dept. of Transportation, 2000d).

The Congress mandated this program as an experimental program aimed at learning the potential of different value pricing approaches for reducing congestion. Value pricing, also known as congestion pricing or peak-period pricing, entailed fees or tolls for road use which vary by level of congestion. Fees were typically assessed electronically to eliminate delays associated with manual toll collection facilities.

The Value Pricing Pilot Program, and its predecessor the Congestion Pricing Pilot Program, provided states, local governments, and other public entitles 80%

federal matching funds to establish, maintain, and monitor pricing projects. By 2004, about $29 million had been obligated to 15 states for 36 projects. These funds were in addition to $30 million obligated under the Congestion Pricing Pilot Program.

Four broad categories of pricing strategies were implemented or planned under the program: newly imposed tolls on exiting toll-free facilities; tolls on lanes added to existing highways; variable tolls on existing or newly built roads, bridges, and tunnels; and pricing strategies that did not involve tolls (e.g., usage-based vehicle charges, market pricing of employer-provided parking spaces, and payments to households to reduce car use) (US Dept. of Transportation, 2004c).

The projects in the program provided evidence that some pricing strategies could be politically and publicly acceptable, could keep congestion from occurring on priced lanes, could change travel behavior, could improve usage of existing highway capacity, and could provide additional funding for transportation improvements (US Dept. of Transportation, 2004c).

Conferences on Refocusing Transportation Planning for the 21st Century

The passage of TEA-21 retained most of the core transportation programs from ISTEA and the relationships among federal, state, and metropolitan areas. However, it provided added emphasis in the areas of streamlining and improving the transportation planning process using emerging planning tools and approaches; operations and management (including intelligent transportation systems); coordination of service providers (including welfare to work and social equity considerations); inclusion of freight planning; and early consideration of environmental impacts (including sustainability and environmental justice).

As a result of these new emerging issues, FHWA and FTA requested that TRB conduct two conferences on Refocusing Transportation Planning for the 21st Century. The conferences were to engage a broad range of stakeholders, reviewed the lessons that had been learned under ISTEA, and identify research, analytical, and programmatic issues under TEA-21. These conferences represented a continuation of the series of similar meetings dating back to 1957 that focused on the clarification and specification of the institutional and programmatic structure of the transportation planning process (Transportation Research Board, 2000).

The first conference led to the identification of key trends, issues, and general areas of research. The overriding umbrella issue that surfaced from the first conference was the need for a more robust transportation planning process to address the emerging problems identified by the conferees. The cross cutting issues areas included development of a customer- and user-based planning process; linking planning to the political process; creating a vision for the community and defining the role of transportation in achieving the vision; understanding current and future movement of freight; technical processes, including models, were unsatisfactory; role and impact of technology on transportation; land use and transportation; determining institutional issues; professional development; connecting linkages to other problem areas; and encouragement of certain transportation solutions or outcomes of the planning process.

The first conference also projected a vision for each subject area 10 years in the future and the actions needed to reach that vision as well as the research needs in those areas. The second conference took the research needs identified in the first conference and developed specific research recommendations to address these issue areas that formed a National Agenda for Transportation Planning Research.

The conference also raised a number of concerns about the future of the transportation planning process. Will the increasing demands on and complexity of the process conflict with the need for relevance and ability to turn around issues and analyses quickly? Will technology assist in addressing complex transportation problems? And, are existing institutions properly structured to handle the rapid pace of change? The conferees were concerned that the number of institutional issues were increasing faster than they were being solved. These conferences demonstrated how complicated and wide ranging the transportation planning process had become by the turn of the century.

National Transportation Policy Architecture for the 21st Century

As the new century was approaching, the US DOT undertook a review of the nation's transportation decision-making process and its ability to respond to the issues that would be facing transportation in the twenty-first century. This review took place 25 years after the National Transportation Trends and Choices report produced under Transportation Secretary William T. Coleman Jr. (US Dept. of Transportation, 1977c).

A report, The Changing Face of Transportation, was produced that reviewed developments in the nation's transportation system over the previous 25 years and looked 25 years into the future (US Dept. of Transportation, 2000e). The report evaluated national transportation policies and programs, reviewed recent transportation trends, identified important transportation issues, and evaluated actions to improve travel service in each travel market, including intercity passenger, intercity freight, urban transportation, rural transportation, and international transportation.

In addition, the department organized a number of "2025 Visioning Sessions," with various stakeholder groups to learn their issues, concerns, and options for the future. A forum on decision-making was held with transportation leaders to discuss the needs and possibilities for the future. And, an International Transportation Conference was to be held to highlight US DOT's accomplishments and obtain feedback from its international partners.

The final report from this process, Transportation Decision Making: Policy Architecture for the 21st Century, recognized that at the threshold of a new century and a new millennium, the process of globalization had broadened horizons and changed the way the world grew, developed, communicated, learned, and cared for the planet and for each other (US Dept. of Transportation, 2000f). It has also influenced government to streamline programs, encouraged privatization of many functions and responsibilities, and recognized that problems are best addressed through interjurisdictional and interinstitutional collaboration, public involvement, and holistic approaches. For transportation, this new world of change demanded a new way of thinking about transportation's place and contribution to the larger purposes it served. It demanded new tools, new alliances, and a new architecture for determining the intricate choices that transportation entailed and created.

The motivation for crafting the policy architecture was to enhance US DOT's stewardship role in future decades. The decision-making roles of public and private sectors defined and the emerging issues and concerns set the stage for building the department's stewardship role. The report established a framework for making decisions specifically aimed at future outcomes and impacts on the people, organizations, and service of the US transportation system in 2025.

The policy architecture for the future had to encompass the entire transportation enterprise, which included federal, state, and local agencies, transportation providers, interest groups, labor unions, and the general public, to improve decision-making and address the issues and concerns in the future. All of these entities must work together to make decisions on future investments, operations, and funding to assure that the nation continued to have the finest transportation system in the world. Transportation decision-making over the previous two decades had evolved to become more multimodal, more inclusive of stakeholders, more flexible in the use of transportation funds, more decentralized to allow decisions to be made by those closer to the problems, and more dependent upon private providers.

The five core principles of decision-making formed the key aspects for effective decision-making in the future:

1. *Holistic*: Transportation decision-making should recognize and foster appropriate tradeoffs among individual transportation choices, industry forces, and societal goals.
2. *Collaborative and consensus building*: Transportation decision-making should use an open and inclusive process, providing an opportunity for all parties and stakeholders to engage the issues and influence the outcomes.
3. *Flexible and adaptive*: The transportation decision-making process should be able to respond quickly and effectively to changing conditions and unpredictable, unforeseen events.
4. *Informed and transparent*: Transportation decisions should be made openly and based on the best information and analysis available.
5. *Innovative*: Transportation decisions should promote a continuing climate of innovation that reflects vision and speeds the movement of new ideas and products into service.

The report concluded that transportation decision-making would need to evolve in the future by actively engaging all stakeholders from the beginning to the end; giving greater attention to consensus building and conflict resolution; forging global cooperation and new partnerships; increasing integration of local and regional transportation planning with commercial concerns; environmental and equity issues, and other social needs and national priorities; and changing structures, organizations, and processes so they are more responsive to customers and more appropriate to new methods of operation.

Chapter 15
Moving Toward Performance-Based Planning

The new century ushered in a drive to preserve and effectively operate the transportation system, assure that expenditures achieved solid results, and find adequate resources to meet growing needs. Demand for transportation funds were increasing faster that resources could be provided. The twenty-two month battle over the passage of the Safe, Accountable, Flexible, and Efficient Transportation Equity Act – A Legacy for Users (SAFETEA-LU) was emblematic of the need for additional resources and the limitation of new funding.

The use of performance measures to guide decision making received a new impetus from federal legislation and the reality of constrained resources. Performance-based transportation planning and decision making was gained advocates for effectively guiding transportation investment and operational decisions. There was also new interest in assuring that the existing system was adequately maintained and refurbished. Asset management was used to allocate not only money to program areas, projects, and activities but also for the deployment of other resources such as staff, equipment, materials, information, and real estate.

In an effort to find additional sources of funds, there was renewed interest in attracting private-sector funding into transportation projects and in public–private partnerships. New and expanded mechanisms for accessing private funds were created by SAFETEA-LU. Moreover, there was a strong drive for the use of pricing mechanisms to manage traffic congestion and raise additional revenues for transportation investment. A number of urban areas initiated high occupancy toll (HOT) lanes and other pricing strategies.

This period came to a close with a v of the 50th anniversary of the act that launched the Dwight D. Eisenhower System of Interstate and Defense Highways. Significant changes occurred over that 50-year period and the planning and construction of the system facilitated some of them. It will remain for future researchers ad analysts to write the final chapters on the impact that the system had on the nation.

E. Weiner, *Urban Transportation Planning in the United States, Third Edition*,
doi:10.1007/978-0-387-77152-6, © Springer Science+Business Media, LLC 2008

Asset Management

By 2000, more than half of all highway capital outlays were for system preservation. The focus of the national highway program was changing from expansion to preservation and operation. This change in focus had been occurring in an environment that was characterized by high user demand, stretched budgets, declining staff resources, and a transportation system that was showing the signs of age. The need to manage the highway system in a results-oriented, cost-effective manner had become evident. The concept of "asset management" was created to address that need (U.S. Dept. of Transportation, 1999a).

Transportation asset management is a set of guiding principles and best practice methods for making transportation resource allocation decisions and improving accountability for these decisions. The term "resource allocation" not only covers the allocation of money to program areas, projects, and activities but also covers

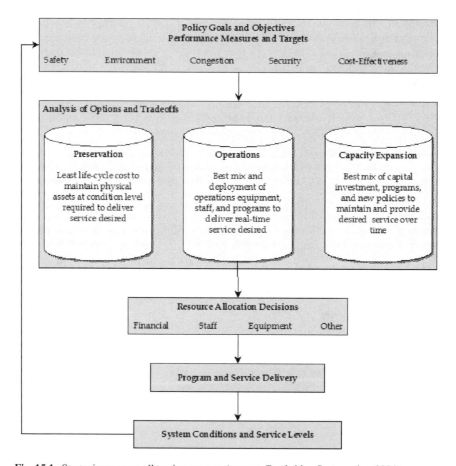

Fig. 15.1 Strategic resource allocation process (source: Cambridge Systematics, 2004)

deployment of other resources that add value (staff, equipment, materials, information, real estate, etc.). Asset management is a framework to relate investment to the performance of the transportation system. Up to this point, asset systems had been viewed separately. Pavement engineers were responsible for pavements; bridge engineers were responsible for bridges, etc. And each group worked with its own set of data. But, the full potential of asset management could only be reached when systems are managed together (Cambridge Systematics, 2004).

Asset management is concerned with the entire life cycle of transportation decisions, including planning, programming, construction, maintenance, and operations. It emphasizes integration across these functions, reinforcing the fact that actions taken across this life cycle are interrelated. It also recognizes that investments in transportation assets must be made considering a broad set of objectives, including physical preservation, congestion relief, safety, security, economic productivity, and environmental stewardship (Fig. 15.1). FHWA in cooperation with AASHTO developed guides and training sources for states and metropolitan areas to adopt asset management practices (Cambridge Systematics, 2004).

Some states contracted out their asset management functions. In 1997, the Virginia Department of Transportation (VDOT) established the first public–private interstate highway asset management project in the nation. Washington, DC established the first urban performance-based roadway asset management contract which featured annual evaluations of the program. Since then, several other states and municipalities contracted out elements of their highway asset management activities.

Conference on Performance Measures in Planning and Operations

For nearly a decade, there was a growing interest in the development and use of performance measures to guide investment decisions at all levels of government. Several factors encouraged this trend toward using performance measures in transportation planning and programming, including:

- A desire to increase the accountability of public expenditures
- The need to communicate results to customers and to get their support for investments by focusing on results in the face of reduced resources
- Responsiveness to federal and state statutes

ISTEA and TEA-21 directed a focus on performance by articulating planning factors, encouraging (and sometimes requiring) management systems, fiscally constraining capital improvement programs, and linking the plans to these programs, while many state legislatures moved toward performance-based budgeting. Simultaneously, there has been a strong aversion by many transportation professionals to have the dialogue on transportation performance controlled by people who did not have direct responsibility for the system. Responding to this trend of growing interest in the topic, TRB and transportation agencies sponsored a Conference on Performance Measures to Improve Transportation Systems and Agency Operations (Transportation Research Board, 2001).

The conferees concluded that performance measures should be based on the information needs of decision makers and should address the goals of both the agency and the larger community. Performance measures must be integrated into the decision-making process; otherwise, performance measurement would be simply an add-on activity that did not affect the agency's operation. Experience showed the importance of first identifying the goals and objectives to be addressed by the performance measures. Buy-in from customers, stakeholders, decision makers, top management, and front-line employees was critical for initial acceptance and continued success of the performance measures.

No one set or number of performance measures can fit all agencies. It was important to use multimodal or mode neutral performance measures. The level of detail and the reporting cycle of the performance measures must match the needs of the decision makers. The presentation of performance measures data must be carefully designed. The information must be easily understood, and the data analysis and presentation must provide the information necessary to improve decision making.

Increasing demands on, broader goals set for, and limited resources available to transportation agencies stimulated the development of performance measurement programs. Consequently, performance measures were considered not a fleeting trend but a permanent way of doing business that eventually would be used at all levels of transportation agencies.

The Alameda Corridor

The Ports of Los Angeles and Long Beach, California, taken together, make up the United States' largest international trade gateway, handling $200 billion in cargo annually (35% of all US waterborne containers). Dramatic increases in the level of international trade caused significant freight congestion at these ports, delaying the transfer of goods, increasing local traffic congestion, and generating ripple effects for shippers across the nation (Los Angeles County Economic Development Commission).

Planning to address these issues began in October 1981, when the Ports Advisory Committee (PAC) was created by the Southern California Association of Governments (SCAG). PAC members included local elected officials, as well as representatives of the ports of Los Angeles and Long Beach, the US Navy, Army Corps of Engineers, affected railroads, trucking industry, and the Los Angeles County Transportation Commission (LACTC). The first phase of their work focused on highway improvements, while the second phase was concerned with the impacts of projected train traffic on communities north of the ports. In August of 1989, a Joint Powers Authority was created to have design and construction responsibility for the Alameda Corridor. The Alameda Corridor Transportation Authority (ACTA) is governed by the cities of Los Angeles and Long Beach, the ports of Los Angeles and Long Beach, and the Los Angeles County Metropolitan Transportation Authority.

After more than two decades of planning and 5 years of construction, the Alameda Corridor freight rail expressway opened on time and on budget on 15

April 2002. The Alameda Corridor is a 20-mile freight rail expressway between the neighboring ports of Los Angeles and Long Beach and the transcontinental rail yards and railroad mainlines near downtown Los Angeles. The centerpiece is the Mid-Corridor-Trench, a below-ground railway that is 10–mile long, 30–ft. deep and 50–ft. wide. By consolidating 90 miles of branch rail lines into a high-speed expressway, the Alameda Corridor eliminated conflicts at more than 200 at-grade railroad crossings where cars and trucks previously had to wait for long freight trains to slowly pass. It also cut by more than half, to approximately 45 min, the time it takes to transport cargo containers by train between the ports and downtown Los Angeles. The Alameda Corridor is operated by a unique partnership between the ports of Los Angeles and Long Beach, Burlington Northern and Santa Fe Railway and Union Pacific Railroad.

The project was constructed at a cost of $2.4 billion. It was funded through a unique blend of public and private sources, including $1.16 billion in proceeds from bonds sold by ACTA; a $400 million loan by the US Department of Transportation; $394 million from the ports; $347 million in grants administered by the Los Angeles County Metropolitan Transportation Authority; and $130 million in other state and federal sources and interest income. Debts are retired with TEU-based fees paid by the railroads for transportation of cargo on the Alameda Corridor and for cargo trans-ported into and out of the region by rail even if the Alameda Corridor is not used.

Since the start of operations, the Alameda Corridor has handled an average of 35 train movements per day – a figure consistent with earlier projections for this stage of operations. Usage is projected to increase steadily as the volume of international trade through the ports grows. The ports project the need for more than 100 train movements per day by the year 2020. The Alameda Corridor can accommodate approximately 150 train movements per day. The Alameda Corridor is intended primarily to transport cargo arriving at the ports and bound for destinations outside of the five-county Southern California region (imports) or originating outside the region and shipped overseas via the ports (exports). This accounts for approximately half of the cargo handled by the ports. The other half of the cargo handled by the ports is bound for or originates in the region, and that cargo is transported primarily by truck.

Freight Analysis Framework

The transportation of freight in the US was predominantly an interstate activity. The 1993 Commodity Flow Survey showed that shipments crossing state bounda-ries accounted for about 73% of the ton-miles and 55% of the value of commodity movements by truck. While freight transportation had been a leading sector in terms of productivity improvements, there were growing concerns regarding the ability of the freight transportation system to support the future increases in freight movements and national economic growth.

Techniques for freight transportation planning, especially at the regional level, had not been as well developed as they were for passenger transportation planning.

To some degree, this could be attributed to the greater complexity of the freight transportation system in terms of the spatial and temporal diversity of freight generation activities and movement, and the large portion of the freight transportation system in the private sector. States were interested in freight movements across their borders but there was no source of information on current movements or forecast of future flows (Fekpe et al., 2002).

In an attempt to fill this void, the Federal Highway Administration developed the Freight Analysis Framework (FAF). The FAF was a comprehensive national data and analysis tool for freight flows for truck, rail, water, and air modes. The FAF also forecasted freight activity to 2010 and 2020 for each of these modes.

The FAF project involved three major technical steps: development of a physical FAF network, development of domestic and international freight flows and linking them to the FAF network, and development of forecasts for 2010 and 2020. The FAF highway network drew upon state-specific databases and data from federal highway inventories in the Highway Performance Monitoring System (HPMS). The FAF information on freight flows was based upon freight transportation data from both public and private sources, notably the 1993 CFS, and proprietary private data. Because of data gaps, some of the FAF freight flows were synthesized by using models. The FAF estimates of commodity volume and value for 2010 and 2020 were based upon proprietary economic forecasts (Meyburg, 2004).

The FAF described domestic and international freight movements within the United States, by commodity and mode, on a network of FAF transportation facilities for 1998, 2010, and 2020. The FAF database contained freight flow information at the county-to-county level and aggregated to the state-to-state level. The FAF database was used to generate a variety of freight flow maps, which were available to state and local agencies. They showed flows by truck, rail, and waterway, as appropriate. The FAF map for each port or border crossing showed the inland movement of international freight by truck in 1998.

Analyses from the FAF showed that the nation's transportation system carried over 15 billion tons of freight valued at over $9 trillion in 1998 (Table 15.1). Domestic freight movements accounted for nearly $8 trillion of the total value of shipments. By 2020, the US transportation system is expected to handle cargo valued at nearly $30 trillion. The nation's highway system handled 71% of the total tonnage and 80% of the total value of US shipments in 1998. Air freight moved less than 1% of total tonnage but carried 12% of the total value of shipments in 1998. The FAF forecasted that domestic freight volumes would grow by more than 65%, increasing from 13.5 billion tons in 1998 to 22.5 billion tons in 2020, with the air and truck modes will experience the fastest growth. International trade accounted for 12% of total US freight tonnage in 1998 and was forecasted to grow faster than domestic trade, nearly doubling in volume between 1998 and 2020 (U.S. Dept. of Transportation, 2002a).

The FAF was a valuable tool in understanding and analyzing the freight sector of the nation's transportation system. Nevertheless, its usability was limited due to its lack of transparency in the derivation of its estimates and was thereby most useful for national scale analyses (Meyburg, 2004).

Table 15.1 US freight shipments by tons and value

Mode	Tons (millions)			Value (billions $)		
	1998	2010	2020	1998	2010	2020
Total	15,271	21,376	25,848	9,312	18,339	29,954
Domestic						
Air	9	18	26	545	1,308	2,246
Highway	10,439	14,930	18,130	6,656	12,746	20,241
Rail	1,954	2,528	2,894	530	848	1,230
Water	1,082	1,345	1,487	146	250	358
Total Domestic	13,484	18,820	22,537	7,876	15,152	24,075
International						
Air	9	16	24	530	1,182	2,259
Highway	419	733	1,069	772	1,724	3,131
Rail	358	518	699	116	248	432
Water	136	199	260	17	34	57
Other[a]	864	1,090	1,259	NA	NA	NA
Total International	1,787	2,556	3,311	1,436	3,187	5,879

[a]Note: Modal numbers may not add to totals due to rounding; NA = not available; The "Other" category includes international shipments that moved via pipeline or by an unspecified mode (U.S. Dept. of Transportation, 2002a)

Central Texas Regional Mobility Authority

As was the case with many states, Texas highways were becoming more congested on a daily basis and their growing population was expected to exacerbate the problem. The state had only the resources to construct one-third of its needed transportation projects using traditional funding methods. State gas tax revenues and federal funds were not expected to increase at a rate that was fast enough to provide funding to build the highway capacity to meet this future demand. As part of a series of strategies to address this shortfall, the Texas Legislature authorized the creation of Regional Mobility Authorities (RMAs) in 2001.

A RMA was a local transportation authority that can build, operate, and maintain toll roads. RMAs provided a new, more flexible way to construct critical mobility improvements by allowing the use of local dollars to leverage revenue bonds. Individual or multiple counties could form an RMA to address local transportation needs more quickly than would be possible under traditional methods, and excess revenues could be used for other transportation projects in the area. RMAs could issue revenue bonds, set toll rates and, in partnership with a taxing entity, establish a taxing district to assist with transportation financing. The Legislature authorized the Texas Transportation Commission (TTC) to convert parts of the state highway system to toll roads and transfer them to RMAs. RMAs also had the power of eminent domain – the right to take private property for transportation projects. The formation of an RMA was initiated at the local level. Local officials could request the TTC to authorize the creation of a regional mobility authority to construct, maintain, and operate a local turnpike project.

The Central Texas Regional Mobility Authority (CTRMA) was the first RMA to be created under this new authority. It was formed by Travis and Williamson Counties, encompassing the metropolitan area of Austin, and was approved by the TTC. The CTRMA was created as an independent government agency in January 2003. Their mission was to implement innovative multimodal transportation solutions that reduced congestion and created transportation choices that enhanced quality of life and economic vitality. The Mobility Authority was overseen by a seven-member Board of Directors with the Chairman appointed by the governor. The County Commissioners of Travis and Williamson County each appointed three board members. Projects developed by CTRMA had to be included in the region's adopted long-range transportation plan and transportation improvement program developed by the Capital Area Metropolitan Planning Organization (CAMPO), the official transportation planning body for Central Texas.

As CTRMA was the first regional mobility authority in Texas, it was an important test case, marking the beginning of a new era of creatively financed road projects in the state. It shifted the financing of highway projects from the traditional "pay-as-you-go" approach. It represented a new approach in the interaction between government and the private sector (Strayhorn, 2005).

The creation of RMAs was not without controversary. RMAs were not directly accountable to the people of Texas. No voter approval was required for their creation; neither for the selection of their board members nor for the selection and funding of their toll projects. Any potential conversion of a highway that was funded through traditional means, such as the gasoline tax, to a toll facility was considered to be double taxation. There was also serious concern regarding a RMA's influence on the transportation development of an urban region in contrast to that of the established MPO for the region.

Bus Rapid Transit

With the growing costs of constructing rail-transit systems and the need for more cost-effective transit systems, attention turned to using buses to provide high quality transit service. These Bus Rapid Transit (BRT) systems combined the quality of rail transit and the flexibility of buses. A central concept of BRT was to give priority to bus transit vehicles using specialized roadways that included fixed guideways (such as expressways, busways, and streets designated for the exclusive use of buses) or nonfixed guideways (such as lanes barrier-segregated from other traffic by physical barriers, exclusive bus lanes on normal roadways, or even mixed traffic lanes that incorporated features like off-lane boarding or signal prioritization). Reducing the number of stops, providing limited-stop service, or relocating stops to areas where there was less congestion was also used to speed service, although potentially with the disadvantage of increasing walk time. All of these techniques not only reduced in-vehicle time but also, by improved the reliability of service, reduced waiting time.

Automatic vehicle location systems were used to manage bus service to regularize the intervals between buses, thereby minimizing passenger waiting time. They implemented vehicle tracking systems that used satellites or roadside sensors and permitted "next vehicle" information displays at stations, automated stop announcements for passengers, traffic signal priority, and enhanced safety and security. New fare collection policies reduced or eliminated on-vehicle fare purchase to speed boarding. Off-board fare collection systems included passes, prepurchased tickets, or "smart cards" that relied on microchip technology.

Improved vehicles were employed with low floors, wide aisles, and distinctive design, color or graphics. Low-floor buses permitted easy entrance and exit, complied with the requirements of the Americans with Disabilities Act (ADA) of 1990, and reduced the boarding time for persons using mobility aids. More and wider doorways also facilitated the rapid entry and exit of passengers, as did well-designed interior space. Along with distinctive design, these features were designed to help overcome negative perceptions of buses. Using marketing techniques also made the public aware of service improvements, and also helped to improve the public image of buses.

BRT systems were designed to promote a transit-oriented land development pattern. The attractiveness of transit was to be improved by making the land use policy more oriented to developing and maintaining pedestrian-friendly areas. In the long run, land use policy coordinated with transit investments was intended to help make transit trips more convenient by locating attractors conveniently adjacent to transit corridors and stations.

BRT projects in various cities used different combination of these elements in their applications. In 1999, FTA formed the BRT Consortium consisting of communities interested in implementing BRT. Seven of the 18 consortium members had some form of BRT: Los Angeles, Miami, Honolulu, Boston, Pittsburgh, Chicago, and Charlotte. The remaining consortium members all expected to initiate BRT revenue operations within the following 4 years. FTA provided technical assistance and guidelines to community and transit leaders who were interested in BRT as a means to improve their regular bus service or respond to transportation needs in a corridor that require a major capital investment. FTA in conjunction with TRB published TCRP Report 90: Bus Rapid Transit, as a two-volume set which identified the potential range of bus rapid transit (BRT) applications through 26 case studies and provided planning and implementation guidelines for BRT (Levinson, 2003).

Transportation Security

On 11 September 2003, terrorists crash two airliners into the World Trade Center in New York City killing 3,500 persons. This event triggered a number of wide ranging programs to improve the security of the nation and its transportation systems. Attacks involving elements of the transportation system were neither new

Table 15.2 Worldwide violent attacks on transportation by mode 1998

Mode	Incidents (%)	Deaths (%)	Injuries (%)
Bus	205 (20%)	647 (39%)	1,029 (47%)
Highways	242 (24%)	579 (34%)	336 (15%)
Rail	105 (10%)	161(10%)	607 (28%)
Maritime/piracy	220 (21%)	105 (6%)	37 (1%)
Aviation	75 (7%)	77 (5%)	13 (1%)
Pipelines	124 (12%)	74 (5%)	154 (7%)
Bridges	22 (2%)	11 (1%)	14 (1%)
Subways/other	40 (4%)	3 (–%)	4 (–%)
Total	1,033 (100%)	1,657 (100%)	2,194 (100%)

(Source: U.S. Dept. of Transportation, 1999b)

nor focused on any particular target. A summary of attacks on transportation world-wide shown in Table 15.2 demonstrated that they were widespread and often deadly (U.S. Dept. of Transportation, 1999b).

In February 2003, to focus on the protection of the nation's transportation systems, the White House released The National Strategy for the Physical Protection of Critical Infrastructures and Key Assets. This document provided a strategic basis for developing and implementing national strategies to protect and secure the nation's infrastructure assets, including transportation, from physical attack. The report contained these near-term security priorities:

- *Planning and resource allocation* – which included collaborative planning involving public- and private-sector stakeholders
- *Securing critical infrastructure* – which included transportation as one of the 11 critical infrastructure sectors

The document also described the importance of protecting the nation's critical infrastructure to preserve our nation's economy and way of life (Dornan and Maier, 2005).

With the passage of SAFETEA-LU, safety and security were identified as separate factors to be considered in both metropolitan and statewide planning processes. This change in the planning factors required transportation planners at state and local levels to address security in the transportation planning process and more completely consider and promote security enhancement early in the program and plan development processes. Most states and MPOs had just begun to consider security in all its aspects.

At this initial stage of including security in the transportation planning process, there were six elements that are needed to be addressed:

- *Prevention* – preventing a potential attacker from carrying out a successful attack
- *Mitigation* – reducing the harmful impact of an attack as it occurs and in the immediate aftermath
- *Monitoring* – recognizing that an attack is underway, characterizing it, and monitoring developments

- *Recovery* – facilitating rapid reconstruction of services after an attack
- *Investigation* – determining what happened in an attack, how it happened, and who was responsible
- *Institutional learning* – conducting a self-assessment of organizational actions before, during, and after the incident (Meyer, 2002)

States and MPOs stated to grapple with the far reaching and resources intensive responsibility. Work continue at the federal, state, and local level to better prepare, coordinate, and develop effective responses to threats to the security of the nation's transportation systems.

Transit Capacity and Quality of Service Manual

Until the publication of TCRP Web Document 6: Transit Capacity and Quality of Service Manual, First Edition (TCQSM), the transportation profession lacked a consolidated set of transit capacity and quality of service definitions, principles, practices, and procedures for planning, designing, and operating vehicles and facilities. This was in contrast to the highway mode, where the Highway Capacity Manual (HCM) defined quality of service and presented fundamental information and computational techniques related to quality of service and capacity of highway facilities. The HCM also provided a focal point and structure for advancing the state of knowledge. It was anticipated that the TCQSM would provide similar benefits. "Transit capacity" was a multifaceted concept that dealt with the movement of people and vehicles; depended on the size of the transit vehicles and how often they operate; and reflected the interaction between passenger traffic and vehicle flow. "Quality of service" was an even more complex concept that must reflect a transit user's perspective and must measure how a transit route, service, facility, or system was operating under various demand, supply, and control conditions (Kittelson and Associates, Inc., 1999).

The first edition of the TCQSM (1) included market research on what potential users would like to see in a TCQSM, (2) assembled and edited existing information on transit capacity, and (3) provided results of original research on measuring transit quality of service. The First Edition, released in 1999, introduced an "A" to "F" classification framework for measuring transit availability and comfort/convenience at transit stops, along transit routes, and for transit systems as a whole.

The Transit Capacity and Quality of Service Manual was designed to be a fundamental reference document for public transit practitioners and policy makers. The manual contained background, statistics, and graphics on the various types of public transportation, and it provided a framework for measuring transit availability and quality of service from the passenger point of view. The manual contained quantitative techniques for calculating the capacity of bus, rail, and ferry transit services, and transit stops, stations, and terminals. Example problems were included. Table 15.2 shows the range of achievable capacities for various transit modes and the highest observed North American values.

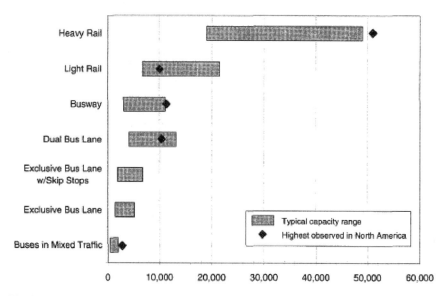

Fig. 15.2 Achievable capacity peak direction (passengers/hour) (source: Kittelson and Associates, Inc., 1999)

The second edition expanded upon the original edition by arranging for transit agencies, metropolitan planning organizations, and others to apply and evaluate, in their own environments, the quality of service concepts and thresholds and supplementing the material on service and capacity implications of service for persons with disabilities. "Planning Applications" chapters were added to the bus- and rail-transit capacity chapters, and an entirely new part on ferry capacity was added. Other major changes included expanded sections on transit-priority treatments, BRT, and commuter-rail capacity; and a new section on ropeway (e.g., aerial tramway, funicular, and cable-hauled people-mover) capacity. Also, the stop, station, and terminal capacity part was expanded to address system interactions of different station elements and the sizing of station facilities to accommodate certain "event" conditions. Demand-responsive transit quality of service has been given a chapter of its own, with measures entirely separate from fixed-route transit (Kittelson and Associates, Inc., 2003).

TRB established a Committee on Transit Capacity and Quality of Service to be responsible for guiding the long-term development and evolution of this manual.

Clean Air Rules of 2004

From 1970 to 2003, the VOC and NOx emissions that caused the formation of ground-level ozone decreased 54% and 25%, respectively; despite significant increases in vehicle miles traveled (VMT) and energy consumption. In 2003, ozone levels nationwide were the lowest they had been since 1980. Only 51 areas comprised of 221 counties remain in nonattainment. Since 1980, significant improvements in ozone levels were measured across the country. One-hour levels had been reduced by 29%. Yet ozone continued to be a pervasive air pollution problem, affecting many areas across the country and harming millions of people, sensitive vegetation, and ecosystems.

In 2004, EPA issued five Clean Air Rules to further improve air quality. Three of the rules specifically addressed the transport of pollution across state borders (the Clean Air Interstate Rule, Clean Air Mercury Rule, and Clean Air Nonroad Diesel Rule). In April 2004, EPA announced nonattainment designations under the Clean Air Ozone Rules for those areas that exceeded the health-based standards for 8-h ozone. EPA designated 474 counties in 31 states as nonattainment under the 8-h ozone standard. These designations and classifications took effect for most areas on15 June 2004. State, tribal, and local governments had to prepare a plan which described their efforts to reduce ground-level ozone. Transportation conformity requirements for the 8-h standard for most areas applied on 15 June 2005.

It also established a process for transitioning from implementing the 1-h standard for ozone to implementing the more protective 8-h ozone standard, attainment dates for the 8-h standard, and the timing of emissions reductions needed for attainment. In November 2005, EPA promulgated the second phase of the implementation rule which explained how attainment demonstrations and modeling, reasonable further progress, reasonably available control measures, reasonably available control technology, new source review, and reformulated gasoline must be addressed in 8-h ozone nonattainment areas.

In January 2005, EPA announced nonattainment designations under the fifth rule for those areas that exceeded the health-based standards for $PM_{2.5}$. State, tribal, and local governments must prepare a plan which describes their efforts to reduce $PM_{2.5}$. Transportation conformity requirements for the $PM_{2.5}$ standard will apply on 5 April 2006. In November 2005, EPA proposed a rule to implement the $PM_{2.5}$ standard. The proposal explained how EPA proposes to address attainment demonstrations and modeling, reasonably available control measures, reasonably available control technology, its policy on precursors, and new source review in $PM_{2.5}$ nonattainment areas.

States had until 2007 (three years from the date of designation) to submit State Implementation Plans (SIPs) to EPA. The SIP must outline the control strategies and technical information to demonstrate how and when the area would achieve attainment of the standard. Attainment dates are to be established based on nonattainment classifications (marginal, moderate, serious, severe, and extreme).

Scenario Planning

Long-range transportation plans were required to be financially constrained to existing and proposed funding sources that could reasonably be expected to be available. As a result, the long-range planning process was limited in its ability to analyze long-term alternative futures for an area. Where States and MPOs sought to carry out this activity, they turned to scenario planning.

Scenario planning was a strategic planning process that developed alternative futures as a means of determining an image of what a community would like to be in the future and an implementation plan to get there. The process involved transportation professionals, decision makers, business leaders, and citizens working together to analyze and shape the long-term future of their communities.

Using a variety of tools and techniques, participants in scenario planning assessed trends in key factors such as transportation, land use, demographics, health, economic development, and the environment. The participants brought the factors together in alternative future scenarios, each of these reflecting different trend assumptions and tradeoff preferences. In the end, all members of the community reached agreement on a preferred scenario. This scenario became the long-term policy framework for the community's evolution, was used to guide decision-making, and would become embodied in the long-range transportation plan.

Scenario planning thereby provided an analytical framework and process for analyzing complex issues and responding to change. It allowed participants to assess transportation's impact on their communities and the implications of different ways to accommodate growth. By improving communication and understanding in a community, scenario planning facilitated consensus building by giving communities the capacity to participate actively in planning, and ensured better management of increasingly limited resources (Ways and Burbank, 2005).

In general, the steps in a scenario planning process started with the identification of the primary issues or decisions facing the region. Next was the identification of the "driving forces," those major sources of change that impact the future. The participants then needed to consider how the driving forces could combine to determine future conditions. Based on this information, scenarios were created about future conditions that conveyed a range of possible outcomes including the implications of different strategies in different future environments. The scenario planning process then analyzed the implications of the various scenarios. The devised scenarios were measured against each other by comparing indicators relating to land use, transportation demographics, environment, economics, and technology. Finally, a preferred alternate scenario was selected.

The use of scenario planning grew through the 1990s and into 2003. Some 80 land use-transportation scenario planning were identified nationwide. Motivations for undertaking scenario planning clustered projects around issues related to growth and its impacts on various measures of quality of life. Scenario planning projects tended to utilize 3–4 scenarios that used centers or clustering as a common archetype with density and location of activities as the primary variables. These projects utilized traditional travel forecasting models with a shift toward GIS-based assessment tools in the more recent years. Of these projects, 27 resulted in adoption of a transportation plan and another 20 resulted in the adoption of a general or comprehensive plan (Bartholomew, 2005).

Public–Private Partnerships

The widening gap between transportation infrastructure requirements and the ability to fund them through traditional public revenue sources resulted in many states considering additional options to funding transportation programs. In addition, the federal share of highway funding had dropped from 28.6% in 1976 to 22.4% in 1998, while the state and local share had increased from 71.4% to 77.6% during this period.

This need to find new revenues sources lead to the emphasis on "public–private partnerships." Public–private partnerships were not a new concept to transportation infrastructure development. For highways, the private sector historically had an important role in highway construction operation and financing. Many of the earliest major roadways in the US were private toll roads. In the early years of the Republic, the importance of highways for westward expansion and trade was recognized and an era of road building began. This period was marked by the development of private turnpike companies to construct essential highways that would operate as toll roads.

During the decade of the 1990s a number of new funding approaches were developed to supplement traditional funding mechanisms and facilitating public–private partnerships. In 1994, the "Test and Evaluation" Program, known as TE-045, paved the way for innovation by providing states with more flexible ways to blend federal and nonfederal highway funds and leverage existing federal funds. The National Highway System Designation Act of 1995 and TEA-21 expanded the toolbox with several innovative mechanisms including State Infrastructure Banks (SIBs), Grant Anticipation Revenue Vehicles (GARVEEs), and TIFIA (Cambridge Systematics, Inc., 2002b).

These innovative finance initiatives were designed to accelerate projects by reducing inefficient and unnecessary constraints on a states' management of federal highway funds and expand investment by (1) removing barriers to private investment in surface transportation infrastructure, (2) encouraging the introduction of new revenue streams, particularly for the purposes of retiring debt obligations, and (3) reducing financing and related costs, thus freeing up the savings for investment into the transportation system itself. Table 15.3 shows which tools were designed to address each of the innovative financing purposes (Cambridge Systematics, Inc., 2002b).

Table 15.3 Changes in national travel characteristics 1956–2004

	1956	2004	Percent Change 1956–2004
Population	165 Million	288 Million	75
Gross domestic product	$427 Billion	$11,446 Billion	2,582
Driver licenses	77.7 Million	199 Million	156
Motor vehicles	65.1 Million	237 Million	264
Vehicle miles of travel	63.1 Million	2,960 Billion	369
Gasoline consumed (Gals)	55.6 Million	179 Billion	222

These innovative finance programs added new revenue sources to the traditional funding sources for taxes and used charges. The base of the pyramid in Fig. 15.3 represents the majority of highway projects that continued to rely primarily upon grant-based funding because they did not generate revenues. Various federal funds management techniques, such as advance construction, tapered match, and grant-supported debt service, helped move these projects to construction more quickly. When circumstances supported the advisability of debt financing (as opposed to pay-as-you-go grant funding), these projects were able to use GARVEE-style debt instruments, in which future federal highway apportionments were used to pay debt service and other debt-related costs (U.S. Dept. of Transportation, 2004d).

The mid-section of the pyramid represents those projects that were at least partially financed with project-related revenues, but could also require some form of public credit assistance to be financially viable. State Infrastructure Banks offered various types of assistance in the form of low-interest loans, loan guarantees, and other credit enhancements to state, regional, and local projects. State loans of federal grant funds, known as Section 129 loans, were another possibility. And the new TIFIA Federal credit program was designed to assist large-scale projects of regional or national significance that might otherwise be delayed or not constructed at all because of their risk, complexity, or cost.

The peak of the pyramid reflects the very small number of projects that were able to secure private capital financing without any governmental assistance. These relatively few projects were developed on high-volume corridors where the revenues from user fees were sufficient to cover capital and operating costs.

These innovative finance initiatives gained in popularity as experience with their use expanded and funding concerns grew and experience with their use expanded.

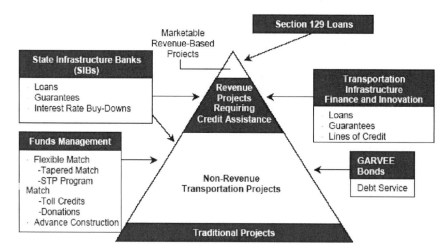

Fig. 15.3 Innovative finance tools for surface transportation projects (U.S. Dept. of Transportation, 2004e)

From 1995 to 2004, projects using these techniques supported over $30 billion in transportation investments (U.S. Dept. of Transportation, 2004e).

Norman Y. Mineta Research and Special Programs Improvement Act

On 30 November 2004 President Bush signed into law the Norman Y. Mineta Research and Special Programs Improvement Act. The purpose of the act was to provide the DOT with a more focused research organization and establish a separate operating administration for pipeline safety and hazardous materials transportation safety operations. The act was designed to allow DOT to more effectively coordinate and manage the department's research portfolio and expedite implementation of cross-cutting, innovative technologies. The act also reflected the department's commitment to the safety of the nation's pipeline infrastructure and continuing emphasis on the safe and secure transport of hazardous materials throughout the transportation network.

The act established the Research and Innovative Technologies Administration (RITA) and the Pipeline and Hazardous Materials Safety Administration (PHMSA). BTS became part of RITA as the central locus of the DOT's research and development capability, including the statistical and research operations within BTS, RITA would have the wherewithal to ensure that research dollars were used most effectively and tying them closely to the DOT's strategic goals. Reflecting the increasingly intermodal nature of transportation, RITA was a cross-cutting administration, bringing together research and analytical capabilities that were fragmented across the department.

RITA's functions under the act were to: coordinate and advance transportation research efforts within DOT; support transportation professionals in their research efforts through grants and consulting services, as well as professional development through training centers; and inform transportation decision makers on intermodal and multimodal transportation topics through the release of statistics, research reports, and a variety of information products via the Internet, publications, and in-person venues such as conferences.

Transportation–Air Quality Conformity

The Clean Air Act Amendments and surface transportation legislation linked transportation and air quality planning to assure that the National Ambient Air Quality Standards (NAAQS) would be met. The process that linked them was the transportation/air quality conformity determination. States were required to develop SIPs detailing their plans to meet the NAAQS within the legislated deadlines. A conformity determination was made to assure that federally assisted projects or actions conformed to the SIP.

No project could cause or contribute to new NAAQS violations, nor increase the frequency or severity of any existing violations of any standard, nor delay the timely attainment of any required NAAQS. The process recognized that transportation-related air quality issues had to be analyzed on a system-wide basis and be controlled through regional strategies to be effective. The Clean Air Act Amendments of 1990 expanded the "sanctions" where states fail to carry out requirements of the act including withholding of federal funding for highway projects.

The conformity determination was made for the long-range transportation plan, for the shorter term Transportation Improvement Program (TIP), and for the individual transportation project. No project could be included in the plan or TIP unless the funding to implement that project could reasonably be expected to be available. As a result, the Clean Air Act Amendments of 1990 created a major challenge to transportation planners to continue to provide urban mobility while meeting the requirements to improve air quality under tight time deadlines. Consequently, transportation/air quality conformity became driving force in and a major concern of the metropolitan and statewide transportation planning processes. Many in the transportation community expressed concern at the potential impact of these conformity determinations in delaying or altering new highway projects (Weiner, 2005).

Conformity determinations were the means of enforcing SIPs for achieving air quality standards, once SIPs had been adopted. If conformity determinations were not made, the SIP might not be implemented as intended, significantly weakening the Clean Air Act's effectiveness. While much emphasis had been placed on the problems potentially caused by areas incurring a lapse in conformity, the need to make conformity determinations affected transportation decisions in all nonattainment and maintenance areas. In this respect, conformity served an important tool for on-going planning and coordination between transportation and air quality officials as well as providing a means of enforcing the act. Conformity lapses occurred in 63 areas in 29 states and Puerto Rico between 1997 and 2004. Most of these areas returned to conformity quickly without major effects on their transportation programs: only five areas had to change transportation plans in order to resolve a conformity lapse (McCarthy, 2004).

The debate regarding proposed changes in conformity tended to be colored by the camp (air quality or transportation) to which one belonged. Those who focus on the need to modify the process generally have concluded that conformity determinations were interfering with or delaying needed transportation improvements. Those whose primary concern was air quality, however, tended to view the process as requiring a necessary analysis of air quality impacts before the commitment of large sums of public money to specific highway or transit projects (McCarthy, 2004).

Energy Policy Act of 2005

After four and a half years of debate, the Congress finally passed and the President signed into law the Energy Policy Act of 2005 on 8 August 2005. The act was a comprehensive energy plan to encourage conservation and energy efficiency;

expand the use of alternative and renewable energy; increase the domestic production of conventional fuels; and invest in modernization of the nation's energy infrastructure. Several of the provisions related to the transportation sector.

The act authorized full funding for the President's Hydrogen Fuel initiative. The initiative was created to develop, by 2015, hydrogen powered vehicles that would be suitable for mass production in 2020. Hydrogen was to be produced from diverse, affordable sources. Similarly, the program was to permit a commitment by 2015 to building hydrogen infrastructure that would be in place by 2020.

No new fuel efficiency standards were required. However, NHTSA was required to do a 1-year study of feasibility and effects of reducing use of fuel for automobiles by model year 2014, by a significant percentage of the amount of fuel consumed by automobiles. The report was to consider alternatives to current law (e.g., CAFE), consider the effects of fuel cells, and consider how automobile manufacturers could contribute to increasing fuel economy (Rypinski, 2005).

The act authorized offers of tax incentives to consumers to purchase energy-efficient hybrid, clean diesel, and fuel cell vehicles. It required a new, multiyear rulemaking by the DOT to increase fuel economy standards for passenger cars, light trucks, and SUVs. And, it established a new renewable fuel standard that required the annual use of 7.5 billion gallons of ethanol and biodiesel in the nation's fuel supply by 2012. It also extended Daylight Saving Time by approximately 4 weeks.

The act authorized the establishment of a competitive grant program under the auspices of "Clean Cities" to provide no more than 30 geographically dispersed cost-shared grants for the acquisition of alternate fuel or fuel cell vehicles, including transit or school buses, airport ground support equipment, neighborhood electric vehicles, mopeds, ultra-low sulfur vehicles, or alt fuel infrastructure. The act also authorized programs for fuel cell bus transit demonstration, clean diesel school buses, clean diesel truck retrofit and fleet modernization, fuel cell school buses, fuel efficient locomotive technologies, and conserve by bicycling. In addition, the act required a study of the link between energy security and vehicle miles traveled. It was to be a study of the linkages, if any, between land use patterns, and energy consumption and the potential benefits of transportation and land use planning in limiting fuel consumption (Rypinski, 2005).

The Energy Policy Act of 2005 demonstrated the nation's commitment to find alternatives to the use of gasoline as the primary fuel for transportation, and accelerated the research and development needed to move toward a hydrogen economy.

Safe, Accountable, Flexible, Efficient Transportation Equity Act: A Legacy for Users

The Transportation Equity Act for the Twenty-First Century (TEA-21) expired on 30 September 2003. The Congress debated for nearly 2 years on its successor. They passed 14 extensions to TEA-21 before passing the Safe, Accountable, Flexible, Efficient Transportation Equity Act: A Legacy for Users (SAFETEA-LU) in July 2005. President Bush signed it into law on 10 August 2005. The major points of contention were the total level of funding and the distribution of funds among the states especially between the donor and donee states. Many felt that the total level of funding should have been much higher which would have provided sufficient funding to accommodate both donor and donee states. However, the forecast of available revenues going into the Highway Trust Fund over the authorization period would not be adequate to support this higher level. With the administration unwilling to increase the gas tax or provide additional General Revenues to the highway programs, a compromise was eventually reached at a lower funding level.

Nevertheless, SAFETEA-LU provided $286.4 billion over 6 years for the nation's highways, public transportation and safety programs which was a 30% increase over TEA-21 levels. SAFETEA-LU continued the core transportation programs from TEA-21 while emphasizing targeted programs in several areas including freight, financing, and safety.

The National Highway System (NHS) program was funded at $30.5 billion through 2009. The formula to distribute funding was continued, based on lane-miles of principal arterials (excluding Interstate), vehicle-miles traveled on those arterials, diesel fuel used on the state's highways, and per capita principal arterial lane-miles. The act expanded eligibility of NHS funding to include environmental restoration and pollution abatement to minimize the impact of transportation projects, control of noxious weeds and aquatic noxious weeds, and establishment of native species.

The 46,000 mile Dwight D. Eisenhower National System of Interstate and Defense Highways retained a separate identity within the NHS. The Interstate Maintenance (IM) program, established under the Intermodal Surface Transportation Efficiency Act of 1991 (ISTEA) to provide for the on-going work necessary to preserve and improve interstate highways, was retained. Authorizations totaling $25.2 billion were provided through 2009, and would continue to be distributed by formula based on each state's lane-miles of interstate routes open to traffic, vehicle-miles traveled on those routes, and contributions to the Highway Account of the Highway Trust Fund attributable to commercial vehicles. A total of $500 million of authorized funds was available at the discretion of the Secretary for high-cost, ready-to-go IM projects.

The Surface Transportation Program (STP), established by ISTEA, provided flexible funding that may be used by states and localities for projects on any federal-aid highway, including the NHS, bridge projects on any public road, transit capital projects, and public bus terminals and facilities. The act expanded STP eligibilities to include advanced truck stop electrification systems, high accident/high congestion intersections, and environmental restoration and pollution abatement, control of noxious weeds and aquatic noxious weeds, and establishment of native species. A total of $32.5 billion in STP funds was authorized through 2009. Funds would continue to be distributed among the states based on lane-miles of federal-aid highways, total vehicle-miles traveled on those federal-aid highways, and estimated contributions to the Highway Account of the HTF.

Each state had to set aside a portion of their STP funds (10% or the amount set aside in 2005, whichever is greater) for transportation enhancements activities.

The set-aside of 10% previously required for safety construction activities (i.e., hazard elimination and rail-highway crossing improvements) was eliminated beginning in 2006, as these activities were funded separately under the new Highway Safety Improvement Program.

The Bridge program was broadened in scope to include systematic preventative maintenance, and freed from the requirement that bridges must be considered "significantly important." A total of $21.6 billion was authorized for this program through 2009 to enable states to improve the condition of their eligible highway bridges over waterways, other topographical barriers, other highways and railroads. The requirement that each state spend at least 15% of its bridge apportionment for bridges on public roads that were not federal-aid highways (off-system bridges) was retained, but the 35% cap was removed. The discretionary bridge program was funded only through 2005; beginning in 2006, $100 million was to be set aside annually to fund designated projects.

SAFETEA-LU provided funding totaling over $2.8 billion to fund transportation projects of national interest to improve transportation at international borders, ports of entry, and in trade corridors. A new Coordinated Border Infrastructure Program provided $833 million in funding, to be distributed by formula, to expedite safe and efficient vehicle and cargo movement at or across the land border between the US and Canada and the land border between the US and Mexico. To further promote economic growth and international or interregional trade, the National Corridor Infrastructure Improvement Program provided $1.948 billion in discretionary funding for construction of designated highway projects in corridors of national significance.

A new program, Projects of National and Regional Significance, provided funds to transportation infrastructure projects that had relevance and produced benefits on a national or regional level. Benefits could include improving economic productivity, facilitating international trade, relieving congestion, and improving safety. In addition, over 5,000 specified projects were identified in the sections under High Priority Projects and Transportation Improvements. SAFETEA-LU authorized a new Freight Planning Capacity Building program for research, training, and education to support enhancements in freight transportation planning, funded at $875,000 per year.

In SAFETEA-LU, metropolitan and statewide transportation planning processes were continued, but some changes were made. Safety and security were identified as separate items to be considered in both metropolitan and statewide planning processes. Consultation requirements for states and MPOs were significantly expanded. MPOs and states had to consult "as appropriate" with "State and local agencies responsible for land use management, natural resources, environmental protection, conservation, and historic preservation" in developing long-range transportation plan. As part of transportation plan and TIP development, MPOs had to employ visualization techniques to improve communication with stakeholders. States also had to employ visualization techniques in the development of the long-range statewide transportation plan. Requirements were added for plans to address environmental mitigation, improved performance, multimodal capacity, and enhancement activities, and to ensure that tribal, bicycle, pedestrian, and disabled interests were represented in the process.

SAFETEA-LU revised the planning factor related to environment for the metropolitan planning process to add "promot[ing] consistency between transportation improvements and State and local planned growth and economic development patterns." Metropolitan transportation plans also had to include operational and management strategies to improve the performance of the existing transportation facilities to relieve vehicular congestion and maximize the safety and mobility of people and goods. MPOs had to develop and utilize a "participation plan" that provided reasonable opportunities for the interested parties to comment on the content of the metropolitan transportation plan and metropolitan TIP. The transportation improvement program (TIP) was to be updated at least every 4 years in nonattainment and maintenance areas, and at least every 5 years in attainment areas. The funds set-aside for metropolitan planning were increased from 1 to 1.25% of the finds for the core highway programs, and a 30-day time limit for states to reimburse MPOs was imposed. The long-range transportation plan and the TIP remained separate documents.

The statewide planning process was to be coordinated with metropolitan planning and statewide trade and economic development planning activities. Additionally for the long-range statewide transportation plan, states had to consult with federally-recognized tribal agencies responsible for land use management, natural resources, environmental protection, conservation, and historic preservation. Two or more states could enter into planning agreements or compacts for cooperative efforts and mutual assistance. The statewide plan had to include measures to ensure the preservation and most efficient use of the existing system. The statewide transportation improvement program (STIP) was to be updated at least every 4 years.

SAFETEA-LU changed the due date for the Infrastructure Investment Needs Report (formerly the Highways, Bridges and Transit Conditions and Performance Report) to 31 July 2006, and every 2 years thereafter, and the report had to include any information necessary for comparison with conditions and measures in previous reports.

SAFETEA-LU authorized $110 million for ITS research from 2005 to 2009, and $122 million for ITS deployment during FY 2005 only. SAFETEA-LU also established a new Real-Time System Management Information Program to provide, in all States, the capability to monitor, in real-time, the traffic and travel conditions of the major highways of the US and to share that information to improve the security of the transportation system, address congestion problems, support improved response to weather events and surface transportation incidents, and facilitate national and regional highway traveler information. States could use NHS, STP, and CMAQ funds for planning and deployment of real-time monitoring elements.

SAFETEA-LU enhanced and clarified provisions governing HOV lanes. States were required to establish occupancy requirements for HOV lanes, with mandatory exemptions for motorcycles and bicycles unless they created a safety hazard, and optional exemptions for public transportation vehicles, low-emission and energy-efficient vehicles, and High Occupancy Toll (HOT) vehicles (otherwise-ineligible vehicles willing to pay a toll to use the facility).

SAFETEA-LU incorporated changes aimed at improving and streamlining the environmental process for transportation projects. These changes, however, came with some additional steps and requirements on transportation agencies. The provisions included a new environmental review process for highways, transit, and multimodal projects, with increased authority for transportation agencies, but also increased responsibilities (e.g., notice and comment requirements related to defining project purpose and need and determining the alternatives). A 180-day statute of limitations was added for litigation, but it was pegged to publication of environmental actions in the Federal Register, which required additional notices. There were several delegations of authority to states, including delegation of Categorical Exclusions for all states, as well as a 5-state delegation of the US DOT environmental review authority under NEPA and other environmental laws.

The air quality conformity process was modified to provide greater flexibility in transportation planning and air quality conformity, without reducing protection for air quality, including the establishment of a 4-year cycle for conformity determinations and allowing conformity findings to be based on a 10-year horizon under certain circumstances.

The Congestion Mitigation and Air Quality Improvement (CMAQ) program was continued at a total funding level of $8.6 billion through 2009 to provide a flexible funding source to state and local governments for transportation projects and programs to help meet the requirements of the Clean Air Act. Funding was available for areas that did not meet the NAAQS as well as former nonattainment areas that were in compliance. SAFETEA-LU required the US DOT to evaluate and assess the effectiveness of a representative sample of CMAQ projects, and maintain a database.

The Transportation, Community, and System Preservation Program (TCSP) was created by TEA-21 to address the relationships among transportation, community, and system preservation plans and practices and identify private-sector-based initiatives to improve those relationships. Under SAFETEA-LU, this discretionary grant program was authorized at $270 million through 2009 to carry out eligible projects to integrate transportation, community, and system preservation plans and practices. SAFETEA-LU also established a new Nonmotorized Transportation Pilot program, authorized at a total of $100 million through 2009, to fund pilot projects to construct a network of nonmotorized transportation infrastructure facilities in four designated communities. The purpose was to demonstrate the extent to which walking and bicycling could represent a major portion of the transportation solution in certain communities.

SAFETEA created a new Equity Bonus Program which had three features – one tied to Highway Trust Fund contributions and two that were independent. First, built on the TEA-21's Minimum Guarantee concept, the program ensured that each state's return on its share of contributions to the Highway Trust Fund (in the form of gas and other highway taxes) was at least 90.5% in 2005 building toward a minimum 92% relative rate of return by 2008. In addition, every state was guaranteed a specified rate of growth over its average annual TEA-21 funding level, regardless of its Trust Fund contributions. Third, selected states were guaranteed a share of apportionments and High Priority Projects not less than the state's average annual share under TEA-21.

SAFETEA-LU made it easier and more attractive for the private sector to participate in highway infrastructure projects to help close the gap between highway infrastructure investment needs and resources available from traditional sources. SAFETEA-LU established a new State Infrastructure Banks (SIBS) program which allowed all states to enter into cooperative agreements with the US DOT to establish infrastructure revolving funds eligible to be capitalized with federal transportation funds.

The Transportation Infrastructure Finance and Innovation Act (TIFIA) program was modified to encourage broader use of TIFIA financing by lowering the project cost threshold to $50 million and by expanding the eligibility to include public freight rail facilities or private facilities providing public benefit for highway users, intermodal freight transfer facilities, access to such freight facilities and capital investment for intelligent transportation systems (ITS). SAFETEA-LU expanded the bonding authority for private activity bonds by adding highway facilities and surface freight transfer facilities to a list of other activities eligible for tax exempt facility bonds. These bonds were not subject to the general annual volume cap for private activity bonds for state agencies and other issuers, but were subject to a separate national cap of $15 billion.

SAFETEA-LU provided states with increased flexibility to use tolling, not only to manage congestion, but to finance infrastructure improvements as well. The Value Pricing Pilot Program was continued, funded at $59 million through 2009, to support the costs of implementing up to 15 variable pricing pilot programs nationwide to manage congestion and benefit air quality, energy use, and efficiency. A new set-aside totaling $12 million through 2009 had be used for projects not involving highway tolls. A new Express Lanes Demonstration Program allowed a total of 15 demonstration projects to permit tolling to manage high levels of congestion, reduce emissions in a nonattainment or maintenance area, or finance added interstate lanes for the purpose of reducing congestion. Tolls charged on HOV facilities under this program had to use pricing that varied according to time of day or level of traffic; for non-HOV, variable pricing was optional.

SAFETEA-LU established the Highway Safety Improvement Program (HSIP) as a core program, separately funded for the first time, with flexibility provided to allow states to target funds to their most critical safety needs. A total of $5.1 billion was provided for 2006–2009. Of this amount, $880 million was set aside for the Railway–Highway Crossing program, with the remainder to be distributed by formula based on each state's lane-miles, vehicle miles traveled, and number of fatalities. $90 million was to be set aside annually for construction and operational improvements on high-risk rural roads. The HSIP required states to develop and implement a strategic highway safety plan and submit annual reports to the Secretary that described at least 5% of their most hazardous locations, progress in implementing highway safety improvement projects, and their effectiveness in reducing fatalities and injuries.

A new Safe Routes to School program was created to enable and encourage primary and secondary school children to walk and bicycle to school. Both infrastructure-related and behavioral projects were to be geared toward providing a safe, appealing environment for walking and biking that would improve the quality of children's lives and support national health objectives by reducing traffic, fuel consumption, and air pollution in the vicinity of schools.

SAFETEA-LU authorized a total $52.6 billion for mass transportation programs over the 6-year period 2004–2009 compared to $36 billion authorized by TEA-21. Just over 80% of the funds were derived from the Mass Transit Account, with only New Starts, Research and FTA Administration coming from the General Fund. All existing programs were continued, with two new programs added beginning in 2006: the New Freedom Program and the Alternative Transportation in National Park and Public Lands Program.

The basic program structure and formulas for FTA's programs were largely unchanged. However, the Urbanized Area Formula program was augmented. A new Small Transit Intensive Cities Formula program starting at $35 million in 2006 was created for urbanized areas under 200,000 with higher-than-average levels of transit service. In addition, a new Growing States and High Density States Formula program starting at $388 million in 2006 was created that allocated funds based on forecast population in 2015 (to allow grantees to develop transit improvements ahead of increased population) and state population density in excess of a benchmark (to address extraordinary transit needs in high density states). Rural funding is increased significantly (nearly double that in TEA-21), and a portion of the increase was allocated to address low-density rural states needs.

Program requirements for major New Starts projects generally remain unchanged. The statutory federal share remains at 80%; however, FTA would no longer be able to withhold approval of preliminary engineering or final design based on a lower proposed federal share than any previous FTA policy (i.e., 60% at that time). Projects would have to receive summary ratings at one of five levels ("high" to "low"), rather than the three previous levels ("Highly Recommended," "Recommended," and "Not Recommended"). The reliability of travel and cost forecasts was added as new "project justification" considerations, and economic development benefits had to also be evaluated. The annual New Starts Report requirement remained; however, the mid-year Supplemental Report requirement was eliminated. Alternatives Analysis activities were to be funded from a separate discretionary program.

Beginning in 2007, a new funding category was to be created for New Starts projects that requested less than $75 million in New Starts funds and had a total project cost of less than $250 million. Other federal funds could also be used for these projects. These projects were to be subject to a simplified project development process and simplified rating criteria. Non-Fixed Guideway Corridor Improvements (e.g., BRT) were allowed under the new Small Starts program. The exemption from the rating process for projects under $25 million was eliminated.

SAFETEA-LU established a New Freedom Formula Grant Program for capital and operating costs of services and facility improvements in excess of those required by the Americans with Disabilities Act. Funds were allocated based on the number of persons with disabilities to designated recipients in areas over 200,000 (60%), and to states for areas under 200,000 (20%) and for nonurbanized areas (20%). States and designated recipients had to select grantees competitively, and projects had to be included in the locally developed human service transportation coordinated plan. Up to 10% of the funds could be used for planning, administration, and technical assistance. The Job Access and Reverse Commute Program was continued, but as a formula program, structured much the same as the New Freedom Program.

A number of changes were made to enhance the coordination of human service transportation. More flexible matching requirements were included in the Urbanized, Rural, Elderly and Disabled, Job Access and Reverse Commute, and New Freedom grant programs, which allowed social service agency funds to match FTA funds. This flexibility was shown to enhance coordination in existing fund-matching programs. In addition, a plan for coordinating human service transportation and FTA funded public transportation had to be developed by 2007 before grants could be received under the Elderly and Disabled, Job Access and Reverse Commute, and New Freedom programs.

SAFETEA-LU established a new discretionary program for planning and capital costs of public transportation in National Parks and other federal public lands ($22 million in 2006). The program was to be managed cooperatively between DOT and Department of the Interior (DOI)/National Park Service (NPS). Projects were to include a variety of alternative transportation services that supplemented automobile access.

SAFETEA-LU provided $3.1 billion to fund driver behavior programs from 2005 to 2009 to be administered by the National Highway Traffic Safety Administration SAFETEA-LU authorized $897 million for 2006–2009 for State And Community Highway Safety Grants to support State highway safety programs, reduce traffic crashes and resulting deaths, injuries, and property damage. A state could use the funds only for highway safety purposes; at least 40% of these funds were to be used to address local traffic safety problems. A state was eligible for these formula grants by submitting a Performance Plan, which established goals and performance measures to improve highway safety in the state, and a Highway Safety Plan, which described activities to achieve those goals. SAFETEA-LU required assurances from states that they would implement activities in support of national highway safety goals, including national law enforcement mobilizations; sustained enforcement of statutes addressing impaired driving, occupant protection, and speed; annual safety belt use surveys; and development of timely and effective statewide data systems.

SAFETEA-LU established a new Safety Belt Performance grant program funded at $498 million for 2006–2009 to encourage the enactment and enforcement of laws requiring the use of safety belts in passenger motor vehicles. SAFETEA-LU authorized $515 million for 2006–2009 for an amended Alcohol-Impaired Driving Counter Measures Incentive grant program to encourage states to adopt and implement effective programs to reduce traffic safety problems resulting from individuals driving while under the influence of alcohol.

SAFETEA-LU established a number of research programs including Future Strategic Highway Research Program (FSHRP), Two Surface Transportation Congestion Relief Solutions Research initiatives, a Surface Transportation-Environmental

Cooperative Research Program (STEP), a National Cooperative Freight Transportation Research Program, and continued the Advanced Travel Forecasting Procedures Program (TRANSIMS). SAFETEA-LU increased annual funding for the University Transportation Centers program to $69.7 million from 2005 to 2009. It also provided $7.75 million annually to develop and test commercial remote sensing products and spatial information technologies.

SAFETEA-LU required a large number of studies. In addition, it established two commissions tasked with making recommendations regarding the future of the surface transportation programs. The first, the National Surface Transportation Policy and Revenue Study Commission, to be chaired by the Secretary of Transportation was to conduct a study of current conditions and future needs of the surface transportation system and develop a conceptual plan to ensure that the surface transportation system continued to serve the Nation's needs. The second, the National Surface Transportation Infrastructure Financing Commission, was to complete a study of Highway Trust Fund revenues and the use of these revenues for future highway and transit needs.

Forum on Road Pricing and Travel Demand Modeling

Road pricing was becoming increasingly prominent as a source of revenue to renew and expand highway infrastructure, as a revenue stream that could bring private money to public infrastructure investments, and as a mechanism for managing traffic congestion and its impacts. Legislative changes also made pricing more attractive by eliminating some federal prohibitions. In addition to extending the Value Pricing Pilot Program, SAFETEA-LU expanded the opportunities for road pricing by allowing states to convert existing HOV lanes to HOT lanes.

Regardless of the primary or dual-motivation of a pricing or toll policy, transportation planners had to be able to analyze and model the effects and impacts of the pricing policy on travel demand. Planners had to either rely on their own past experiences, peer city experiences, or travel demand models to predict travel demand, forecast patronage, and estimate the revenue stream – usually 20 or more years into the future.

For these reasons, a forum of experts in road pricing and demand forecasting was held to assess the state of practice to plan, predict, and make decisions about road pricing schemes. The specific intent of the forum was (1) to provide a setting for travel demand modelers to share experiences representing road pricing in forecasting models and (2) to develop ideas for needed research in this field (U.S. Dept. of Transportation, 2006).

Forecasting traveler responses to pricing was a challenge because of the large errors in both demand and cost estimates associated with infrastructure projects in general, and transportation facilities in particular. The market for accurate forecasting was expanding beyond government agencies once private money was being invested in road systems. The private sector required accuracy in forecasts because of the risk of real money losses. At the same time, private investors appeared better able than government to address and accommodate forecast uncertainty.

The forum revealed a lack of confidence in the ability of existing demand forecasting methods and their application to satisfactorily analyze pricing options. The scrutiny of private investors occurred at a level seemingly higher than the skepticism applied to strictly public choices. Investors and their advisors routinely reduced forecasts of revenues for proposed toll-financed facilities by 25% to guard against excessive optimism that may have been occurred in travel forecasts. Financiers appeared to have confidence in the revenue forecasts of only a few consultants, who used proprietary techniques not subject to the scrutiny of peer review and publication.

The tools used by these consultants were concerned not only with making forecasts more accurate, but also with finding ways to protect investors from the consequences of large forecasting errors. This resulted in an active market for risk analyses to manage the uncertainty in forecasting. The use of subjective probabilities, meta-analysis of many outcomes in the knowledge base, and Monte Carlo techniques to utilize historical information on forecasting errors offered ways to use available knowledge to test and improve the accuracy of demand and revenue forecasts. Mainstream transportation planning and decision making could also benefit from the regular and systematic application of such methods of risk management.

Many felt, that in some applications, the state of the practice in travel forecasting was well behind the state of the art. Together, these points suggested a growing need for investments in and improvements to methods for forecasting traveler responses to road pricing and the feasibility of tolled facilities. To meet these requirements would require: better data, more realistic models, and skilled modelers.

Better data to identify, quantify, and model the impacts of existing pricing schemes were essential to understanding behavioral relationships and building the next generation of models. To be useful, data had to describe a stimulus–response situation that was similar to the forecast case. Data had to capture the complexity of travel choices; for example, in response to price changes, travelers may change modes, times of travel, routes, trip chains, destinations, activity patterns, and in the long run, auto ownership and location. And there should be information on the price paid as well as attitudes and willingness to pay.

Models with realistic fidelity were essential to produce accurate forecasts. Traveler decision processes were complex, dynamic, and iterative, and thus it was not logical to expect models to be simple. Time of day was a key variable in the response to time-varying road pricing schemes. These and other characteristics of the decision process were likely to lead us to activity- and tour-based models, dynamic traffic assignment, and microsimulation. In the long term, road pricing could be expected to produce land use impacts calling for advanced location modeling.

Modelers also contributed to forecast quality. Their experience and credibility brought wisdom and creativity to their work and influenced the quality certification that goes along with the forecast. A good modeler had a greater impact on decisions than the model results alone, for the modeler brings experience, perspective, and judgment to bear on the numbers.

The conference suggested a transition path to new and better forecasting tools that balanced realistic complexity with ease of use. In the short term, the effort should be focused on extending the application of state of the art tools, e.g., activity-based modeling and dynamic traffic assignment. There should also be discussions of ethical issues in forecasting through professional forums and more frequent peer reviews to drive out intentional or careless bias in predictions. The intermediate term should see the growing use of truly dynamic, integrated models that better reflect the complexity of traveler decisions. In the longer term, there should be an investment in the development of a household-activity-based modeling system that can be applied rapidly in new places through the use of generic and parametric activity databases, stronger understanding of model and parameter transferability, and automated network coding.

Interstate 50

6 June 2006 marked the 50th anniversary of the federal law that created the Dwight D. Eisenhower System of Interstate and Defense Highways. This 46,508-mile network of superhighways transformed the nation and the economy. It was the largest public works project ever undertaken in the country. The Interstate Highway System revved up the economy, forever changing the way people and freight moved, and facilitated international trade. It stretched the link between homes and jobs – for better and for worse – and redefined the relationship between urban and rural America. It put Americans within a few days' drive of practically everyone else in our nation, altering the willingness to travel. And, the system as brought huge changes to lifestyles, although some of the changes have been controversial. Table 15.4 shows some of the changes in travel characteristics that have occurred since the Interstate System began.

The wide, relatively straight roadways in the Interstate Highway System were designed to be faster and safer than the two-lane roads that preceded them. The highways were designed for 75–80 mph. However, the actual speed limits were set by the states and varied by location around the country. The geometric standards were established by AASHTO. In addition to being designed to support automobile and truck traffic, the interstate highways were designed for use in military and civil defense operations within the US.

The original cost estimate for the system that was used during debate leading up to the Federal-Aid Highway Act of 1956 was $27 billion. It was based on a report by the US Bureau of Public Roads (BPR), which covered only the 37,700 miles designated in 1947. The final estimate of the total cost of the Interstate System issued in 1991 would be $128.9 billion, with a federal share of $114.3 billion. This estimate covered only the mileage (42,795 miles) built under the Interstate Construction Program. It excluded turnpikes incorporated into the Interstate System within the mileage limitation and the mileage added as a logical addition or connection outside the limitation but financed without Interstate Construction funds.

Table 15.4 Innovative finance purposes

Purpose	Approach	Tools
Accelerate projects	Identify and reduce inefficiencies/ unnecessary barriers in federal-aid grants management	• Advance construction • Partial conversion of advance construction • Tapering • Toll credits • Flexible match
	Create and conduct outreach on new models for borrowing to leverage new and existing revenue streams	• Grant anticipation revenue vehicles • State Infrastructure Banks (SIBs) • Transportation Infrastructure Finance and Innovation Act (TIFIA) Federal Credit Program
Expand investment	Reduce barriers to attracting private contributions to federal-aid projects, including investment of at-risk equity	• Flexible match • TIFIA
	Encourage identification of new revenue streams, in part by creating new borrowing options that facilitate the use of project-based revenues to retire debt obligations	• TIFIA • Section 129 loans • SIBs
	Lower cost or more flexible borrowing options	• Section 129 loans • SIBs • TIFIA

(Source: Cambridge Systematics, Inc., 2002b)

The increased cost resulted from several factors. An additional 2,300 miles of urban routes had been designated in 1955. In addition, design standards were stricter beginning in 1956, and compliance with essential environmental requirements enacted in the 1960s added to the cost of projects. As might be expected, inflation was a major factor as well.

The total mileage of the system in 2003 was 46,773. There were approximately: 14,750 interchanges, 55,512 bridges, 82 tunnels, and 1,214 rest areas along the Interstate System. All but five state capitals are directly served by the Interstate System. Those not on the system are Juneau, Alaska; Dover, Delaware; Jefferson City, Missouri; Carson City, Nevada; and Pierre, South Dakota. The interstates comprised less than 1% of the nation's roads but carried more than 24% of travel, including 41% of total truck miles traveled.

The Dwight D. Eisenhower System of Interstate and Defense Highways facilitated the emergence of automobile-oriented postwar suburban development patterns, often referred to as "urban sprawl." The construction of the system peaked at a time when GIs were returning home and the Congress made available low interest V.A. loans for new homes. The combination of these factors has had a permanent impact on the development patterns in the nation. Clearly, the Interstate System had major economic, social, and environmental impacts on the nation. These impacts have been hotly debated and will continue to do so for years to come.

Logo Celebrating the 50th Anniversary of the Dwight D. Eisenhower system of interstate and defense highways. (Source: US Dept. of Transportation, Federal Highway Administration)

National Strategy to Reduce Congestion on America's Transportation Network

Despite the many hundreds of billions of dollars the federal government spent on transportation infrastructure and upkeep, the extent and intensity of congestion had worsened in the nation's largest metropolitan areas. Whether in the form of trucks stalled in traffic, cargo stuck at overwhelmed seaports, or airplanes circling over crowded airports, congestion costs America an estimated $200 billion a year by 2006. Highway congestion in particular increased dramatically over the previous two decades, and was on its way toward becoming a major problem in medium-sized cities within the next 10 years.

In May 2006, Secretary Mineta unveiled the National Strategy to Reduce Congestion on America's Transportation Network at the National Press Club (U.S. Dept. of Transportation, 2006). Under this initiative, there were six major components, each of which showed potential to both reduce congestion in the short term and build the foundation for successful longer term congestion-reduction efforts.

1. *Relieve urban congestion.* The department would seek to enter Urban Partnership Agreements with model cities, pursuant to which the cities will commit to the following actions (1) implementing a broad congestion pricing or variable toll demonstration; (2) creating more efficient and responsive public transit systems that tailor services specifically for rush-hour commuters; (3) working with major area employers to expand telecommuting and flex scheduling; and (4) utilizing advanced technological and operational approaches to improve system performance, support regional efforts to expand the provision of real-time traveler information, improve traffic incident response, improve arterial signal timing, and reduce the obtrusiveness of highway construction work zones. The department will commit discretionary resources to support these actions.

2. *Unleash private-sector investment resources.* The department would work to reduce or remove barriers to private-sector investment in transportation infrastruc-

ture by (1) encouraging states to enact laws that enable public–private partnerships (PPPs) and (2) utilizing existing federal program authorities and SAFETEA-LU implementation to encourage formation of public–private partnerships.

3. *Promote operational and technological improvements.* The department would work to advance low-cost operational and technological improvements that increase information dissemination and incident response capabilities by (1) encouraging states to utilize their federal-aid formula funds to improve operational performance, including providing better real-time traffic information to system users; (2) emphasizing congestion-reducing technologies in the implementation of the Intelligent Transportation Systems program; and (3) promoting best practices and identifying private-sector partnering and financing opportunities to improve incident and intersection management.

4. *Establish a "Corridors of the Future" competition.* The department would accelerate the development of multistate, multiuse transportation corridors by (1) fast-tracking major congestion reducing corridor projects that received funding in SAFETEA-LU; (2) competitively selecting 3–5 major growth corridors in need of long-term investment; and (3) convening a multistate process to advance the development of these corridors.

5. *Target major freight bottlenecks and expand freight policy outreach.* The department would address congestion in the nation's freight system by (1) working with all relevant stakeholder groups to forge consensus on a path toward increasing freight capacity in Southern California; (2) engaging shippers, freight carriers, and logistics firms through a series of "CEO Summits," structured around the Department's National Freight Policy Framework; and (3) working with the Department of Homeland Security to prioritize operational and infrastructure improvements at the nation's most congested border crossings.

6. *Accelerate major aviation capacity projects and provide a future funding framework.* The department would address congestion in the aviation system by (1) designing and deploying the Next Generation Air Transportation System – a modernized aviation system with greater capacity and less congestion; (2) improving efficiency and reducing delays at New York City's LaGuardia Airport; (3) giving priority treatment and agency resources to projects that enhance aviation system capacity; and (4) streamlining environmental reviews for aviation capacity projects.

With regard to the first component of this initiative, 27 urban areas applied to enter into Urban Partnership Agreements. In August 2007, the Secretary announced five final urban partners: Miami, Minneapolis/St. Paul; New York City; San Francisco; and Seattle. The department also selected the final corridors to be designated as the Corridors of the Future under the Corridor of the Future Program (CFP). DOT selected the six corridors that would best achieve all of the goals of the CFP, reducing congestion, increasing freight reliability, and enhancing the quality of life: Interstate 5 – A Roadmap for Mobility; Interstate 10 – National Freight Corridor; Interstate 15 – A Corridor without Borders; Interstate 69; Interstate 70 – Dedicated Truck Lanes; and Interstate 95. The department was carefully monitoring the progress of these projects.

Metropolitan Travel Forecasting: Current Practice and Future Direction

In 2003, the Transportation Research Board conducted a peer review of the travel demand modeling of the Metropolitan Washington Council of Governments' (MWCOG) Transportation Planning Board (TPB), the MPO for Washington, DC (Transportation Research Board, 2003). In the course of this review, it became apparent that little information was available to practitioners to assist them in making judgments about state-of-the-practice techniques for model development and application. Although the NRC committee that conducted the review was charged with assessing whether the modeling of the MWCOG TPB was state of the practice, the committee had to rely on its judgment in making this assessment, rather than on detailed information about how key technical issues are treated by the MPO's peers.

Consequently, US DOT funded a TRB study to gather information needed to determine the national state of practice in metropolitan area travel demand forecasting by MPOs and state departments of transportation. A committee was formed to carry out this work. The committee was tasked with assessing the state of the practice in travel demand forecasting and identifying shortcomings in travel forecasting models, obstacles to better practice, and actions needed to ensure the use of appropriate technical approaches. This report provides the requested assessment and recommendations for improvement and is designed for officials and policy makers who rely on the results of travel forecasting. A separate report commissioned by the committee is intended for readers with an interest in the technical details of current practice (Transportation Research Board, 2007).

The findings summarized above reveal that most agencies continue to use a trip-based three- or four-step modeling process that, while improved during the past 40 years, has remained fundamentally unchanged. These models have basic, documented deficiencies in meeting current modeling needs. There are also deficiencies in current practice – particularly data gaps – that will not be resolved by switching to more advanced models. The institutional environment for travel modeling has devolved much of the responsibility for the development of travel models to the states and MPOs, although the federal government retains a strong interest in the area. Advanced models that better meet the needs of MPOs have been developed and satisfactorily implemented by some metropolitan areas. There are, however, considerable barriers to fundamental change, including resource limitations, practitioners' uncertainty as to whether new practices will be better than those they replace, a lack of coordination among stakeholders, and inadequate investment in the development and transfer of new techniques. Accordingly, the pace of fundamental change in the field of travel forecasting has been very slow.

The committee recommended the development and implementation of new modeling approaches to demand forecasting that are better suited to providing reliable information for such applications as multimodal investment analyses, operational analyses, environmental assessments, evaluations of a wide range of policy alternatives, toll-facility revenue forecasts, and freight forecasts, and to meeting federal and state regulatory requirements. In addition, the committee recommended that:

- MPOs should establish their own national cooperative research program
- MPOs should conduct formal peer reviews of their modeling practice
- The federal government should substantially increase funding for models development and implementation
- The federal government should include the results of peer reviews in their MPO certification process
- A national steering committee should be formed to coordinate travel model activities among the federal and state governments and MPOs
- A national travel forecasting handbook should be developed and kept current
- Studies should be performed to compare the performance of conventional and advanced models (Transportation Research Board, 2007)

Chapter 16
Concluding Remarks

Fifty years have elapsed since the passage of the Federal-Aid Highway Act of 1956 launched the Dwight D. Eisenhower System of Interstate and Defense Highways. And, more that 40 years have elapsed since the Federal-Aid Highway Act of 1962 initiated the continuing, comprehensive, and cooperative urban transportation planning process. Since these acts were passed, there have been major changes in the nation and, to some extent, these acts enabled some of those changes. Transportation planning has evolved with the nation's changing issues and concerns. It is remarkable how enduring the transportation planning process has been. The basic fundamentals identified in the 1962 act are still relevant today.

Urban transportation planning evolved from highway and transit planning activities in the 1920s and 1930s. These early efforts were directed at constructing transportation facilities including a national network of all-weather highways. In carrying out this task, engineers and planners focused on improving the design and operation of individual transportation facilities. As travel demand grew, the focus was aimed at upgrading and expanding these facilities.

Early urban transportation planning studies during the 1950s and 1960s were carried out by separate planning groups often under the state highway department With the passage of the 1962 Federal-Aid Highway Act of 1962, Memorandum of Agreements were signed between local governmental agencies and the states to carry out the urban transportation planning process. These urban transportation studies were primarily systems-oriented with a 20-year time horizon and region-wide in scope. This was largely the result of legislation for the National System of Interstate and Defense Highways which required that these major highways be designed for traffic projected 20 years into the future. As a result, the focus of the planning process through the decade of the 1960s was on this long-range time horizon and broad regional scale.

Gradually, starting in the early 1970s, the focus of planning processes turned toward shorter term time horizons and the corridor-level scale. This change came about as the result of the realization that long-range planning had been dominated by concern for major regional highway facilities with only minor attention being paid to lesser facilities and the opportunity to improve the efficiency of the existing system. This shift was reinforced by the increasing difficulties and cost in constructing new facilities, growing environmental concerns, and the Arab oil embargo.

E. Weiner, *Urban Transportation Planning in the United States, Third Edition*,
doi:10.1007/978-0-387-77152-6, © Springer Science+Business Media, LLC 2008

Also, the Urban Mass Transportation Assistance Act of 1970 provided the first capital grants for transit.

Early efforts with programs such as TOPICS and express bus priorities eventually broadened into the strategy of transportation system management. TSM encompassed a whole range of techniques to increase the utilization and productivity of existing vehicles and facilities. It shifted the emphasis from facility expansion to provision of transportation service. The federal government took the lead in pressing for changes that would produce greater attention to TSM. At first there was considerable resistance. Neither institutions nor techniques were immediately able to address TSM options. A period of learning and adaptation was necessary to redirect planning processes so that they could perform this new type of planning. During the 1980s, urban transportation planning had become primarily short-term oriented in most urbanized areas.

By the early 1990s, there were major changes underway that would have significant effects on urban transportation and urban transportation planning. The era of major new highway construction was over in most urban areas. However, the growth in urban travel was continuing unabated. With only limited highway expansion possible, new approaches needed to be found to serve this travel demand. Moreover, the growth in traffic congestion was contributing to degradation of the urban environment and urban life, and needed to be abated. Previous attempts at the selected application of transportation system management measures (TSM) had proven to have limited impacts on congestion, providing the need for more comprehensive and integrated strategies. In addition, a number of new technologies were reaching the point of application, including intelligent transportation systems (ITS).

Many transportation agencies entered into strategic management and planning processes to identify the scope and nature of these changes, to develop strategies to address these issues, and to better orient their organization to function in this new environment. They shifted their focus toward longer term time horizons, more integrated transportation management strategies, wider geographic application of these strategies, and a renewed interest in technological alternatives. Approaching the year 2000, the focus of urban transportation planning shifted to addressing growing congestion, meeting the NAAQS, reducing global warming, and supporting sustainable development.

There were also changes to make the urban transportation planning process more inclusive in the manner decision making occurred. For most of the century, transportation decisions were made by engineers and planners in government organizations. With the passage of the Federal-Aid Highway Act of 1962 and its successors, pubic officials participating on MPOs gained some control of transportation decisions within their urban areas. Successive federal surface transportation acts increased the flexibility in the use of highway and transit funds. They also increased the ability of urban areas to make transportation development and financing decisions for their respective areas.

With the passage of ISTEA, other stakeholders and private citizens had to be given a reasonable opportunity to comment on the long-range transportation plans and the shorter term transportation improvement programs. The regulations implementing the legislation required a formal proactive and inclusive public involvement process that provided ample opportunity for community participation. Reinforcing this expansion of participatory decision-making process was an Executive Order that required the environmental impact process under NEPA be used to address environmental justice issues. Under that process, federal actions and projects had to be analyzed to assure that including human health, economic, and social effects did not fall disproportionately on minority communities and low-income communities. As the public gained more influence over transportation decisions in their affected areas, public interest groups became more sophisticated in their participation in the transportation planning process.

Through its evolutionary development, the urban transportation planning process had been called upon to address a continuous stream of new issues and concerns, methodological developments, advances in technology, and changing attitudes. Usually it was the requirements from the federal government to which the planning process was responding. Major new issues began affecting urban transportation planning in the latter half of the 1960s and on through the 1970s. The list of issues included safety, citizen involvement, preservation of park land and natural areas, equal opportunity for disadvantaged persons, environmental concerns (particularly air quality), transportation for the elderly and handicapped, energy conservation, and revitalization of urban centers. More recently these have been joined by concerns for deterioration of the highway and transit infrastructure and its effect on economic growth. Traffic congestion, air quality, global warming, environmental justice, sustainable development, asset management, and transportation security have now become the major concerns of urban transportation planning.

During this same period there have been advocates for various transportation options as solutions to this vast array of problems and concerns. They ran the gamut from new highways, express buses, heavy and light rail transit systems, pricing, automated guideway transit, telecommuting, paratransit, brokerage, dual-mode transit, ITS, and maglev. It was difficult at times to determine whether these options were advanced as the answer to all of these problems or for just some of them. Transportation system management was an attempt to integrate the short-term, low capital options into reinforcing strategies to accomplish one or more objectives. Transportation demand management seeks to merge various strategies to affect travel behavior and its effects on congestion and air quality. Alternatives analysis was designed to evaluate tradeoffs among various major investments options as well as transportation management techniques. However, broader evaluation approaches are needed to assess effects of a wide array of strategies on travel demand, land development, and environmental quality.

Transportation planning techniques have also evolved during this time. Procedures for specific purposes were integrated into an urban travel forecasting process in the early urban transportation studies in the 1950s. Through the 1960s improvements in planning techniques were made primarily by practitioners, and these new approaches were integrated into practice fairly easily. The FHWA and UMTA carried out extensive activities to develop and disseminate analytical techniques and computer programs for use by state and local governments. The Urban

Transportation Planning System (UTPS) became the standard computer battery for urban transportation analysis by the mid-1970s.

Starting in 1970s new travel forecasting techniques were being developed for the most part by the research community largely in universities. These disaggregate travel forecasting approaches differed from the aggregate approaches being used in practice at the time. They used new mathematical techniques and theoretical bases from econometrics and psychometrics that were difficult for practitioners to learn. Moreover, the new techniques were not easily integrated into conventional planning practices. Communication between researchers and practitioners was fitful. While researchers were developing more appropriate ways to analyzing this complex array of issues and options, practitioners stayed wedded to the older techniques. The gap between research and practice is only gradually being closed.

Microcomputers have become integrated into all aspect of urban transportation planning and the use of GIS is spreading. But, few agencies have the resources to develop their own software and are left to the vagaries of the commercial market. Moreover, microcomputers are now available to smaller agencies and even interest groups. This provides the opportunity for analyses to be carried out by these organizations but may increase the difficulty of achieving consensus.

The 1990s brought new challenges to urban transportation planning organizations. After a decade of decentralization of authority and responsibility, urban transportation planning was faced with the problems of low-density land development patterns, congestion and air pollution which need to be addressed at the regional scale or even on a statewide basis. The institutional arrangement in most urban, however, areas did not lend itself to the coordination and integration of the various elements needed to bring about more efficient land use patterns. The institutional arrangement was fragmented vertically between various levels of government; horizontally among the large number of local units of government; and functionally among transportation, land use, air quality, and other service areas. There was little effort aimed at merging these institutions in most urban regions. In a few instances, states began to provide some institutional integration. But, increased coordination between air quality and transportation planners will be needed if the requirements of the 1990 Clean Air Act Amendments are to be met.

The demands on urban transportation planning are now greater than ever. The range of issues that need to be addressed is continuing to lengthen. Analytical requirements are more comprehensive and exacting than previously was true. Some states have requirements beyond those of federal agencies. However, little effort is being made to assist urban transportation planning agencies to meet these demands and requirements. Funding for research and development has gradually declined and the funding for urban transportation planning had not kept pace with increasing requirements. The Travel Model Improvement Program (TMIP) was one modest effort to fill these needs.

The budgets of urban transportation planning agencies are still tight. There is little money for methodological development or research. Data bases in many areas are old and agencies face difficulties in collecting large-scale regional data sets such as home-interview, origin-destination surveys. The NPTS and Census' UTPP have provided an opportunity for the updating of older data bases at a reduced cost. However, many urban transportation planning agencies had not upgraded their travel forecasting procedures for some time and a large scale effort will be needed to carry out this task.

The new century has ushered in a renewed concern owing to limitations on resources to address transportation issues. The focus has again shifted to preserving and effectively operating the transportation system, to assuring that expenditures achieved solid results, and to finding adequate resources to meet growing needs. Interest in private sector financing to bolster public funds has increased. Widening public involvement in the transportation planning process has accelerated. And new issues continue to appear on the horizon to be addressed by transportation planners.

All of this demonstrates that urban transportation planning is still dynamic and changing to further adapt to new issues and needs.

References

1,000 Friends of Oregon, 1997, Making the Connections – A Summary of the LUTRAQ Project, February.

Advisory Commission on Intergovernmental Relations, 1995, MPO Capacity: Improving the Capacity of Metropolitan Planning Organizations to Help Implement National Transportation Policies, Washington, DC, May.

____, 1974, Toward More Balanced Transportation: New Intergovernmental Proposals, Report A-49, U.S. Government Printing Office, Washington, DC.

Advisory Council on Historic Preservation, 1986, Section 106, Step-by-Step, Washington, DC, October.

Allen, John, 1985, "Post-Classical Transportation Studies," Transportation Quarterly, Volume 39, No. 3, July.

Allen-Schult, Edith and John L. Hazard, 1982, "Ethical Issues in Transport – The U.S. National Transportation Study Commission: Congressional Formulation of Policy," Transport Policy and Decisionmaking, Volume 2, Martinus Nijhoff, The Hague, The Netherlands, pp. 17–49.

American Association of State Highway and Transportation Officials, 1973, A Policy on Design of Urban Highways and Arterial Streets - 1973, Washington, DC.

American Association of State Highway and Transportation Officials, 2003, A Manual of User Benefit Analysis for Highways, 2nd Edition, Washington, DC, August.

American Public Transportation Association, 2007, 2007 Public Transportation Fact Book - 59th Edition, Washington, DC.

____, 1978, A Manual on User Benefit Analysis of Highway and Bus-Transit Improvements – 1977, Washington, DC.

____, 1984, A Policy on Geometric Design of Highways and Streets – 1984, Washington, DC.

____, 1987a, Understanding the Highway Finance Evolution/Revolution, Washington, DC, January.

____, 1987b, Action Plan For the Consensus Transportation Program, Washington, DC, May.

____, 1988, Keeping America: The Bottom Line – A Summary of Surface Transportation Investment Requirements 1988–2020, Washington, DC, September.

____, 1990, A Policy on Geometric Design of Highways and Streets, Washington, D.C.

____, 2004, A Policy on Geometric Design of Highways and Streets, 5th Edition, Washington, DC.

American Association of State Highway Officials, 1950, Policies on Geometric Highway Design, Washington, DC.

____, 1952a, Road User Benefit Analyses for Highway Improvements (Informational Report), Washington, DC.

____, 1952b, "A Basis for Estimating Traffic Diversion to New Highway in Urban Areas," 38th Annual Meeting, Kansas City, Kansas, December.

____, 1954, A Policy on Geometric Design of Rural Highways, Washington, DC.

____, 1957, A Policy on Arterial Highways in Urban Areas, Washington, DC.

____, 1960, Road User Benefit Analyses for Highway Improvements (Informational Report), Washington, DC.

____, 1966, A Policy on Geometric Design of Rural Highways - 1965, Washington, DC.

American Planning Association, 1979, Proceedings of the Aspen Conference on Future Urban Transportation, American Planning Association, Chicago, IL, June.

American Public Transit Association, 1989, 1989 Transit Fact Book, Washington, DC, August.

____, 1994, Transit Funding Needs 1995–2004, Washington, DC, May.

____, 1995, 1994–95 Transit Fact Book, Washington, DC, February.

Arrillaga, Bert, 1978, "Transportation Pricing Program of the Urban Mass Transportation Administration," Urban Economics: Proceedings of Five Workshops on Pricing Alternatives, Economic Regulation, Labor Issues, Marketing, and Government Financing Responsibilities, U.S. Department of Transportation, Washington, DC, March, pp. 13–15.

Arthur Andersen & Co., 1973, Project FARE, Urban Mass Transportation Industry Reporting System, Volumes I–V, U.S. Department of Transportation, Urban Mass Transportation Administration, Washington, DC, November.

Aschauer, David A., 1989, "Is Public Expenditure Productive?" Journal of Monetary Economics, Volume 23, No. 2, March, 177–200.

Bartholomew, Keith, 1995, A Tale of Two Cities, Transportation, Volume 22, No. 3, Kluwer, Dordrecht, The Netherlands, August, pp. 273–293.

——, 2005, Integrating Land Use Issues Into Transportation Planning: Scenario Planning, University of Utah, Salt Lake City, Utah.

Bauer, Kurt W., 1963, "Regional Planning in Southeastern Wisconsin," Technical Record, Volume 1, No. 1, Southeastern Wisconsin Regional Planning Commission, Waukesha, Wisconsin, October–November.

Beimborn, Edward, Harvey Rabinowitz, et al., 1991, Guidelines for Transit Sensitive Suburban Land Use Design, U.S. Department of Transportation, Washington, DC, July.

Bennett, Nancy, 1996, "The National Highway System Designation Act of 1995," Public Roads, Volume 59, No. 4, U.S. Department of Transportation, Federal Highway Administration, Spring.

Bloch, Arnold J., Michael B. Gerard, and William H. Crowell, 1982, The Interstate Highway Trade - In Process, 2 Volumes, Polytechnic Institute of New York, Brooklyn, NY, December.

Booth, Rosemary and Robert Waksman, 1985, National Ridesharing Demonstration Program: Comparative Evaluation Report, U.S. Department of Transportation, Transportation Systems Center, Cambridge, MA, August.

Bostick, Thurley A., 1963, "The Automobile in American Daily Life," Public Roads, Volume 32, No. 11, U.S. Department of Commerce, Bureau of Public Roads, Washington, DC, December.

——, 1966, "Travel Habits in Cities of 100,000 of More," Public Roads, Volume 33, No. 12, U.S. Department of Commerce, Bureau of Public Roads, Washington, DC, February.

Bostick, Thurley A., Roy T. Messer, and Clarence A. Steele, 1954, "Motor-Vehicle-Use Studies in Six States," Public Roads, Volume 28, No. 5, U.S. Department of Commerce, Bureau of Public Roads, Washington, DC, December.

Brand, Daniel and Marvin L. Manheim, Eds., 1973, Urban Travel Demand Forecasting, Special Report 143, Highway Research Board, Washington, DC.

Briggs, Dwight, Alan Pisarski, and James J. McDonnell, 1986, Journey-to-Work Trends Based on 1960, 1970 and 1980 Decennial Censuses, U.S. Department of Transportation, Federal Highway Administration, Washington, DC, July.

"Bronx River Parkway – Historic Overview," http://www.nycroads.com/roads/pkwy_NYC.

Brown, William F. and Edward Weiner, Eds., 1987, Transportation Planning Applications: A Compendium of Papers Based on a Conference Held in Orlando Florida in April 1987, U.S. Department of Transportation, December, 1987.

Bureau of the Budget, Executive Office of the President, 1967, "Coordination of Federal Aids in Metropolitan Areas Under Section 204 of the Demonstration Cities and Metropolitan Development Act of 1966," Circular No. A-82, Washington, DC, April 11.

——, 1969, "Evaluation, Review, and Coordination of Federal Assistance Programs and Projects," Circular No. A-95, Washington, DC, July 24.

Cabot Consulting Group, 1982, Transportation Energy Contingency Planning: Transit Fuel Supplies Under Decontrol, U.S. Department of Transportation, Washington, DC, May.

Calongne, Kathleen, 2003, Problems Associated With Traffic Calming Devices, Seconds Count, Boulder, CO, January.

Cambridge Systematics, Inc., 2002a, Transportation Asset Management Guide, National Cooperative Highway Research Program Project 20–24(11), American Association of State Highway and Transportation Officials, Washington, DC, November.

____, 2002b, Performance Review of U.S. DOT Innovative Finance Initiatives – Final Report, U.S. Department of Transportation, Federal Highway Administration, Washington, DC, July.

——, 2004, FHWA Asset Management Position Paper – White Paper, U.S. Department of Transportation, Federal Highway Administration, Washington, DC, April.

Cambridge Systematics, et al., 1992, Characteristics of Urban Transportation Systems, Revised Edition, U.S. Department of Transportation, Federal Transit Administration, Washington, DC, September.

Campbell, M. Earl, 1950, Route Selection and Traffic Assignment, Highway Research Board, Washington, DC.

Chappell, Charles W. Jr. and Mary T. Smith, 1971, "Review of Urban Goods Movement Studies," Urban Commodity Flow, Special Report 120, Highway Research Board, Washington, DC.

Charles River Associates, Inc., 1988, Characteristics of Urban Transportation Demand: An Update, U.S. Department of Transportation, Urban Mass Transportation Administration, Washington, DC, July.

Chicago Area Transportation Study, 1959–1962, Study Findings, (Volume I), December, 1959; Data Projections, (Volume II), July 1960; Transportation Plan, (Volume 3), April 1962, Harrison Lithographing, Chicago, IL.

Clinton, William J., 1994a, Principles for Federal Infrastructure Investment, Executive Order 12893, Federal Register, Volume 59, No. 20, January 31, pp. 4233–4235.

____, 1994b, Executive Order on Federal Actions to Address Environmental Justice in Minority Populations and Low-Income Populations, White House Memorandum, February 11.

____, 1994c, Federal Actions to Address Environmental Justice in Minority Populations and Low-Income Populations, Executive Order 12898, Federal Register, Volume 59, No. 32, February 11, pp. 7629–7633.

Clinton, William J. and Albert Gore Jr., 1993, The Global Climate Action Plan, The White House, Washington, DC, October.

Cole, Leon Monroe, Ed., 1968, Tomorrow's Transportation: New Systems for the Urban Future, Prepared by U.S. Department of Housing and Urban Development, U.S. Government Printing Office, Washington, DC, May.

Comptroller General of the United States, 1976, Effectiveness, Benefits, and Costs of Federal Safety Standards for Protection of Passenger Car Occupants, U.S. General Accounting Office, Washington, DC, July 7.

COMSIS Corp., 1984, Quick Response System (QRS) Documentation, Prepared for the U.S. Department of Transportation, Federal Highway Administration, Washington, DC, January.

——, 1990. Evaluation of Travel\Demand Management Measures to Relieve Congestion, Prepared for U.S. Department of Transportation, Federal Highway Administration, Washington, DC, February.

COMSIS Corp., et al., 1993, Implementation/Effective Travel Demand Managing Measures, Prepared for the U.S. Department of Transportation, Institute of Transportation Engineers, Washington, DC, June.

Cook, Kenneth E., Margaret A. Cook, and Kathleen E. Stein-Hudson, 1996, "Conference on Major Investment Studies in Transportation (MIS)," Transportation Research Circular No. 463, September.

Cooper, Norman L. and John O. Hidinger, 1980, "Integration of Air Quality and Transportation Planning," Transportation and the 1977 Clean Air Act Amendments, American Society of Civil Engineers, New York, NY.

Council on Environmental Quality, 1978, National Environmental Policy Act – Regulations, Federal Register, Volume 43, No. 230, November 29, pp. 55978–56007.

Creighton, Roger L., 1970, Urban Transportation Planning, University of Illinois Press, Urbana, IL.

Cron, Frederick W., 1975a, "Highway Design for Motor Vehicles – An Historical Review, Part 4: The Vehicle Carrying of the Highway," Public Roads, Volume 39, No. 3, December, pp. 96–108.

____, 1975b, "Highway Design for Motor Vehicles – An Historical Review, Part 2: The Beginnings of Traffic Research," Public Roads, Volume 38, No. 4, March, pp. 163–174.

Detroit Metropolitan Area Traffic Study, 1955/56, Part I: Data Summary and Interpretation; Part 2: Future Traffic and a Long Range Expressway Plan, Speaker-Hines and Thomas, State Printers, Lansing, MI, July and March.

Diamant, E.S., et al., 1976, Light Rail Transit: State of the Art Review, De Leuw, Cather and Co., Chicago, IL, Spring.

Domestic Council, Executive Office of the President, 1972, Report on National Growth – 1972, U.S. Government Printing Office, Washington, DC, February.

——, 1976, 1976 Report on National Growth and Development – The Changing Issue for National Growth, U.S. Department of Housing and Urban Development, U.S. Government Printing Office, Washington, DC, May.

Dornan, Daniel L. and Patricia M. Maier, 2005, Incorporating Security into the Transportation Planning Process, Surface Transportation Security, Volume 3, Transportation Research Board, Washington, DC.

Dunphy, Robert T. and Ben C. Lin, 1990, Transportation Management Through Partnerships, Urban Land Institute, Washington, DC.

Dutch Ministry of Transport and Public Works, 1986, Behavioural Research for Transport Policy (The 1985 International Conference on Travel Behaviour), VNU Science, Utrecht, The Netherlands.

Dyett, Michael V., 1984, "The Land-Use Impacts of Beltways in U.S. Cities: Lessons For Mitigation," in: Land-Use Impacts of Highway Projects – Proceedings of the Wisconsin Symposium on Land-Use Impacts of Highway Projects, Alan J. Horowitz, Ed., Wisconsin Department of Transportation, Milwaukee, WI, April.

Engelke, Lynette, Ed., 1995, Fifth National Conference on Transportation Planning Methods Applications, Volumes 1 and 2, Texas Transportation Institute, Arlington, TX, June.

Environmental Justice Resource Center, 1996, Conference on Environmental Justice and Transportation: Building Model Partnerships – Proceedings Document, Clark Atlanta University, Atlanta Georgia, June.

Envision Utah, 2000, Envision Utah Quality Growth Strategy and Technical Review, Salt Lake City, UT.

Ewing, Reid, 1999, Traffic Calming: State of Practice, Institute of Transportation Engineers and U.S. Department of Transportation, Federal Highway Administration, Washington, DC, August.

Faris, Jerry, Ed., 1993, Fifth National Conference on Transportation Planning Methods Applications, Volumes 1 and 2, Tallahassee, FL, September.

Feiss, Carl, 1985, "The Foundation of Federal Planning Assistance – A Personal Account of the 701 Program," APA Journal, Chicago, IL, Spring.

Fekpe, Edward, Mohammed Alam, Thomas Foody, and Deepak Gopalakrishna, 2002, Freight Analysis Framework Highway: Capacity Analysis Methodology Report, Battelle, Washington, DC, April 18.

Ferguson, Eric, 1990, "Transportation Demand Management: Planning, Development, and Implementation," Journal of the American Planning Association, Volume 56, No. 3, Autumn.

Fertal, Martin J., Edward Weiner, Arthur J. Balek, and Ali F. Sevin, 1966, Modal Split – Documentation of Nine Methods for Estimating Transit Usage, U.S. Department of Commerce, Bureau of Public Roads, U.S. Government Printing Office, Washington, DC, December.

Fisher, Gordon P., Ed., 1974, Goods Transportation in Urban Areas – Proceedings of the Engineering Foundation Conference, Berwick Academy, South Berwick, Maine, August 5–10, 1973, U.S. Department of Transportation, February.

____, 1976, Goods Transportation in Urban Areas – Proceedings of the Engineering Foundation Conference, Santa Barbara, California, September 7–12, 1975, U.S. Department of Transportation, May.

——, 1978, Goods Transportation in Urban Areas – Proceedings of the Engineering Foundation Conference, Sea Island, Georgia, December 4–9, 1977, U.S. Department of Transportation, June.

Fisher, Gordon P. and Arnim H. Meyburg, Eds., 1982, Goods Transportation in Urban Areas – Proceedings of the Engineering Foundation Conference, Easton, Maryland, June 14–19, 1981, U.S. Department of Transportation, January.

Fitch, Lyle C., Ed., 1964, Urban Transportation and Public Policy, Chandler, San Francisco, CA.

Gakenheimer, Ralph A., 1976, Transportation Planning as Response to Controversy: The Boston Case, MIT, Cambridge, MA.

Gakenheimer, Ralph and Michael Meyer, 1977, Transportation System Management: Its Origins, Local Response and Problems as a New Form of Planning, Interim Report, Massachusetts Institute of Technology, Cambridge, MA, November.

Garrett, Mark and Martin Wachs, 1996, Transportation Planning on Trial: The Clean Air Act and Travel Forecasting, Sage, Thousand Oaks, CA.

Garvin, Alexander, 1998, "Are Garden Cities Still Relevant?", Proceeding of the 1998 Planning Conference, AICP Press, American Planning Association, Chicago, IL.

Gatti, Ronald F., 1969–1989, Radburn – The Town For The Motor Age, The Radburn Association, Radburn, NJ.

Georgia Regional Transportation Authority, 2003, "Background and History," http://www.grta.org, August 21.

Giuliano, Genevieve and Martin Wachs, 1991, Responding to Congestion and Traffic Growth: Transportation Demand Management, Reprint, No. 86, Sage, Thousand Oaks, CA.

Goldner, William, 1971, "The Lowry Heritage," Journal of the American Institute of Planners, Volume 37, March, 100–110.

Gortmaker, Linda, 1980, Transportation and Urban Development, U.S. Conference of Mayors, U.S. Government Printing Office, Washington, DC, October.

Grant, Michael and Chester Fung, 2005, "Congestion Management Systems: Innovative Practices for Enhancing Transportation Planning," ICF Consulting, Submitted for presentation at the 85th Annual Meeting of the Transportation Research Board, Washington, DC, November 21.

Hanks, James W. Jr. and Timothy J. Lomax, 1989, Roadway Congestion in Major Urban Areas – 1982 to 1987, Texas Transportation Institute, College Station, TX, October.

Harris, Britton, Ed., 1965, "Urban Development Models: New Tools for Planning," Journal of the American Institute of Planners, Volume 31, No. 2, May.

Harvey, Greig and Elizabeth Deakin, 1991, Toward Improved Regional Modeling Practice, National Association of Regional Councils, Washington, DC, December.

——, 1992, "Part A – Air Quality and Transportation Planning: An Assessment of Recent Developments," Transportation and Air Quality, Searching for Solutions, A Policy Discussion Series, Number 5, U.S. Department of Transportation, Federal Highway Administration, Washington, DC, August.

——, 1993, A Manual of Regional Transportation Modeling Practice for Air Quality Analysis, National Association of Regional Councils, Washington, DC, July.

Hassell, John S., 1982, "How Effective Has Urban Transportation Been?," in: Urban Transportation: Perspectives and Prospects, Herbert S. Levenson and Robert A. Weant, Eds., Eno Foundation For Transportation, Westport, CT.

Hawthorn, Gary, 1991, "Transportation Provisions in the 1990 Clean Air Act Amendments of 1990," ITE Journal, April.

Hawthorn, Gary and Elizabeth Deakin, 1991, Conference Summary – Best practices for Transportation Modeling for Air Quality Planning, National Association of Regional Councils, Washington, DC, December.

Heanue, Kevin E., 1977, "Changing Emphasis in Urban Transportation Planning," Presented at the 56th Annual Meeting of the Transportation Board, Washington, DC, January.

——, 1980, "Urban Transportation Planning – Are New Directions Needed for the 1980s?," Presented at the American Planning Association Conference, San Francisco, CA, April.

Hedges, Charles A., 1985, "Improving Urban Goods Movement: The Transportation Management Approach," Transportation Policy and Decisionmaking, Volume 3, Martinus Nijhoff, The Netherlands, pp. 113–133.

Hemmens, George C., Ed., 1968, Urban Development Models, Special Report 97, Highway Research Board, Washington, DC.

Hensher, David A. and Peter R. Stopher, Eds., 1979, Behavioral Travel Modeling, Croom Helm, London.

Herman, Frank V., 1964, Population Forecasting Methods, U.S. Department of Commerce, Bureau of Public Roads, Washington, DC, June.

Hershey Conference, 1962, Freeways in the Urban Setting, Sponsored by American Association of State Highway Officials, American Municipal Association, and National Association of County Officials, Automotive Safety Foundation, Washington, DC, June.

Higgins, Thomas J., 1986, "Road Pricing Attempts in the United States," Transportation Research: Part A, Volume 20A, No. 2, Pergamon, London, England, March, pp. 145–150.

——, 1990, "Demand Management in Suburban Settings: Effectiveness and Policy Considerations," Transportation, Volume 17, Kluwer, The Netherlands, pp. 93–116.

Highway Research Board, 1965, Highway Capacity Manual – 1965, Special Report 87, Washington, DC.

——, 1971a, Demand-Actuated Transportation Systems, Special Report 124, Washington, DC.

——, 1971b, Urban Commodity Flow, Special Report 120, Washington, DC.

——, 1971c, Use of Census Data in Urban Transportation Planning, Special Report 121, Washington, DC.

——, 1973a, Organization for Continuing Urban Transportation Planning, Special Report 139, Highway Research Board, Washington, DC.

——, 1973b, Demand-Responsive Transportation Systems, Special Report 136, Washington, DC.

Highway Users Federation and the Automobile Safety Foundation, 1991, The Intermodal Surface Transportation Efficiency Act of 1991 – A Summary, Washington, DC, December.

Highway Users Federation for Safety and Mobility, 1988, Beyond Gridlock: The Future of Mobility as the Public Sees it, Washington, DC, June.

——, 1990, Proceedings of the National Leadership Conference on Intelligent Vehicle Highway Systems, Washington, DC.

Highways and Urban Development, Report on the Second National Conference, Williamsburg, Virginia, 1965, Sponsored by American Association of State Highway Officials, National Association of Counties, and National League of Cities, December.

Holmes, E.H., 1962, "Highway Planning in the United States" (unpublished, Madrid, Spain).

——, 1964, "Transit and Federal Highways," Presented at The Engineers' Club of St. Louis, U.S. Department of Commerce, April 23.

——, 1973, "The State-of-the-Art in Urban Transportation Planning, or How We Got Here," Transportation, Volume I, No. 4, March, pp. 379–401.

Holmes, E.H. and J.T. Lynch, 1957, "Highway Planning: Past, Present, and Future," Journal of the Highway Division, Proceedings of the ASCE, Volume 83, No. HW3, July, 1298–1 to 1298–13.

Homburger, Wolfgang S., Ed., 1967, Urban Mass Transit Planning. University of California Institute of Transportation and Traffic Engineering, Berkeley, CA.

Horowitz, Alan J., 1989, Quick Response System II Reference Manual – Version 2.3, Prepared for the U.S. Department of Transportation, Federal Highway Administration, Washington, DC, February 1.

Howard/Stein-Hudson Associates, Inc. and Parsons Brinckerhoff Quade and Douglas, 1996, Public Involvement Techniques for Transportation Decision-making, U.S. Department of Transportation, Federal Highway Administration and Federal Transit Administration Washington, DC, September.

Hu, Pat S. and Timothy R. Reuscher, 2004, Summary of Travel Trends - 2001 National Household Travel Survey, U. S. Department of Transportation, Federal Highway Administration, Washington DC, December.

Hu, Patricia S. and Jennifer Young, 1992, 1990 National Personal Transportation Survey – Summary of Travel Trends, U.S. Department of Transportation, Federal Highway Administration, Washington, DC, March.

Humphrey, Thomas F., 1974, "Reappraising Metropolitan Transportation Needs," Transportation Engineering Journal, Proceedings of the American Society of Civil Engineers, Volume 100, No. TE2, May.

Institute of Traffic Engineers, 1965, Capacities and Limitations of Urban Transportation Modes, Washington, DC.

Institute of Transportation Engineers, 1976, Trip Generation, An Informational Report, Washington, DC.

Institute of Transportation Engineers, 2003, Trip Generation - 7th Edition, Washington, DC, January.

____, 1979, Trip Generation, An Informational Report, 2nd Edition, Washington, DC.

____, 1982, Trip Generation, An Informational Report, 3rd Edition, Washington, DC.

____, 1987, Trip Generation 4th Edition, Washington, DC.

____, 1991, Trip Generation, 5th Edition, Washington, DC.

——, 2003, Trip Generation, 7th Edition, Washington, DC, March.

Insurance Institute for Highway Safety, 1986, Status Report (Special Issue: U.S. Safety Acts), Volume 21, No. 11, Washington, DC, September 9.

International Association for Travel Behavior, 1989, Travel Behaviour Research: Fifth International Conference on Travel Behaviour, Gower, Hants, England.

Kirby, Ronald F. and Arlee T. Reno, 1987, The Nation's Public Works: Report on Mass Transit, The Urban Institute, National Council on Public Works Improvement, Washington, DC, May.

Kirby, Ronald F., Kiran V. Bhatt, Michael A. Kemp, Robert G. McGillivray, and Martin Wohl, 1975, Para-Transit: Neglected Options for Urban Mobility, The Urban Institute, Washington, DC.

Kittelson & Associates, Inc., et al., 1999, "Highlights of the Transit Capacity and Quality of Service Manual: 1st Edition," Research Results Digest, Transit Cooperative Research Program, No. 35, November.

——, 2003, "Transit Capacity and Quality of Service Manual – 2nd Edition," TCRP Report 100, Transit Cooperative Research Program, Transportation Research Board, Washington, DC.

Klinger, Dieter and Richard Kuzmyak, 1985–1986, Personal Travel in the United States: 1983–1984 National Personal Transportation Study, Volumes 1 (August, 1986) and 2 (September, 1986), and Survey Data Tabulations (November, 1985), COMSIS Corp., U.S. Department of Transportation, Federal Highway Administration, Washington, DC.

Kret, Ellen H. and Subhash Mundle, 1982, Impacts of Federal Grant Requirements on Transit Agencies, National Cooperative Transit Research & Development Program Report 2, Transportation Research Board, Washington, DC, December.

Kuehn, Thomas J., 1976, The Development of National Highway Policy, University of Washington, August.

Kulash, Damian, 1974, Congestion Pricing: A Research Summary, The Urban Institute, Washington, DC, July.

Lansing, John B. et.al., 1964, Residential Location and Urban Mobility, Institute for Social Research, The University of Michigan, Ann Arbor, MI, June.

Lansing, John B., 1966, Residential Location and Urban Mobility – A Second Wave of Interviews, Institute for Social Research, The University of Michigan, Ann Arbor, MI, January.

Lansing, John B. and Gary Hendricks, Automobile Ownership and Residential Density, Institute for Social Research, The University of Michigan, Ann Arbor, MI. June.

Lee, R.B., W. Kudlick, J.C. Falcocchio, E.J. Cantilli, and A. Stefanivk, 1978, Review of Local Alternatives Analyses Involving Automated Guideway Transit, Urbitran Associates, New York, NY, February.

Levinson, Herbert S., 1978, Characteristics of Urban Transportation Demand – A Handbook for Transportation Planners, Wilbur Smith and Associates, for U.S. Department of Transportation, Washington, DC, April.

——, 1979, Characteristics of Urban Transportation Demand – Appendix, Wilbur Smith and Associates, for U.S. Department of Transportation, Washington, DC, January.

Levinson, Herbert S., et al., 1973, Bus Use of Highways: State of the Art, National Cooperative Highway Research Program Report 143, Highway Research Board, Washington, DC.

Levinson, Herbert, et al., 2003, Bus Rapid Transit, Volume 1: Case Studies in Bus Rapid Transit and Volume 2: Implementation Guidelines, Transit Cooperative Research Program, Transportation Research Board, Washington, DC.

Lieb, Robert C., 1976, Labor in the Transit Industry, Northeastern University, Boston, MA, May.

Lindley, Jeffrey A., 1987, "Urban Freeway Congestion: Quantification of the Problem and Effectiveness of Potential Solutions," ITE Journal, Volume 57, January, pp. 27–32.

——, 1989, "Urban Freeway Congestion Problems and Solutions: An Update," ITE Journal, Volume 59, December, pp. 21–23.

Liss, Susan, 1991, 1990 Nationwide Personal Transportation Study – Early Results, U.S. Department of Transportation, Federal Highway Administration, Washington, DC, August.

Lomax, Timothy J., Diane L. Bullard, and James W. Hanks Jr., 1988, The Impact of Declining Mobility in Major Texas and Other U.S. Cities, Texas Transportation Institute, College Station, TX, August.

Lookwood, Ian, 1997, "ITE Traffic Calming Definition," ITE Journal, July.

Los Angeles County Economic Development Commission, "California's Global Gateways".

Loukaitou-Sideris, Anastasia and Robert Gottlieb, 2003, "Putting Pleasure Back in the Drive: Reclaiming Urban Parkways for the 21st Century," Access, University of California, Transportation Center, No. 22, Spring.

Lowry, Ira S., 1964, A Model of Metropolis, The RAND Corporation (RAND Research Memorandum RM-4035-RC), Santa Monica, CA, August.

Mabee, Nancy and Barbara A. Zumwalt, 1977, Review of Downtown People Mover Proposals: Preliminary Market Implications for Downtown Application of Automated Guideway Transit, The Mitre Corporation, McLean, VA, December.

Marple, Garland E., 1969, "Urban Areas Make Transportation Plans," Presented at the 1969 American Society of Civil Engineers Meeting of Transportation Engineering.

Maryland Department of Transportation, 1998, Thinking Beyond the Pavement, Baltimore, MD, May.

McCarthy, James E., 2004, "Transportation Conformity Under the Clean Air Act: In Need of Reform?," Congressional Research Service Reports RL32106, Washington, DC, November 17.

McFadden, Daniel L., 2002, "The Path to Discrete Choice Models," Access, University of California Transportation Center, Berkeley CA, No. 20, Spring.

Meck, Joseph P., 1965, The Role of Economic Studies in Urban Transportation Planning, U.S. Department of Commerce, Bureau of Public Roads, US. Government Printing Office, Washington, DC, August.

Metropolitan Transportation Commission, 1979a, BART in the San Francisco Bay Area – Summary of the Final Report of the BART Impact Program, U.S. Department of Transportation, Washington, DC, December.

——, 1979b, BART in the San Francisco Bay Area – The Final Report of the BART Impact Program, U.S. Department of Transportation, Washington, DC, September.

Meyburg, Arnim H., 2004, Letter Report on the Freight Analysis Framework, Committee on the Future of the Federal Highway Administration's Freight Analysis Framework, Transportation Research Board, Washington, DC, February 9.

Meyer, Michael, 1983, "Strategic Planning in Response to Environmental Change," Transportation Quarterly, Volume 37, No. 2, April.

——, 2002, The Role of Metropolitan Planning Organizations in Preparing for Security Incidents and Transportation Response, Georgia Institute of Technology, Atlanta, GA.

Miller, David R., Ed., 1972, Urban Transportation Policy: New Perspectives, Lexington Books, Lexington, MA.

Mills, James R., 1975, "Light Rail Transit: A Modern Renaissance," Light Rail Transit, Special Report 161, Transportation Research Board, Washington, DC.

Mitchell, Robert B. and Chester Rapkin, 1954, Urban Traffic: A Function of Land Use, Columbia University Press, New York, NY.

Moler, Steve, 2002, "A Hallmark of Context-Sensitive Design," Public Roads, Volume 65, No. 6, U.S. Department of Transportation, Federal Highway Administration, Washington, DC, May/June.

Moyer, David D. and Barry L. Larson, Eds., 1991, Proceedings of the 1991 Geographic Information Systems (GIS) for Transportation Symposium, American Association of State Highway and Transportation Officials, Washington, DC, April.

Muller P.O., 1995, "Transportation and Urban Form: Stages in the Spatial Evolution of the American Metropolis," in: The Geography of Urban Transportation, Hanson, S., Ed., 2nd Edition, The Guilford Press, New York.

MultiConsultant Associates, Inc. 1999, Nationwide Personal Transportation Survey Symposium, Search for Solutions – A Policy Discussion Series, Number 17, U. S. Department of Transportation, Federal Highway Administration, Washington DC, February.

National Committee on Urban Transportation, 1958–59, Better Transportation for Your City: A Guide to the Factual Development of Urban Transportation Plans (with 17 procedure manuals), Determining Street Use (Manual 1A), Origin - Destination and Land Use (Manual 2A), Conducting a Home Interview Origin - Destination Survey (Manual 2B), Measuring Traffic Volumes (Manual 3A), Determining Travel Time (Manual 3B), Conducting a Limited Parking Study (Manual 3C), Conducting a Comprehensive Parking Study (Manual 3D), Maintaining Accident Records (Manual 3E), Measuring Transit Service (Manual 4A), Inventory of the Physical Street System (Manual 5A), Financial Records and Reports (Manual 6A), Cost Accounting for Streets and Highways (Manual 6B), Standards for Street Facilities and Services (Manual 7A), Recommended Standards, Warrants and Objectives for Transit Services and Facilities (Manual 8A), Developing Project Priorities for Transportation Improvements (Manual 10A), Improving Transportation Administration (Manual 11A), Modernizing Laws and Ordinances (Manual 12A), Public Administration Service, Chicago, IL.

National Council on Public Works Improvement, 1986, The Nation's Public Works: Defining the Issues (Report to the President and the Congress), Washington, DC, September.

———, 1988, Fragile Foundations: A Report on America's Public Works (Final Report to the President and Congress), U.S. Government Printing Office, Washington, DC, February.

National Research Council, 1994, Curbing Gridlock: Peak-Period Fees to Relieve Traffic Congestion, Volumes 1 and 2, Transportation Research Board Special Report 242, National Academy Press, Washington, DC.

National Transportation Policy Study Commission, 1979a, National Transportation Policies Through The Year 2000, U.S. Government Printing Office, Washington, DC, June.

____, 1979b, National Transportation Policies Through The Year 2000 – Executive Summary, U.S. Government Printing Office, Washington, DC, June.

N.D. Lea Transportation Research Corporation, 1975, Lea Transit Compendium – Reference Guide, Volume II, No. 1, N.D. Lea Transportation Research Corporation, Huntsville, AL.

Neuman, Timothy R., et al., 2002, A Guide to Best Practices for Achieving Context Sensitive Solutions, National Cooperation Highway Research Program Report 480, Transportation Research Board, Washington, DC.

O'Connor, Rita, Marcy Schwartz, Joy Schaad, and David Boyd, 2000, "State of the Practice: White Paper on Public Involvement," Committee on Public Involvement in Transportation, Transportation in the New Millennium – State of the Art and Future Directions, Transportation Research Board, Washington, DC, January.

Orski, C. Kenneth, 1982, "Private Sector Involvement in Transportation," Urban Land, Urban Land Institute, Washington, DC, October.

Paparella, Vincent F., 1982, An Administrative History of the Development of the FHWA/UMTA Joint Urban Transportation Planning Regulations, U.S. Department of Transportation, Urban Mass Transportation Administration, Washington, DC, February.

Parker, Elizabeth A., 1991, "Major Provisions to Restructure the Highway Program," Transportation Quarterly, Vol. 45, No. 1, Eno Foundation for Transportation, Inc., Westport, CN. pp. 55–66.

Parker, Elizabeth A., 1977, Major Changes in the Urban and Rural Highway and Transit Programs, Department of Transportation, Washington, DC.

Payne-Maxie Consultants and Blayney-Dyett, 1980, The Land Use and Urban Development Impacts of Beltways, 4 Volumes, U.S. Department of Transportation and U.S. Department of Housing and Urban Development, Government Printing Office, Washington, DC, October.

Peat Marwick Main & Co., 1989, Status of Traffic Mitigation Ordinances, Prepared for U.S. Department of Transportation, Urban Mass Transportation Administration, Washington, DC, August.

Pisarski, Alan, E., 1987a, Commuting in America – A National Report on Commuting Patterns and Trends, Eno Foundation for Transportation, Inc., Westport, CT.

____, 1987b, The Nation's Public Works: Report on Highways Streets, Roads and Bridges, National Council on Public Works Improvement, Washington, DC, May.

——, 1996, Commuting in America II – The Second National Report on Commuting Patterns and Trends, Eno Transportation Foundation, Inc., Lansdowne, VA.

Polytechnic Institute of New York, 1982, The Interstate Highway Trade-In Process, Brooklyn, New York, NY, December.

Pratt, Richard H. and John H. Copple, 1981, Traveler Response to Transportation System Changes, 2nd Edition, Barton-Aschman Associates, Inc., for U.S. Department of Transportation, Federal Highway Administration, July.

Pratt, Richard H., Neil Pedersen, and J. Mather, 1977, Traveler Response to Transportation System Changes – A Handbook for Transportation Planners: Edition 1, R.H. Pratt Associates, U.S. Department of Transportation, Federal Highway Administration, Washington, DC, February.

Pratt, Richard H., et al., 2000, Traveler Response to Transportation System Changes – Interim Handbook, Transit Cooperative Research Program Web Document 12, Transportation Research Board, Washington, DC, March.

Putman, Stephen H., 1979, Urban Residential Location Models, Martinus Nijhoff, Boston, MA.

——, 1983, Integrated Urban Models, Pion, London, England.

Rabinowitz, Harvey and Edward Beimborn, et al., 1991, The New Suburb, US. Department of Transportation, Washington, DC, July.

Reagan, Ronald, 1981a, Federal Regulation, Executive Order 12291, Federal Register, Volume 46, No. 33, February 17, 1981, pp. 13193–13198.

——, 1981b, Postponement of Pending Regulations, White House Memorandum, January 29.

____, 1982, Intergovernmental Review of Federal Programs, Executive Order 12372, Federal Register, Volume 47, No. 137, July 16, 1982, pp. 30959–30960.

Reno, Arlee T. and Ronald H. Bixby, 1985, Characteristics of Urban Transportation Systems, 6th Edition, System Design Concepts, Inc., for U.S. Department of Transportation, Urban Mass Transportation Administration, Washington, DC, October.

Reno, Arlee, Richard Kuzmyak, and Bruce Douglas, 2002, Characteristics of Urban Travel Demand, Transit Cooperative Research Program Report 73, Transportation Research Board, Washington, DC.

Rice Center, 1981, Urban Initiatives Program Evaluation, Houston, TX, March 12.

Rosenbloom, Sandra, 1975, Paratransit, Special Report 164, Transportation Research Board, Washington, DC.

Ryan, James M. and Donald J. Emerson, et al., 1986, Procedures and Technical Methods for Transit Project Planning, U.S. Department of Transportation, Urban Mass Transportation Administration, Washington, DC, September.

Rypinski, Arthur, 2005, Energy Policy Act of 2005 – Listing of Provisions Potentially Affecting the Department of Transportation – Based upon Conference Committee Report of 27 July 2005, U.S. Department of Transportation, Washington, DC, August 3.

Sagamore Conference on Highways and Urban Development, 1958, Guidelines for Action, Conference Sponsored by American Municipal Association, American Association of State Highway Officials, Highway Research Board, and Syracuse University, October.

Salvesen, David, 1990, "Lizards, Blind Invertebrates, and Development," Urban Land, Volume 49, No. 12, Urban Land Institute, Washington, DC, December.

Sanders, David and T. Reynen, 1974, Characteristics of Urban Transportation Systems: A Handbook for Transportation Planners, De Leuw, Cather and Co./U.S. Department of Transportation, Urban Mass Transportation Administration, Chicago, IL/Washington, DC, May.

Schaeffer, Eric N., 1986, "Transportation Management Organizations: An Emerging Public/ Private Partnership," Transportation Planning and Technology, Volume 10, Gordon and Breach/Science Publishers, Inc., London/New Hampshire, NH, pp. 257–266.

Schmidt, Robert E. and Earl M. Campbell, 1956, Highway Traffic Estimation, Eno Foundation for Highway Traffic Control, Saugatuck, CT.

Schrank, David and Tim Lomax, 2005, The 2005 Urban Mobility Report, Texas Transportation Institute, The Texas AM University System, College Station, Texas, May.

Schrank, David L., Shawn M. Turner, and Timothy J. Lomax, 1993, Estimates of Urban Roadway Congestion – 1990, Texas Transportation Institute, Texas Department of Transportation, Austin, TX, March.

Schreiber, Carol, 1991, Current Use of Geographic Information Systems in Transit Planning, Prepared for U.S. Department of Transportation, Urban Mass Transportation Administration, Washington, DC, August.

Scott, James A., Ed., 1975, Transportation (Special Issue on Paratransit), Volume 4, No. 4, Elsevier, Amsterdam, The Netherlands, December.

Second Conference on Application of Transportation Planning Methods, 1989, University of North Carolina at Charlotte, April.

Shieftain, Oliver and Raymond H. Ellis, 1981, Federal, State and Local Responses to 1979 Fuel Shortages, Peat, Marwick, Mitchell & Co., Washington, DC, February.

Shrouds, James M., 1991, "Transportation Provisions of the Clean Air Act Amendments of 1990," Presented at the National Association of Regional Councils: National Briefing on New Clean Air Act, Washington, DC, February 2.

———, 1995, Challenges and Opportunities for Transportation Implementation of the CAE of 1990 and the IS TEA of 1991, Transportation, Volume 22, No. 3, Kluwer, Dordrecht, The Netherlands, August, pp. 193–215.

Silken, Joseph S. and Jeffery G. Mora, 1975, "North American Light Rail Vehicles," Light Rail Transit, Special Report 161, Transportation Research Board, Washington, DC.

Silver, Jacob and Joseph R. Stowers, 1964, Population, Economic, and Land Use Studies in Urban Transportation Planning, U.S. Department of Commerce, Bureau of Public Roads, Washington, DC, July.

Smirk, George M., Ed., 1968, Readings in Urban Transportation, Indiana University Press, Bloomington, IN.

Sousslau, Arthur B., 1983, Transportation Planners' Guide to Using the 1980 Census, COMSIS Corporation, U.S. Department of Transportation, Federal Highway Administration, Washington, DC, January.

Sousslau, Arthur B., Maurice M. Carter, and Amin B. Hassan, 1978a, Manual Techniques and Transferable Parameters for Urban Transportation Planning, Transportation Forecasting and Travel Behavior, Transportation Research Record 673, Transportation Research Board, Washington, DC.

Sousslau, Arthur B., Amin B. Hassan, Maurice M. Carter, and George V. Wickstrom, 1978b, Travel Estimation Procedures for Quick Response to Urban Policy Issues, National Cooperative Highway Research Program Report 186, Transportation Research Board, Washington, DC.

Sousslau, Arthur B., Amin B. Hassan, Maurice M. Carter, and George V. Wickstrom, 1978c, Quick Response Urban Travel Estimation Techniques and Transferable Parameters – User's Guide, National Cooperative Highway Research Program Report 187, Transportation Research Board, Washington, DC.

Southeastern Wisconsin Regional Planning Commission, 1965–66, Planning Report No. 7 – Land Use - Transportation Study, Inventory Findings – 1963 (Volume 1), May 1965; Forecasts and Alternative Plans (Volume 2), June 1966; Recommended Land Use and Transportation Plan – 1990 (Volume 3), November 1966, Waukesha, Wisconsin.

Spear, Bruce, et al., 1977, Application of New Travel Demand Forecasting Techniques to Transportation Planning: A Study of Individual Choice Models, U.S. Department of Transportation, Federal Highway Administration, Washington, DC, March.

——, 1979, Service and Methods Demonstration Program Annual Report, U.S. Department of Transportation, Urban Mass Transportation Administration, Washington, DC, August.

——, 1981, Service and Methods Demonstrations Program Report, U.S. Department of Transportation, Urban Mass Transportation Administration, Washington, DC, December.

Stopher, Peter, 1991, "Deficiencies in Travel Forecasting Procedures Relative to the 1990 Clean Air Act Amendment Requirements," Presented at the Annual Transportation Research Board meeting, Washington, DC, January.

Stopher, Peter R. and Arnim H. Meyburg, Eds., 1974, Behavioral Modeling and Valuation of Travel Time, Special Report 149, Transportation Research Board, Washington, DC.

——, 1976, Behavioral Travel-Demand Models, DC, Heath, Lexington, MA.

Stopher, Peter and Martin Lee-Gosselin, 1996, Understanding Travel Behavior in an Era of Change, Pergamon, New York, NY, August.

Stopher, Peter R., Arnim H. Meyburg, and Werner Brog., Eds., 1981, New Horizons in Travel-Behavior Research, DC, Heath, Lexington, MA.

Strayhorn, Carole Keeton, 2005, Central Texas Regional Mobility Authority: A Need for A Higher Standard, Special Report, Texas Comptroller of Public Accounts, Austin, TX, March.

Swerdloff, Carl N. and Joseph R. Stowers, 1966, "A Test of Some First Generation Residential Land Use Models," Land Use Forecasting Concepts, Highway Research Record Number 126, Highway Research Board, Washington, DC.

Sword, Robert C. and Christopher R. Fleet, 1973, "Updating An Urban Transportation Study Using the 1970 Census Data," Highway Planning Technical Report, No. 30, U.S. Department of Transportation, Federal Highway Administration, Washington, DC, June.

Texas Transportation Institute, 1972, Urban Corridor Demonstration Program Evaluation Manual, U.S. Department of Transportation, Washington, DC, April.

——, 1997, Activity-Based Travel Forecasting Conference, June 2–5, 1996, Summary, Recommendations, and Compendium of Papers, U.S. Department of Transportation and U.S. Environmental Protection Agency, Washington, DC, February.

The President's Council on Sustainable Development, 1996, Sustainable Development: A New Consensus for Prosperity, Opportunity, and a Healthy Environment for the Future, Washington, DC, February.

Third National Conference on Transportation Planning Applications, 1991, Texas State Department of Highways and Public Transportation, April.

Transportation Alternatives Group, 1990, Future Federal Surface Transportation Programs: Policy Recommendations, Washington, DC, January.

Transportation Research Board, 1974a, Demand-Responsive Transportation, Special Report 147, Washington, DC.

——, 1974b, Demand-Responsive Transportation Systems and Services, Special Report 154, Washington, DC.

——, 1974c, Census Data and Urban Transportation Planning, Special Report 145, Washington, DC.

——, 1975a, A Review of Urban Mass Transportation Guidelines for Evaluation of Urban Transportation Alternatives, A Report on the Conference on Evaluation of Urban Mass Transportation Alternatives, Washington DC, February 23–26.

——, 1975b, Light Rail Transit, Special Report 161, Washington, DC.

——, 1977, Urban Transportation Alternatives: Evolution of Federal Policy, Special Report 177, Washington, DC.

——, 1978, Light Rail Transit: Planning and Technology, Special Report 182, Washington, DC.

——, 1982a, Light Rail Transit: Planning, Design and Implementation, Special Report 195, Washington, DC.

——, 1982b, Urban Transportation Planning in the 1980s, Special Report 196, Washington, DC.

_____, 1984a, Future Directions of Urban Public Transportation, Special Report 200, Washington, DC.

_____, 1984b, Travel Analysis Methods for the 1980s, Special Report 201, Washington, DC.

_____, 1984c, Census Data and Urban Transportation Planning in the 1980s, Transportation Research Record 981, Washington, DC.

_____, 1985a, Light Rail Transit: System Design for Cost-Effectiveness, State-of-the-Art Report 2, Washington, DC.

_____, 1985b, Proceedings of the National Conference on Decennial Census Data for Transportation Planning, Special Report 206, Washington, DC.

_____, 1985c, Highway Capacity Manual, Special Report 209, Washington, DC.

_____, 1987, Research for Public Transit - New Directions, Special Report 213, Washington, DC.

_____, 1988, A Look Ahead – Year 2020, Special Report 220, Washington, DC.

_____, 1990a, Transportation and Economic Development – 1990, Transportation Research Record No. 1274, Washington, DC.

_____, 1990b, In Pursuit of Speed: New Options for Intercity Passenger Transportation, Special Report 233, Washington, DC, November.

_____, 1993, Moving Urban America, Special Report 237, Washington, DC.

_____, 1994, Highway Capacity Manual, 3rd Edition, Special Report 209, Washington, DC.

_____, 1995a, Institutional Aspects of Metropolitan Transportation Planning, Transportation Research Circular Number 450, Washington, DC, December.

_____, 1995b, Expanding Metropolitan Highways – Implications for Air Quality and Energy Use, Special Report 245, Washington, DC.

_____, 2000, Refocusing Transportation Planning for the 21st Century, Conference Proceedings 20, National Academy Press, Washington, DC.

_____, 2001, Performance Measures to Improve Transportation Systems and Agency Operations, Conference Proceedings 26, Report of a Conference – Irvine, California, October 29–November 1, 2000, National Academy Press, Washington, DC.

_____, 2003, Letter Report from TRB Committee for Review of Travel Demand Modeling by the Metropolitan Washington Council of Governments, Washington, DC, September 8.

——, 2007, Metropolitan Travel Forecasting: Current Practice and Future Direction, Special Report 288, Washington, DC.

Transportation Systems Center, 1977, Light Rail Transit: State of the Art Review, U.S. Department of Transportation, Washington. DC, May.

Tyndall, Gene R., John Cameron, and Chip Taggart, 1990, Strategic Planning and Management Guidelines for Transportation Agencies, National Cooperative Highway Research Program Report 331, Transportation Research Board, Washington, DC, December.

Upchurch, Jonathan, 1989, "The New Edition of the Manual on Uniform Traffic Control Devices: An Overview," ITE Journal, Volume 59, No. 4, April.

U.S. Congress, 1939, Toll Roads and Free Roads, House Document No. 272, 76th Congress, First Session, U.S. Government Printing Office, Washington, DC.

_____, 1944, Interregional Highways, (Message from the President of the United States Transmitting a Report of the National Interregional Highway Committee), House Document No. 379, 78th Congress, Second Session, U.S. Government Printing Office, Washington, DC.

_____, 1968a, 1968 National Highway Needs Report, Committee Print 90–22, 90th Congress, Second Session, U.S. Government Printing Office, Washington, DC, February.

_____, 1968b, Supplement to the 1968 National Highway Needs Report, Committee Print 90–22A, 90th Congress, Second Session, U.S. Government Printing Office, Washington, DC, July.

_____, 1970, National Highway Needs Report With Supplement, Committee Print 91–28, 91st Congress, Second Session, U.S. Government Printing Office, Washington, DC, September.

_____, 1972a, Report to Congress on Section 109(h), Title 23, U.S. Code – Guidelines Relating to the Economic, Social, and Environmental Effects of Highway Projects, House Document No.

45, 92nd Congress, Second Session, U.S. Government Printing Office, Washington, DC, August.

——, 1972b, Part 1 of the 1972 National Highway Needs Report, House Document No. 92–266, 92nd Congress, Second Session, U.S. Government Printing Office, Washington, DC, March 15.

——, 1972c, Part 2 of the 1972 National Highway Needs Report, House Document No. 92–266, Part II, 92nd Congress, Second Session, U.S. Government Printing Office, Washington, DC, April 10.

——, 1975, The 1974 National Highway Needs Report, House Document No. 94–45, 94th Congress, First Session, U.S. Government Printing Office, Washington, DC, February 10.

——, 1981, The Status of the Nation's Highways: Conditions and Performance, House Document No. 97–2, 97th Congress, First Session, U.S. Government Printing Office, Washington, DC, January.

——, 1989, The Status of the Nation's Highways and Bridges: Conditions and Performance, House Document No. 101–2, 101st Congress, First Session, U.S. Government Printing Office, Washington, DC, January.

U.S. Congress, Office of Technology Assessment, 1975, Automated Guideway Transit – An Assessment of PRT and Other New Systems, U.S. Government Printing Office, Washington, DC, June.

U.S. Congress, Senate, 1962, Urban Transportation – Joint Report to the President by the Secretary of Commerce and the Housing and Home Finance Administration, Urban Mass Transportation – 1962, 87th Congress, Second Session, U.S. Government Printing Office, Washington, DC, pp. 71–81.

U.S. Department of Commerce, Bureau of Public Roads, 1944, Manual of Procedures for Home Interview Traffic Studies, U.S. Government Printing Office, Washington, DC.

——, 1950, Highway Capacity Manual – Practical Applications of Research, U.S. Government Printing Office, Washington, DC.

——, 1954a, Highways in the United States, U.S. Government Printing Office, Washington, DC.

——, 1954b, Manual of Procedures for Home Interview Traffic Studies – Revised Edition, Washington, DC, October.

——, 1957, The Administration of Federal-Aid for Highways, U.S. Government Printing Office, Washington, DC, January.

——, 1962, Increasing the Traffic-Carrying Capability of Urban Arterial Streets: The Wisconsin Avenue Study, U.S. Government Printing Office, Washington, DC, May.

——, 1963b, Calibrating and Testing a Gravity Model for Any Size Urban Area, U.S. Government Printing Office, Washington, DC, July.

——, 1963c, Instructional Memorandum 50-2-63, Urban Transportation Planning, Washington, DC, March 27.

——, 1963d, Highway Planning Program Manual, Washington, DC.

——, 1964, Traffic Assignment Manual, U.S. Government Printing Office, Washington, DC, June.

——, 1965a, Highway Progress, (Annual Report of the Bureau of Public Roads, Fiscal Year 1965), U.S. Government Printing Office, Washington, DC, October.

——, 1965b, Traffic Assignment and Distribution for Small Urban Areas, U.S. Government Printing Office, Washington, DC, September.

U.S. Department of Energy, 1978, The National Energy Act – Information Kit, Washington, DC, November.

U.S. Department of Housing and Urban Development, 1978a, A New Partnership to Conserve America's Communities – A National Urban Policy, Urban and Regional Policy Group, U.S. Government Printing Office, Washington, DC, March.

——, 1978b, The President's 1978 National Urban Policy Report, U.S. Government Printing Office, Washington, DC, December.

——, 1980, The President's 1980 National Urban Policy Report, U.S. Government Printing Office, Washington, DC, August.

U.S. Department of Transportation, 2006, National Strategy to Reduce Congestion on America's Transportation Network, Department of Transportation, Washington, DC, May.

——, Volpe National Transportation Systems Center, 2006, Expert Forum on Road Pricing and Travel Demand Modeling – Proceedings, Washington, DC.

——, Federal Highway Administration, 2004a, National Bicycling and Walking Study – Ten Year Status Report, Washington, DC, October.

——, Federal Highway Administration and Federal Transit Administration, 2004b, The Metropolitan Transportation Planning Process: Key Issues A Briefing Notebook for Transportation Decisionmakers, Officials, and Staff, Transportation Planning Capacity Building Program, Washington, DC, May.

——, Federal Highway Administration, 2004c, Report on the Value Pricing Pilot Program Through March 2004, Washington, DC.

——, Federal Highway Administration, 2004d, Report to Congress on Public-Private Partnerships, Washington, DC, July.

——, Federal Highway Administration, 2004e, Highway Finance and Public-Private Partnerships – New Approaches to Delivering Transportation Services, Washington, DC, December.

——, Federal Highway Administration, 2002a, "Freight Analysis Framework," Freight News, Washington, DC, October.

——, Federal Highway Administration, 2002b, State Infrastructure Bank Review, Washington, DC, February.

——, Federal Highway Administration, 2000a, MUTCD 2000 – Manual on Uniform Traffic Control Devices – Millennium Edition, Washington, DC, December 18.

——, ITS Joint Program Office, 2000b, National Intelligent Transportation Systems Program Plan – Five-Year Horizon, Washington, DC, August.

——, Federal Transit Administration, 2000c, Report on Job Access and Reverse Commute Program – Report of the Secretary of Transportation to the United States Congress Pursuant to 49 U.S.C. 3037(k)(2)(b), Washington, DC.

——, Federal Highway Administration, 2000d, 2000 Report on the Value Pricing Pilot Program, Washington, DC, July.

——, 2000e, The Changing Face of Transportation, Washington, DC.

——, 2000f, Transportation Decision Making: Policy Architecture for the 21st Century, Washington, DC.

——, Federal Highway Administration, 1999a, Asset Management Primer, Washington, DC, December.

——, Office of Intelligence and Security, 1999b, Worldwide Terrorist and Violent Criminal Attacks Against Transportation – 1998, Washington, DC.

——, 1998, A Summary – Transportation Equity Act for the 21st Century, Washington, DC, July.

——, 1997a, Environmental Justice in Minority and Low-Income Populations: Incorporation of Procedures Into Policies, Programs and Activities, DOT Order 5610.2, Federal Register, Volume 62, No. 72, April 15, pp. 18377–18381.

——, Federal Highway Administration, 1997b, An Evaluation of the U.S. Department of Transportation State Infrastructure Bank Pilot Program – SIB Report to Congress, Washington, DC, February 28.

——, Federal Highway Administration, 1997c, Flexibility in Highway Design, Washington, DC, July.

——, 1996a, Building Livable Communities Though Transportation, Washington, DC, October.

——, Federal Transit Administration, 1996b, Planning, Developing, and Implementing Community-Sensitive Transit, Washington, DC, May.

——, Federal Highway Administration and Federal Transit Administration, 1996c, Statewide Transportation Planning Under ISTEA – A New Framework for Decision Making, Washington, DC.

_____, 1996d, A Progress Report on the National Transportation System Initiative, Washington, DC, December.

_____, Federal Highway Administration and Federal Transit Administration, 1995, A Guide to Metropolitan Transportation Planning Under ISTEA – How the Pieces Fit Together, Washington, DC.

_____, Federal Highway Administration, 1994, National Bicycling and Walking Study Final Report – Transportation Choices for a Changing America, Washington, DC, April.

_____, 1993a, Transportation Implications of Telecommuting Washington, DC, April.

_____, Federal Highway Administration and Federal Transit Administration, 1993b, Statewide Planning; Metropolitan Planning; Rule, Federal Register, Volume 68, No. 207, October 28, pp. 58040–58079.

_____, Federal Highway Administration and Federal Transit Administration, 1993c, Management and Monitoring Systems, Interim Final Rule, Federal Register, Volume 58, No. 229, December 1, pp. 63442–63485.

_____, Federal Transit Administration, 1992a, Intermodal Surface Transportation Efficiency Act of 1991 – Flexible Funding Opportunities for Transit, Washington, DC, April 30.

_____, 1991a, Transportation for Individuals With Disabilities, Federal Register, Volume 56, No. 65, April 4, pp. 13856–13981.

_____, 1991b, A Summary – Intermodal Surface Transportation Efficiency Act of 1991, Washington, DC, December.

_____, 1990a, National Transportation Strategic Planning Study, Washington, DC, March.

_____, 1990b, Moving America: New Directions, New Opportunities, A Statement of National Transportation Policy, Washington, DC, February.

_____, 1990c, Report to Congress on Intelligent Vehicle-Highway Systems, March.

_____, Federal Railroad Administration, 1990d, Assessment of the Potential for Magnetically Levitated Transportation in the United States, Washington, DC, June.

_____, 1989a, Moving America: New Directions, New Opportunities, Volume 1: Building the National Transportation Policy, Washington, DC, July.

_____, 1989b, Moving America: A Look Ahead to the 21st Century, Washington, DC.

_____, Urban Mass Transportation Administration, 1988a, The Status of the Nation's Local Mass Transportation: Performance and Conditions, Washington, DC, June.

_____, Urban Mass Transportation Administration, 1987a, The Status of the Nation's Local Mass Transportation: Performance and Conditions, Washington, DC, June.

_____, Urban Mass Transportation Administration, 1987b, Charter Service, Federal Register, Volume 52, No. 70, April 13, pp. 11916–11936.

_____, 1987c, Fact Sheet-Surface Transportation and Uniform Relocation Assistance Act of 1987 (P.L. 100-17), Washington, DC, April 10.

_____, Federal Highway Administration, 1987d, Highway Performance Monitoring System Analytical Process, Volumes 1–3, Washington, DC, December.

_____, Federal Highway Administration and Urban Mass Transportation Administration, 1987e, Environmental Impact and Related Procedures, Federal Register, Volume 52, No. 167, August 28, pp. 32646–32669.

_____, Urban Mass Transportation Administration, 1986a, Charter Bus Operations; Proposed Rule, Federal Register, Volume 51, No. 44, March 6, pp. 7892–7906.

_____, 1986b, Nondiscrimination on the Basis of Handicap in Department of Transportation Financial Assistance Programs, Federal Register, Volume 52, No. 100, May 23, pp. 18994–19031.

_____, Urban Mass Transportation Administration, 1984a, "Stanley Announces Policy for New Fixed Guideway Systems," (News Release), UMTA 16–84, May 18.

_____, Urban Mass Transportation Administration, 1984b, Urban Mass Transportation Major Capital Investment Policy, Federal Register, Volume 49, No. 98, May 18, pp. 21284–21291.

_____, Urban Mass Transportation Administration, 1984c, Private Enterprise Participation in the Urban Mass Transportation Program, Federal Register, Volume 49, No. 205, October 22, pp. 41310–41312.

____, Urban Mass Transportation Administration, 1984d, The Status of the Nation's Local Public Transportation: Conditions and Performance, Washington, DC, September.

____, Federal Highway Administration, 1984e, Highway Performance Monitoring System Field Manual, Washington, DC, January.

____, 1983a, Intergovernmental Review of the Department of Transportation Programs and Activities, Federal Register, Volume 48, No. 123, June 24, pp. 29264–29274.

____, Urban Mass Transportation Administration, 1983b, ACT Socio-Economic Research Program Digest, Washington, DC, March.

____, Federal Highway Administration and Urban Mass Transportation Administration, 1983c, Urban Transportation Planning, Federal Register, Volume, 48, No. 127, June 30, pp. 30332–30343.

____, Urban Mass Transportation Administration, 1983d, Microcomputers in Transportation Software and Source Book, Washington, DC, September.

____, Urban Mass Transportation Administration, 1983e, Microcomputers in Transportation Selected Readings: Getting Started in Microcomputers, (Volume 1); Selecting a Single User System, (Volume 2), Washington, DC.

____, 1983f, Nondiscrimination on the Basis of Handicap in Programs Receiving Financial Assistance from the Department of Transportation, Federal Register, Volume 48, No. 175, September 8, pp. 40684–40694.

____, 1983g, Fact Sheet-Surface Transportation Assistance Act of 1982 (P.L. 97-424), Washington, DC, January 13.

____, Urban Mass Transportation Administration, 1982a, Paratransit Policy, Federal Register, Volume. 47, No. 201, October 18, pp. 46410–46411.

____, Urban Mass Transportation Administration 1982a, Charter Bus Operations and School Bus Operations (ANRPM), Federal Register, Volume 47, No. 197, October 12, pp. 44795–44804.

____, 1981a, Nondiscrimination on the Basis of Handicap, Federal Register, Volume 46, No. 138, July 20, pp. 37488–37494.

____, Federal Highway Administration and Urban Mass Transportation Administration, 1981b, Air Quality Conformity and Priority Procedures for Use in Federal-Aid Highway and Federally-Funded Transit Programs, Federal Register, Volume 46, No. 16, January 26, pp. 8426–8432.

____, Urban Mass Transportation Administration, 1981c, Charter Bus Operations, Federal Register, Volume 46, No. 12, January 19, pp. 5394–5407.

____, Urban Mass Transportation Administration, 1981d, National Urban Mass Transportation Statistics: First Annual Report, Section 15 Reporting System, Washington, DC, May.

____, Federal Highway Administration, 1980–1983, 1977 Nationwide Personal Transportation Study, Characteristics of 1977 Licensed Drivers and Their Travel (Report No. 1, October 1980); Household Vehicle Ownership (Report No. 2, October 1980); Purposes of Vehicle Trips and Travel (Report No. 3, December 1980); Home-to-Work Trips and Travel (Report No. 4, December 1980); Household Vehicle Utilization (Report No. 5, April 1981); Vehicle Occupancy (Report No. 6, April 1981); A Life Cycle of Travel by the American Family (Report No. 7, July 1981); Urban/Rural Split of Travel (Report No. 8, June 1982); Household Travel (Report No. 9, July 1982); Estimates of Variances (Report No. 10, November 1982); Person Trip Characteristics (Report No. 11, December 1983), Washington, DC.

____, Federal Highway Administration, 1980a, Federal Laws and Material Relating to the Federal Highway Administration, U.S. Government Printing Office, Washington, DC.

____, Federal Highway Administration and Urban Mass Transportation Administration, 1980b, Environmental Impact and Related Procedures, Federal Register, Volume 45, No. 212, October 30, pp. 71968–71987.

____, 1980c, Energy Conservation by Recipients of Federal Financial Assistance, Federal Register, Volume 45, No. 170, August 29, pp. 58022–58038.

____, Federal Highway Administration, 1980d, A Study of the Administrative Effectiveness of the Department of Transportation Ridesharing Programs, Washington, DC, May.

____, Federal Highway Administration and Urban Mass Transportation Administration, 1980e, "Interstate Withdrawal and Substitution; Revision of Regulations," Federal Register, Volume 45, No. 204, October 20, pp. 69390–68400.

____, Federal Highway Administration, 1979a, America's Highways, 1776–1976, A History of the Federal-Aid Program, U.S. Government Printing Office, Washington, DC.

____, Urban Mass Transportation Administration, 1979b, Urban Mass Transportation Act of 1964, as amended through December 1978, and Related Laws, U.S. Government Printing Office, Washington, DC.

____, 1979c, Energy Conservation in Transportation, Washington, DC, January.

____, 1979d, The Surface Transportation Assistance Act of 1978, Washington, DC, August.

____, 1979e, "Improving the Urban Transportation Decision Process," (Memorandum from the Federal Highway Administrator and Acting Deputy Urban Mass Transportation Administrator), Washington, DC, October 11.

____, 1979f, Nondiscrimination on the Bases of Handicap in Federally-Assisted Programs and Activities Receiving or Benefiting from Federal Financial Assistance, Federal Register, Volume 44, No. 106, May 3l, pp. 31442–31482.

____, Urban Mass Transportation Administration, 1979g, Urban Initiatives Program, Program Guidelines, Federal Register, Volume 44, No. 70, April 10, pp. 21580–21583.

____, Urban Mass Transportation Administration, 1978a, Policy Toward Rail Transit, Federal Register, Volume 43, No. 45, March 7, pp. 9428–9430.

____, Federal Highway Administration, 1978b, Manual on Uniform Traffic Control Devices, Washington, DC.

____, Federal Highway Administration, 1977a, Computer Programs for Urban Transportation Planning – PLANPAC/BACKPAC General Information Manual, U.S. Government Printing Office, Washington, DC, April.

____, Urban Mass Transportation Administration, 1977b, Urban Mass Transportation Administration - Statistical Summary, U.S. Government Printing Office, Washington, DC.

____, 1977c, National Transportation Trends and Choices – to the Year 2000, U.S. Government Printing Office, Washington, DC, January 12.

____, Urban Mass Transportation Administration, 1977d, Urban Mass Transportation Industry Uniform System of Accounts and Records and Reporting System, General Description (Volume 1), Washington, DC, January 10.

____, Urban Mass Transportation Administration, 1977e, Uniform System of Accounts and Records and Reporting System, Federal Register, Volume 42, No. 13, January 19, pp. 3772–3779.

____, 1976a, Urban System Study, Washington, DC.

____, Urban Mass Transportation Administration, 1976b, Major Urban Mass Transportation Investments, Federal Register, Volume 41, No. 185, September 22, pp. 41512–41514.

____, Urban Mass Transportation Administration and Federal Highway Administration, 1976c, Transportation for Elderly and Handicapped Persons, Federal Register, Volume 41, No. 85, April 30, pp. 18234–18241.

____, Urban Mass Transportation Administration, 1976d, Charter and School Bus Operations, Federal Register, Volume 41, April 1, pp. 14123–14131.

____, Federal Highway Administration and Urban Mass Transportation Administration, 1975a, Planning Assistance and Standards, Federal Register, Volume 40, No. 181, September 17, pp. 42976–42984.

____, 1975b, 1974 National Transportation Report: Current Performance and Future Prospects, U.S. Government Printing Office, Washington, DC, July.

____, Urban Mass Transportation Administration, 1975c, Major Mass Transportation Investments, (Proposed Policy), Federal Register, Volume 40, No. 149, August 1, pp. 32546–32547.

____, 1975d, A Statement of National Transportation Policy (By the Secretary of Transportation), U.S. Government Printing Office, Washington, DC, September 17.

____, Federal Highway Administration, 1975e, National Highway Inventory and Performance Study Manual – 1976, Washington, DC, July.

____, Federal Highway Administration, 1974a, Progress Report on Implementation of Process Guidelines, Washington, DC, May 10.

____, 1974b, A Study of Mass Transportation Needs and Financing, Washington, DC, July.

____, Federal Highway Administration, 1972–1974, Nationwide Personal Transportation Study, Automobile Occupancy (Report No. 1, April 1972); Annual Miles of Travel (Report No. 2, April 1972); Seasonal Variations of Automobile Trips and Travel (Report No. 3, April 1972); Transportation Characteristics of School Children (Report No. 4, July 1972); Availability of Public Transportation and Shopping Characteristics of SMSA Households (Report No. 5, July 1972); Characteristics of Licensed Drivers (Report No. 6, April 1973); Household Travel in the United States (Report No. 7, December 1972); Home-to-Work Trips and Travel (Report No. 8, August 1973); Mode of Transportation and Personal Characteristics of Tripmakers (Report No. 9, November 1973); Purpose of Automobile Trips and Travel (Report No. 10, May 1974); Automobile Ownership (Report No. 11, December 1974); Washington, DC.

____, Federal Highway Administration, 1972a, Policy and Procedure Memorandum 90–4, Process Guidelines (Economic, Social and Environmental Effects on Highway Projects), Washington, DC, September 21.

____, 1972b, 1972 National Transportation Report: Present Status- Future Alternatives, U.S. Government Printing Office, Washington, DC, July.

____, Urban Mass Transportation Administration, 1972c, External Operating Manual (UMTA Order 1000.2), Washington, DC, August.

____, 1972d, An Analysis of Urban Highway Public Transportation Facility Needs, Volumes 1 and 2, Washington, DC, April.

____, Federal Highway Administration, 1970a, Stewardship Report on Administration of the Federal-Aid Highway Program 1956–1970, Washington, DC.

____, Federal Highway Administration, 1970b, Highway Environment Reference Book, Washington, DC, November.

____, Federal Highway Administration, 1969a, Policy and Procedure Memorandum 20-8, Public Hearings and Location Approval, Washington, DC, January 14.

____, Federal Highway Administration, 1969b, 1968 National Highway Functional Classification Study Manual, Washington, DC, April.

____, Federal Highway Administration, 1968, Instructional Memorandum 50-4-68, Operations Plans for "Continuing" Urban Transportation Planning, Washington, DC, May 3.

____, Federal Highway Administration, 1967a, Policy and Procedure Memorandum 50-9, Urban Transportation Planning, Washington, DC, June 21.

____, Federal Highway Administration, 1967b, Guidelines for Trip Generation Analysis, U.S. Government Printing Office, Washington, DC, June.

____, Federal Highway Administration, 1967c, Instructional Memorandum 21-13-67, Reserved Bus Lanes, Washington, DC, August 18.

____, and U.S. Department of Housing and Urban Development, 1974, Report to the Congress of the United States on Urban Transportation Policies and Activities, Washington, DC.

U. S. Department of Commerce, Bureau of Public Roads, 1970, Directory of Urbanized Areas, Washington, DC.

U.S. Environmental Protection Agency, 1990, Clean Air Act Amendments of 1990 – Detailed Summary of Titles, Washington, DC, November 30.

——, 1993, Air Quality: Transportation Plans, Programs, and Projects; Federal or State Implementation Plan Conformity; Rule, Federal Register, Volume 58, No. 225, November 24, pp. 62188–62253.

U.S. Federal Works Agency, Public Roads Administration, 1949, Highway Practice in the United States of America, U.S. Government Printing Office, Washington, DC.

U.S. General Accountability Office, 2005, Highway Congestion – Intelligent Transportation Systems' Promise for Managing Congestion Falls Short, and DOT Could Better Facilitate Their Strategic Use, Washington, DC, September.

U.S. General Accounting Office, 1997, Transportation Infrastructure – States' Implementation of Transportation Systems, Washington, DC, January 13.

U.S. Housing and Home Finance Administration and U.S. Department of Commerce, 1965, Standard Land Use Coding Manual, U.S. Government Printing Office, Washington, DC, January.

Vickrey, William, 1959, "Economic Justification For Peak-Hour Charges," Statement to the U.S. Congress Joint Committee on Washington Metropolitan Problems, November 11.

Vonderohe, Alan, Larry Travis, and Robert Smith, 1991, "Implementation of Geographic Information Systems (GIS) in State DOTs," NCHRP Research Results Digest, Transportation Research Board, Washington, DC, August.

Voorhees, Alan M., 1956, "A General Theory of Traffic Movement," 1955 Proceedings, Institute of Traffic Engineers, New Haven, CT.

Voorhees, Alan M. and Associates, Inc., 1974, Status of the Urban Corridor Demonstration Program, U.S. Department of Transportation, Washington, DC, July.

——, 1979, Guidelines for Assessing the Environmental Impacts of Public Mass Transportation Projects, U.S. Department of Transportation, Washington, DC.

Vuchic, Vukan R., 1981, Urban Public Transportation: Systems and Technology, Prentice-Hall, Englewood Cliffs, NJ.

Wachs, Martin, 1990, "Regulating Traffic by Controlling Land Use The Southern California Experience," Transportation, Volume 16, 241–256.

Wagner, Frederick A., 1978, Evaluation of Carpool Demonstration Projects – Phase I Report, U.S. Department of Transportation, Federal Highway Administration, Washington, DC, October.

Walmsley, Anthony, 2003, "The Henry Hudson Parkway Scenic Byway Initiative, History," http://www.henryhudsonparkway.org/hhp/history2.htm, April.

Washington Center for Metropolitan Studies, 1970, Comprehensive Planning for Metropolitan Development, Prepared for U.S. Department of Transportation, Urban Mass Transportation Administration, Washington, DC.

Watson, Peter L. and Edward P. Holland, 1978, "Congestion Pricing: The Example of Singapore," Urban Economics: Proceedings of Five Workshops on Pricing Alternatives, Economic Regulation, Labor Issues, Marketing, and Government Financing Responsibilities, U.S. Department of Transportation, Washington, DC, March, pp. 27–30.

Ways, Sherry B. and Cynthia Burbank, 2005, "Scenario Planning," Public Roads, Volume 69, No. 2, U.S. Department of Transportation, Federal Highway Administration, Washington, DC, September/October.

Webster, Arthur L., Edward Weiner, and John D. Wells, 1974, The Role of Taxicabs in Urban Transportation, U.S. Department of Transportation, December.

Weiner, Edward, 1974, "Urban Issues in the 1974 National Transportation Study," Presented at the ASCE/EIC/RTAC Joint Transportation Engineering Meeting, Montreal, Canada, July.

——, 1975b, "Urban Area Results of the 1974 National Transportation Study," U.S. Department of Transportation, Washington, DC, January.

——, 1975c, "The Characteristics, Uses, and Potentials of Taxicab Transportation," Transportation, Volume 4, No. 4.

——, 1976a, "Assessing National Urban Transportation Policy Alternatives," Transportation Research, Volume 10, Pergamon, London, England, pp.159–178.

——, 1976b, "Mass Transportation Needs and Financing in the United States," Transportation, Volume 5, Elsevier, Amsterdam, The Netherlands, pp. 93–110.

——, 1979, "Evolution of Urban Transportation Planning," in: Public Transportation: Planning, Operations, and Management, Chapter 15, G. Gray and L. Hoel, Eds., Prentice-Hall, Englewood Cliffs, NJ.

——, 1982, "New Directions for Transportation Policy," Journal of the American Planning Association, Volume 48, No. 3, Summer.

——, 1983, "Redefinition of Roles and Responsibilities in U.S. Transportation," Transportation, Volume 17, Martinus Nijhoff, The Hague, The Netherlands, pp. 211–224.

——, 1984, "Devolution of the Federal Role in Urban Transportation," Journal of Advanced Transportation, Volume 18, No. 2.

____, 1989, "Summary – Second Conference on Application of Transportation Planning Methods," Proceedings of the Second Conference on Applications of Transportation Planning Methods, University of North Carolina at Charlotte, June.

____, 1993a, "Upgrading Travel Demand Forecasting Capabilities," Proceedings of the Fourth National Conference on Transportation Planning Methods Applications, May 3–7.

____, 1993b, "Upgrading Travel Demand Forecasting Capabilities," The Urban Transportation Monitor 1993, Volume 7, No. 13, July 9.

____, 1994, "Telework: A Vital Link to Transportation, Energy, and the Environment," Proceedings of the Telework '94 Symposium: The Evolution of a New Culture, November 15.

——, 2005, "Transportation Policy in USA," in: Handbook of Transport Strategy, Policy and Institutions, Chapter 44, Kenneth J. Button and David A. Hensher, Eds., Elsevier, San Diego, CA.

Weiner, Edward and Fredrick W. Ducca, 1996, "Upgrading Travel Demand Forecasting Capabilities: The U.S. DOT Travel Model Improvement Program," TR News, No. 186, September–October.

Wells, John D., Norman J. Asher, Richard P. Brennan, Jane-Ring Crane, Janet D. Kiernan, and Edmund H. Mantell, 1970, An Analysis of the Financial and Institutional Framework for Urban Transportation Planning and Investment, Institute for Defense Analyses, Arlington, VA, June.

Wells, John D., et al., 1974, The Economic Characteristics of Urban Public Transportation Industry, Institute for Defense Analyses, U.S. Department of Transportation, Washington, DC, February.

Index

Printed in the United States of America